PARADISE RETURNED
&
Other Poems

PARADISE RETURNED
&
Other Poems

Kedar Nath Sharma

Allied Publishers Pvt. Ltd.

NEW DELHI • MUMBAI • KOLKATA • CHENNAI • NAGPUR
AHMEDABAD • BANGALORE • HYDERABAD • LUCKNOW

Allied Publishers Private Limited

Regd. Off.: 15 J.N. Heredia Marg, Ballard Estate, **Mumbai**–400001
Ph.: 022-42126969 • E-mail: mumbai.books@alliedpublishers.com

47/9 Prag Narain Road, Near Kalyan Bhawan, **Lucknow**–226001
Ph.: 0522-2209942 • E-mail: lko.books@alliedpublishers.com

F-1 Sun House (First Floor), C.G. Road, Navrangpura,
Ellisbridge P.O., **Ahmedabad**–380006
Ph.: 079-26465916 • E-mail: ahmbd.books@alliedpublishers.com

3-2-844/6 & 7 Kachiguda Station Road, **Hyderabad**–500027
Ph.: 040-24619079 • E-mail: hyd.books@alliedpublishers.com

5th Main Road, Gandhinagar, **Bangalore**–560009
Ph.: 080-22262081 • E-mail: bngl.books@alliedpublishers.com

1/13-14 Asaf Ali Road, **New Delhi**–110002
Ph.: 011-23239001 • E-mail: delhi.books@alliedpublishers.com

17 Chittaranjan Avenue, **Kolkata**–700072
Ph.: 033-22129618 • E-mail: cal.books@alliedpublishers.com

60 Shiv Sunder Apartments (Ground Floor), Central Bazar Road,
Bajaj Nagar, **Nagpur**–440010
Ph.: 0712-2234210 • E-mail: ngp.books@alliedpublishers.com

751 Anna Salai, **Chennai**–600002
Ph.: 044-28523938 • E-mail: chennai.books@alliedpublishers.com

Website: www.alliedpublishers.com

ISBN: 978-81-8424-914-9

Illustrations and Cover designed by Harsh Vardhan Arya

Published by Sunil Sachdev and printed by Ravi Sachdev at
Allied Publishers Pvt. Ltd., (Printing Division), A-104 Mayapuri Phase II,
New Delhi-110064.

A.P.J. Abdul Kalam

Rashtrapati Bhavan
New Delhi - 110004

29 March 2007

Dear Shri Kedar Nath Sharma,

Thank you for your letter and sending me your poem "Paradise Returned". It is indeed a beautiful and creative work.

My best wishes to you.

Yours sincerely,

(A.P.J. Abdul Kalam)

Shri Kedar Nath Sharma
Poet & Journalist
1, Shivalik Apartments
Opp. D-Block, Saraswati Vihar,
Pitampura, Delhi–110 034

Poetry of Great Intensity and Flavour

K.N. Sharma's 'Paradise Returned & Other Poems' is a fine anthology of moving and revealing poems of considerable merit. The book comprises one long – 38 pages – title poem and several short poems. These concern a variety of themes from nature, contemporary events, religious and deeply felt experiences. Thus the poems cover numerous motifs.

'Paradise Returned' as some other 'pieces' point to some influences on the poet, he candidly acknowledges them. However these outside impressions are not allowed to impose any pattern on the raw material. The poet seems to assimilate splendidly whatever he borrows from other books/authors. Nowhere does this hamper the flow or freshness of his creative venture.

Here is a clear development of art from 'The Whiff' and his earlier sojourn into literary world. Whether the theme or scene has Indian or the US background, the treatment is both original and natural. K.N. Sharma, in his own way is a 'bard of passion and of mirth'. His poetry delights and lifts, surprises and shakes. At times Sharma takes up simple, day to day occurrences or ordinary topics as examples in 'We Sell Truth', 'Bush to Sadam', 'Our Mule', 'Living a Burden', 'A Mosquito Murmurs', and 'Death is a Siren', and so on. But in each case things are finely examined "Within the ring fence" of an idea since everything seems to pass through the 'Cruciable of Imagination.'

In "Paradise Returned", various episodes and beliefs have been artistically presented adequately dramatized. Yet all along the poem flows naturally, retaining their pace, passion and precision. The poet conforms to his area of experiences and understanding, he knows that he knows. His poems, therefore, are like powerful arrows originating from heart and directly striking the target, hitting the nail on the head. Free from clutches of literary jargons or burdensome allusions, it is the poetry characterized by intensity, spontaneity and simplicity.

One feels that poets like K.N. Sharma, P.C. Katoch, D.C. Chambial, O.P. Bhatnagar and R.K. Singh (who have several good collections to their credit) deserve wides readership (national/ international) and more importantly, in depth critical studies at M.Phil./Ph.D. levels.

Dr. Atma Ram
Former Advisor Education
Director Education
Himachal Pradesh

Paradise Returned

Paradise Returned by Kedar Nath Sharma is neither John Milton's Paradise Lost nor Paradise Regained, but an attempt to be at the basis of human religion, what's the ways which ultimately lead to Him and what we are for actually. The poet churns the things for to arrive at some conclusion. The victory by the bloody sword cannot live for long and it is bound to end up in blood. Narrower outlooks can never take us close to God and never does He preach for violence to spread a religion. A mere cling to conservatism and orthodox views is not going to do any good to us. How much pious or virtuous are we from our within? Such a thing is but *Blakian, Hopkinsian, Herbertian and Trahernean. The main thing is our innocence which we have defiled so much perhaps. God is in piety, in our karma and in our karma lies in the dharma of human life.

Apart from choosing a noble topic to write upon, the poet plays with wit, irony, humour, conceit and satire. If it is not Miltonic in essence, so much so holy, it is of course Don Juanic or Don Quixotic. To view it otherwise, Paradise Returned is Alexander Popean and John Drydenian. He wants to cleanse the muck staining it. The soul is the temple of God and He dwells in here. The other point of deliberation may be that some Coleridgean Kubla Khan under the spell of opium is here doing the rounds. The other thing is this that the poet has definitely imbibed what it is prevalent in existentialism, nothingness, agnosticism, skepticism and atheism. One should keep it in mind that these are also the remarkable ways of approaching the Lord. In these isms, lies the questioning of the existence of God. What is God? Where does He lie in? Where is the paradise and the gates of it? Where is the Inn of God? Is man a Pilgrim? These are the questions which engage so much so of our space. The quest after God may be another theme of this poem under discussion. The poet banks upon the asked questions of life and living and we cannot help without them. Some Nachiketa or inquisitive Siddhartha seems to be the protagonist of the poem. The poet draws heavily from the scriptural stock dawning upon knowledge, wisdom, piety, pity, charity, chastity, purity, virtue, morality, service and ethics. The Kathopnishad seems to be the centre of the Nachiketa, Vajashrava and Yama's tripartite talks. The unity of religion he talks about and the cultural synthesis which he dreams about may be a poetical chimera of his. Sometimes confutes and confronts and sometimes assimilates in. American transcendentalism may be one of the likes of K.N. Sharma.

There is no doubt in it to say that the thing he seeks to deliberate upon is the unity of all religions, but the fanatics, zealots and the loyal people of God are bent upon wreaking havoc. It is very difficult to say who is an infidel and who a faithful. The mole in the midst of beards will say it who the thief is in reality. The people religiously blind are the most dangerous breed of man. An inter-faith meeting is the thing which poet Sharma hints towards, but the candle of hope will finally extinguish it out itself. The proverbs themselves tell us a lot more, service to man is service to God and charity begins at home as for example.

The present day world has greatest fears from the fanatics and it is none but these people who turn up as terrorists. The religious ghost makes them play the roles they desire to enact otherwise it would not have. To put it in the Marxistic idiom, religion is the opium of the people and this is absolutely correct with regard to these rugged people of rugged faiths. To change a little bit, they are under the ganja puffs and smokes, talking of heaven and faith under its redness. And here in this work, the poet seems to hold Geneva talks and meets with Gods and their incarnations one by one. There is something of rebel as a poet in him and it is but a P.B. Shelleyian characteristic. Apart from, I can mark the influences of Salman Rushdie and Taslima Nasrin working as hangovers.

Kedar Nath Sharma has applied the narrative form in writing the whole spectacle and it falls short of being termed 'An interview with Gods'. The journalistic and the poetic halves are perhaps trying to come to term herein. Wit, conceit, irony, satire and intellect seem to be the properties of the poet and he frolicks and gambols with these. The theological discourse which he writes down is but a different one standing at variance with the one that is metaphysical. The poet uses in general the light mode in writing his poetic stuffs. Sometimes the lines seem to be too loose to be called poetry. Whatever be our criticism of his poetry, his verse-lines follow the course of their own. The poet sometimes gives the meditational tips and how to keep fit work-out here and there. The poet is of the view that the world will not turn into a paradise as long as the fundamentalists and fanatics continue to live in and inhabit it. How to eliminate them and who would be their terminators? As you sow, so you reap goes the adage, and they are reaping what they have held with them so far personally. The cluster bombs falling over, casualties taking place and they go running for cover. Who can but say who are really holy and faithfuls? The poet takes up what it goes in the making of a fanatic-cum terrorist without fearing the expected backlash.

Bijay Kant Dubey
Head Deptt. of English
Chandrakona Vidyasagar Mahavidyalaya
Chandrakona Town, Paschim Medinipur
West Bengal-721201
Coordinator
Netaji Subhash Open University
Chandrakona Vidyasagar Mahavidyalaya
Study Centre (G-03) Paschim Medinipur

Preface

The litterateurs, particularly poets, everywhere hearken to the world philosophy to endow pragmatism and a tinge of learning to their works. Similitude and symbolism are the most important trappings poets make use of for embellishing their art.

Naturally, therefore, poets of the English language in the western world have recourse to western philosophy and mythology which germinated in Greece nearly six hundred years before Christ. But the Hindu philosophy which is millenniums older than that is a rich source inviting Indian poets, nay even the poets of the whole world, to make use of in their works.

The western thought process has been influenced by the philosophers such as Heraclitus and Democritus and then by the greats like Socrates, Plato and Aristotle. Plato had differentiated between the ideas and the senses. He believed in the transmigration of the soul as we Hindus do.

The concepts of various philosophers and thinkers sway the general public and the poets and the writers alike. Therefore over the ages different concepts such a Hellenism, Neoplatonism, cosmic consciousness, polytheism and Semitism have remained in vogue from time to time. The ideas of thinkers like John Locke, David Hume, Voltaire, Rousseau, and Immanuel Kant have influenced the authors. The Romantics like Hans Christian Andersen, E.T.A. Hoffman were not only pathfinders but also trendsetters. They influenced the literature all over the world. The thoughts of George Wilhelm Friedrich Hegel were called Hegelianism. Kierkegaard gave importance to the individual as against the system in the nineteenth century. However, the most revolutionary thinker was Karl Marx the protagonist of communism and class struggles of the mid nineteenth century. He had become the craze of the authors and influenced the prose and poetry all over the world.

Charles Darwin's theory of evolution enunciated in his book the Origin of Species had become world famous. Then Sigmund

Freud, a neurologist conceived of psychoanalysis and coined the notorious phrase Oedipus Complex. Many male and female authors have chosen Freudian sexual concepts as a sure fire channel of instant fame all over the world including India. The authors in the twentieth century were influenced by the theory of existentialism put forth by Friedrich Nietzsche and Jean Paul Sartre. Certain authors stretched existentialism to such an extent that it came to be called Surrealism. Certain authors have also adopted analytical philosophy or logical empiricism.

Sartre's wife Simone de Beauvoir wrote the book Second Sex and became the protagonist of feminism. She did not find any difference between men and women and considered both the sexes equal. Many authors particularly the women everywhere lapped up her thinking.

Materialism is the latest fad of both the scientists and writers seeking cogent explanation of what matter is. A ceaseless research by the scientists about the creation of the universe has resulted in the conclusion that this universe is a multiverse. The entire human thinking is now futuristic and the authors are writing science fiction and the scientists are proving what was earlier called fiction and fancy.

The poem **Paradise Returned** is an effort to seek replies to what the seers/philosophers have been telling us for centuries. We are told that the soul is immortal, knowing the self (i.e. the soul) and merging with our source, God, should be our aim. I somehow cannot swallow it all without cogitating. I refuse to be a slave of the religion without exploring veracity of its canons. If the soul is everything why did God create the body? What was the necessity to create the entire universe and make the material things manifest? To me life is a reality because before and after it I know nothing and will know nothing unless God had endowed me with the capacity to recall my past and foresee the future. Hindu seers admonish that I can do it all, but as I am, I find myself incapable of verifying their assertions. It might take many lives I am told. But how do I know it? Therefore the world opinion about terrorism and what the terrorist have been doing in Kashmir and elsewhere in the world, moved my mind. The theology of the Jihadees committing them to their heinous methodology with the conviction to reach paradise and the civilized world determined to dispatch them to their destination had propelled me to visit paradise alive. Therefore I decided about exploring the veracity of such people's convictions and our own mythology and philosophy. With that food for thought I started writing this poem at my son's house at Gurnee, Illinois, a suburban town of Chicago, U.S.A. in August 2003 and finished it in Delhi. Hindu philosophy and scientific thinking juxtaposed with each other creating turmoil within me. Einstein's (a German-American scientist who died in 1955) theory of relativity that all motion is relative, that light has the constant velocity and that space-time are a four dimensional continuum (Oxford Dictionary) flashed Manu (Indian Seer and author of Manusmriti) in my mind. Manu had divided time into four ages i.e. Satyug, Traita, Doapar and Kaliyug in that order.

Space too is unlimited and Vedic seers had opined that the earth is in the middle of the fourteen worlds (lokas). The seven worlds below the earth are:

Atala, Vitala, Sutala, Talaatala, Rasaatala, Mahatala and Paatala.

The six lokas above the earth are:

Bhuvarloka, Suvarloka, Maholoka, Janoloka, Tapoloka and Satyaloka.

There is no mention of the Swaragloka (Paradise) although Satyaloka is considered to be the paradise. I do not know how other religions have divided the space but all of them are sure of paradise, and the terrorists most of all. My sojourn in the paradise is a scrutiny of some concepts of various religions. I hope the readers would like it.

The rest of the poems in this volume are my usual random reflections about current events, my personal experiences and perceptions.

Kedar Nath Sharma

This book is most respectfully dedicated to

Mr. Vijay Mundhra

in everlasting gratitude

Acknowledgements

I am grateful to Dr. D.C. Chambial Editor of Poetcrit for publishing in his magazine some of the poems included in this volume.

I am obliged to Mr. P.C. Mathur, the Editor of Indian Book Chronicle, Jaipur, for publishing the complete Paradise Returned in the May-June, 2010 issue.

I am also grateful to Prof. V. Bhaskar Rao of Warangal, Andhra Pradesh for translating the poem Paradise Returned into Telugu after reading it in the Indian Book Chronicle.

I am beholden to Mr. R.N. Malhotra, the Proprietor of Malhotra Photostat for going through the manuscript of this book. It is my third collection of poems, which he has gone through.

But I am immensely obliged to Dr. Atma Ram who was Director of Education and then Advisor Education, Government of Himachal Pradesh, for going through the manuscript. He is a well-known educationist of the country, a renowned literary critic, and a litterateur who is conversant with various religions. I had sent the manuscript for his scrutiny. He has done a heartening analysis.

Dr. Bijay Kant Dubey, Head, Department of English, Chandrakona Vidyasagar Mahavidyalaya, Chandrakona Town, Paschim Medinipur, West Bengal-721201 has written nicely about my poetry. I am highly obliged to him.

Above all I express my heartfelt gratitude to His Excellency the President of India, Dr. A.P.J. Abdul Kalam, himself a poet and a genius par excellence, for appreciating on 29.3.2007 the poem Paradise Returned from Rashtrapati Bhavan, New Delhi.

The beautiful illustrations have been done by Mr. Harsh Vardhan Arya, a well known Hindi poet of Delhi. He has illustrated the works of other authors also and commands great respect both as a poet and as a painter. He is a Youngman so I am sure that a very bright future awaits him. I am very highly obliged to him for his commendable contribution to my effort.

I am also grateful to Allied Publishers Pvt. Ltd. for publishing this book.

The inquisitive readers who want to check the veracity of my experiences of Paradise may like to refer to the following books:

1. Manusmrti with commentary by Pt. Rameshwar Bhatt published by Chaukhamba Sanskrit Pratishthan, Delhi.
2. Bhaktiyog and Rajyog with Patanjali's Yogasutra by Swami Vivekananda published by Rama Krishan Muth, Nagpur.
3. Vedic Healing-1 by Guru Shree Hariharan Vadhyar.
4. Sophie's World by Jostein Gaarder (a Norwegian author) published by Berkley Books, New York.
5. Among the Believers (An Islamic Journey) by V.S. Naipaul.
6. Heroes & Icons/Time 100 (Person of the Century) published by Time Books, New York, in the year 2000.
7. An article entitled A New Face of Gay Power by John Cloud Cody, published in October 13, 2003 issue of Time, New York.
8. How Did It Really Happen? by The Reader's Digest Association Inc. Pleasantville, New York/Montreal.
9. Marne Ke Baad Kiya Hogaa? (What will happen after death?) by Maulana Mohammed Ashiq Ilahi Buland Shahari published by Siraj Publications, Delhi-110006.
10. a. Wayside Gardens—Catalog Spring 1999 Hodges, South Carolina, USA.
    b. New Roses, 1999, Jackson & Perkins Medford, Oregon, USA.
    c. Paradise Water Garden—a complete guide to water gardening Whitman, Massachusetts, USA.

Stimulation for visiting Paradise was provided by J.R.R. Tolkien's fantasy books—The Silmarillion, The Hobbit and The Lord of the Rings.

Kedar Nath Sharma

Contents

Paradise Returned

I

Einstein has opined:
Time and space are relative.
That reminds me of Vedic scriptures
and of Nachiketa knocking at the doors of Death alive.
So I decided to probe it all myself.
My daily Vedic prayer enthused me:
O Lord,
Lead us from the untruth to the truth
From Darkness to Light
From death to immortality!
I took refuge in yogic meditation.

My thoughts perturbed me.
Vedas say: we are not alone
in the entire cosmos
which is not a universe
but is a multi-verse.
There are twelve more Lokas
besides the earth—Bhooloka.
and the swarag loka—paradise.
Moreover other religions too are true.
Prophet Mohammed has decreed:
those who kill the infidels go to paradise.
Therefore the suicide terrorists
are all flocking to the heaven.
The rest of the world is determined
to send them all to where they intend to go.
Naturally heaven must be chockfull.

So I prayed and prayed.
God appeared before me
in his cosmic shape—Virat Roop.
He had hundreds of faces
including those of seers of all faiths.
I implored my own Lord Krishna
who seemed to be smiling.
He immediately blessed: Tatha-astu (be it so)!
I was overjoyed to visit paradise
on tourist visa.
But then how to travel?

American shuttle has had several accidents
traveling a fraction of our own solar system
whereas paradise is far beyond
millions of more galaxies.
I myself cannot jump more than one foot above the earth
and know not the art of levitating or flying
as did our ancient seers.
Narada could stride
from one loka to the other in a jiffy.
It is not a fiction.
Scientists and doubting Thomases
will have to delve deep
into the Vedic lore to seek the light.
But poor me what do I do?
How will Krishna's word come true?
I implored him again and he commanded:
Close your eyes - I did.
Open your eyes - I did.
Lo and behold I was at the gate of paradise
a trillion light years away
left to fend for myself.

I implored my own Lord Krishna.

II

Someone at the gate asked,
O earthling, how have you reached here alive?
With Lord Krishna's grace, I replied.
You can't enter this way,
it is meant for the immortals.
Go to the 1001th gate named Rebirth
and present your credentials.
I had just heard a voice and not its source.
I had to rub my eyes again and again
till I could blear through
the dazzling light of almost hundred suns.
Nothing was clear and water flowed from the eyes.
Was I weeping or going blind?
I could not guess but cried:
O, Lord what have you done?
Just then a cool breeze wafted my face
and I started seeing clearly.
I saw a group of angels
wearing saffron or white robes of monks
with green or white sashes dangling
down their left shoulders
to the right sides of their bodies
but they had different leg gears.
The one that spoke to me had a dhoti on
and trod on wooden sandals.
His glad cherubic face and generous smile
made me speak:
alive as I am I have to go back
to earth after a brief sojourn.
He started talking to me in Sanskrit
but I requested him
to speak to me either in Hindi or in English,
please note that I am America returned.

Angel:
We appear before the beholder, in the garb he wants to see us.

Soon you will be paradise returned, he quipped.
I could only make my lips curl up into a smile.
He informed: paradise is very vast—
fourteen times larger than the earth.
But there are no means of transport.
You have to walk or fly all your own
as we do.
So there is no noise and no pollution here.
It is one country and not many as on the earth.
There are no states either.
We have counties.
Here where you stand is the district of the immortals.
Being a Hindu you would like
to visit the district of Rebirth.
But there are no walls or boundaries
once you enter a gate you can go everywhere.
There are no separate religious entities such as
Christians, Jews, Muslims, Hindus etc. here.
There are no deterrent injunctions of almighty God
Who stays detached here too.
He would stir only if there is any commotion.
There are no houses or hotels here.
You don't have to cook and to eat.
The climate here is such that none falls ill
as there are no diseases
and none feels hunger or thirst.
But if you want to relish anything
you can have the earthly food of your choice
just by wishing for it but only vegetarian—
you don't have to kill anything living
for your own living.
There is no birth or death here.
Ther are no marriages, so no couples.
What a dull place! I thought.
The angel could read my mind.

He admonished: no, no, not dull.
It is gay and interesting.
Gay? Are many Americans here?
O, no!
Gay means happy, the lesbians and the gays
of the earth never come here.
They go to the hell.
The sexes are made by God
for procreation and not recreation.
How can you vouch for it?
I am omniscient, he replied.
Nothing is unknown to me.
How do you know my language?
I was not taught any.
I am primordial and can speak the languages
of the inhabitants of other thirteen Lokas too
where life exists in the entire cosmos.
The scientists will not believe you
without cogent evidence, I said.
Yes, it is how God has divined.
The scientists go by what they see
in the matter and probe it.
The spiritualists can know
by communicating directly with God.
Both can do that by labouring hard.
What is the name of God here in paradise?
He is the Creator—the names are given
to him by the seekers.
You call him Lord Krishna.
Are you not a seeker? I asked.
I am a part of him, as invisible as the soul—
the life force.
I don't believe—you are talking to me.
I am talking to you for your help, he averred.
Come and touch me!

Do you feel anything solid?
I was convinced—I could feel nothing
and yet I saw him.
So I exclaimed:
Is it Maya?
Do I dream?
Neither, you are face to face with God's power.
But you are wearing the robes of a Hindu monk.
How can nothingness wear such clothes?
I am not wearing anything.
All those living in paradise are naked souls
fractions of the Creator.
We appear before the beholder
in the garb he wants to see us.
You are a Hindu, I appear before you as such.
I fell on his feet and implored:
please forgive me, an ignorant creature.
Kindly do help me see the paradise
and let me return safely to where I belong.
The perpetual smile of his face
reassured me.
Go wherever you like, he said.
Henceforth you can walk, float or fly
As you may like till you go back home.
But I have come here for the first time
I need some guide to show me round.
I may meet certain souls
whose language I may not understand.
The angel replied:
those who reach here after death
automatically know the world languages.
However, the queries arising in your mind
will be answered by me promptly.
But being a living man you may feel hungry
or bored by the prevailing nothingness here.

You will see and enjoy whatever you wish for.
because nothing is bought or sold.
You wont find the feuds of isms
such as capitalism and the now almost dead communism.
We all bask in God's munificent grace.
So you need not worry about any
Government officials bothering you.
There is no dictator here.
There is no democracy or monarchy either.
No pick pockets, no beggars
informed the angel dispelling all my fears.

III

Thus assured I entered the very next gate and walked
on the sight seeing tour of paradise.
But there was nothing visible.
There was effulgence everywhere.
I could see no temple, no mosque,
church, synagogue, dargah or whatever.
What is this heaven?
Why do religionists advise us to aspire for it?
There was no singing of God's panegyrics:
Kirtan, aarti, hymns, psalms or azans
only light and nothing else
What a swarg lok!
prompt came the sound of the
familiar voice to my mortal ears.
All the places of worship are man made.
But God's name is commercialized
and politicized by the fundamentalists
everywhere on the earth, I blurted out.
There was silence. So I moved ahead
Wishing to see the high rise buildings
like those of the earth.

But paradise has no buildings.
Yet soon the Sears Tower of Chicago
and 1483 feet high twin Petronas Towers
of Kuala Lumpur loomed before my eyes.
I could see even down town Los Angeles,
Beverly Hills and dazzling Las Vegas.
Then jumped before my eyes
The smoking and crumbling Twin Towers
of the World Trade Centre of New York.
I could even see the suicide Islamic pilots
killing themselves in the swirling fires
like those of hell, on the wild earth.
Immediately the name of prophet Mohammed
flashed in my mind.
I was shell shocked to see a bearded man
with a white skull cap on head appear before me
Who are you?
I am prophet Mohammed you have just called
I am sorry I could not recognize you.
But the fault is your own
as you have banned icon worship by your followers.
Had I seen even one picture of yours
I would have recognized you.
I was inspired by God
so I said what I said, he replied.
But how come you are in paradise?
You should have been lying dead
somewhere else called Barzakh till resurrection
which has still not happened.
All your dead followers must be awaiting
the same somewhere in some
unknown galaxy in the multi-verse.
And what about those suicide bombers,
the Jihadis aspiring for paradise
killing themselves in your name
all over the world?

They should have been with you here
but you are all alone.
Are you not proving yourself wrong?
And what have you to say about your own outcastes:
the Shiites, the Bahais and the Ahmedias
(Ahmed was born in 1838 at Qadian
in the Indian Punjab, you may know)?
How can you blame me for what has happened
after my exit from the scene?
And I don't interpret Koran
for the Mullahs in the mosques.
They do it to suit their needs,
Mohammed commented.
O, yes that reminds me
of your own predilection for Aisha
your thirteen year old wife
whom you had married when you were
in your mid fifties.
The poor girl was left alone in the desert
with a handsome soldier for a night
when you had marched ahead
during your early military escapades
in the year 626 or 627.
Ali your cousin and son-in-law
wanted her to be discarded for adultery.
But because of your infatuation for her
you had ordained that four eye witnesses
were needed to prove adultery.
Since there was none you declared her pious.
Following your foot prints your aged followers
marry young girls of the age of their granddaughters
from the poor Muslim households.
You must be proud of that!
Your love for polygamy has made
your religion spread fast.

But it will not any more
because your chauvinists have challenged
the formidable America.
The Americans the most powerful people today
will haunt them everywhere on the earth
till at least 2020 by which time
the hydrogen based motor fuel
will replace the gasoline,
the money spinner of the Muslims
making Islam go back to the desert days.
There is time still for you to warn
your followers of the impending disaster.
Kindly advise them to study science also
and not just Koran.
Prophet Mohammed nodded in affirmation.
I quoted:
La illaha illal Allaho,
Muhammad ur Rasool Allah!
You know its meaning very well yet I translate:
There is no God but Allah.
Muhammad is the prophet of Allah!
By limiting God only to the word Allah
you have negated the names given to
God by other religions and have made
Islam narrow in outlook.
The prophet replied: no, don't misinterpret,
I had said God is one and I had named
him Allah. God will remain God with any name.
Satisfied I wished him Islam-a-lekam
and floated ahead.
Suddenly Rehmatullah my teacher
Who had taught me Urdu in the fourth standard
before 1947 appeared before me.
A lanky six footer with hollow cheeks
gave a loving smile.

I could recognize him only when
he asked, can you spell
Rauza Taj Mahal properly even today or not?
I exclaimed, "Oh, sir, namaskar!
Glad to meet you in Swarg Lok.
But according to your religion
you should have been awaiting resurrection—
you are here?"
That is not a mystery, he replied.
I was hiding behind the statue
of Lord Hanuman when I was beheaded
by the angry Hindu zealots
in the temple of our town.
So Lord Hanuman brought me personally here
because I was holding him very fast.
It is a pleasant surprise! I said.
So there must here be other pious Muslims also?
Yes, there are saints Mouinddin Chisti,
Hazrat Nizzamuddin, Kalimullah Wali
and Amir Khusro too with countless others.
Is poet Mohammed Iqbal also here?
No, I have not seen him, replied Rehmatullah
and said, "Iqbal had sung:
Saare Jehan se achcha Hindustan Hamara,
but he was the first to float the idea
of Pakistan in his speech
to the Indian Muslim League in 1930.
Poor fellow had died in 1938
nine years before the birth of Pakistan.
But for him and Jinnah
My family and I would have continued to live happily.
I wish Allah had not created religious fanatics.
Quest for God makes a man mad,
whereas God is everywhere.
It is the soul that makes every creature live
even the tiniest of the bugs.

Without soul man cannot live
so man should first delve in the self
and converse with his soul
as soul is an eternal pilgrim.
Bodies of all beings are just mortal shells.
Time exists and space exists
because soul exists and soul is a fraction of God.
Whole paradise in inhabited by bodiless souls."
When Rehmatullah had finished, I said:
well, sir, a thinker like you
deserves to be in heaven. Bye!

IV

I was bored of the all pervading light
and my eyes craved for something
as pleasant as the Mughal Garden of Raisina Hill.
I soon found myself in a valley of flowers
where I could recognize roses,
the heralds of love, I had seen on the earth:
French perfume and lace, sun flares
peace, Tropicana, harlequins,
baby blanket, or weeping tree roses.
But the sweet smelling were only
the Indian red roses.
Then floated past my eyes
the beds of perennial lupines
spiking in blue, purple, pink, red and white;
rows of large hollyhocks having single
flowers on tall stalks;
the cosmos of various hues;
double gold daisies;
hibiscus blooms of clear pink
propped on lush, dark green foliage;
flox, emerald blue or coral eyes, pink
or white delight, cuddly marigolds,

Garden in Heaven

lilacs, giant hydrangeas and floribundas;
petunia, giant doubles, pink and purple waves
and razzle dazzle; sun runner with
countless radiant yellow blooms
open atop a dark green mat of foliage;
dragon fly, as if kiln fired, were eye catching
There was sweetly scented honey suckle
blooming profusely with
sweet peas and sweet smelling jasmine,
narcissus, water and ball lilies
with thousands of other flowers
which I could not recognize, danced
with the languid air.
Signifying beginning of life were ferns
such as caladiums, ostrich fern, deer fern,
piceas, junipers, pictum and toothed wood ferns.
Then there were anarchist carnations
and chrysanthemums symbolizing death.
There were giverny arches
and Versailles arbors skirted by
Lillian golden stardust with yellow angel's trumpets.
There were pompous dahlias
shadowed by double red bougainvilleas.
Ornamental grasses such as pampas,
punila, variegata, red baron and
fargesia of the bamboo breed.
Then I saw rain forests followed by
mango, maple and magnolia glades,
pine, poplar and peepal glens,
banyans, bananas all bonsai.
And elms and oaks adorned by
Thuja spring groves, cypresses and cacti.
Poor me, I knew not the names of
all botanical beauties of the paradise.
Dazzled, I exclaimed:
paradise is indeed paradise!

V

Swarag Lok is the highest of all Lokas.
It must have been created first of all!
No, came the reply of the familiar voice,
all lokas were created together
the big bang way in the primeval explosion
with cosmic hum symphony of OM.
Lord God who stays still higher
in the Braham Lok in cosmic sleep
creates several galaxies while
breathing out strings of energy.
He had first created three powers
for creating, preserving and annihilation.
The creator Brahama was born
in a lotus flower that rose from God's navel.
Don't tell me the story of Shrimad Bhagwat Puran
and the other ancient Hindu lore,
just because I am Hindu, I replied.
Other religions have their own such myths.
Pat came the reply:
myths are just stories
which science does not believe in.
The scientists' theory of big bang
is the closest to the reality.
Even Christianity is not off the track.
Noah is the preserver like the Hindu Vishnu
who protects all the creatures of God
in all the floods which occur after every Kalpa.
His ark is not a boat of wood.
It is God's munificent power
to protect to preserve.
Abraham does not sacrifice a goat
but through him man is advised
to discard avarice and ego.

Those who misread the parable kill goats.
It is better not to read than to misread.
That is why Buddha advised the people
long before that, not to kill any living beings.
But Christian God takes seven days
to create the world, I asked.
Not at all, the voice replied.
It is the relativity of Time and Life
in consonance with Space
without which reckoning of time
would be chaotic.
Therefore science and all religions
agree to a seven day week.
You see, even science is not irreligious.
I see, I said. It is swarag lok
But I don't see the Hindu God Indra
and his courtiers, the cabinet and the courtesans:
Maneca, Rambha, Urvashi et al, here?
There was laughter and the voice said:
God Indra is God's coordinating power
controlling five elements: Agni (fire),
Vayu (air), Varun (water) etc. which sustain life
with Prithvi (earth) and the Akaash (ether).
He is not a philanderer as presumed
by some who misinterpret.
And the nymphs are nothing but
replicas of female energy controlling the world.
But Hindu's supreme God (Braham)
is always sleeping whereas I do not see
either day or night here in swarag
and no soul sleeps here, I asked.
It is no riddle, the voice quipped.
The supreme soul in his astral body
has his eyes half open, ever vigilant.
He too neither sleeps nor wakes.

And the nymphs are nothing but
replicas of female energy controlling the world.

He just winks at the end of
a regular cycle of time
for realignment with space
when the great floods occur
to annihilate and to start again.
I don't trust I commented
because I cannot live that long
to watch what you say.
There was silence.

VI

Suddenly a big lotus flower
spread before me like a hammock.
I stepped into it and fell asleep.
I dreamt: my body was disintegrating,
there were no bones, no flesh,
no form, no shape.
I was just like the other inhabitants of paradise—
a speck of light, a small string of energy
without the pull of gravity.
I heard God saying:
I had created you to live in the world
to leave it better than when you were born.
I had endowed you with:
compassion and passion
love and hatred,
forbearance and anger,
discernment and discretion,
above all a brain to make use of.
You have been indulging
in negativity—the dark side of duality.
O, God! My Lord! I implored:
Good and bad are your own gifts to the world.
What would happen if negativity
which is half of your creation vanished?

Who would then worship you?
The world will cease to be the world
and you will have to start afresh
by creating a Noah and his ark.
So long as you, God, live
nature and its objects will continue eternally.
Life and death will survive.
Can you undo yourself?
Suddenly I was jolted out of sleep
and found my lotus hammock rocking violently.
Fearing I might get injured or be killed
I jumped out of it
and fell on the back of a white swan
which flew nearby.
Oh, what a dangerous place is heaven!
I could have been killed
that lotus was more scary
than the roller coasters of California's
Disney Land.
Now the swan was flying fast.
It brought me to the Christian part of paradise.

VII

Flashed on the bright sky
(The sky in paradise is not azure)
in golden hue, were the words of
the psalm 46:1
"God is for us a refuge and strength,
a help that is readily to be found during distress."
I read these words several times and asked:
why should we seek God
only during distress?
He is with us all the time.
Why not befriend him,

can someone explain?
Suddenly Jesus Christ
appeared before me and said,
"God is indeed everywhere with us
but in distress he is more of an anchor."
I immediately folded my hands
and bowed before him.
I am gratified to see you in person.
May I have the privilege,
if you forgive my intransigence
to ask a few pertinent questions
crowding my mind?
He nodded his permission.
Reverend sir, a great religion
connected with you is prevalent
in the world for over two thousand years.
Those who felt doomed crucified you
because of your rising popularity at the time.
Some people think that you had not died
on the cross but were rescued
by your followers and had reached India
where you died at ripe old age
and were buried in a grave in Kashmir.
What is the fact?

I had acquired a stage in spirituality
that I could transmigrate myself
like the Hindu sages.
So the death of my body was insignificant.
Since my devotees were hysterical
I had to oblige them too. he informed.
I felt convinced.

You had set up a body of spiritualists
which was first called a Congregation

and subsequently a church.
But now there are so many churches:
Roman Catholic, Apostolic, Presbyterian,
Protestant, Baptist, Lutheran, Episcopal,
and I know not how many more.
Why so many churches?
He replied:
They represent so many interests
of different humans who choose
what they like for their own weal.
And sir, you had advised people
to lead straight life as pious
married men and women.
Roman Catholics did not permit even abortion.
But there are many unmarried Christian mothers.
Even adolescent girls indulge in sex
and many undergo abortions too.
Not only that, homosexuality is rampant.
The apex court of USA, a Christian country,
has legalized sodomy.
Not only the Christian society
even the church priests are homosexual.
A gay priest has been elected
Episcopal Bishop in August, 03.
This fad of homosexuality is being aped
by the so-called modernists
in the developing societies too.
Is it a good sign?
No, it is a sign of a sick society
and augurs doom for the Christian world
and for others too.
The governments should nip this evil
before it rips the fabric of God's creation apart.
The faddists should be crucified, observed Christ.
Having said this he went behind the curtain of light.

VIII

The spectacle of light merging with the light
made me think that paradise is nothing
but the land of the spirits of the dead.
It could therefore be the Hades of Greek mythology
but it is not the underworld, I started cogitating.
Just then a saint wearing ochre jumper
and a cap dangling down to his ears
appeared and remarked: It would be wrong
to call it Hades though the souls of the dead inhabit here.
It is paradise, the reservoir of
God's immense energy, his potent power.
But who are you? May I know your name?
I am Guru Nanak, said the resplendent spirit.
I am the same whose turbaned pictures
you keep in your books. My cap was replaced
with a turban only in the twentieth century
by Sobha Singh, an artist, who lived at Andreta
in district Kangra of India. He was an ardent Sikh.
Gurudev ! I bow before you. You and other saints:
Sai Baba and father Agnelo inspire me
and bless me that is why I am here
face to face with you in paradise.
Gurudev you had started the Sikh religion
though born a Hindu, I said.
I did not like the social mores
then prevalent in the country.
People liked what I said and they followed me.
I was against social discrimination.
Mostly the indigent and the socially deprived
liked my approach to God.
Many became my disciples (Shishyas)
and started calling me the guru.
With the passage of time they came to be called Sikhs.

Gradually the movement became
protestant Hindu religion and was named Sikhism
by a staunch patriot named Guru Gobind Singh
who made the harassed to rise
and to gird up their loins against the tyranny.
Sensing the need of the hour he started calling
the valiant Singhs, the ferocious lions,
to intimidate the religious bigots and
the human predators of the time, Nanak replied.
But you had made the people
believe in karmas like the Hindus,
and thus in destiny, unlike the tenth Guru
who had made men self reliant, I observed.
These are the karmas of the previous lives
which make a soul shed its astral body
and be born in a gross body
to reap what it had sown.
Science too talks about cause and effect.
It is not obscurantism.
This concept makes the God fearing
act noble in their lives.
But religion is man made
and is not ordained by God.
He wants humans to be humane.
If they violate his creatures in any way
they add to their karmas and taste the fruit.
God does not like sycophants.
He likes abiding beings, said Nanak and vanished.

IX

I felt frustrated by his sudden exit
when I was enjoying his company.
But then things were not in my control
as they are not on the earth too.

One thing was, however, certain:
Time and space lose their dimensions
in paradise.
Here time loses its circumambience
and space its circumference.
They merge here as they blend in our dreams.
But paradise is not a dreamland.
It is impassive whereas in our dreams
we do not fail to feel
and can fly away
to be everywhere and here too
being invisible like the air around.
I felt that even the seers consigned to paradise
very much like to live on earth.
God drafts them on assignments
in our world.
Therefore comparing life
with a dream is erroneous
because dreams are transient
both on the earth and in the heaven
like the one in lotus hammock.
And life is as real as
a flight in a jet
or on the back of a swan in paradise.
It must be lived discerningly.
Beyond that God does not need
anything in return from his creatures.
He is not a trader.
He rules from far beyond paradise
but his divinity dwells everywhere.
His incarnates can be seen by the seekers
in whatever form they like.
The climate in paradise is salubrious
though no sun rises there.
There is no night either.

So I could not see any stars.
There are no clouds, no rain,
no heat, no cold.
Yet souls survive
in their non-terrestrial nothingness
wallowing in the celestial hum of the Word—Om.
There is no birth,
no age, no death,
no children cry
no youth pry.
There is no anger,
no wars, no WMDs,
no hunger, no craze.
There is no jealousy,
no struggle for power
so no politics.
There is complete nothingness
visible to the mortal eyes.
No living mortal can live in paradise.
One must die to be there
to delve in divine snugness.
But I could find nothing to enchant me.
I held my breath pensively
and suddenly felt floating and flying
across paradise
without any sense of
east or west, north or south.
All sides, in or out, left or right
are man made on the earth below.
I flew fast without any power
or will of my own
and reached a place
where I thought I saw a banyan tree
large and lofty with its roots
dangling down from no where

to everywhere
wherever I could see.
It presented a spectacle
of God's grandeur to be seen nowhere on the earth.
I plumped down on the ethereal
surface of paradise
to see more wonders.

X

On a swing of the tangled roots
of the banyan tree I saw
a saint meditating in lotus pose.
I went near him and sought his blessings.
Reverend swami ji, what is this strange tree
and the swinging dais of the roots
from where you meditate?
He replied:
This is the tree of life with its roots
straddling all over the cosmos
without getting roots and yet planted deep.
All heavenly bodies hang like that
all around as I do.
Swami ji my mind is cluttered.
My brain is stuffed.
I know not waste management
nor do I have a broom.
I wish I could cleanse it!
But how?
Stop thinking, he advised
and give your mind a holiday.
Let your brain sit on a strike
to make you learn to meditate
and to make yourself to be knowing nothing.
I wish I were a mystic!
I exclaimed.

I saw a banyan tree—
its roots dangling down from nowhere.

You have to be nothing but yourself.
Just rein in your mind
and don't let it gallop or trot.
When you start scanning
the hollowness of your head
you will find it cleaned
and flush with light.
You will then be at peace with yourself
perfectly peaceful, calm and serene,
he mutered.
The vision dissolved.
I was disappointed because
I could not know who he was
I just thought of Manu
and was soon flicked off vertically
to the feet of a hoary meditating figure
who opened his eyes and peeking at me
asked, "What do you want? I am Manu."
I was overawed, yet I murmured:
In your book Manusmriti you had
divided time into four ages.
To Kaliyug, the iron age to which
I belong, you had ascribed 1200 years.
But we find that Iron Age has been
continuing for nearly five thousand years.
How had you faulted in your calculations?
You had also created four castes
but today they are countless.
Time is one unit Manu replied.
It can't be divided as you attribute it to me.
The primeval world was good.
Brahma had assumed goodness to degenerate
in about twelve thousand years
which was the perimeter of one cycle of time
fixed by him.

This cycle has moved countless times.
In the present Iron Age human nature
has degenerated faster and longer
and human nature has never been in my purview.
Humans are themselves responsible for it
because of their karmas
so the present Iron Age has prolonged.
God had created four categories (castes) of humans considering
the instincts and
inclinations of persons and not
according to their birth.
Those who subsist by using their mouth
were called Brahmins;
those who relied on their arms
were called Kashtriyas;
those who make use of their legs
were named Vaishyas;
those who treaded on their feet
to make a living were called Shudras.
Now remember that mouth, arms, legs and feet
denote intellectual prowess of the individuals
and not just parts of human body.
All this is described in the Vedas
and I had only made matters simpler
in my book.
I quipped: but modern Indian politicians
blame you for it.
They are ignorant.
You should guide them,
replied Manu and suddenly
I slumped down to the lower parts of paradise.
What a perplexing experience!
But I had found that paradise lies
in tiers and is multidimensional.
Thinking of politicians made me remember

Chanakya the economist,
Chanakya the statesman.
How can a politician reach paradise?
I asked myself.
Just then I was pushed forward in time
to third century B.C.
A figure appeared before me
and said, "I am Chanakya."
I quipped: venerable Brahmin
I had never expected to meet a politician here.
He replied: Mean politicians
of the Indian brand these days
cannot reach here.
But I was not depraved.
I hated proud rulers called kings,
had groomed Chandragupt
to be an ideal ruler.
I had advised men in my Niti Shastra
to be humble enough and to learn
even from animals and birds.
I had said:
Be bold like a lion;
Imbibe self-restraint of a crane;
Be cocksure and an early riser,
fair patriarch and self-dependent
like a cock.
Man must also be cautious like a crow
be daring, watchful and lay aside
some means for the rainy day
and must meet his mate secretly.
Man must also be dogged, faithful,
content and sleep light like a dog;
be assiduous like an ass
unmindful of oppression
and remain contented like him.

Leave aside animals, modern politicians
don't learn anything from history even.
They are thus bound to inhabit in hell.
Can you offer them some advice? I asked.
None to the incorrigible, he replied,
and melted away in translucence.

XI

Are there no women in paradise?
I thought. Several said the Voice
and a lady with a lute in her hand
stood before me.
She said, she was Meera and added
souls have no sex, Nature has.
Saint Meera you worshipped Lord Krishna,
why didn't you worship Lord Ram? I asked.
Ram, Krishna, Shiv, Allah, God
and thousands of others are the names of
one Super Soul the greatest super power
the cause of all that one can see, feel and touch.
Worship him by any name
you will find him, was her reply.
You discarded your husband for Krishna
was that good?
It is only the body that relates,
not a soul.
Can I meet God?
You have met the souls
his molecules, you can meet him too.
Just carry on. I could see her no more
since I had thought about Ram
Tulsi Das instantly stood before me.
I said, I have read your biography of Lord Ram.

It is a melodious poetic account about the graces of God and
the tribulations
that he underwent during his incarnation
and sojourn on earth.
Why should God act like a man
when he can wield his powers
even without being visible
as he does through natural calamities?

He does it to make man have faith in him.
In floods mountains crumble
elephant die and yet an ant can survive
to make man exclaim: God is great!
Ram was very rash with Sita, his consort
and you too had said:
servitors, animals and women
need to be admonished.
So you and Ram seem odd to the modern man.

Ram was not at all harsh with Sita.
He was advising wives to be reasonable
and not aspire for improbables
like the skin of a golden deer.
If they do, they would suffer as Sita did.
That is why I had advised
to enforce discipline on the three
to bring harmony in the society.

Why was Sita made to walk through fire?
I asked.

A woman is a mother like mother earth,
a spring from which sprouts humanity.
If defiled mankind would be depraved.
A pure woman is the progenitor
of a healthy society,

A profligate breeds a sickly one.
Ram was presenting ideals.
Sita's fire test was a benchmark
of a woman's chastity
and of an unpolluted society.
Moreover fire should not be
considered only an agent combustible.
It also means social restraints,
which a pious woman must observe.
Sexual freedom for both men and women
would be like wild earth where only
jungles grow and weeds boom brightly.

Ram was born in Ayodhya.
As an incarnation he was
the God of all mankind.
Is it good to limit him to Ayodhya
making him the God of Hindus alone?
I asked.

Ram is just one name of one universal God.
He should not be solicited
for parochial purposes,
doing so would be belittling him.

I rejoined:
Thank you poet the great,
I envy you but am not endowed
with the faculties you possessed.
I don't have your melody.
But there was no reply
and he was no more visible.

I regretted my incompetence to see
the souls in the heaven as long as
I wished.

So I desired to meet someone
who could teach me to acquire
that super sensory power
to seek, to meet, to hold.
I sought some Guru like swami Vivekananda.
Just then the Swami in his ochre robes
and a turban stood before me
and said:
you can get what you desire
by being selfless.
Selflessness is the sine qua non
of a real religion.

Serve Lord Shiva's beings without any motive
and you will meet him in person
and hold Him eternally.
You might visit several temples
and undertake countless pilgrimages
still you can't be trusted
like a cheetah in spite of his
colourful coat of stripes.
Only love and hate not anybody
for none is high and none is low.
An ant and a god are equal.

The star of India's destiny had set
on the day she had coined the word
'Malechch' which means
impure or untouchable and
had started looking down upon
Lord Shiva's other creatures.
Remember that purity, patience, dedication
and love will make you a true receptacle
of His divinity.

You must also acquire boldness,
self control, renunciation and faith.
Become the architect of your own destiny.
Avoid disputes about religion
as they betray a lack of spirituality
and showcase puerility.

I had once written to sister Nivedita:
I'm the fear of the fear,
The terror of terror,
I am the fearless, I am unique.
I am the rule of destiny
the wiper out of facts.
I used to call myself condensed India.
You too can be that and can meet God and me
on the earth too.

He was no more visible
but had convinced me
that man can be near God
even while living on earth
and should stop aiming to reach paradise.
He can make a heaven or a hell
in his own mind
as had John Milton opined.
So I burst out:
Tomorrow or tomorrow or tomorrow
the day will come
when all earthlings with aplomb
would like to stay on the earth
created by God for them.
With pleasures sublime
and would stop worrying God
to inhabit them all in his heaven,
the heaven where no living beings go.

only the souls of the dead can soar
leaving all hopes and aspirations,
dreams and emotions,
their hatred and their love
in the world below.
The paradisians have no feelings,
they need no tears,
have no purpose for laughter,
have no need for pleasure,
they shun all treasures,
for there are no wants,
simple deathless and birth less souls
resplendent with light
lie passive in the powerhouse of paradise.
The very concept of paradise
is the handiwork of dreamers and repudiates
God and his plans.
Without it
the priests and the preachers would be left jobless.
making religions worthless.
So the wise must act wise,
discard the notion of paradise,
learn to be grateful to God
who has made this earth for them
and they must make itself a paradise
the land of their dreams.
Suddenly I found myself
at my own home
reclining in a rocking chair.

Our Mule

The animal eunuch,
she was called Mule
because she was indeed a mule
the beast of burden
serving a family of shopkeepers:
my maternal grandfather
and his son.

She felt homogenous
among two cows,
two buffaloes and their offsprings
living under one roof
munching hay
sleeping and snoozing
She often slept standing—
a trait of horses and the like.

Ever since I was a boy of ten or more
my uncle used to ask me
to put fodder before her
and take her to the pond
for drinking water.
She had thus come to recognize me.
But she would not like
to be disturbed when after a long journey
she munched her grassy meal.
She would prick her ears backward
to express her annoyance
and look threateningly towards me,
I would feel scared.

She would obey me when she liked
or disdain me when she wanted.

I compromised till I grew up.
She would sometimes behave the same way
with her master, my uncle too.
He would then flail her
with a long staff or stop feeding her wet grams
which she relished when put in a bag
hung by her ears.
After such incidents I often saw
tears rolling down her long temples.

The mules are the hybrid cross breed
of a mare and an ass.
They are barren and would never conceive
but one in thousands might;
necessitating caesarian by a veteran vet
or die during delivery
a painful death.
But they are wiser than
their male counterparts
and even their father—the donkey.

The mule I am talking about
was a thinking creature and moody too.
Once while I was on her back
the boy of twelve or so
she had missed her footfall
on an uneven path
and had to bend her left knee
but her right stood the ground firmly.
With a sudden jerk I had fallen down.
As soon as she stood erect
she kept standing and waited
for me to gather myself up again.
She dutifully took me home.

On another such occasion
she had left me fallen on the ground
without affliction.
When she reached home
without me with all her harness on
my uncle had brought her back
and she had to carry me grudgingly home.

The Beas river those days
had not been bridged or dammed
and people crossed it on large boats
rowed by sailors with bamboos long.
I often had to cross the river
to fetch merchandise from Datarpur
on my mule's back to Khatiar
over-looking the present day Pong Dam.
She would board the boat
like a seasoned traveller
and carry me and the merchandise
home quite safe.

I also used to take her for grinding wheat
into flour at the hydro-flour-mill (Gharat)
by the river side.
She would take me to the right mill
my uncle's favourite one.

I used to travel long journeys
on her back because
the narrow gauge train
had its own timings
but was miles away from the country side
and the buses could be seen
in towns alone.

So quadrupeds were the handy transport
for those who could afford.
I was once asked to take my mother home
to my native place from the granny's house
and bring the mule back,
a distance of about forty miles.

The journey was done in two days.
One night was spent midway,
at a rented house where
we used to live for several years,
our mule was familiar with this place.
On the return journey
I was alone with her.
When we reached the midway
she, as her won't, turned on the way
to our rented house.
But I prodded her by digging
my shoe heels on her flanks.
She obeyed unwillingly till
she reached another way leading
to our midway night rest.
Here she became adamant
and insisted on breaking the journey.
I was expected back on that very day
but the mule knew nothing about human worries.
After she had walked for a while
on the way of her choice
I had to strike hard her flanks with my heels.

In that human and animal struggle
a chronic carbuncle at the top of her
right leg was burst with my kicking
and the pus and blood had trickled out copiously.
She felt the pain but was helpless

to trudge on the onward journey
with tears flowing down her eyes.
With dismay or may be annoyance
she let her lose her way
but as the day wore away
she became conscious of the impending night
and I too was worried
and had to seek guidance from other travellers.
It soon became dark but I was able to bring
her to the right track.
She trudged on through the hilly forest
of pines and wild animals
late into the night.

Whether she was afraid or not
I could not know but sitting on her back
I was praying to Lord Hanuman
and reached home at bed time.
I then realized the folly of my stubbornness.
She died nearly thirty years ago
But I remember her far sightedness.
I think that animals are often wiser than men
and mules are not foolish.

During the second world war
the mules were sacrificed
to serve the Allied forces
and the war concluded by the use
of man made nukes.
Certainly some animals are more humane
than men.
The mules are courageous, bold and faithful.
They like to be understood and loved.
All animals do.

God is Bewildered

God is bewildered
and knows not
where his creation is headed.
He finds man turned fiend.
He knows not
why there is darkness at noon
even when the sun is shining.
Has the midnight sun of Scandinavia
leased its darkness
to the noon in Asia?
It is an eclipse
so whatever was bright
is now slight.

Self-mortification, fasting,
singing and dancing
to please God
are man's pastimes,
his diversions,
a camouflage for hypocrisy.
God is anxious to know
why man is so odious.
He had not intended him thus.
Is the creation
greater than the creator?

I am not Dead Yet

I am not dead yet
and may not be for you for ever
if you are sure of your eternity
You don't trust God,
I don't trust destiny.
So you hate me.
I pity you,
You curse me.
What a conundrum!
Contradiction is a component of life.
If life is not so simple
it is not complex too.
You make it
you may live it too.
You may break it
still you have to live it.
There is no way out.
Not even death
that will come when it will come.

Wind Surfing

Beside the Malibu Hills
on the Pacific shore
the young and not too young
were wind surfing on the evening tide
that lashed angrily against the rocks
lifting the daring in her splashing arms
carrying them on their small sail boards
first to the rocks as if to thrash them
and then receding back to the ocean and
leaving them in leg deep waters
in sudden spasmodic contraction.

Some were flown legs up and heads down
leaving others topsy-turvy
in nowhere state
thrown up by the convulsive ocean
like unwanted things
abandoned on the roads of LA.
The wild ocean seemed to be playing
with little nothings.
But with their bravado
they made mockery of the mighty sea
tumbling in and out of itself
as if in a binging spree.

Life is not a Serious Affair

Human life is not a serious affair
in my country
it can spend itself
like worms.
And death is lighter still.
The dead are carried shoulder high
for cremation
in the name of Ram,
the eternal truth,
who is mimicked yearly
but not emulated.

Living a Burden: Dying a Crime

If you die a slow death
by starvation
none will pay attention.
But if you decide to
end your pain caused
by starvation
through a fast death way
the state will sue you
for suicide.
Why not? Our civil society
is so civil!
If you are dying of cancer
you can wriggle through the murk
as long as you may,
that is your privilege
because you don't have money.
Our society is mercifully
merciless!
Praise be to its parsimony!

A Mosquito Murmurs

A mosquito murmurs in my ears
and pleads for bleeding me
while a fly twists over head
and waltzes free.
Rats prance about in my house sniffing
and roaches caper loose.
Lilies ravishing red
bloom lavishly in the vases
for days few.
I simply watch and scan the scampering
And try to smell the non smelling scents
and take things lying down
to do nothing.
Am I not great?
Any comments?

It is Great to be Labyrinthine

It is great to be labyrinthine.
To be straight is as worthless
as a scare crow
that trembles and teeters
even with a slight characterless
air which cannot claim its existence.
And the deadwood device
cannot scare even a fly
what to talk of a crow.
Be dubious, cumbersome,
winding and crooked.
Be robed like an onion
which can never be naked
and can never be dressed.
But don't be straight.
Your words should have other meanings
than what you mean.
You will be understood
after you have done the damage
or have had an impact.
That is what you crave for.
That is what you aim at?
Isn't it?
Be a nothing ipso facto
and yet lead the masses
in Bharat!

O, Time!

O, time you are so young
as you were 68 years ago,
only I am shriveled.
Those who call you old
grow old
then collect themselves and fold
to go beyond your hold
to restart measuring you
once more.
But in my present innings
will you wait for me
till I reverse the figures
to 86 and even more?
This world is vivacious
so varied, so varying!
It engrosses pleasingly.
But you remain unchanged.
Still they blame:
Times are changing
to forget that they are themselves changing
not you.
They pluralize you
but you are always single,
steadfast
neither sad nor happy.
They tarnish you
for their own vacillating moods.
You are neither black nor dark,
neither golden nor copper.
You are shapeless, colourless,
still they divide you
in their own fashions

which they call ages, eras
and feign to consign you
to their own archives.
You carry nothing and leave nothing behind
Do you?

Death is a Siren

Death is a siren,
which sounds but is not heard.
I have lived the morning
I have delved in the night.
Between them both I have shelved the day
the peaceful or turbulent or resonant.
The journey has been vibrant
and meandering most.
Miry, dusty and pock marked
have been the ways;
I have trudged on
Graduating the milestones of death.

Life is a Thrill

Life is a thrill.
You have sometimes
to hang upside down
or walk on all fours
to fool failure
squirrels like feeding from the bird feeder.
You have to lie low, flat
imperceptible, crushed under
to survive to live on.
You have to fly,
you have a cruise
you have to cringe,
you have to row
you have to hoe;
to threat, to be threatened
laugh and scowl
be fair and foul
kill, to be killed
and yet survive.
Life is a mechanized excitement
as at the Six Flags
in the states of Stars and Stripes
where life is made easy
tediously!
But life is still as simple
as lived in Brazilian Amazon
by the Flecheiros.
So hang on
and live vivaciously.

You have sometimes to hang upside down
or walk on all fours.

Nature's Wake-Up Call

Some of them start singing
much early in the morning;
they are the few early warblers.
But their full orchestra
plays at dawn.
Crowding the little leafy trees
outside the window of my room
(The room is narrow but the window is wide
it is grasping.)
they goad the others to ecstasy.
These little, little birdies sing
a mystic Mass or a hymn.
Do they implore God
or
does the simple Nature mystifies herself?
The bigger birds too intone one by one:
the koel,
the mynah
the dove
the crow.
They all mark their presence
in the Nature's wake-up call.

They all mark their presence in the Nature's wake–up call.

We Live Every Day

We live every day
but shall die just once.
I can sing about life
but know nothing about Death.
If somehow I were to resurrect
I would know what it is like to die.
While I lie dead
I shall meet Death face to face
(Unlike Nachiketa who met him alive)
and probe him inside out;
shall tell him that man
worships God because of him.
If Death dies
I shall have nothing to fear;
I shall be a living immortal.
People made immortal
as a fruit of God worship
long to be reborn as living beings
to know this world
to know themselves
and stay awed by God,
or is it Death?

Koel's Love

I heard the mellifluous song
in the dead of night around two in the morning.
A koel at that unnatural hour
is never heard.
What must have propelled her?
A cocky crow might have barged into her habitat
because an apathetic mother
she allows the crow to hatch her eggs.

She is a seasonal singer
flipping from one mango tree to the other
in summer months.
She is a mango maniac
in love with that fruit
right from its blooming stage
and gauche greenness.

I haven't seen her eat this fruit.
She merely fondles it
and does not even peck it.
She simply salivates over it
leaving a black spot
on its skin to sweeten it.

The exuberance of love
must have made her mad
to sing out loud at that hour
heralding the selfless love
in an opiate state.

I Ride a Lion

During the nights in summer
I sleep and wake
and sleep and wake again
and in between
take twin tumblers of water
every time before I go to sleep again.

On one such night
the other day, past midnight
I dreamt:
I stood on the foot of a hill
where a runnel ran
silently by and beyond it lay
sedgy expanse hemmed by
a forest wild.

From the mouth of a cleft rock
on the hill above me
growled a lion
as if he had had a hearty meal.
When I looked up to him
he jumped down and stood before me
like a pet horse
for me to ride.

As soon as I sat astride him
he jumped up to his cave
and flew from there to land
beyond the river
on the sand soaked with water.

He jumped down and stood before me
Like a pet horse for me to ride.

He growled again and I dismounted
to find me standing
where I stood before
I rode the lion
watching the river and the ferny forest
dense and deep.

Ah!
My desires soaring and settling down
at the nowhere land
where I usually stand!

Oh That!

Oh that somebody could love me!
Love lies in the purse,
dwells not in the heart.
Thicker the wallet, cosier the love.
The heart stops breathing
sans the blood of bread.
Lust for lucre makes the heart moist,
it dries up with slobbering sentiments.
You can buy love at the mall
but my pocket has been meshed and small.

The Long Road Lies Ahead

The long road lies ahead of me,
I feel that
all its curls and curves have ended.
I have left two sign posts behind
In New England.
The road may dip
or heave up in its onward journey
but I think I can weather it all
and tread on.

Fortune and Misfortune

Fortune and misfortune
are sisters true
akin in nature and deeds too.
They dwell and deal together.
They play and ply at will.
But man brands them:
miss and amiss.
He falls ill in his misfortune
to bolster doctor's fortune.
He dies on his dooms day
in undertaker's heyday.

Fortune and misfortune,
miss and amiss

Will You Remember Me

Will you remember me
when I am dead?
You may or you may not
it will touch me not
because the dead will be dead
Even while I am living
you have cajoled me
to serve your purpose
have never come to me just for me.
Once you have extracted what you want
you have done away with me
just for that time.

We are Slaves of Our Conscience

We are slaves of our conscience
or conscience is our guide.
Conscience spurs us
and we prance.
Dead conscience stinks
like rotten thoughts.
Conscious or unconscious
when we ignore it
we drift down hill
motivating our mind
to go perfidious.
Conscience is like a seed
which sprouts unseen
in human mind to make a man,
an angel or a devil.

We Sell Truth

We sell Truth
and buy a lot of lies.
We do globalize
as the world in neighbourhood lies.
Do you know what we gain?
Dollars! No Euros–u rue
don't you?
And the tongue we talk in
is English which is lame and plastered
yet runs smooth and gibberish.
We are skinny white
and hearty black.
We have our God baptized
all others' Gods are not divine.
We trade in souls.
We buy men whole.
We fly above the skies.
We drive down the hole.

Come Sweet Sleep

Come sweet sleep
slip over me, have a crush on me.
Enclose me in your cozy arms
and take me away from
the flurry around
so that I may cease to be
me!
Sleep you are living and vibrant
but impalpable and invisible.
I wish I could hug you, kiss you.
Can you make that?
I would like to feel refreshed
for, your touch is so mesmerizing.
Hiss a lullaby to make me dream
that I exist.
Sleep come sleepily upon me
because wakefulness
is not always awakening.

White Oaks and Lazy Lake

White oaks, nay maples
fifty feet high or more
hug its deck
and a lazy lake dimples
to kiss its posterior
on Gurnee's Knottingham Drive
in the lake county
in the vicinity of Chicago.
It is named 1376
where live he, she, me and mine
with hopes, aspirations and prayers;
waiting for the third generation
to creep to crawl
to laugh to shriek
to jump with joy
to excel and exclaim
Hi, Hi!
And to let giggles explode
the neighbourhood!

White oaks, nay maples
hug its deck.

The Feel Good Factor

Many hopes haunt men here,
multitudes of aspirations
lie asphyxiated
in the four walls of our tenement
where every room
is decked with a door,
a wide window: that many loopholes
for fraudulence and depravity.
Life has been close to history
with nothing new or strange.
The poor can see the mansions
but have no huts to live in.
Food rots in warehouses
feeds not the poor tummies.
Nature has been natural
with floods and quakes.
Only Death (Yamah) does not ride a buffalo.
It travels on vehicles new
like express trains
to kill and carry the dead away.
Devilry and perjury
corrode the social fabric diligently
to make us gloat about
the feel good factor.

Death (Yamah) does not ride a buffalo.

The Moody April

The summery April
dawns to make the Gulmohar
flare up fiery red
making the murky daylight glow.

The boughs of mango trees
blister with drop-lings emerald green
promising pulpy sweetness
of mouthful luscious fruit.

The bulbs of lilies lying
underneath the earth
sprout up in slender stems
and bloom to pistillate into balls
once a year.
Merry, parsimonious Nature!

April is a moody month
blows hot and cold
when it likes
showing Nature's pleasures
and gorgeous grace.

God is in the Temple

God is in the temple
let us go and worship Him there.
at home we are
parents, grandparents
and children
But the Divine lives there
where we have installed him,
God loves congregation,
domestic solitude is not conducive to Him.
He wants the man to please him
to seek his grace and benevolence.
Otherwise why should He have
created the man?
Remember that God is nearer the church,
the mosque but farther from man.
And man is immortal till his death.
Summum Bonum—Pra-tattwa?

It is Good

It is good to live.
It is good to die.
It is good to smile.
It is good to sigh.
Every thing is good as it is.
It is good to be good.
It is good to be sly.
All humans are different
a few things are alike.
Air cannot be fair all the time.
Only humans don't have moods
birds, animals and reptiles
are moody too.
Man can be unmanly
or feminine
and women unwomanly too.
There are beings asexual
God's technical failures.
How can then scientists be perfect
when cloning and propagating?

My Brain

My brain is restless
but I lie akimbo on the bed.
I cannot sleep
and want not to be awake
perforce I study the ceiling
that glares upon me.
The ceiling that can be
as high as the astral sky
or as low
as my lowly height.
My mind is a vast ocean
my heart is just a drop.
What a peak, what a flop!

At the Monica Beach

At the Monica beach
on the Pacific ocean
overlooked by promenade
just at noon in the month of May
I saw a sea lion squatting
on Californian sand
neither wet nor dry.
There were a few more humans
eyeing the animal,
which did not mind my grabbing it
in my lens.
It seemed to be thoughtful
and yet curious
looking at us all
in a state of thrall
having sailed out of its watery home
to rejoice at our sight
in drenched delight.

The sea was silent on the shore
but was heard growling far away.
A solitary ship sailed
eastward, from this western coast.
The earth seemed moving westward
and the sun to the east.

A solitary ship sailed
eastward from the western coast at the Monica Beach

Blood Suckers

Blood suckers plenteous
roam in my room
sting me, hurt me, pain me
with no respite.
Such tiny nothings!
Just a clap is enough for them each.
When they go, they leave
a bloody smear behind
with a stingy memory of piercing pain.
Nature's creatures they are
as we are.
Why cant we be different?

Awake, Awake!

Awake, awake
and shake off sloth
to see that life is calling you!
No bones are old
there is no dead end.
May be Time is long
but life is one.
The here and after
the now and ever
are yours to grab.
To pick and have
in every breath
at every stride
all that you aspire.
So stride, stride!

Brother & Bother

Brother and bother
are simply 'r' consonant apart,
'ar' prods 'es' to selfishness
being alphabetic neighbours
to make the former bothersome.
He is pride, I'm not proud.
He is immortal, I see my door.
He gloats:
all heritage belongs to him
none else can claim it.
His standing's high
his shadows sublime;
all others are midgets
wallowing in slime,
he alone exudes golden glare.
He philosophizes:
Greatness is not achieved,
it is assumed.
He has crammed this conviction
into his mind's moat
and let it cosily bloat.
There it stank, stinks
and will continue so
to emit hate.
His values are vaunted
and practices puerile.
May he progress all the while!

It is a Pleasure

It is a pleasure when we swagger.
It is measure when we show off.
A vaunt becomes a mountain
which, the wise can refrain.

A snail is the slowest pedestrian
carrying the load of life on its back.
The fastest are those who are light
but sail haughtily
rowing with knotted oars of life.
The wise know it all
and do not gloat.

The fastest are those who are light
but sail haughtily
rowing with knotted oars of life.

Awake, Arise, Advance

Awake, arise, advance
march, march and move fast.
The time is short
but the goal's far off.
Our ancestors have done much.
We must do much more.
Shake hands with Success.
Let not pleasures or hurdles detain you.
Establish a benchmark
for the future to emulate,
for you to be pleased
but not to gloat over,
for the nation to be proud of
and for the world to note.

The Butterfly that You Carry

The butterfly that you merrily carry
on your shoulder today, my dear
will soon weigh a metric tonne
turning all your pleasure
into misery.
You are of open heart,
liberal and adoring;
all those good graces of yours
will leave you with sour memories.
Leash, leash, the wise have warned
lest it should be too late.
The journey is long
with ups and downs and changing weather,
so befriend prudence;
your good intentions
must not become liabilities.

Para-Tattva (Summum Bonum)

I have heard a blind man say:
God is deaf, I implore him
to have mercy on me but
He does not listen.
And the deaf says:
God is blind otherwise
He would look at me
and have mercy.
The lame looks at god's pictures
His cosmic form—the Virat Roop
and says:
He has so many arms but only two legs
so He can't spare any for me;
moreover I feel ashamed
To ask for what He Himself
does not have.
The dumb flashes his arms
the left to the right
and the right to the left
but I follow him not.
He sees my helplessness
and touches his thumb to the index finger
making the sign of zero,
with the right hand and with the left
points to his tongue
and then waves the thumb
signifying nothing.
The scientist says:
It is only at times of disasters
That I feel God may be around.

But a hermit opines:
the flowers bloom,
the winds blow
and all things around
with you and me
are all his creations.
Close your eyes to see within
grope, grope and grope
till you see a light sparkle.
He will soon appear before you
in the shape you want to see
Him.
Have faith and you will find.

Truth Stifles

Truth stifles
but half truths may gain some currency
where falsehood reigns.
During democracy of just
over five decades young
this is what India has gained.
What else can one hope for
from a decadent culture?
In a resurgent country
where men have majored
in intrigues
learnt to manufacture
mannequins of truth
to drape with flimsy garbs.

At the fag end of the twentieth century
when the world was moving
towards unity of the universal man
with Time squeezed and
distances dissolved
one small man called V.P.
catapulted to the apex.
Chose to immortalize himself
by shattering the societal fabric
into shreds of castes.
No none can stitch the entire thing
together again.

Night Life

I have seen fireflies waltzing
in the forests slight
during night,
and the glow worms
frolicking on the pools and ponds
like the stars twinkling
on the calm surface of crystal lakes
reclining in the palms of hills—
that is night life in Nature's lap.

But in the city at night
painted biped butterflies
blooming, bouncing and
clinging with their cuddly limbs
to the lusty masculine arms
warmed up with elixir
made of malt or grapes,
under the tiny lights
peeping through the ceiling
of the jaunty rendezvous.

Dear Rohan

Rohan our lovely lissome rose
blooming at the end of March
has come to us with fragrance sweet
Bringing the foursome close.

Cute and cuddly, just eight months old
he has put our ageing on hold.
His wordless carols and
garrulous grumble
make us fumble
to catch their core,
but joyously make us
love him more 'n' more.

Sitting in his stroller
on a walk on Minuteman trail
he sings sweet songs without fail.
His gibberish chatter and silky smiles
make us walk for miles and miles
to push him fly on swings awhile
when he laughs in his soulful style.

Infant Appeals

Our little rosy Rohan
his granny calls him Mohan
when he trills and squeals
his infant appeals
for milk or feed
whatever else indeed,
we know not what.
He makes us fret
to make our guess
without fume 'n' fuss.
We do hurry up soon
to hear his winsome croon.

Ten Months Old Rohan

He blooms like peony white
of corolla close
and smiles to glow
like a summer rose.
He crawls around
in search profound
to pick up any crumb
with his feeble fingers
and the tiny thumb.
He loves out-doors
and on the swing
his heart outpours.
He walks on the walker
through the house
like a knight on his horse.
He loves olive oil massage
but shuns the closing
garrulous garage.
He likes to bathe
but grudges to be stripped
and then be dressed.
He loves to hear his granny sing
when she feeds him anything.
He dotes to scratch
his grand pa's face.
Enjoys his papa's shoulder race.
At night he wakes up
time and again
to make his mom play
with him again.
Who is he, who is he
this baby discreet?
He is ten months old Rohan sweet.

You Are Sure to Shine

Vrinda we remember you every day,
see your photos at the Facebook
uploaded by your mom.
Just one and a half years old
you loved to walk
avoiding the pram
to let your cousin enjoy it more.
You know no envy.
You loved the story books
to be read to you but of your choice,
your choice sublime,
our tastes mattered not.
You love to dance and play the music
to make your granny dance
to tunes you like the most.
Fast learner
with prodigious grasp
you are sure to shine in life.
May you make the country proud!

Crane Beach—Atlantic Ocean

On an autumn day, Crane Beach at Ipswich in Massachusetts
was sparsely swarmed by small children
chaperoned by their parents in swimsuits.

Far off two small sail boats seemed as if doodling or fishing
but nearby a young man maneuvering
his tiny, snarling, snorting boat appeared to be playing
for the gallery in reckless enjoyment.

A young mother with her four-year old son
was making a sand castle topped by
spiraling mini minarets.
After having finished it she called her son
to pose for copious photos.
The castle is beautiful someone said.
She gloated; she has been making such castles
for the last thirty years since her childhood.
Her kinetic son was agog and capering,
swish-swashing the thin sea water
at the margin with his restless feet.

With tucked up trousers I was wading through
knee-deep waters rippling silently by
when a seven-year old boy said,
"It is a crab, I want to have it."
I reached him and did see a hard shell stuck in sand.
"It is alive," the boy said.
A kick of my toes could not dislodge it,
but it stirred a bit and I said,
"It is alive, you can take it."
He dared not and left to meet his parents.
I continued pressing my toes hard but in vain.

After several hard pushes
It took its pincers out and sailed away.
But I was aghast when I saw only
The posterior of another crab
With the rest of its body stuck in the sand deep.
It may be a female crab,
May be they were mating for procreation,
Only a marine scientist could know that.
I came away with a guilty conscience.
Only the sea gulls loitered around.

Bush to Saddam

When I say
you are bad – you are bad
The world may agree
or it may not,
I have condemned you
so be condemned.
You are arrogant,
you are dangerous.
You can annihilate the whole world
but before you do that
be prepared to lick the dust
I will choose your successor
who will say yes sir!
That will bring peace on earth.
Till you do that
I shall drain you out.
Stifle you, strafe you.
kill you
or make you leave your land.
Don't confront
but try to understand
that I am the only one
the U-ass-aye!
You Sad damn!

Critical Theory in the Twenty-First Century

Critical Theory in the Twenty-First Century

DARROW SCHECTER

BLOOMSBURY
NEW DELHI • LONDON • OXFORD • NEW YORK • SYDNEY

First Published in India 2017
First published by Bloomsbury Academic in 2013

Bloomsbury Academic
An imprint of Bloomsbury Publishing Plc
Bloomsbury is a registered trade mark of Bloomsbury Publishing Plc

This edition published with permission from Bloomsbury Publishing Plc
50, Bedford Square, London, WC1B3DP

Library of Congress Cataloging-in-Publication Data
Schecter, Darrow.
Critical theory in the twenty-first century / by Darrow Schecter. pages cm
Includes bibliographical references and index.
ISBN 978-1-4411-6432-2 (hardcover : alk. paper) – ISBN 978-1-4411-0546-2
(pbk. : alk. paper) 1. Civil society. 2. Differentiation (Sociology)
3. Political science. I. Title.
JC337.S335 2013 142–dc23
2013005983

ISBN 978 93 86606 32 7
10 9 8 7 6 5 4 3 2 1
For sale in the Indian subcontinent only

Bloomsbury Publishing India Pvt. Ltd
Second Floor, Building No. 4
DDA Complex LSC, Pocket C – 6 & 7
Vasant Kunj, New Delhi 110070
www.bloomsbury.com

Exclusively Distributed in India by:
Manohar Publishers & Distributors
4753/23, Ansari Road
Darya Ganj, New Delhi 110002
Tel.: 23284848, 23289100
Email: sales@manoharbooks.com, manoharbooks@gmail.com

Design by Newgen Knowledge Works (P) Ltd., Chennai, India
Printed and bound in India

For Jarret, and serious clowning

Contents

Acknowledgements

This book attempts to make a contribution to the renewal of critical theory. It draws on the work of the first generation of Frankfurt School thinkers without simply restating their main positions on key questions that continue to be relevant to the study of society. I have received a great deal of help in recent years from undergraduate and postgraduate students at the University of Sussex, such as Matthew Bisset, Arianna Bove, Steve Conway, Alex Elliot, Erik Empson, Verena Erlenbusch, Alastair Gray, Carla Ibled, Ralph Kellas, Alastair Kemp, Claire Kennard, Peter Kolarz, Angelos Koutsourakis, Natalie Leeder, Chris Malcolm, Charles Masquelier, Andrew Mitchell, Teodor Mladenov (congratulations!), Simon Mussell, Chris O'Kane, Alastair Riggs and many others. I'd especially like to thank Patrick Wheatley and Charles Whitehouse.

I also take this opportunity to thank the faculty teaching on the Sussex Social and Political Thought (SPT) programme, especially Andrew Chitty and Luke Martell. My most abiding debt at Sussex is to Gordon Finlayson, who is a great teacher, thinker, and the guiding force of SPT. I'd also like to thank a number of colleagues at other universities for their advice, including Heiko Feldner, Eric Jacobson, Raul Digon Martin, Mark McNally, Drew Milne, William Outhwaite, Jaroslav Skupník, Chris Thornhill, Fabio Vighi and Chris Wyatt.

Many thanks go to Marie-Claire Antoine, Kaitlin Fontana, Ally-Jane Grossan and Matthew Kopel at Bloomsbury. Marie-Claire has moved on since initiating the *Critical Theory and Contemporary Society* series, and will surely be missed by her Bloomsbury colleagues. It was a pleasure to work with her, and I wish her all the best in everything she does.

The help of friends has also been indispensable. A number of the ideas in this book have been developed in conversation with Fernand Avila, Joan Contreras Castro, Costantino Ciervo, Jean Demerliac, Luca Lavatori, Volker Lorek, Mand Ryaïra, Imke Schmincke (Glückwunsch!) and Céline Surprenant.

Thanks once again, Francis and Diana, for every day.

Introduction

(I)

A series of books on critical theory and contemporary society cannot repackage the main ideas of the Frankfurt School thinkers and insist on their permanent relevance. This would be very much against the spirit of the thinkers in question as well as an inadequate response to current socio-economic and political realities. Although some of the main aims of critical theory as it was originally formulated are discussed in the chapters that follow, this is done in order to emphasize that the need for non-eclectic yet multidisciplinary social enquiry links critical theory today with the guiding principles of the people who founded the Institute for Social Research in Frankfurt in 1924.[1] Beyond this methodological point of continuity, however, it is doubtful that one can simply update or slightly adjust the theories of the totally administered society, one-dimensional humanity, the authoritarian personality, the culture industry, etc., in order to 'fit' the evolution of global capitalism and what is now sometimes referred to as world society.[2] The continued resonance of some of the main ideas of the first critical theorists, and in particular the contemporary relevance of T. W. Adorno's critique of identity thinking analysed in Chapter Three, stems from the ongoing need to combat academic specialization and to re-articulate the macroeconomic concerns of Smith, Ricardo, Marx and Keynes in conjunction with pressing issues in sociology, legal theory, philosophy, political theory, media studies,

---

[1]For an extensive overview of the origins of the Institute and the ideas of its main thinkers, see Rolf Wiggershaus, *The Frankfurt School*, Cambridge, MIT Press, 1994. For a more succinct account see Darrow Schecter, *The History of the Left from Marx to the Present: Theoretical perspectives*, London, Continuum, 2007, chapter 3.

[2]The term world society appears in the work of the systems theory of Niklas Luhmann (1927–98). See his *Macht* [*Power*], Stuttgart, Enke, 1975, pp. 90–1, and 'Globalization or World Society: How to Conceive of Modern Society', *International Review of Sociology*, 7 (1997), pp. 67–80.

history, aesthetic theory, film studies and psychoanalysis. This detailed work of re-articulation is offered in the other volumes of Continuum/Bloomsbury's *Critical Theory and Contemporary Society* series. *Critical Theory in the Twenty-First Century* acts as a general introduction to those more specifically focused contributions.[3] The present volume is designed to provide a broad framework for re-conceptualizing critical theory so that it is open to various sociological realities that have been the subject of increased theoretical attention since 1968, as, for example, in the area of disability studies, while also being able to think, rather than merely classify or condemn, political phenomena such as terrorism. These are phenomena that the first generation of Frankfurt School theorists, confronted first with fascism and then with the post-war rise of consumerism and popular culture, never really encountered for fairly obvious historical reasons.[4] Moreover, these are areas of conflict and potential change that are often largely neglected by many of the more aesthetic approaches to critical theory found in the literature and philosophy departments of many universities across Europe and North America. If it is possible to speak of a 'linguistic turn' in social and political theory, it is also perhaps justified to speak in terms of the 'literary turn' of critical theory. This literary turn has undoubtedly borne fruits, especially as a result of the theoretical research linked with Jameson's particular readings of Marx and Adorno, and Derrida's development of deconstruction.[5] But it has also led to a prioritizing of notions of incommensurable otherness, divine justice, traces of the forgotten, etc., at the expense of political economy and investigations of power, contingency, functional differentiation, etc., with the inevitable consequence that normative ideals tend to marginalize sociological analysis in many literary approaches to critical theory.[6] The first generation of critical theorists indeed

---

[3]Already published in the series are William Outhwaite, *Critical Theory and Contemporary Europe* (2012), and Fabio Vighi, *Critical Theory and Film* (2012). Forthcoming titles in 2013 include: Heiko Feldner, *Critical Theory and the Contemporary Crisis of Capital*, and David M. Berry, *Critical Theory and the Digital*.

[4]The term popular culture is used in this context to denote something historically and sociologically distinct from traditional culture as well as folk art. While there are relatively clear points of demarcation between popular and folk culture, it is not so easy to distinguish between popular culture and what is at times referred to as youth culture. These issues are dealt with by Simon Adam and Howard Horne in *Art into Pop*, London, Methuen, 1987, and especially in Greil Marcus, *Lipstick Traces: A Secret History of the Twentieth Century*, Cambridge, Harvard University Press, 1989.

[5]A good example is provided by Alex Thomson in *Deconstruction and Democracy: Derrida's Politics of Friendship*, London, Continuum, 2005. Also see Fredric Jameson, *Marxism and Form: Twentieth Century Theories of Literature*, Princeton University Press, 1971, and *Late Marxism, or the Persistence of the Dialectic*, Cambridge, Harvard University Press, 1982.

[6]These tendencies clearly do not obviate the need for literary approaches to critical theory altogether. Terry Eagleton and Drew Milne (eds) offer a very reliable guide to the debates on

may have sought to deconstruct the fact/value dichotomy. If it is clear that the deconstructive work in question is not accomplished by declaring the dichotomy to be the simple result of reification, fetishism, or even of the division of labour, it is equally apparent that one will not understand the issues involved in the current financial crisis with exclusive recourse to notions like alterity. In short, it is neither a question of transcending the fact/value dichotomy nor of achieving the right balance of normative and sociological elements understood as heterogeneous factors that round out a complete picture. One must think in terms of the constellations in which a plurality of phenomena constitutes complex contexts where the factual and normative are not easily disentangled. For example, normative criteria stipulating what ought to be and empirical criteria registering the rules governing existing practices converge in a field such as law. Should law be conceived of as an autonomous system with discernible boundaries and autonomous codes, or should it be seen instead as a specific instance of political power deriving from the more general exercise of state power? Or does law act as a conduit between system and life-world without belonging exclusively to either? These and many other questions need to be addressed with sensitivity to the historical evolution of specific societies in ways that project beyond the rigid dichotomization or awkward fusion of facts and norms. The *Critical Theory and Contemporary Society* series introduced by this volume seeks to re-articulate critical theory outside of such narrow and outdated parameters.

Some observers may wish to argue that the time for critical theory has in fact passed with the publication of Jürgen Habermas' *Theory of Communicative Action* (1981) and the alleged linguistic turn in social and political thought referred to above. Proponents of this view might say that critical theory was conceived of as intellectual resistance to fascism and as a subsequent warning not to forget the possibility of new variants of authoritarian populism, despite the apparent social harmony accompanying much of the post-World War II economic boom period.[7] According to this view, the dangers in a

---

Marxism, critical theory and literature in *Marxist Literary Theory*, Oxford, Blackwell, 1996. For a good summary of the relations between critical and literary theory in the work of Fredric Jameson, Terry Eagleton, Raymond Williams and others, see Razmig Keucheyan, *Hémisphère gauche: une cartographie des nouvelles pensées critiques*, Paris, La Découverte, 2010, pp. 38–9 and 294–301. Keucheyan provides an excellent sourcebook that is reviewed in detail by Laurent Jeanpierre in *Le Monde des Livres*, 2 July 2010, p. 8.

[7]This period is often described with the French notion of the 30 glorious years ('les Trente Glorieuses'), to denote the period of steady growth and nearly full employment which came to an end with the oil crises of the 1970s and the subsequent election of Thatcher, Reagan and Kohl. The austerity imposed by the governments of those political leaders found its counterpart in the frustrations of the first Mitterand government, which was forced to retreat on virtually all of its major socio-economic reforms because of the threat of capital flight and the pressure on

postcolonial global world are more likely to be postmodern relativism, 'end of history' complacency, 'clash of civilizations' bigotry, ecological disaster and terrorism, such that what is really required is a new kind of postmodern cosmopolitanism rather than a renewal of modernism or critical theory as such.[8] Yet the ongoing economic crises that have intensified since 2008 suggest that a number of the phenomena first diagnosed by Marx and Simmel and subsequently taken up by the Frankfurt School, the regulation school, and other currents of thought, are far from being resolved or outdated.[9] In the most recent chapter of the ongoing historical struggle between governments and states, on the one hand, and financial markets and capital, on the other, it appears that trade unions and social-democratic political parties are losing their former capacity to distil and partially reconcile normative ideals and sociological realities, and it is far from certain that this dynamic is adequately captured with terms like globalization or cosmopolitanism.[10] At first glance the centrist evolution of European social democracy and the declining political influence of trade unions in Europe and North America could be interpreted as part of a wider series of processes leading to the arrival of a post-industrial and post-ideological world order. On closer inspection, it appears that there has been renewed struggle over legal control of nationally based private capital within states, parallel struggles over international capital between states, and

---

the Franc imposed by international financial markets, though at that time few people used the term 'globalization' to describe this phenomenon. See Robert Boyer and Jean-Pierre Durand, *L'après-fordisme*, Paris, Syros, 1993.

[8]There are also those who argue that with the possible exception of Franz Neumann's *Behemoth* (1944), first-generation critical theory was not even very adept at theorising fascism, to say nothing of post-World War II social and political phenomena. For a representative of this line of interpretation, see Michael Schäfer, *Die Rationaliät des Nationalsozialismus: Zur Kritik philosophischer Faschismustheorien am Beispiel der kritischen Theorie*, Weinheim, Beltz, 1994. For a more positive assessment of the Frankfurt School's interpretations of fascism, see William Scheuerman, *Between the Norm and the Exception: The Frankfurt School and the Rule of Law*, Cambridge, MIT, 1994.

[9]The regulation school provides an interesting example of the need to re-articulate critical theory since, although rigorous and analytical, regulation theory tends to be too narrowly focused on the economic dimensions of capitalist crisis. An excellent collection of the main representatives of this approach to the study of contemporary industrial society is found in Robert Boyer and Yves Saillard (eds), *Theorie de la régulation: L'état des savoirs*, Paris, La Découverte, 1995.

[10]For a critical examination of cosmopolitanism in the works of thinkers like David Held and Seyla Benhabib, see Sophie Heine, *Oser penser à gauche: pour un réformisme radical*, Brussels, Éditions Aden, 2010, chapter 3, part 3. It is not inconceivable that European social-democratic parties will go the way of the former Euro-communist parties if, that is, they continue to suffer dwindling electoral fortunes and have difficulties in identifying a well-defined set of groups and classes to represent. See Jean-Christophe Cambadélis, 'Le moment social-démocrate', *Le Monde*, 13 October 2006, p. 21. Perhaps the more general point is that it is far from clear today if critical theory is left-wing theory, since what it means to be on the left today is also a matter of much contention.

an additional battle on the part of state capital itself for the control of credit and markets within and across the boundaries of existing nation-states. The recent political upheavals related to credit allocation and financial speculation offer a pertinent case in point.

It now seems clear that when banks lend money to borrowers in ways that tend to lead to the formation of pockets of blocked credit, the banks can incur massive debts that blur the already problematic distinction between the real economy of production and the virtual economy of speculation. At some point during the course of 2008 it became apparent in North America, for example, that the sub-prime credit used to pay family mortgages created personal debts that were not going to be paid back to creditors in the allotted time frame. This placed private lenders in difficulties that were eventually palliated by the US Treasury, thus leading, in a number of important cases, to what was effectively the nationalization of major banks. In an economic equivalent of the state of exception, the 'laws' of supply and demand were suspended so that the health of private firms and banks could be maintained with public money provided at unusually low rates of interest. In what could be interpreted as a flagrant case of money laundering with a friendly face, these bail-outs became public deficits for states that in their turn have been forced to borrow money as well as impose austerity policies on citizens who have been politely informed that their pensions are not really safe, that they may have to work to a later age in life than previously stipulated in collective bargaining agreements, and that they will have to do so under decidedly more precarious conditions than they had done in recent decades. The irony does not stop there, however, since in notable cases it is the very banks that incurred debts which are now increasing their leverage (and indirect political control) over government policy by lending money to financially stricken states at normal and even high rates of interest. If in 2008 it appeared for a brief time that social-democratic Keynesian measures were going to be reintroduced by states with enhanced legitimacy and better planning resources, things looked very different by 2010. Depending on the source of information on the subject of financial crisis, states are not generally regarded as sources of potential planning and mediation between public collective goods and private interests, but are seen, instead, as inefficient squanderers in need of market discipline. The private firms and financial markets which depleted public economic resources in the first place seem somehow to exist in a space insulated from social and political criticism, thus making a renewal of critical theory indispensable in order to grasp the character of the forces shaping current policy and decisively influencing our understanding of what is politically possible in the twenty-first century.

At the moment governments and states are often portrayed in the mainstream media as responsible for the public debt crisis which actually began with the banks and their credit policies. The antidote to the crisis also appears to be removed from rigorous analysis and generally consists in the single 'acceptable' solution to the problem of 'unproductive' labour: cutting back government spending on health, public housing, education, pensions, legal aid, etc. In addition to the long-term problems of retirement and pensions, there are the immediate issues of unemployment and prolonged recession that often accompany fiscal austerity. Single possible solutions are usually imposed and authoritarian, and necessarily dismiss or ignore other real alternatives. It is nonetheless doubtful if the notion of the authoritarian personality complex developed by first-generation critical theorists provides an adequate explanation of the phenomena involved, or if this concept illuminates the specific responses on the part of the great numbers of people affected by decisions over which they have relatively little control. Indeed, one can say that these 'decisions' are really more like commands. It is moreover difficult to say if ostensibly cosmopolitan dialogue on the part of high profile academics and media figures at conferences is going to be able to consolidate the bases of international civil society against the IMF and financial market pressure on governments.[11] A theoretical analysis of these phenomena cannot stop at an economic diagnosis of the issues at hand, since there are clearly other factors involved. This underlines the need for non-eclectic multidisciplinary social enquiry that is neither normatively naïve nor irrelevant to normative concerns in the manner of some versions of empiricism and positivist social science. To date the crisis has been widely accepted as a kind of socio-economic Tsunami or similar natural event somehow taking place outside the scope of creative political intervention. It is thus unsurprising that it is met with fear, resignation, and reactions that correspond more to human interest responses to natural catastrophes (anecdotes about resilient pensioners who keep smiling rather than giving in, etc.), than to the analyses of engaged research. It is curious too that it is rarely mentioned in the commercial academic press that even the most drastic cuts in government spending will do little to alter the fact that most of the goods and services on offer in the so-called developed world can be produced at lower cost in the developing world. A political response, in

[11]The fact that banks across Europe and North America have been stabilized by state treasuries cannot really conceal the fact that this amounts to a resurrection of former national currencies. The implicit nationalism and corresponding defensiveness of leaders like Merkel and Zapatero indicate that a rational debate on these matters has yet to ensue. This is to say nothing of the way an entire nation-state such as Greece has been made to feel irresponsible and guilty for rather standard spending policies, while little attention is paid to the evidently close relations between banking elites and cabinet circles in places like Britain.

contrast to a panicked reaction, might be that ecologically sound, slow-growth economies could be considered as an alternative to coercing consumers to accept passively the eternal return of more sophisticated models of what are basically the same commodities. Hence one is entitled to ask if austerity is the rational reaction to this state of affairs, or if austerity is simply reactionary in an almost literal political and psychological sense of reaction formation. There is no objective reason why the global economy has to be organized as a series of competing trade blocks, so that rationality is pared down to its instrumental dimension and consists for the most part in governments slashing spending on public goods, and states imposing longer working lives on their citizens. It can be shown that such non-thinking obeys the dictates of a flawed reality principle rather than the open-ended questioning and listening that distinguishes thought from adaptation to external pressure. This raises a number of questions about critical theory and political action that will be taken up in this book and in the series more generally.

(II)

At the risk of some schematization, one might designate the period from the *Communist Manifesto* and the upheavals of 1848 to the early 1960s as one in which Marxism and the Russian Revolution provide the main lines of political and intellectual orientation for many independent thinkers, militant trade unions, and most socialist and communist political parties in Western and Central Europe. To intellectuals of the post-World War II period such as Jean-Paul Sartre, for example, Marxism constitutes the insuperable intellectual and political horizon of humanity, by which he means that the socialization of production and exchange is the condition for a truthful as opposed to an ideological translation into praxis of the ideals of 1789. Until the late 1960s and early 1970s, that translation seemed to many observers to be confronted with extremely difficult but ultimately resolvable problems, despite the authoritarian turn of the 1917 Revolution and Stalin's ascension to uncontested power in Russia in the late 1920s. The events in former East Germany and Hungary in 1953 and 1956 confirmed the hypothesis that the transition from centralized authoritarian socialism (dictatorship of the proletariat) to decentralized libertarian socialism (socialism with political as opposed to mainly repressive police functions) would indeed be punctuated with crises. But during the first two decades of the post-World War II period, many intellectuals on the left of the political spectrum such as Brecht and Sartre supported the former USSR in spite of its obvious flaws, perhaps in the conviction that without this backing, it might appear inevitable that the legislation of merely *formal* equality and the manifestation of only sporadic instances of fraternity was humanity's political *fate*, and in the fear that the sequel to 1789 might be indefinitely postponed if the world's first workers' state was not defended.[12]

The simultaneous invocation of formalism and fate is not fortuitous in this context. It hints at Horkheimer and Adorno's thesis that a formal as opposed to a substantive solution to the problems of knowledge, freedom, equality and justice might mean a potential epistemological and political retreat to pre-1789 positions on reason and individual autonomy, despite, that is, the official declaration that democracy and the rule of law must take the place of feudal hierarchy and religious dogma. In other words, socially mediated explosions of fate in the guises of arbitrary authoritarianism and politico-bureaucratic tyrannies have taken over individual lives at precise historical junctures since the French Revolution. Horkheimer and Adorno suggest that there is a discernible tendency for this to happen if formal freedom is institutionalized as informal oppression. That is, they hint that formal freedom is either too formal or not formal enough unless it serves as a preliminary step towards substantive freedom. It could be argued that the young Marx meant as much in distinguishing between the political emancipation achieved in 1789, and the coming human emancipation of an anticipated second revolution to follow.[13] The young Marx implies that the formal freedoms won in 1789 would eventually have to become substantive, so that the principles of political democracy could penetrate into social life. Hence it is in a sense logical that German and Russian Marxists were happy to call themselves social democrats, at least, at any rate, until 1914. It became clear to many by the 1950s that the 1917 revolution in Russia came too late to deliver political emancipation, and, by extension, came too early in order to be the harbinger of human emancipation. Nonetheless, Lukács and countless others continued to look to Marxism–Leninism for the correct combination of objective sociological realism and subjective political normativity. At stake was the defence of an epistemology capable of addressing the problems raised by Marx in 1843–4

[12]On the interrelatedness of philosophical, political and aesthetic questions, see Fredric Jameson, *Marxism and Form: Twentieth-Century Dialectical Theories of Literature*, Princeton, Princeton University Press, 1971, as well as his *Brecht and Method*, London, Verso, 1998.

[13]As in the case of many of the other members of the Frankfurt School, Adorno's epistemological and political position with regard to Marx is not all that straightforward. While both are obviously critics of capitalism, Adorno's critique of epistemology differs from Marx's critique of political economy in a number of important respects. A number of important points of clarification can be found in Frank Böckelmann, *Über Marx und Adorno: Schwierigkeiten der spätmarxistischen Theorie*, Freiburg, ça ira, 1998.

in relation to the French Revolution and the possibility of a decisive break with feudalism and mythology in the name of reason and autonomy.[14]

As the 1960s unfolded, however, hopes for a revolutionary sequel to 1789 came mainly in the guise of support for a renewal of Marxist thought against its degeneration into state ideology in the USSR and its satellite states in Eastern Europe. Militants on the left may have been willing to overlook episodes such as the role of the Soviet Union in the fall of Spain to Franco's forces during 1936–9, the Molotov–Ribbentrop Pact, and Khrushchev's revelations in 1956 about the pathological aspects of Stalin's dictatorship. But the suppression of the Prague Spring in former Czechoslovakia in 1968 seemed to mark the end of any hope of reforming the system that eventually did collapse in 1989–90. Qualified support for a renewal of certain dimensions of Marxist thought and action in the context of the argument to be developed in the following chapters of this book means something more epistemologically relevant than simple political advocacy of communism or some other easily identifiable alternative to capitalism and formal democracy, and it certainly does not mean nostalgia for the old state-socialist regimes that disappeared with the end of the Cold War. The link between Marxism and critical theory that remains of interest today is captured by the particular strand of Marx's work that is taken up in different ways by Simmel, the Frankfurt School, and Foucault, and can be presented in this introduction as part of what is sometimes referred to as the unfinished project of modernity.[15] As will become clear in subsequent chapters, modernism need not be synonymous with authoritarian planning or privileged epistemological subjects. The grand narratives of Enlightenment and Progress may well have failed in some measure. It will be argued that there are good grounds to think that communicative and aesthetic reason have not failed, but must be re-articulated in order to gain visibility and credibility. Chapters One and Two explain the role that certain elements of modernist epistemology could play in such a re-articulation.

The Frankfurt School thinkers support the modernist project to the extent that they see why there is a great deal more to the demise of feudalism – and the possible end of naturalized forms of domination – than the rise of the disenchanted world of the Protestant ethic and the homogenized rhythms

---

[14]Schecter, *The History of the Left from Marx to the Present*, pp. 54–60, and *The Critique of Instrumental Reason from Weber to Habermas*, London, Continuum, 2010, chapter 2.

[15]In response to Habermas' *Der philosophische Diskurs der Moderne* [*The Philosophical Discourse of Modernity*], Frankfurt, Suhrkamp, 1985, Seyla Benhabib and Maurizio Passerin d'Entrèves edited a volume entitled *Habermas and the Unfinished Project of Modernity: Critical Essays on the Philosophical Discourse of Humanity*, Cambridge, MIT, 1997. It will be seen in Chapter Two that the approach to modernity offered in this book differs from both that of Habermas and that of Benhabib and d'Entrèves.

of mass production.[16] The *de-naturalization* of forms of feudal authority in which people's places are determined at birth in a preordained and therefore authoritarian hierarchy has a hand in undermining religious faith and cultural tradition. Hence the gradual process of de-naturalization plays an important role in shaking the foundations of two of the primary sources of Western art in the period following the end of the classical world and preceding the advent of secular humanist aesthetics, Enlightenment and industrialization. In a parallel vein, there are observable signs of gradual *differentiation* between the spheres of modern Western societies. If one broadly follows Marx, Simmel, Weber, and especially Luhmann, it seems clear that money and capitalism can be understood sociologically as key factors influencing the differentiation of religious authority, political power, law, economic function and art. To paraphrase and slightly modify the argument in *The Dialectic of Enlightenment*, it could be said that money and capitalism play a major role in the transition from feudalism to modernity, but the processes furthering the demise of tradition and supposedly natural subordination need not necessarily result in alienation and disenchantment *if*, that is, critique, rational debate, and a broadly conceived and widely diffused praxis of modernist aesthetics can replace what is oppressive about naturalized identities and tradition without, thereby, transforming traditional socio-economic and political relations into mainly capitalist and commercial ones. The full implications of this 'if-possibility' for politics and aesthetics are still being sounded out today and offer key guidelines for the formulation of the tasks of critical theory in the twenty-first century.[17]

Following Walter Benjamin's argument in *The Work of Art in the Age of Mechanical Reproduction* (1935), one could say that individual creativity and

---

[16]The plausibility of this interpretation of first-generation critical theory admittedly rests on a setting aside of the more apocalyptic pronouncements found in *The Dialectic of Enlightenment* (1944) and *Minima Moralia* (1951), where Horkheimer and Adorno at times abandon their modernism in favour of a meta-historical narrative in which the price for the demise of myth and tradition is construed as a closed system of administrative rationality, bureaucratic power and money. I follow paths suggested by other parts of their oeuvre which indicate that disenchantment is not the necessary consequence of post-traditional epistemology and politics.

[17]Modernist aesthetics like André Breton's vision of surrealism are rational in a Freudian–Marxist sense of sounding out unknown epistemological territory, and are not to be confused with posturing or provocation for its own sake. Speaking about the aims of surrealism at an international congress of writers in Paris in 1935, Breton states that 'Marx said "change the world." Rimbaud said "change life." For us these two demands express the same imperative.' Surrealism can thus be seen as an attempt to create a political symmetry between collective use values and individual aesthetic values. Breton thinks that these distinct but dialectically related aspects of reality can be mediated and do achieve a kind of fleeting synthesis in Rimbaud's poetry. Breton's comments on Marx and Rimbaud at the writers' congress are reprinted in *Position politique du surréalisme*, Paris, Pauvert, 1971, p. 68.

autonomy have almost invariably been mediated by religion, tradition and a mythological orientation towards nature hovering between wonder and fear which is reflected in rigid social norms and largely un-accountable forms of political authority. The age of industrial production presents an historically unique chance for humanity to combine liberation from material scarcity with liberation from oppressive social structure – the possibility of genuine individual and collective autonomy – *if*, once more, autonomy is not subordinated to secular mythologies that come to replace the traditional ones whose approaching end is heralded by Nietzsche's notion that 'God is dead'.[18] While the events of 1989–90 really could have been the occasion to launch the project again without the threat of nuclear war, humanity was quickly confronted instead with the imposition of a 'new world order' under the auspices of global capitalism which, from a critical standpoint, may indeed be regarded as an example of secular myth. However counter-intuitive and offensive it may seem to those who were forcibly separated from friends by the Berlin Wall, the particular manner in which the Cold War was concluded was in demonstrable ways a political defeat for humanity and Enlightenment rather than the unequivocal triumph of human rights over totalitarian dictatorship. Today that demonstration needs to be elaborated with an eye towards re-articulating the affirmative dimension of critical social theory, beginning with the writings of Marx and Nietzsche, among others.[19]

It makes little sense to juxtapose Marx, the revolutionary theorist of communism, with Nietzsche, the reactionary postmodern defender of aristocratic values, as is often done. Both thinkers can instead be seen as precursors of critical theory who analyse the material, cultural and political factors required to test the hypotheses that (1) humanity only sets itself tasks that it is objectively capable of achieving, and (2) the necessary conditions for the achievement of autonomy are slowly being fulfilled and attaining real historical visibility. However much they might style themselves as opponents of Hegel's idealism, and however much they might reject the notion of the state as objectified *Geist*, they concur with the author of the *Phenomenology* in one important respect. All three implicitly agree to different degrees that

---

[18]As is well known, for Benjamin these secular mythologies include capitalist forms of economic growth, natural and positive law, un-reflective notions of progress and linear conceptions of time. See his 'The Work of Art in the Age of Mechanical Reproduction', in *Illuminations*, New York, Schocken, 1976a, and Samuel Weber's *Benjamin's Abilities*, Cambridge, Harvard University Press, 2008, especially chapter 17 (pp. 250–80), entitled 'Closing the Net: Capitalism as Religion'.

[19]The most fruitful synthesis of Marx and Nietzsche is still to be found in the writings of Gilles Deleuze and Félix Guattari. See in particular Deleuze's *Nietzsche et la Philosophie*, Paris, Presses Universitaires de France, 1962 as well as his *Foucault*, Paris, Les Éditions de Minuit, 1986.

the basis for the answers to normative questions about human freedom is offered by history and society rather than abstract morality, metaphysics, theology or simply chance, and, moreover, that this possibility is peculiar to modern humanity existing under socio-economic conditions of objectively possible post-scarcity. There is a corollary to the claim that the conditions of autonomy can be known and are socio-historical rather than abstractly moral: the phenomena that prevent the transition to freer forms of socio-economic and political organization can also be known and subjected to critique and transformation, that is, the failure to realize determinate political possibilities in practice is not simply a question of God's will, bad luck, destiny, inevitable decline, spontaneously coordinated supply and demand or, to bring the matter up to date, economic Tsunamis. Hence it will be shown in the course of the chapters to come that the political potential signalled by the differentiation of religious faith, political authority, economic function and aesthetic vision remains provisionally unrealizable *if* the spaces and possibilities opened by de-traditionalization and de-naturalization are closed down by the prevalence of instrumental over other forms of reason, and it will be shown too that this is an historical-analytical argument and not a speculative one. Part of what this entails is to show how and why the three *if*-clauses above refer to missed transitions and still possible transitions in contrast to what one might call *as if* epistemologies, such as those implied by the categorical imperative and the kingdom of ends, the veil of ignorance and the ideal speech situation.[20] In an essay on instrumental reason written in 1965 and published in 1969 entitled 'Subject and Object', Adorno states that the critique of knowledge (*Erkenntniskritik*) is also social critique (Kritik an der Gesellschaft) and vice versa. This statement may still be regarded as a precise definition of critical theory in the twenty-first century, and informs the approach adopted in this book. But the statement must also be re-phrased bearing in mind two caveats that qualify the issue.[21]

First, the role of Marxism in *Erkenntniskritik* is much more uncertain now than it was in 1965, when there was a relatively easily identifiable symmetry between being a Marxist, being an intellectual, being on the left, regarding

---

[20]These speculative models are respectively associated with Kant, Rawls and Habermas. See Kant, 'Perpetual Peace: A Philosophical Sketch', in Hans Reiss (ed.), *Kant: Political Writings*, Cambridge, Cambridge University Press, 1970, pp. 93–130; John Rawls, 'Justice as Fairness: Political not Metaphysical', *Philosophy and Public Affairs*, 14 (1985), pp. 223–51; and Habermas, *Theorie des kommunikativen Handelns* [*The Theory of Communicative Action*], Vol. 2, Frankfurt, 1981, pp. 447–88. For an analysis of the problems raised by these thinkers see Darrow Schecter, 'Liberalism and the Limits of Justice: Kant and Habermas', *King's College Law Journal*, 16 (2005b), pp. 99–119.

[21]Theodor W. Adorno, *Stichworte: Kritische Modelle 2* [*Critical Models*], Frankfurt, Suhrkamp, 1969, p. 158.

the working classes as the privileged agents of social transformation, and, until 1968 or thereabouts, being politically active as an anarchist, socialist, communist or trade unionist. This symmetry forms the basis of the much invoked unity of theory and praxis in Western Marxism that is often associated with Lukács' programmatic statement in the essay 'Reification and Proletarian Class Consciousness' in *History and Class Consciousness* (1923). Within Lukács' framework, the relation between theory and praxis can be altered with a revolutionary change in consciousness. Or, as he was forced to concede when he abjured the essay under duress by the Bolshevik leadership of the Third International, it can be bridged through adherence to the party, where failure to adhere is tantamount to false consciousness in the guise of reformism, revisionism, or, by 1928, social fascism.[22] The spectacularly obvious problems with this position should not distract contemporary critical theory from the more pertinent but less apparent flaw, which is that there are tremendous conceptual and practical problems implied by the notion that there can be any mechanical or direct conversion of theory into practice or quantity into quality. This idea conveniently brackets out what is both potentially liberating (genuine autonomy) and debilitating (postmodern relativism and passivity) in what one can loosely designate as the modern or late-modern period. The reality of this conflict implied by the clash between potential emancipation from socially mediated dependence versus passive adaptation to the dictates of oppressive institutions and norms indicates that despite all appearances, politics in the form of choices, deliberation, values and decisions continues to exist beyond the now hackneyed parliamentary instantiations of left, right and supposed third ways. For a critical theorist like Adorno, theory and praxis are fused rather than properly mediated in the work of thinkers such as Lukács.[23] What proper mediation might mean in this context is also not directly apparent and requires more detailed clarification in later chapters. But for now it will suffice to say that one could only posit a direct theory–praxis ensemble in Lukács' manner if it was unproblematic and non-tautological to say something like 'the exploiters exploit the exploited'. The derivation of 'correct' praxis from the 'right' theory might then consist in the dominated dominating the dominators in their turn. The complexities of modern societies immersed in the ongoing processes of de-naturalization

---

[22]Lukács, 'Verdinglichung und das Bewusstsein des Proletariats' ['Reification and Proletarian Consciousness'], in *Geschichte und Klassenbewusstsein: Studien über marxistische Dialektik* [*History and Class Consciousness*] (1923), Amsterdam, De Munter, 1967, pp. 218–20. For an analysis of the main lines of Western Marxism, see Schecter, *The History of the Left from Marx to the Present*, chapter 2, and Martin Jay, *Marxism and Totality*, Cambridge, Polity, 1984.
[23]Theodor W. Adorno, 'Erpresste Versöhnung' ['Reconciliation under Duress'] (1958) in *Noten zur Literatur*, Frankfurt, Suhrkamp, 1981, pp. 251–80.

and differentiation defy such easy congruities. But this does not mean that exploitation and domination are chimerical, or that critique and transformation are impossible and undesirable. In terms of the argument developed here it is worth considering if the apparent breakdown of the symmetry uniting the Marxist, intellectual and left-wing activist in one person is related to the equally apparent fragmentation of social classes and the crisis of what used to be known as 'class politics'. While many observers regard these phenomena as signs of postmodern apathy, it may be the case that class is in some real measure an historical descendent of the more recognizably naturalized category of caste, that is, a condition that one is born into, with minimum chances to escape or change. The end of a particular practice of class politics may be part of the ongoing de-naturalizing and differentiating transitions from caste to class and beyond, and thus might signify the possible beginning of a new theory and praxis of libertarian socialism in which a plurality of forms of property and diverse forums of decision-making are required precisely because de-naturalized societies are too complex and too de-centred to steer by small numbers of socio-economic and political elites, and, as the financial crisis indicates, one cannot count on spontaneous steering through the processes that Luhmann calls *autopoiesis*.[24]

This suggests that the processes that begin with caste society and then class society need not finish with the currently prevailing populism of authoritarian mass society, although it is likely that they will continue to do so as long as the possibility of transition from a class society to a classless society remains eclipsed by the identitarian logic of populist forms of democracy. This claim is defended in detail in Chapter Three. One might ask in what ways the decline of class is related to the same set of phenomena that explain the declining role of social-democratic and other political parties in mediating between society and government. Those mediations could become more spontaneous and flexible, not in spite of complexity, but because complexity requires such agility of movement and elasticity of response.[25] Chapters

---

[24]Niklas Luhmann, *Macht* [*Power*], Stuttgart, Ferdinand Enke, 1975, pp. 81–9. For an overview of Luhmann's theory of *autopoiesis* and other main concepts, see Michael King and Chris Thornhill, *Niklas Luhmann's Theory of Politics and Law*, London, Palgrave Macmillan, 2003, and the essays collected in Wolfgang Burckhardt (ed.), *Luhmann Lektüren*, Berlin, Kulturverlag Kadmos, 2010.

[25]Hence it may well have seemed in 1989–90 that the 'velvet revolutions' of those years proved beyond the shadow of a doubt that modern societies are too complex to be steered from a single-party centre, which is why the reform movements that proliferated in the alternative public spheres of Eastern Europe were led by informal networks and associations rather than by political parties. Yet from the vantage point afforded by the financial crises of 2008–10, it is plausible to maintain that these societies (and ours) are also too complex to be steered by two-party or multiparty 'democratic' political systems. More provocative still, it might be argued that if narrowly defined criteria of growth are allowed dogmatically to determine what constitutes

Four and Five show how mediation in this sense is possible, thus making a contribution to the renewal of critical theory. The book also indicates that one of the identifiable, non-speculative conditions for the realization of this possibility is a series of political decisions and legal measures taken to discard the permanent growth model of quantitative economic expansion that continues to shackle production to the necessity of undercutting competitors on a world scale, regardless of the environmental consequences, in favour of qualitative innovation that takes into account the reality of finite natural resources and consumer preferences. These measures are needed to prevent environmental ruin and the flooding of markets with wasteful and unwanted goods that are destroyed after quick shelf lives.[26]

Second, exploitation and domination must be re-conceptualized without a leading epistemology like Marxism or a privileged subject of change like the working class, though without embracing the view that life simply happens to people across classes, races, etc., in a haphazard way. In other words, what remains of *Erkenntniskritik* and the study of social transformation without an obvious epistemological foundation or primary agent of transformation?[27] Should state-funded universities and research centres continue to constitute the core of scientific and intellectual production, or has this function been 'outsourced', in a manner of speaking, to the general intellect of the multitude? These are difficult questions, but one can safely say that if critical theory in the twenty-first century is obliged to dispense with privileged epistemological doctrines and subjects, it cannot dispense with an epistemological approach to distinguishing between autonomy and more or less 'successful' modes of adaptation to social power, or between an imposed command and a collective decision, or, in more general terms, between the actual and the possible. *Critical Theory in the Twenty-First Century* attempts to sketch the

---

efficiency and well-being, a modified single-party system like the Chinese model may be the most 'successful'. Relevant and illuminating thoughts on this topic are provided by Wang Hui, *The End of the Revolution: China and the Limits of Modernity*, London, Verso, 2009, pp. 6–66.

[26]This perspective is elaborated by the authors of the essays in section 3 of Iring Fetscher and Alfred Schmidt (eds), *Emanzipation als Versöhnung: Zu Adornos Kritik der Warentausch-Gesellschaft und Perspektiven der Transformation* [*Emancipation as Reconciliation*], Frankfurt, Verlag Neue Kritik, 2002. They indicate that democratically elected consumer councils remain the key to instituting these measures, before hapless recourse to post hoc boycotts that inevitably look cumbersome and ineffective.

[27]The questions are dealt with in an innovative way in some contemporary social theory. See for example, Luc Boltanski, *De la critique. Précis de sociologie de l'émancipation*, Paris, Gallimard, 2009; Robin Celikates, *Kritik als soziale Praxis. Gesellschaftliche Selbstverständigung und kritische Theorie*, Frankfurt, Campus, 2009, as well as the essays in Beat Ringger (ed.), *Zukunft der Demokratie: Das postkapitalistische Projekt*, Basel, Rotpunkt, 2008; and the contributions to Klaus Dörre (ed.), *Soziologie, Kapitalismus, Kritik: Eine Debatte*, Frankfurt, Suhrkamp, 2009, especially those of Hartmut Rosa in that volume.

broad outlines of such an approach, bearing in mind that history and society indicate the possible answers to questions about autonomy, commands versus decisions and other key issues. This entails research about key moments of transition and political choice, rather than speculation about who the new revolutionary subjects might be, or musings about which supposedly timeless conceptions of human essence might be reinvigorated in time to rescue intellectual political tradition.

1

Dialectics, de-naturalization and social differentiation (I): From the public sphere to the emergence of civil society

Chapters One and Two chart the theoretical, historical and sociological background required to understand how and why critical theory emerges. Following this preamble, Chapters Three to Five attempt to set out the broad lines of a critical social theory with relevance for the twenty-first century. Before the reconstructive work undertaken in the second part of the book begins, the first two chapters set the stage and briefly substantiate a number of issues touched on in the introduction, such as the claim that it is possible to distinguish between potential autonomy from unnecessary ignorance and dependence, on the one hand, and more or less successful modes of passive adaptation to unnecessarily rigid norms, on the other. This claim is linked to another hypothesis sketched in the introduction. The corollary to the thesis that the conditions of autonomy can be known and are socio-historical and cultural rather than abstractly moral or narrowly juridical, is that the phenomena which actively prevent the transition to freer forms of socio-economic and political organization (such as financial crisis or failure of the educational system, depending on context in every instance) can be known, subjected to critique, and eventually transformed. The failure to realize determinate political possibilities in practice is not simply a question of God's will, individual or species destiny, the eruption of completely unpredictable social volcanoes or economic Tsunamis, etc., because each historical epoch indicates in different ways that humanity is not simply at the mercy of occult forces or secretly ordained hierarchies. This is not to say that there is no such thing as contingency or the exercise of social power issuing from contingency and uncertainty. But it does suggest there are more and less instrumentally rational ways of facing unpredictability and difficult choices. Societies accrue knowledge and planning capabilities as instances of monetary as well as non-monetary wealth, and indeed, a thinker like Hegel regards the capacity of the modern state to mediate public and private law as the ongoing institutionalization of such accumulated juridical, political and cultural knowledge. This point could be elaborated into a lengthy investigation of the rise and development of modern states and constitutions that is beyond the scope of this introduction to critical theory.[1]

What is an immediately pressing issue is assessing the extent to which the state can still be relied on to store and transmit this knowledge, and the mediation of private and public law remains the central task of politics. The relevant point for the discussion in this and subsequent chapters is that societies do not simply adapt to environmental scarcity and human conflict with purely technical or financial means. It seems clear that wealth and resources are not exclusively quantifiable or natural, and that there is a verifiable tendency for industrial societies to evolve as a series of simultaneous and plural processes characterized by polyvalent learning, individual choices and collectively binding decisions.[2] Hence the terms learning, steering and planning are decidedly not synonymous with vaguely defined notions of progress or strictly balance sheet indicators of economic growth as a self-legitimizing means and end. They refer to the processes and institutions in and through which the relations between humanity and nature are mediated. In a variety of ways the first generation of Frankfurt School critical theorists claim that the specific ways in which these technical and non-technical processes are politically organized and socially embedded will have a great impact on the construction of reality principles informing prevalent conceptions of educational deficits, socio-economic dependence, political possibility and human emancipation. Just as the term socio-economic dependence refers to a set of phenomena which includes class but is not reducible to what are sometimes called class identity or class politics, human emancipation has a broader connotation than simply redistributive justice. While narrowly

---

[1]See for example, David Sciulli, *Theory of Societal Constitutionalism: Foundations of a Non-Marxist Critical Theory*, New York, Columbia University Press, 1992, and Chris Thornhill, 'Legality, Legitimacy and the Constitution: A Historical-Functionalist Approach', in Chris Thornhill and Samantha Ashenden (eds), *Legality and Legitimacy: Normative and Sociological Approaches*, Baden-Baden, Nomos, 6 (2010), pp. 29–56. The ideas in this important article are developed in greater detail in Thornhill, *A Sociology of Constitutions: Constitutions and State Legitimacy in Historical-Sociological Perspective*, Cambridge, Cambridge University Press, 2011.

[2]Klaus Eder, *Die Vergesellschaftung der Natur: Studien zur sozialen Evolution der praktischen Vernunft* [*The Socialisation of Nature*], Frankfurt, Suhrkamp, 1988, chapters 1 and 4.

legalistic conceptions of justice can accommodate aspirations to negative liberty (liberty as non-infringement) and claims for redistributive justice (justice as punishment), it is unlikely that they can facilitate the realization of individual potential or the expansion of what a thinker like Gilles Deleuze might refer to as micro-political creativity.[3] Existing social systems tend to regard such notions as matters of individual choice not susceptible to legal reform, so that any attempt to promote a positive conception of the good can be dismissed in advance as paternalist, interventionist, or undecidable in juridical terms. One of the questions to be taken up in Chapters Four and Five is whether or not this tendency on the part of late modern social systems can be attributed to the fact that they operate amidst the vestiges of early modern liberal-democratic political institutions and suppositions. Critical theory in the twenty-first century has to evolve so that it can address the inadequacies of prevailing notions of dependence, and at the same time develop a differentiated conceptual vocabulary capable of analysing systems as too formal, not formal enough, or both. While an excess of formalism is likely to be dogmatic and raises some of the problems related to paternalist interventionism, an insufficient degree of formalism raises issues connected with relativism and juridical undecidability. The second part of this chapter suggests that critical theory can best approach theoretical and institutional questions of form with a method capable of drawing attention to the socio-historical dimension of dialectics, while tempering the emphasis which theories of performance and recognition tend to give to its individual, subjective dimension.[4]

---

[3]Gilles Deleuze, *Spinoza et le problème de l'expression* [*Spinoza and the Problem of Expression*], Paris, Minuit, 1968, pp. 248–51, and Manola Antonioli, 'La machination politique de Deleuze et Guattari', in Alain Beaulieu (ed.), *Gilles Deleuze*, Paris, Presses Universitaires de France, 2005, pp. 76–91.

[4]For a detailed and textually informed discussion of first-generation critical theory with specific reference to methodological issues, see Anastasia Marinopoulou, *The Concept of the Political in Max Horkheimer and Jürgen Habermas*, Athens, Nissos, 2008, and her *Dialogues in Modern Epistemology* in Continuum's *Critical Theory and Contemporary Society* series, Continuum, New York and London, 2014. The terms *salariat*, hegemony and *habitus* have been developed as part of the project to widen the notion of socio-economic dependence beyond the limited explanatory power offered by the concept of class. One usually associates hegemony with Gramsci and *habitus* with the sociology of Pierre Bourdieu. Gramsci and Bourdieu advance our understanding of *stratification* in the sense that they remain committed to the notion that society is divided into classes that consciously seek to dominate each other, which means that they at times also miss aspects of *differentiation*. Problems with assumed stratification are discussed in Chapters Four and Five, but for now one must remain aware of the fact that modern societies are stratified as well as differentiated, that is, that stratification has not yet become a redundant category of analysis.

In somewhat overdrawn terms, it makes a great deal of difference if scarcity is regarded as a demon to be exorcised as well as a God to be placated, or if, by contrast, the deliberate marginalization of scarcity is approached as a simultaneous chance to institutionalize new forms of collective freedom and of individual self-overcoming. The implication is that the particular mode of production engaged to overcome scarcity is a crucial factor in determining whether production will serve to bring about the highest degree of freedom from natural as well as institutionally imposed necessity, including socially necessary labour time, thus making socially mediated self-overcoming a real possibility, or if production becomes the measure of productivity. In the latter case one has a tautological end in itself in analytical terms which in practical terms translates into the domination of the producers and the perpetuation of unnecessarily rigid norms dictating the terms defining what constitutes public and private wealth. These are obviously two very different scenarios. There is therefore a great deal more at stake than an academic argument if it can be shown that the first scenario can prevail over the second through a series of collective decisions. While such conscious and rational planning may well sound like either wishful thinking or dictatorship, the possibility of a gradual but palpable evolution towards the formulation of binding rational and consensual decisions has its origins in the emergence of the modern public sphere as a unique historical space not subordinated to economic necessity or the exercise of traditional political command. The appearance of this space documents the possibility that post-traditional authority can evolve towards the entrenchment of rationalized power in a Weberian–Luhmannian sense of the legal-rational domination of unbridled systems, but might equally become rational and legitimate in a far less arbitrary and instrumental sense.[5] In what follows, this possibility will be interpreted as one salient part of a collective learning process at a specific juncture in European history, where two related possibilities accompanying social differentiation materialize for the first time. First, the struggle against scarcity and poverty no longer has to be an all-consuming necessity shaping economic as well as extra-economic communicative norms. Second, authority can be re-imagined beyond the hypothetical state of nature framework, that is, political legitimacy can be re-conceptualized in its political and pluralist dimensions rather than in fictional terms as ahistorical

[5]Andreas Fischer-Lescano and Gunther Teubner describe this phenomenon in terms of 'totalizing social systems'. They develop this concept in chapter 13 of their fine book, *Regime-Kollisionen: Zur Fragmentierung des globalen Rechts* [*Regime Collisions*], Frankfurt, Suhrkamp, 2006. See Philipp Schuler, *Rationalität und Organisation: Ein Vergleich zwischen Max Weber and Niklas Luhmann*, Norderstedt, Grin, 2007, for an interesting comparison between Weber on organizational dynamics and Luhmann on the different degrees of autonomy that social systems may or may not have.

spontaneity and imagined unanimity.[6] Hence the discussion in this chapter begins with a quick look at the discernible methodological innovation signalled by the shift from reliance on the state of nature in the writings of the social contract theorists, to the incipient sociology found in the writings of Kant, Hegel and Marx on the public sphere and civil society.

Natural rights, the state of nature and political philosophy in question

It can be argued that Kant occupies a kind of last outpost position among the state of nature and social contract theorists. It is from this vantage point that the ground is prepared for Hegel, Marx and a non-speculative historical approach to understanding the different possible modalities of transition implied by the shift from political emancipation and the destruction of feudal organic hierarchies, emblematically symbolized by the French Revolution, to the anticipated post-capitalist forms of human emancipation discussed in Marx's writings of 1843–4, which to this day remain for the most part anticipated. If realized in practice, such a transition would signify a non-ideological, qualitative diminution in the degree of human dependence on nature and authoritarian political tradition, made possible by coordinating increased productive capacity with the capacity for increasingly specialized media of communication and dissemination of information.[7] The coordination in question is not comparable to the patently false supposition that supply

---

[6]Hence one can understand the widespread fetish of nature and natural hierarchy, notions of imagined community, and fictional accounts of ahistorical spontaneity as different aspects of traditional thinking that are incongruent with secular authority. See Jürgen Habermas, *Strukturwandel der Öffentlichkeit: Untersuchungen zu einer Kategorie der bürgerlichen Gesellschaft* [*The Structural Transformation of the Public Sphere*] (first published in German by Luchterhand in 1962), Frankfurt, Suhrkamp, 1991. In the introduction to the 1991 edition of the book (pp. 45–50), Habermas stresses that the 'velvet revolutions' of 1989 and other sociological developments in complex industrial societies had forced him to re-think the capacity of the public sphere to function as a space for the generation of norms of communication independent from both economic criteria of profitability and political demands for order and administrative predictability. In his estimation this kind of non-authoritarian coordination is better understood as a vital part of civil society. He goes on to develop the sociological and juridical implications of this concept in detail in *Faktizität und Geltung* [*Between Facts and Norms*], Frankfurt, Suhrkamp, 1992a.

[7]This argument is made by several of the authors included in Jürgen Fohrmann and Arno Orzessek (eds), *Zerstreute Öffentlichkeiten: Zur Programmierung des Gemeinsinns*, Munich, Wilhelm Fink, 2002. See in particular Niels Werber, 'Kommunikation ohne Interaktion: Thesen zu einem zweiten Strukturwandel der Massenmedien', in Fohrmann, Jürgen and Arno Orzessek (eds), *Zerstreute Öffentlichkeiten: Zur Programmierung des Gemeinsinns*, Munich, Wilhelm Fink, 2002, pp. 43–51.

and demand are spontaneously adjusted by an invisible hand, nor can it be likened to the similarly flawed notion that changes in the economic base of society produce directly corresponding mutations in the ideological, cultural, juridical and political superstructure. It is suggested in this book that increased productive capacity and increasingly specialized media of communication are linked through the social-juridical production of rights. The implication is that rights are not, in the first instance, the legal instantiation of supposedly universal anthropological constants like the capacity for speech, labour, etc., which are imposed on political power. Instead, rights can be seen as constructs that allow complex, post-traditional societies to assess the reserves of power they rely on in order to function in a stable way.[8] It is centrally relevant to critical theory today that stability in this context depends on de-centralized planning rather than hierarchical order or faith in the magical powers of the market. The distant echoes of this contemporary phenomenon are faintly audible in Kant's ideas on law, politics and the public sphere.

Kant's republican version of sovereignty and individual natural rights is preceded by a long history of conflict between pro-papal and early proto-national-monarchical positions which crystallize at decisive moments during the Reformation and its aftermath, in the period roughly spanning the years 1517–1648. Bodin, for example, in his *Six Books of the Republic*, affirms the right of sovereign authority to make laws to which the legislator, re-presented in the person of the monarch, is not directly subject. He thus raises what remains a crucial question for all secular polities in which the authority of the state to mediate between private interests and public goods becomes functionally separated from the authority of the church to mediate between theological doctrine and daily religious ritual. From the moment that this separation is accomplished, a reflexively immanent and constantly modifiable response to the question can take the place of a fixed, dogmatically transcendent and predetermined solution. That is, how can the legal framework for making collective decisions be accepted as legitimate by those individuals, groups, classes and parties who think that they have been disadvantaged by the decisions taken? The simple answer for many thinkers from Bodin to the social contract theorists and beyond to conservative-authoritarian legal theorists like Carl Schmitt, that is, from perspectives both before and well after 1789, is the notion of sovereignty.[9] Before explaining why the notion of a

---

[8]Chris Thornhill, 'Re-conceiving Rights Revolutions: The Persistence of a Sociological Deficit in Theories of Rights', *Zeitschrift für Rechtssoziologie*, 2 (2010), pp. 177–207.

[9]Hasso Hoffmann, *Legitimität gegen Legalität: Der Weg der politischen Philosophie Carl Schmitts* [*Legitimacy against Legality*] (1964), Berlin, Duncker & Humblot, 2002, parts 2 and 3. For an innovative approach to the critique of sovereignty in the theories of Arendt and Foucault, see Claire Edwards, 'Arendt and Foucault: Beyond the Social and Political', DPhil in SPT at the University of Sussex, 2012.

unitary concept of sovereignty is incompatible with reflexive immanence and therefore unsuitable to the realties of complex industrial societies, it might be mentioned that *Six Books of the Republic* (1576) can be seen as an early stage on the path to *Leviathan* (1651) and the historical transition from late medieval practices conceding special privileges to estates, parliaments, corporations, communes, etc., to the positivization of law and the centralization of early modern state authority. In the specific case of the pioneering British road to post-feudalism, this movement is accompanied by the rise of London as a financial and commercial centre, as well as a decisive displacement of power from the almost completely naturalized privilege of the aristocracy, to the more rationalized social power exercised by the gentry and the upper bourgeoisie through control of banking and finance. In relation to the point above concerning rights and reserves of power, however, it may be time to revise a number of existing historical accounts of class domination in light of the concomitant factor of gradual, qualified independence of banking and finance from direct political control and religious interference. If there is an analytical dialectic of insufficient and excess form, there may also be an historical dialectic of social stratification and functional differentiation. An overemphasis on either stratification or differentiation in accounts of the rise and development of capitalism may contribute to a misunderstanding of the issues at stake.[10]

The emergence and partial autonomy of the economy is not an isolated phenomenon at this time, which also witnesses the subordination of the church to the throne under Henry VIII. There are a number of ways of interpreting this conflict. It can be seen as a first step towards the differentiation of political and religious authority within the framework provided by national territories, in a manner analogous to Swiss Calvinism and German Lutheranism, later to be accelerated in Great Britain as a result of the subsequent break with Rome and the ascendance of Anglicanism. The general tendency across Western Europe around this time is that the external political independence of modern nation-states from Rome proceeds in tandem with the internal differentiation of executive power and legislative authority at the national level, bearing in mind that each national context exhibits particular dynamics and peculiarities.[11] There is no need here to summarize the well known events

[10]Hence there is still much collaborative work to be done between historians and sociologists. Although somewhat rudimentary in sociological terms, G. M. Trevelyan's *English Social History*, London, Longmans, 1944, chapters 4–5, offers a thorough account of the period.

[11]Where this independence came relatively late in comparison with Britain, as in the cases of Germany and Italy, it tended to foment an aggressive nationalism accompanied by militarist and in some cases racist rhetoric. This combination of late unification, nationalism and racism eventually became manifest in fascism. On this account fascism is perhaps better explained as a result of

punctuating the conflict between crown and parliament which intensifies with the ascent to the throne of James I and the inevitable clash between his conception of the divine right of kings and demands for parliamentary sovereignty, the ascent of Charles I, and the advent of the Short and Long Parliaments. These developments leading up to the English Civil War are of interest to the extent that they foreshadow a way of thinking about political authority and the state of nature that comes to fruition in the writings of Hobbes and other social contract theorists.[12] It is a way of thinking that is challenged by Kant and especially Hegel's thesis that the simple dichotomy between state of nature and civil society must give way to a more complex picture capable of theorizing the distinctiveness of the early modern public sphere and the historically unique formation of a semi-autonomous system of needs, that is, the modern economy and the division of labour theorized by Hegel and Marx. Feudal authority had been exercised as an aggregate of religious, political and economic power in the form of traditional privilege. By contrast, post-feudal power tends to be disaggregated and dispersed even though, at least with regard to statute, law is gradually becoming positivized and rationalized in a series of processes undermining late medieval corporate particularities, thus pointing forward to 1789. The positivization of law and the simultaneous dispersion of legal jurisdiction in a post-sovereignty direction is an important historical development which informs the argument developed in Chapter Four, where it is explained why the dis-articulation of religion, morality, politics and law need not be framed in the conceptual vocabulary of bifurcated unity and alienation to be overcome in re-appropriated unity. The important point at this juncture is that the state of nature argument may have been somewhat convincing in a period when land ownership was still the major indicator of wealth, and the organic bonds between person, property and status did not undergo major change over the course of several decades. Under such conditions one could think about legality and legitimacy in ideal terms as a function of making stable property relations in civil society out of precarious possessions held in the state of nature. But what happens at

---

failed processes of differentiation, leading to weak and unstable states, than as a sudden reaction to economic crisis or political uncertainty. On the German case and the collapse of the Weimar Republic, see Detlev Peukert, *Die Weimarer Republik: Krisenjahre der klassischen Moderne* [*The Weimar Republic*] (available in English), Frankfurt, 1987. A text with continuing resonance in this regard is Marx's analysis of the dynamics of legislative and executive power in the *Eighteenth Brumaire of Louis Bonaparte*, included in most good collected works editions, for example, in Iring Fetscher, *Studienausgabe Vol IV. Geschichte und Politik 2*, Frankfurt, Fischer, 1990b.

[12]Readers interested in this period can consult the expert investigations offered by Christopher Hill in *The Century of Revolution, 1603–1714*, New York, Columbia University Press, 1966; and Lawrence Stone, *The Crisis of the Aristocracy*, London, Penguin, 1968.

a later stage, when the presupposed unity of person, property and status becomes as doubtful as the at times fanatically defended unity of a national understanding of the *demos*, that is, 'the people', national territory and the state? As will be seen presently, theoretical inquiry is obliged to renounce its ahistorical postulates as well as some of its dogmatic anthropological and religious assumptions.[13]

Kant is often quoted as saying that Hume woke him from his dogmatic epistemological slumbers. But it is also evident that Hobbes' dictum that 'auctoritas, non veritas facit legem' ('authority, not truth, makes the law'), provoked an abrupt end to Kant's political complacency. The initial impetus to refute Hobbes on this matter comes to Kant from Rousseau, for whom democratic politics depend on the imperative that there be no secrets or factions among the citizens of a state. Factions and cliques undermine the transparency needed for the general will, as opposed to the will of all, to emerge. Rousseau's general will manifests truth content beyond the sum of individual wills; while the latter can at times yield erroneous decisions, the former, he insists, is always right. In this way popular sovereignty presupposes the unity of morality and politics required to make democracy possible and the early modern state, now bereft of credible recourse to divine right, legitimate beyond mere legality. According to Rousseau's account of humanity's exit from the state of nature, the fictive social contract making all subsequent contracts valid can not be derived from logic or actual political experience. It rests on an anthropologically based conception of a universal human political being whose autonomy is inseparable from the autonomy of the other members of a secular political community. Kant concludes that it is possible for each individual to leave the state of nature, enter civil society (which prior to Hegel is synonymous with the state), and remain as free as they were before joining. Indeed, this individual is now qualitatively freer due to the moral education one receives only as a citizen.[14]

He agrees with Rousseau's theses on the possible unity of morality and politics, and is also convinced that universally valid moral principles can be derived for all rational and autonomous individual wills. He draws attention to the complementary relation between morals and politics in public debate (*Publizität*), and thinks that this may indicate the best way to refute Hobbes on the question of the origins of law. Kant argues that while reason indicates

---

[13]This deconstructive work is accomplished with elegance of style and power of vision in Gilles Deleuze and Félix Guattari, *Capitalisme et schizophrénie 1: L'Anti-Œdipe* [*Capitalism and Schizophrenia 1: The Anti-Oedipus*], Paris, Minuit, 1973.

[14]Rousseau, *Du contrat social* [*The Social Contract*] (1762), Paris, Éditions Garnier frères, 1960, p. 243.

the boundaries of knowledge and, by extension, the limits of legitimate state intervention in the lives of private citizens, practical reason yields general principles according to which the moral autonomy of individuals can be reconciled with the political necessity of joining all individuals as citizens within a just legal order of potentially international dimensions. As in Rousseau's formulation, though importantly without recourse to the notion of a sovereign general will, Kant believes that individual wills can join to form a republic, without this process resulting in an encroachment upon individual freedom. Rousseau and Kant see that only very instable grounds of political obligation can be secured by juxtaposing freedom and authority, and that what is needed in an era of secular authority is a theory and practice that reconcile them. It is worth noting their differing positions on this crucial issue. While Rousseau responds with a theory of republican sovereignty based on the general will, Kant thinks that the only way to reconcile freedom and authority in non-authoritarian terms is with a theory of negative liberty, that is, with a theory of liberty as non-infringement. But will this approach not quickly reveal itself to be a mainly commercial theory of liberty based on the contractually mediated right to buy and sell property, in the first instance, and then labour power and even votes, in the second? Although this possibility is confirmed as a real sociological tendency in the writings of Marx and then later with the first generation of Frankfurt School theorists, it is already clear to Kant that negative liberty might be problematic. Kant is not entirely happy with his formal and negative solution to the problem of autonomy and authority in ways that are more explicit in Hegel, and which in Kant's case impel him towards the idea of *Publizität*. In clear anticipation of Habermas' theory of communicative action, Kant believes that the sphere of morally autonomous individuals can be coupled – not fused – with the political institutions of the republic through the mediation process achieved by open debate in the public sphere (*Öffentlichkeit*). Kant maintains that although it is extremely difficult for an isolated individual to transcend their natural state of ignorance and isolation, a critical public can initiate a de-naturalizing dynamic through the open exchange of views and opinions. He submits that this exchange results in the formulation of ethical maxims which can exert moral pressure on existing legal statutes as soon as statute respects the need for order without respecting the desideratum of individual autonomy. Hence a great deal is at stake in pinpointing what autonomy actually entails, and specifying its enabling conditions.[15]

---

[15]Kant, 'Beantwortung der Frage: Was ist Aufklärung?' ['What is Enlightenment?'] (1783), in Wilhelm Weischedel (ed.), *Schriften zur Anthropologie, Geschichtsphilosophie, Politik und Pädagogik*, Frankfurt, Suhrkamp, 1977, p. 54. Kant's most important political writings, including 'What is Enlightenment?', are available in translation in Hans Reiss (ed.), *Kant: Political Writings*,

Two qualifying principles inform Kant's idea of a critical public mediating between morally autonomous private individuals and political institutions. First, anticipating Rawls' veil of ignorance, the individuals entitled to participate in public sphere debate should be thought of as being born with a will which, in maturity, can reason independently of their actual political experience. Second, critical reasoning and exchange of views and information is ideally conducted in a realm of freedom, that is, not in a workplace, scientific laboratory or other setting in which a competence-based hierarchy is more appropriate than an assembly of equals. Though it is implicit that the authority of experts should not be challenged in their respective fields of competence, Kant insists that all economically autonomous citizens can assemble and mutually enlighten one another outside of the spheres of technical knowledge and material necessity. In the first case the expert makes private use of his reason and is an unquestioned authority. In the second case he deploys an early manifestation of what Habermas and others will later designate as communicative reason, employed in an ongoing exchange of ideas with one's fellow citizens. Kant's thought registers the historical novelty of a situation in which legal norms can be modified as a result of non-speculative abstraction from both material necessity (anticipated post-scarcity, albeit for a select few within Kant's framework) and the omnipresent possibility of a war of all against all. This raises a number of issues that warrant a very short digression on the subject of autonomy.

To the extent that he quite openly excludes women and salaried workers from the public sphere because of a lack of economic independence, Kant's views seem antiquated and sociologically irrelevant. At a second glance, however, it is striking that in qualifying the conditions that will enable information to be epistemologically reliable and ethically sound, Kant conflates ethical moral autonomy, economic independence and natural reason. This caution to stipulate the terms defining epistemological validity highlights the ambiguity of his position and marks a notable difference between Kant and much of the rest of the social contract tradition in political philosophy. Once subjected to

---

Cambridge, Cambridge University Press, 1970. Important questions are raised by Habermas' attempt to re-articulate Kant, drawing on linguistic pragmatism and a number of other sources, in order to re-ground critical theory beyond what he regards as the dead ends encountered by the first generation. These questions will be taken up throughout this book but can be condensed into the issue of how best to redeem the epistemological and political possibilities offered by de-naturalization in particular and modernity in general. In terms of contemporary relevance, it can be noted that the rise of alternative public spheres in Eastern Europe was an intrinsic part of the 'velvet revolutions' of 1989. It may as yet be too early to say if something analogous began to emerge in North Africa in the spring of 2011, but there are a number of indicators to suggest that this is the case.

critique and revision, Kant's ideas provide evidence for the hypothesis that norms in modern societies can be underwritten by reason rather than force or tradition. This of course leaves open the question what the concept reason might mean, but for the moment one can proceed as follows: if taken literally, Kant undermines even the merely theoretical realization of a rational alternative to tradition by restricting access to rational communication to an elite minority. However, if one bears in mind that the social structure of the historical period in question is rapidly evolving in the directions subsequently theorized by Hegel and then Marx and Simmel, it does not require a fanciful sociological imagination to see that the aggregation of individual ethics, bourgeois forms of independence and instrumental reason can be deconstructed. The conflation can be discarded for sociological reasons, rather than on merely logical grounds or in terms of a development in the history of ideas, without, however, discarding the unique chance of allowing informed dialogue to intrude upon and eventually undermine the archaic privileges of raison d'état couched either as Machiavellian *virtù* or as the procedural stringency of positive law. At that point a completely new set of criteria informing the conditions of law-making and individual autonomy can be introduced. Hence on this reading it is not that the nascent bourgeoisie takes over from the moribund aristocracy and expands an economic system that the bourgeoisie, in its turn, will fail to release from what will become debilitating relations of production (a simplified, if not entirely distorted statement of many versions of historical materialism). Instead of failing chiefly because they evolve into impediments to capitalist production, bourgeois norms come into crisis because they become a barrier to legitimate socio-economic and political inclusion in decisions affecting the autonomy of individual citizens. Exclusion of this kind, which may have been a stabilizing factor in early modernity, later becomes a destabilizing factor manifested in periodic socio-economic crises. From a contemporary perspective it appears that such crises require juridical inclusion in the guise of enhanced social rights and democratic participation, rather than cumbersome technocratic steering of what have clearly become overburdened central state authorities, if, that is, inclusion and participation can be organized in ways that are flexible and decentralized enough to cope with contingency and complexity. At that point rational planning sheds the dirigiste approach characteristic of one-party, and to a lesser extent, multiparty political systems. In broad accordance with a substantially modified Kantian approach taken up in different ways by Habermas, Rawls and others, the potential of reflexivity can only be redeemed under conditions of church–state separation, where the mediation between humanity and nature is no longer tied to speciously stable points of reference external to the historical process, that is, no longer bound to metaphysical criteria of truth in nature or

Heaven.[16] While this initially appears as a triumph for the state vis-à-vis the church, it soon turns out to be problematic for that particular early modern liberal-democratic state form that is structurally ill-suited to acknowledge and adjudicate the conflict and contradictions between the political inclusion of citizens and the socio-economic exclusion of diverse groups, classes, genders and races. This is a problem that even Hegel cannot solve, as will be seen presently, and that Marx does not adequately address.[17]

The potential complementarity of normative and positivist dimensions of modern legality comes into focus here. On the one hand, increasing complexity demands that states recognize more and eventually all citizens as bearers of rights and not, anymore, as incarnations of idiosyncratically fixed locations within a hierarchical chain of being. On the other hand, the transcendence of class-ridden rationality becomes a juridical imperative once it becomes clear that this particular form of reason cannot stand up to rigorous criteria of universality (normative dimension), and that this lack of clarity contributes to unpredictable and arbitrary dynamics between the legislature, executive and judiciary (political sociological dimension).[18] At this point political authoritarianism, which, as stated, may well once have been a stabilizing factor during periods of religious conflict and economic scarcity, is likely to become a destabilizing factor and in any case a relatively short-term measure, as in the case of fascism.[19] The debate on the public sphere introduced by Kant and subsequently developed by social historians and political theorists such as Habermas, Oskar Negt, Alexander Kluge and others is misunderstood if interpreted as a polemic about the end of the Enlightenment and the eclipse of reason, 'class justice', or the ostensible

---

[16]This historical critique of metaphysical timelessness is advanced by Hegel, and then in a more recognizably sociological direction by Wilhelm Dilthey in *Der Aufbau der geschichtlichen Welt* [*The Construction of the Historical World*], 1910, which the author did not manage to finish before his death in 1911, Frankfurt, Suhrkamp, 1981, pp. 235–45.

[17]Jürgen Habermas, 'Reconciliation through the Use of Public Reason: Remarks on John Rawls' Political Liberalism', in Gordon Finlayson and Fabian Freyenhagen (eds), *Habermas and Rawls: Disputing the Political*, London, Routledge, 2011, pp. 25–45.

[18]The evolution of the Weimar Republic (1918–33) from parliamentary republic to presidential regime and from there to dictatorship offers an illuminating case in point. See Melissa Schwartzberg, *Democracy and Legal Change*, Cambridge, Cambridge University Press, 2007, chapter 5.

[19]On these and related arguments see Harold J. Berman, *Law and Revolution: The Formation of the Western Legal Tradition*, Cambridge, Harvard University Press, 1983, part II; Gianfranco Poggi, *The Development of the Modern State: A Sociological Introduction*, Stanford, Stanford University Press, 1978, chapter 4; and Ingeborg Maus, *Rechtstheorie und politische Theorie im Industriekapitalismus*, Munich, Wilhelm Fink Verlag, 1986, chapter 1. It is significant that the emphasis here is on emancipating norms and reason rather than on trying *directly* to emancipate humanity by insisting on some kind of *identity* between social being in class, gender, race, etc., terms, and some highly arbitrary and un-mediated ideal of justice.

need for state-socialist authoritarian forms of levelling equality. It becomes an altogether different debate if channelled towards a series of investigations concerning the possibilities for emancipating norms and reason from patently ideological notions of autonomy, nature and organic unity.[20]

Fundamental to Kant's view of *Publizität* is his insistence that the impetus for the introduction of an ethical core into political legislation must come from the independent private persons in the public sphere who mediate between the private sphere and government, which is part of the reason why he thinks that there can be moral politicians, but no political moralists as such.[21] While he thinks that the rights to property, marriage and family are natural rights deducible from practical reason, the origins of the state and government have to be traced to the fictitious moment when the state of nature is abandoned in order to enter into a contract sanctioning the birth of civil society. Kant asserts that this moment is a necessary fiction, since in real historical terms, states are quite obviously founded on violence rather than spontaneous and unanimous consent. Thus Kant sets up an opposition between inherently rational ethics (moral, individual) and potentially rational law (public, political), and submits that individuals are only free to the extent that they continuously assemble as a critical public, mediating between the private sphere of natural rights and the ultimately violently founded political authority that legally guarantees natural law. In a parallel vein, he maintains that violent disobedience towards violently founded states is illegal and therefore unacceptable and unethical. Instead, open discussion must produce compelling arguments for a change in the law in order to make it conform to the maxims implied by mutually and discursively redeemed claims and counter-claims. He suggests that it would be absurd and self-defeating to announce one's intentions to overthrow a government. More importantly, this kind of confusion would contribute to the collapse of the communicative space of *Publizität*, transparency, and reason opened up by the disarticulation of religious theological dogma and religious art, political authority and feudal land rights. This puts Kant in a somewhat difficult position. While he seems to be aware that it is this dis-aggregation of power and function that makes

[20]Kant, 'Was ist Aufklärung?' ['What is Enlightenment?'] (1783), p. 57; Habermas, *Strukturwandel der Öffentlichkeit* [*The Structural Transformation of the Public Sphere*], chapter 13; Oskar Negt and Alexander Kluge, *Öffentlichkeit und Erfahrung: Zur Organisationsanalyse von bürgerlicher und proletarischer Öffentlichkeit* [*The Public Sphere and Experience*], Frankfurt, Suhrkamp, 1973, chapter 1.

[21]Kant, 'Zum ewigen Frieden' ['Perpetual Peace'] (1795), p. 231; 'Über den Gemeinspruch: Das mag in der Theorie richtig sein, aber taugt nicht in der Praxis' ['Theory and Practice] (1793), pp. 145–51, in *Schriften zur Anthropologie, Geschichtsphilosophie, Politik und Pädagogik* (both essays also available in Reiss, ed.).

authority susceptible to articulate critique, he nonetheless seems to fear the revolutionary effects that rigorous dissent might have. One may suppose that Kant's political pamphlets and essays of 1790–5, such as 'Perpetual Peace' and 'On the Common Saying', were written with the unfolding events of the French Revolution in mind. In these forays into political theory he appears to want to refute Hobbes' notion that authority and not truth is the source of law, yet he recoils before the possibility that when confronted with communicatively validated truth claims, violent conflict between authority and the public sphere might ensue. Hence he seems to enjoin the citizens of the public sphere to 'suffer in non-silence', that is, he retreats to a position which is disappointingly close to Hobbes.[22]

Kant does have a response, however, which is to argue that all maxims resulting from the deliberations of a critical public should be made in accordance with existing forms of law, for it is *the task* (Aufgabe) of politics to harmonize the at times conflicting projects of individuals and groups under a single authority acceptable to all. Kant submits that politics is beholden to the task (rather than duty or law) of addressing the discrepancy between the need for hierarchical enforced order and the rational freedom of an informed and activist public whose members have been released from economic necessity to a significant extent. Even if, within Kant's framework, this transcendence is doubtful and in any case not in the least egalitarian, the potential implications within a changed Kantian framework are of the utmost interest for critical theory in the twenty-first century. If the claims of the public can only be redeemed through *Publizität*, and if the claims acquire universal validity through discussion, they then attain an ethical and rational truth content that makes a change in existing law a moral imperative. This is an imperative which conforms to universal truth criteria, but which cannot be imposed by a publicly sanctioned external force because it derives from the internal laws of conscience. Hence Kant hopes that over time, *Publizität* will eventually make the contrasting claims between individual morality and public law virtually non-existent, and Hobbes' account of legitimacy will be definitively disproved. The brief discussion of modernism at the end of this chapter and the start of the next will indicate why, in the course of the evolution of industrial society, individual private consciousness ceases to offer sufficient criteria for the formulation of reflexive judgements on the legitimacy and rationality of legal and political decisions. In anticipation of that discussion one can say that the

---

[22]Kant, 'Zum ewigen Frieden' ['Perpetual Peace'], pp. 241–4; Hans H. Gerth, *Bürgerliche Intelligenz um 1800*, Göttingen, Vandenhoeck & Ruprecht, 1976, chapters 3 and 4. Again, it is difficult not to think of the relevance of these ideas to the situation in North Africa during the spring of 2011.

truth content of what one might designate as 'the Kantian moment' is bound up with the emergence of the public sphere. If, as Habermas and others submit, the latter undergoes a structural transformation, a corresponding structural transformation of existing economic and political institutions becomes necessary in order to redeem the Enlightenment promise of the possibility of consistently post-feudal, post-traditional authority.[23]

One of the tasks of contemporary critical theory is to deconstruct the institutional logic that presupposes privatized consciousness and personal ownership of property as the unquestioned premises of juridical validity, and, at the same time, reflexively to rethink the possibilities for the mediation of political authority and transcendence of necessity beyond the flawed forms of meritocracy still prevalent in many advanced industrial and post-industrial economies today. In so doing it can set itself apart from the normative abstraction of analytical political theory and the normative silence of systems theory, without, however, having to embrace positions taken up by what remains of social democracy or some woolly version of communitarianism. It is difficult to say in definitive terms if meritocracy has to be made much more egalitarian and sociologically rigorous, or if the concept of merit itself should be re-examined in the light of the reality principles and performance principles that help organize the dynamics of meritocracy in late/organized capitalist societies. With regard to merit and individual vitality, for example, Horkheimer and Adorno reckon that if nature signifies scarcity, the possibility of sudden death, illness, deformity, in short, arbitrary fate, nature also implies spontaneity, sensuous cognition and genuine life beyond mere survival, that is, freedom beyond dogged or even sophisticated self-preservation. In the *Dialectic of Enlightenment* they explain that 'successful' attempts to eradicate nature as fate will almost certainly eliminate nature as freedom. The book indicates that once transposed onto the plane of history and society, the dialectic of nature as fate and nature as freedom becomes one where fleeting moments of emancipation from dependence are offset by various modes of domination which suppress concrete individuals in the name of questionable notions of merit, progress, reason, knowledge and autonomy. In their work the process mediating nature as destiny with nature as discovery and play is a negative dialectic. This dialectic indicates that each collective human emancipation from natural scarcity through competitively organized modes of exploitative production and technological innovation also initiates

---

[23]Kant, 'Zum ewigen Frieden' ['Perpetual Peace'], pp. 250–1; Habermas, *Strukturwandel der Öffentlichkeit* [*The Structural Transformation of the Public Sphere*], pp. 178–95; Stephen K. White, *The Recent Work of Jürgen Habermas: Reason, Justice and Modernity*, Cambridge, Cambridge University Press, 1988, chapter 6.

the domination of individual life by the bureaucratic command and repressive order needed to propel the productive machine that supposedly emancipates collective humanity from scarcity. As one epoch succeeds another, historically mediated fear of nature is transformed into juridically mediated socio-economic and political fear of discriminatory exclusion and forced inclusion. According to Horkheimer and Adorno fear is not transcended in organized capitalism. It is institutionalized in social mechanisms such as the educational system and labour markets, which often conflate the reality principles guiding an antagonistic social order, on the one hand, with a set of fairly arbitrary performance principles, on the other. These perpetuate the simultaneous isolation and homogenization of people by confusing, in practice, what is seemingly efficient within the framework offered by these performance principles, with what is rational and conducive to autonomy.[24]

Theory is complicit in the ongoing and repeated transformation of fate into narrowly conceived performance principles when it fails to insist that conscious and decentralized planning of binding decisions is more than a merely hypothetical possibility when economy and polity are mediated and recoupled rather than identical and fused, as in the former USSR and its satellite states (authoritarian socialist re-feudalization), or arbitrarily separated and then haphazardly re-sutured according to 'growth at all costs' ideology and free market dogma (what is sometimes referred to as casino capitalist re-feudalization, whose defenders have insisted in recent years that the major banks and international corporations 'cannot fail').[25] The dynamics of identity, fusion, separation and mediation relate to the observations made in the introduction about institutional dialectics that are too formal or not formal enough, and these, in turn, are related to theorizing appropriate paradigms in order to describe conditions of autonomy in non-tautological terms, that is, without resorting to the notion that these conditions are simply part of the definition of subjectivity. The point of deconstructing the institutional logic that presupposes privatized consciousness and personal ownership of property as the fundamental premises of juridical validity is

[24]Max Horkheimer and Theodor W. Adorno, *Dialektik der Aufklärung: Philosophische Fragmente* [*The Dialectic of Enlightenment*] (1944), Frankfurt, Fischer, 1995, pp. 21–3. There is a particularly simple and beautiful passage towards the end of the book, in the brief section entitled 'On the Critique of the Philosophy of History', where the authors comment that there is a rational dimension to hope that in qualitative terms exceeds the rationality of instrumental reason. They suggest that it is this non-illusory instance of hope, rather than belief in progress or the march of history, which may be able somehow to safeguard the vital impulse that guides every creature towards the light and towards expression.

[25]Ingeborg Maus uses the term re-feudalization in this sense in *Zur Aufklärung der Demokratietheorie*, Frankfurt, Suhrkamp, 1994, pp. 44–6.

to demonstrate that in complex, functionally differentiated societies, some of the conditions of individual autonomy are external to the individual. This means that they are to some extent historically contingent. But it also means that the conditions of individual autonomy are dependent on institutions that can be transformed, lest ostensibly sophisticated models of contingency resurrect naturalist paradigms of destiny and blind fate. It is not so much that the *Dialectic of Enlightenment* needs to be brought up to date with the modalities of globalization. It is instead a question of exploring the dynamics of de-coupling and re-coupling, of becoming a reflexive subject and overcoming existing forms of reflexive subjectivity. What remains relevant from early critical theory is the attempt to theorize social processes as constellations in their many-sidedness and plurality, and to do this with sensitivity to the particularity of transition periods and structural transformations. In this way one can observe the dialectics of conflict, collective social learning, and juridical evolution, instead of invoking the supposed inevitability of ahistorical, zero sum trade-offs. This is often done in the liberal democracies of Europe and North America in debates about the middle ground between freedom and equality, where it is frequently implied that a worker is a bourgeois without money and education, and that a bourgeois deprived of money and education becomes a worker. According to the identity thinking underlying this institutional logic, every person can be assumed to want the same things 'deep down', so that justice consists in striking a pragmatic balance between freedom and equality that leaves everybody happy in the end. In this instance identity thinking in practice reduces the dialectic of nature as fate and freedom to the re-naturalized ideology of differing talents and their neutral adjudication in a democratic order that in principle champions the right before the good. Horkheimer and Adorno may well have regarded the return to these ultimately premodern theoretical reflexes as indicative of the resurgence of mythological explanation and justification. They certainly are in little doubt about the compatibility of mythological thinking with the relentlessness of the culture industry.[26]

[26]The 'Culture Industry' argument may seem elitist and outdated to many. Yet there is clearly more than an accidental relation between the happy ends of Hollywood films, the speciously neutral means of the justice system analysed by Benjamin, and the assumption that money and education define who has and who has not fulfilled what are widely taken to be the universally accepted criteria of success. If it can be supposed that the people on the movie screen living in a far-off place in a far-off time aspire to the same things as one's neighbours here and now, as the films often suggest, why should it not be assumed that people behind a veil of ignorance will not opt for a safe combination of material incentives and rewards, as mainstream theorists and political parties often assume?

Critical theory can counter myths about universally competitive and consumerist human nature with far more convincing arguments explaining how and why it is not enough that power be divided between the different branches of government and between government and industry. Such division does not suffice to qualify an institutional setting as post-feudal, to say nothing of the end of history or the arrival of postmodernity. Historical research by Habermas, Foucault and others indicates that power in non-authoritarian post-feudal societies and states is dispersed, and that the emergence of the public sphere is linked to the opening up of a political space not directly subordinate to state authority or economic function, thus reflecting the potential pluralism embedded in modern polycentrism. One need not choose either mournful contemplation of the two dialectics of nature or embrace redistributive 'justice' as the only pragmatic 'solution' to the apparent tragic dimension in nature's ambiguity. The theoretical analysis and empirical observation of complex societies suggests that they are characterized by the dispersion of power, and that this reveals a diversity of decentralized political possibilities. An obvious one is offered by neo-liberal de-regulation which in reality does not turn out to be very pluralist or de-centred. It is not even consistently de-regulated as much as it is readjusted defensively to react to the rigours of international competition and the emergence of new centres of economic might such as China. Another plausible outcome entails a creative response to the opportunities offered by the de-centring logic of differentiation, and searches for practical answers to the following question: how is the dispersion of knowledge, power and authority to be organized, mediated and re-coupled in ways that meet rigorously formulated criteria of legitimacy? Within the terms established and bequeathed by the norms of existing private property regimes, such re-organization of energies, resources and mentalities may take on the initial appearance of heavy-handed meddling in the spontaneous production of goods and services, but there is little proof that this need be the case in the longer term (or that capitalist production in its current phase is in any meaningful sense spontaneous in view of the role played by advertising and other factors enlisted to sell commodities). Strict adherence to free market ideology raises many questions, such as those concerning the costs in terms of human potential and missed transitions to different modes of re-coupling that are incurred in the process of large-scale bank bail-outs and other stopgap measures designed to 'keep things moving in the right direction', as if the need for constant economic expansion has become a necessary fiction required to buttress the political fictions of natural origins and unanimous consent in an imaginary past before the existence of public spheres and civil societies.[27]

Another way of saying this is that some of the main conditions for a transition to a society characterized by enhanced autonomy are created to a large extent by objectively possible material post-scarcity, increasing complexity and social differentiation.[28] But this potential remains largely unrealized if the processes in question are not analysed, understood, and, where necessary and possible, corrected and guided with the help of a public that is not beholden to dogmatic growth imperatives or the ritualistic legitimation of centralized power and party leaders. Enhanced autonomy from mediated dependence on external nature and other humanity means maximum independence from scarcity secured without recourse to surplus repression of individual internal nature. A key issue to be explored in Chapters Four and Five is the extent to which law can perform key mediating and re-coupling functions. This will depend on re-conceptualizing the law outside of the frameworks suggested by the theories of (a) juridical populism, according to which law emanates from some kind of collective general will, and (b) juridical autonomy, according to which modern law is a self-creating system that dispenses with normative considerations altogether (both can be critiqued in dialectical terms as simultaneously too formal and not formal enough). This deconstructive possibility is suggested by a series of parallel differentiation and collective learning processes of the kind that prompt

---

[27]The concept that growth could have tremendous costs is often dismissed as a contradiction in terms by the apologists of growth-at-all-costs economies, who seem to be incapable of conceiving of poverty as a relation. In this particular example it is the relation between individual private interests and public services within a system governed by a logic that repeatedly juxtaposes private and public, that is, where growth is simply posited as a necessity and public expenditure is regarded in purely negative terms as a financial cost and a kind of moral burden imposed by the lazy and underperforming. There have been a number of very good investigations of this phenomenon. See for example, Pierre Dardot and Christian Laval, *La nouvelle raison du monde: Essai sur la société néolibérale* [*The World's New Reason*], Paris, La Découverte, 2009; Luc Boltanski and Eve Chiapello, *Le nouvel esprit du capitalisme* [*The New Spirit of Capitalism*], Paris, Gallimard, 1999; and the essays collected in Susan Braedly and Meg Luxton (eds), *Neo-liberalism and Everyday Life*, Montreal, McGill University Press, 2010. For a very readable and acute vision of alternatives to thinking about private, public and economy in neo-liberal terms, see Waldon Bello, *Deglobalization: Ideas for a New World Economy*, London, Zed Books, 2004. Bello's ideas are echoed in a considerable number of contemporary French studies on the possibility of *décroissance* (literally de-growth), that is, economic growth beyond exclusively private and monetary terms.

[28]This argument is developed in detail in relation to Luhmann's systems theory by the essays collected in Alex Demirovic (ed.), *Komplexität und Emanzipation: Kritische Gesellschaftstheorie und die Herausforderung der Systemtheorie Niklas Luhmanns* [*Complexity and Emancipation*], Münster, Westfälisches Dampfboot, 2001. See in particular the contributions by Daniel Barben and Demirovic.

Hegel to reject the simple dichotomy between state of nature and civil society in favour of the more historical and dialectical approach developed in the *Phenomenology* and more explicitly in the *Philosophy of Right*. These processes lead to epistemological and political positions that point beyond Hegel to Marx and Nietzsche. In addition to the evolution of religious and political authority according to increasingly discrete logics, post-feudal political authority and economic function subsequently enter into a similarly discontinuous articulation in relation to one another. Hegel and Marx trace this tendency in their respective accounts of the emergence and development of civil society, which will be very briefly discussed in what follows. But first it should be mentioned that the emergence and consolidation of discrete institutional logics has important, if somewhat ambiguous implications. The first generation of critical theorists were well aware that the emancipation of art and of the truth content of aesthetics from religious tutelage and political control opens up the path towards a potential re-alignment (once again, not fusion) of individual autonomy, collective decision-making processes and political contestation.[29] In retrospect one can say that this potential finds its most potent, if to date only partially realized expression in certain modernist avant-garde movements such as Dada, surrealism, Bauhaus and situationism, which pose the question of *Publizität* in decidedly non-Kantian but certainly not anti-Kantian terms.[30] Such movements indicate that at the juncture in history associated with the Industrial Revolution, the struggle against scarcity and poverty no longer has to be an all-consuming necessity shaping economic

---

[29]On the links between critical theory, modernist aesthetics and radical politics, see Hauke Brunkhorst, *Theodor W. Adorno: Dialektik der Moderne* [*Theodor W. Adorno: The Dialectic of Modernity*], Munich, Piper, 1990; Douglas Kellner, *Critical Theory, Marxism and Modernity*, Baltimore, Johns Hopkins University Press, 1989; Agnes Heller, *A Theory of Modernity*, Oxford, Blackwell, 1999; and Raymond Williams, *The Politics of Modernity: Against the New Conformists*, London, Verso, 2nd edn, 2007. A very illuminating dialogue between some of the main protagonists in the initial debates on modernism and revolutionary politics is contained in Fredric Jameson (ed.), *Aesthetics and Politics: Theodor Adorno, Walter Benjamin, Ernst Bloch, Bertolt Brecht and Georg Lukács*, London, Verso, 2007a. Jameson's 'Afterword' to the volume explains the contemporary relevance of these thinkers and their ideas.

[30]Sascha Bru, *Democracy, Law and the Modernist Avant-Gardes: Writing in the State of Exception*, Edinburgh, Edinburgh University Press, 2009; Ravit Reichman, *The Affective Life of Law: Legal Modernism and the Literary Imagination*, Stanford, Stanford University Press, 2009. It is interesting to note that Galileo's account of scientific validity, which brought him into trouble with the religious–political authority of Roman Catholicism, had a major impact on the formulation of Kant's critical epistemological project, which, broadly following Habermas' reading of Kant during the *Strukturwandel* period, retains a political potential which is by no means insignificant. The links between Kant, the first generation of critical theorists and Habermas are clarified by Rolf Eickelpasch in 'Bodenlose Vernunft: Zum utopischen Gehalt des Konzepts kommunikativer Rationalität bei Habermas', in Rolf Eickelpasch and Armin Nassehi (eds), *Utopie und Moderne* [*Utopia and Modernity*], Frankfurt, Suhrkamp, 1996, pp. 11–50.

as well as extra-economic communicative norms. De-naturalized and post-populist forms of de-centralized authority can then be debated by a creative, activist citizenry whose capacity to revolutionize the imaginary institution of society, to borrow from Castoriadis for a moment, is no longer oppressed by the unnecessary austerity imposed by re-feudalized economies, of which the United States and China offer the prevailing contemporary examples.[31]

Critical theory today can be confident and assertive in maintaining that the emancipation of the imaginary institution of society from religious tutelage and political control is forfeited – and a transition is temporarily missed – if money is allowed to eclipse law as well as aesthetic praxis and other forms of non-instrumental reason, as the principle agent of differentiation and mediation. Hence the present book endeavours to shed new light on the relations between money, law and reason as the three key instances of de-naturalized communication in modern societies. While it is perhaps obvious that money now functions as much more than simply a mechanism of exchange within the world economy, it is less self-explanatory that law and various instances of communicative reason could play much more significant re-coupling roles in complex societies than they do at present. It is naively utopian and un-dialectical to juxtapose starkly a rationalized constellation governed by money with a reasonable one sustained by art, dialogue and communication: instead of setting them up as real and ideal worlds, critique can show where these two constellations intersect, and how the second of the two might be re-articulated in theory and affirmed in practice.[32] The theoretical possibility of non-authoritarian and non-commercial mediation between differentiated spheres is registered in Hegel's *Philosophy of Right* (1821), in which the role of civil society and the system of needs within it is analysed outside of and in deliberate opposition to the social contract/state of nature approach.

---

[31]See Cornelius Castoriadis, *L'institution imaginaire de la société* [*The Imaginary Institution of Society*], Paris, Seuil, 1975, which elaborates the author's experience as a libertarian socialist in the *Socialism or Barbarism* group in the 15 years preceding the publication of this book, which is his most famous contribution to sociological theory. On the organizational parallels between the United States and China, see Wang Hui, *The End of the Revolution: China and the Limits of Modernity*, chapter 1.

[32]It might be objected that language is and has always been the primary denaturalized mode of communication known to humanity, and that, as Habermas shows, language, law and reason are not neatly separable. There is much validity to this objection, but it must also be seen that there has been a literary turn in critical theory and social and political thought that has contributed to the under-theorization of sociological phenomena. Addressing this sociological deficit seems more important than more abstract theorizing about the relations between experience, language and truth. This is not to say that critical theory should be silent about the matter. It is also the case that critical theory is capable of engaging with other paradigms of thought on the issue of language. See for example, Rolf Wiggershaus, *Wittgenstein und Adorno: Zwei Spielarten modernen Philosophierens*, Göttingen, Wallstein, 2001.

Social differentiation and conditions of knowledge external to the subject

In the addition to paragraph 182 of the *Philosophy of Right*, Hegel remarks that 'civil society is the product of the modern world', by which he implies several things. First, he seeks to show that a break must be made with the prevalent ways of thinking about political legitimacy from Bodin to Kant. Necessary fictions such as divine right or the social contract are in fact unnecessary because the appearance of the public sphere marks the beginning of a discernible evolution towards greater social complexity, and therewith, enhanced potential for systemic economic and political self-organization at the pre-state levels of what Hegel refers to in the *Philosophy of Right* as *Sittlichkeit* (usually translated as ethical life, comprised of the family, civil society and the state). Hegel thinks that what is required in the place of unnecessary fictions and generic concepts of legitimacy is a theoretical framework that thinks in harmony with the movement of the historical process. This process offers a contradictory but ultimately comprehensible pattern characterized by conflict, conflict resolution, and successive instances of reconciliation between humanity and nature. These, in turn, provide the bases of anticipated reconciliation between the different parts of a humanity alienated from itself.[33] In Hegel's view the public sphere is a necessary but insufficient condition for reconciliation in either sense. His work systematizes the mounting evidence at this time which suggested that the period of economically independent private citizens (the Kantian moment of private juridical consciousness) was passing with the advent of intensified industrialization and the inexorable evolution towards more comprehensive, dynamic forms of economy. Hegel sees that in the wake of the relatively short historical moment separating him from Kant, mere possession of wealth and property will no longer serve as the fundamental condition of reflexivity or the premise of reliable mediation between familial, economic, corporate and political spheres.[34] This is related to the second point implied by the addition to paragraph 182, namely, that a more complex theoretical framework is needed to analyse the tendencies inherent in qualitatively and quantitatively new modes of exchange registered

---

[33]Perhaps the most famous examples of this notion of alienation in Hegel's work are the now somewhat over-cited sections of chapter 4 of the *Phenomenology* about the reciprocal dependence of master and slave, which have inspired a great deal of subsequent recognition theory. For a reliable summary of those debates, see Simon Thompson, *The Political Theory of Recognition: A Critical Introduction*, Cambridge, Polity, 2006. It will be seen below that there are a number of theoretical ambiguities related to the concept of alienation.

[34]Hegel, *Grundlinien der Philosophie des Rechts* [*The Philosophy of Right*] (1821), Frankfurt, Suhrkamp, 1970a, p. 339.

in the writings of the Scottish Enlightenment thinkers Smith, Ferguson, Hume and Stewart. He also notes that while the dissolution of feudalism was apparently accompanied by a breaking-down of social bonds, incipient industrialization in Western and Central Europe is marked by a plurality of new associations which, while ultimately responsible to state authority, enjoy an unprecedented capacity to organize the integration of individuals on a more rational basis. Hegel has especially positive things to say about the corporations in this regard, although he also warns against their bureaucratization. This prompts him to remark in that same paragraph that although civil society appears as the *difference* between the family and the state, it is a difference that presupposes the *unity* of all the moments of ethical life in the state. This complements his view that a valid contract presupposes a valid state, and merits an explanatory observation.[35]

According to the idea of political freedom and authority expounded by Hegel and other theorists of secular political order, there exists a mediated unity between citizens, law and the state. This constellation of institutional forces binds individual citizens within a territorially demarcated national community, in which the citizens have rights and obligations. The term mediated unity expresses the idea that if there was no unity at all between citizens and the state, representation would be impossible, thus indicating that mediation processes and the possibility of rational representation are closely linked for Hegel and many others. If there was identity between citizens and the state instead of mediated unity, representation would be superfluous. Self-conscious and perfectly coordinated spontaneity would prevail, and there would be no need to mediate theory and practice through government and administration. For Hegel, the truth content of absolute spirit, as this is manifested in philosophy, religion and art, finds its counterpart in the truth content of objective spirit, as this is embodied in abstract right, morality and ethical life. The truth content of ethical life ensures that political representation in the modern state is juridical rather than arbitrary and authoritarian. According to the logic of ethical life analysed in the *Philosophy of Right*, the unity of the family is re-articulated at a higher, richer level in the state. Unity is therefore both the starting and the end point of a contradictory, horizontal and vertical flow of imperfect information in which socio-historical

[35]Ibid., addition to paragraph 182, pp. 339–40. Hegel is able to break with the state of nature/civil society dichotomy, and almost seems willing to consider the discontinuity between conceptual thought, thinking in a more general, sensual sense and institutional reality. Although he concedes that unity between humanity and nature is mediated rather than simple or direct, he will not accept that mediation can be real without producing re-unified configurations of the conceptual and extra-conceptual. Might it not be objected, from Hegel's standpoint, that the non-conceptual is itself a concept? Adorno has several responses that Hegel does not fully anticipate.

being and consciousness are neither fused nor separated. Indeed, the idea of a relation between heterogeneous but nonetheless related elements that are neither fused nor separated illustrates what Hegel means by the mediated unity of humanity and nature in *Geist* (variously translated as mind or spirit).

In his writings on world history and objective spirit Hegel submits that being and conscious being converge, diverge, and converge again. This results in perpetual conflict and new modes of conflict resolution at different levels of society, such that being and consciousness are gradually moving towards a non-oppressive synthesis in fully rational institutions communicating increasingly perfect information, the most powerful example of which is the modern state.[36] Hegel intimates that the phenomenon of *Öffentlichkeit* (publicity/the public sphere) ensures that the public space previously occupied by the symbols and authority of ritualized feudal political tradition and religious authority is kept open and perpetually undefined; it is even enlarged into the antagonistic pluralism of civil society, of which the public sphere is now a part. In Hegel's view the modern state cancels and preserves the moment of truth contained in this largely *negative affirmation* of individual liberty and group interest. Early modern *Öffentlichkeit* within the newly emerging civil society of Europe is therefore not a simple renaissance of ancient republican virtue. The relatively transparent social structure that sustains the historically particular form of activism in the *polis* and later in the Italian city-states is succeeded by a more intricate network of overlapping rationalities which foster individualism and contrasting associational allegiances. But instead of fearing difference and attempting to coerce unmediated unity between citizens and the government of the kind that blatantly failed during the episode of the Terror in the French Revolution, Hegel is confident that private interest and public reason can and do coexist in mediated unity. Mediated unity thus describes the structure of knowledge as well as that of law and politics; it offers the key to a correct interpretation of reality in the broadest sense, of which objective spirit is one notable dimension. The dynamics of private and public lives can simultaneously unfold as long as differentiation is respected and no voluntarist attempts are made to integrate civil society into the state through bureaucratic management and excess steering. It is however intrinsic to Hegel's defence of the state that the epistemological status of mediated disunity represented by civil society is inferior to that of the accumulated

[36]Although this way of phrasing the matter makes Hegel sound like a systems theorist *avant la lettre*, this reading of him is entirely possible and can be supported with evidence from Hegel's texts. In addition to mediating, Hegel's state establishes channels of communication between otherwise discrete logics of practice. See Manfred Riedel, *Theorie und Praxis im Denken Hegels: Interpretationen zu den Grundstellungen der neuzeitlichen Subjektivität*, Frankfurt, Ullstein, 1965, pp. 123–50.

knowledge embodied in the mediating power of the state. This will become a focal point in the young Marx's critique of Hegel's idealism.[37]

In the *Philosophy of Right* the state is not a simple means for the political unification of individuals and the protection of their property, nor is it a means for unifying the nation. The state is mind objectified: it is a means as well as an end, and it is legal as well as legitimate.[38] The immediate question is not whether Hegel had become a conservative advocate of order and authority at this stage of his life. His insistence that one cannot come up with the grounds of political obligation in terms of a contract because a valid contract presupposes a legitimate state is more pertinent. Hegel gives systematic expression to a wider tendency in theorizing about political representation, analysed in more detail in Chapter Three as an instance of institutionalized identity thinking. This is the tendency to make original unity the basis of re-presented unity and the benchmark of the tolerable limits of dissent and alienation. Hence Hegel's assertion that the state is more than a means is bound up with his project to secure the bases of a method for the study of social reality that is more than a passive or neutral method, since for Hegel the dialectic is inherent in the structure of history and the journey of consciousness to self-consciousness objectified in institutions ('mind objectified'). If the state, as an expression of objective spirit external to the individual, is the condition of an individual rational will (rather than the other way round), the dialectic is the condition that enables humanity to understand the mediated character of all things real. In attempting to locate a field outside of the knowing subject as the condition of that subject's understanding, Hegel points the way towards modernist and psychoanalytic accounts of the self as internally fragmented and, to paraphrase Simmel, part of a series of interactive reciprocal exchanges. Hegel offers an alternative to ahistorical fictions and other mythologies, empiricism, scientist positivism and crude materialism. Although it is an idealist alternative, it is one which has a profound impact on modernist thinkers such as Marx and Nietzsche, even if, in the case of Nietzsche, it is largely a negative influence. But wherever one happens to stand in relation to Hegel's idealism, one cannot be indifferent to or dismissive of what he attempts in epistemological terms and this, in turn, is inseparable from the way he thinks about identity, difference and processes of differentiation. In Chapter Three it will be seen that Adorno is critical of idealist dialectics, but like Hegel he is very interested in the possibility of a *method* of inquiry that might be unified with the *object* of inquiry without distorting either. If realized in non-coerced practice, such a

---

[37]Hegel, *Vorlesungen über die Philosophie der Geschichte* [*Lectures on the Philosophy of History*], Frankfurt, Suhrkamp, 1970b, Part IV, section 3, especially paragraph 257.

[38]See Hegel, *Grundlinien der Philosophie des Rechts* [*The Philosophy of Right*] (1821), Part III on ethical life and the pre-eminent role of the state within it.

method would enable humanity to understand its place in the world without fear. What remains of fear could then be analysed and addressed with psychoanalytic and other approaches, instead of re-naturalized, that is, declared to be a trans-historical dimension of the human condition or an ontological feature of being in the world.[39] Naturalistic and ontological explanations tend to be ahistorical and insufficiently dialectical, and as such, they generally fail to explain the phenomena they set out to illuminate. The best response is a critical theory of mediations that, in contrast to Hegel's, is not apologetic of existing social and political institutions. Although residually idealist, such a theory would be more materialist and sociologically relevant than historical materialism and naïve liberal-democratic theory. If for Adorno a critical theory of mediations has to be a negative theory until the external conditions of a reconciled world are met, this means renouncing the affirmation of an already existing subject (the demos or the proletariat) or foundation (state) that can organize the mediations. He thinks that such foundational organization would inevitably be coercive and, in a more profound sense related to anticipated reconciliation, untrue. But it does not entail renouncing a modified version of the dialectical method, which could make an incisive contribution to indicating paths of research concerning the following questions: what might be the possibilities for the realization of a de-centred, plural network of mediations instead of a unified mediating instance?[40] If complexity demands this flexibility – and the contemporary crisis of quite clearly overburdened states provides further evidence of this need for an historically new form of stability – must not the search for order without destabilizing hierarchy constitute a key epistemological priority? Might twelve-tone music and other examples of non-hierarchical order provide the legitimate traces of what may still be redeemed as a fruitful point of departure for this research?[41]

---

[39]Freud and the psychoanalytical method are of great interest here in view of the fact that while Hegel breaks with the social contract theorists in favour of an internally differentiated model of socio-political reality, Freud regards the internal differentiation of the self to be a potentially emancipatory development even if, within a repressive context, such complexity can have de-stabilizing effects on many individuals. See Céline Surprenant, *Freud's Mass Psychology: Questions of Scale*, London, Palgrave, 2003, chapters 5–6; and Jon Mills, 'The I and the It', in Jon Mills (ed.), *Rereading Freud: Psychoanalysis through Philosophy*, Albany, State University of New York Press, 2004, pp. 127–63. There will be more to say about these issues in the course of subsequent chapters. The immediate point at hand is that neither an internally divided self nor the location of the conditions of knowledge and autonomy in a space external to the subject are necessarily pathological or 'alienating'. To say that a phenomenon is internally divided or external to the subject is not to say that it is an illness or a threat.

[40]If method and object can somehow be reconciled without distorting either, it might also be possible to provide accurate explanation in the service of non-antagonistic autonomy. See Adorno, *Negative Dialektik* [*Negative Dialectics*], pp. 125–36.

[41]Theodor W. Adorno, *Philosophie der neuen Musik* (1949), Frankfurt, Suhrkamp, 1976, chapter 1; Simon Jarvis, *Adorno: A Critical Introduction*, Cambridge, Polity, 1998, chapter 5.

Adorno suggests that if Hegel's methodological promise can be redeemed in non-idealist terms without resorting to one-sided materialism, humanity would receive renewed impetus to recommence the Enlightenment project of emancipation from dependence on external nature and suppression of individual, internal nature, that is, what is referred to at the start of this chapter as individual human life. Critical philosophy and modernist aesthetics therefore guide Adorno towards an epistemology that is at once aesthetically theoretical (a method informed by aesthetic/mimetic reason) and theoretically aesthetic (concerned with the objective mediating structures constitutive of socio-historical reality as these are illuminated by such reason), as the title of one of his central epistemological contributions to aesthetic and social theory intimates.[42] Perhaps somewhat less apparent is the juridical and sociological relevance of this approach, which is delineated in Chapters Three to Five. In keeping with the project of locating a field outside of the knowing subject as the condition of subjectivity, Adorno's work helps outline the contours of a method that strengthens the objective, socio-historical dimension of the dialectic while also tempering the individual, subjective dimension bequeathed by Hegel to a great deal of subsequent social and political thought. This includes the many instances in which the influence comes in the form of an ostensible rejection of dialectics.[43] It will be seen in Chapter Two that the qualified recuperation and redeployment of the social, historical and legal dimension of dialectical and constellational thinking follows an aesthetic and modernist reflex, and is of great importance for the renewal of critical theory. The individual-subjective dimension of Hegel's dialectic that is understated by Adorno has often been inflated into a collective-subjective version in the hands of thinkers whose work has the reputation of somehow being incisive, radically democratic, praxis-oriented, etc., as in the case of Lukács. More recently, it has been refashioned into largely academic theories of recognition, performance, etc. While the former have lost a considerable degree of their

---

[42]Theodor W. Adorno, *Ästhetische Theorie* [*Aesthetic Theory*] (published posthumously a year after Adorno's death), Frankfurt, Suhrkamp, 1970, pp. 29–30. Thanks go to Simon Mussell for this point concerning theory that is about aesthetics and also aesthetically theoretical. Also see the arguments sketched in Theodor W. Adorno, *Drei Studien zu Hegel: Aspekte Erfahrungsgehalt Skoteinos, oder Wie zu lesen sei* [*Hegel: Three Studies*], Frankfurt, Suhrkamp, 1963, and Robert B. Pippin, *Idealism as Modernism: Hegelian Variations*, Cambridge, Cambridge University Press, 1997, pp. 160–1, 192–5.

[43]One thinks in the first instance of that particular strain of Nietzsche's genealogical and deconstructive thought that inspires a great deal of post-structuralism, and especially the work of Gilles Deleuze and Felix Guattari. This is by no means to suggest that post-structuralism is politically irrelevant. Like Foucault, Deleuze and Guattari paved the way for Todd May, Saul Neumann and a variety of thinkers and movements associated with global anti-capitalism and *altermondialisme*. See the contributions collected in Duane Rousselle and Süreyyya Evren (eds), *Post-Anarchy: A Reader*, London, Pluto, 2011.

appeal and relevance, the latter, like the predominantly literary approaches to critical theory, suffer from a juridical and sociological deficit that is in urgent need of redress if critical theory is to regain the political impetus it had before the linguistic turn marked by the *Theory of Communicative Action*. As remarked in the introduction of this book, however, to regain cannot simply mean to restate, as Chapters Three to Five seek to demonstrate.[44]

In the third section of the *Philosophy of Right* on ethical life, Hegel maintains that although the family represents a kind of unmediated unity between humanity and nature based on unconditional love and spontaneously generated ethical feeling, the family is more, in rational terms, than brute, ahistorical nature. To the extent that it is based on monogamy and has a definite structure, the family is an instance of historically tested, if far from perfect, communal life underwritten by law and custom.[45] The unmediated unity of the natural familial bond cedes place to mediated disunity in civil society, where instinct and spontaneity are modified by calculation, interest and contract. Although this is a moment of rupture with nature and instinct, it bears a moment of social-juridical truth within it that reveals something about the structure of conflict and compromise at a particular place and time. Unlike Hobbes, Locke, Rousseau and Kant, Hegel ceases to juxtapose a timeless state of nature with a hypothetical account of the birth of civil society. Prior to Hegel's intervention, the reigning distinction among post-feudal political theorists is the social contract-based dichotomy contrasting the ostensibly pre-political state of nature with the origins of political authority. That is, prior

---

[44]Most of the early members of the Institute for Social Research attempted to combine a philosophical interest in Hegel and Marx with studies in political economy, law and sociology. Otto Kirchheimer and Franz Neumann were the most prominent members of the first generation of critical theorists with a sustained interest in law (they were in fact trained and practising lawyers). See William E. Scheuerman, *Between the Norm and the Exception: The Frankfurt School and the Rule of Law*, Cambridge, MIT Press, 1994. Kirchheimer and Neumann's interest in legal theory was later renewed by Habermas in *Between Facts and Norms*. From a contemporary vantage point, one can no longer assume the mediated unity of the people, law and the state. This suggests that it is no longer possible to theorize about the law in the manner of Schmitt, Kirchheimer, Neumann, or even Habermas. This is one of the reasons why the juridical implications of Adorno's ideas are of central interest here.

[45]This is not the place to expound on what could be considered the dubious premises of monogamy and other institutions that make up the fabric of Hegelian ethical life. What is important is giving clear theoretical and empirical contours to the mediations between monogamy, private property, systematic socio-historical exploitation, and, as Hegel does with the civil service of his day, the designation of a decidedly non-universal class as universal. However disparate they may seem, these phenomena cannot be construed as accidental or explainable in terms of base and superstructure. Nor is it a simple case of the symbolic order of society writ large. In a more contemporary context, the task is to examine the premises of notions like merit as these relate to the metaphors of movement and dynamism in concepts such as social *mobility* and economic *growth*.

to Hegel, civil society is synonymous with the state, such that it is not an exaggeration to say that the theory of objective spirit in the *Philosophy of Right* gives theoretical expression to a profound structural transformation of social reality. He explains that if the difference between possession and property is law and the state, this discrepancy implies that the condition of a contractual agreement between the buyer and a seller is their *antagonistic unity* provided by a third instance. The reality of this third instance, which one might also designate as the reality of form and the formality of reality, confirms the integrity of a reality outside of the knowing subject at the same time that it negates any dualistic, undifferentiated methodology trapped in antinomies like humanity/nature, subject/object, reason/instinct, or state of nature/civil society. But as the term antagonistic suggests, it is a deeply flawed unity that combines what is oppressive about relative proximity to nature as fate, with what is exploitative and instrumental in contract. This indicates that although Hegel has few illusions about the virulence of the conflicts in civil society, his account of mediated unity in the state is flawed in ways that Hegel himself may not suspect.

Proximity to nature is not identity with nature: people who have purchased land or houses do not simply have the earth or the constructions in which they live. They enjoy the right to those things, which implies that all property is state property to a significant extent, thus raising two important questions. If humanity's relations with things, land, commodities and with other people are mediated by concepts made real in everyday life, why does the everyday appear to be organized by forces outside of human control? Can the conditions of knowledge and autonomy be seen as simultaneously external to humanity (law and the state) and internal to it (individual consciousness and experience), or are radical contingency and relativism the only alternatives to tradition and faith? Critical theory is of course determined to show why dialectics offers a much more fruitful path than relativism and dogmatism, since the latter are, in effect, two sides of the same false coin. The question which indicates the line of inquiry which would come to be pursued in different ways by Adorno, Benjamin and other modernist thinkers concerns how the mediation processes, rather than the re-appropriation processes (of which redistribution is the weaker version in several senses), are to be organized, that is, given legal form. Rethinking mediation entails interrogating the internal and external conditions under which the negative affirmation and antagonistic unity referred to above might be reformed into positive and plural affirmation without embracing a metaphysical conception of liberty or largely symbolic instances of reconciliation. In Marx's case, framing the matter in this way raises questions about property rights and different possible modes of production. Marx's early writings make a number of profound points in this regard. But Marx thinks in terms of re-appropriating alienated essences, which means that his legacy remains somewhat ambiguous. He appears to agree that the emancipation of art and of the truth content of aesthetic experience from religious tutelage and political control open up several possible paths towards the reconfiguration of individual autonomy and collective decision-making processes in post-liberal democratic terms.[46] But to the extent that he envisages the emancipation of the imaginary institution of society in terms of a reunification of aesthetics, politics and economics, he also seems to be insufficiently wary of the problem of re-feudalization, and a potential retreat to pre-liberal democratic positions on questions of reason and autonomy. These problems are no less real for the fact that they were a frequently used weapon in the ideological arsenal of Cold War critics of the former USSR – nor have they disappeared with the passing of the Soviet Union and the end of the Cold War. But it can be said that only a decentralized and differentiated society will be able to redeem the promise of a truly post-traditional alternative to state socialism and technocratic capitalism, which is why the Hegel–Marx–Adorno dialogue remains of great interest. Part of what it means to fortify the socio-historical dimension of the dialectic in the sense referred to above in relation to Adorno entails specifying the external conditions of knowledge and reconciliation to the greatest extent possible, rather than speculating what kind of individual or collective subject might be able to reunite itself with its 'forces propres', as Marx remarks in *On the Jewish Question* (1843).[47]

Hegel maintains that modern society is characterized by processes of complex differentiation, unprecedented pluralism and contractual association, all of which are related to the emergence of civil society as a sphere of industrial political economy enjoying qualified autonomy vis-à-vis the family and government. Marx agrees that Hegel is correct to regard the emergence of civil society as a part of the movement of social form towards increasing differentiation. But as an acute reader of Ludwig Feuerbach, Marx is also sure that Hegel is wrong to suppose that the state successfully mediates between private people and public citizens. Hence Feuerbach's critique of religion is a key moment on the road from Hegel to Marx and Nietzsche. Feuerbach suggests that in religion, and especially Christianity, humanity tends to project its best qualities and capacities for self-organization (creating,

---

[46]Alan Antliff, *Anarchy and Art: From the Paris Commune to the Fall of the Berlin Wall*, Vancouver, Arsenal Pulp Press, 2007, chapter 1.

[47]'Zur Judenfrage' ['On the Jewish Question'] (1843) in Karl Marx und Friedrich Engels, *Studienausgabe (I): Philosophie*, Iring Fetscher (ed.), Frankfurt, Fischer, 1990, p. 55. At the very end of this essay Marx insists that only when humanity has re-organized its individual forces as social forces not separated from political authority will the transition from political emancipation to human emancipation be possible.

knowing, forgiving, loving, etc.) onto a deity. The consequence is that the realization of those qualities in the real interactions structuring daily life is rendered impossible, and further, that these qualities return to humanity in institutions that collective experience for the most part ceases to recognize as an emanation of its own imaginary institution of society. By the time humanity's best qualities and values come back to it in the rituals and hierarchies of hierarchically organized faith, their secular and social character is obscured by a mysterious rival power that seems to have either fully natural or divine origins. Combining Hegel's method with Feuerbach's anthropology, Marx suggests that whether understood as natural or other-worldly, this rival, alienated force can only exist to the extent that people forget or ignore their own participation in the rituals that consolidate and perpetuate inequality and hierarchy. Following Feuerbach's analysis it seems inevitable to the young Marx that the problem of human emancipation, as opposed to the limited political emancipation from feudalism achieved in the French Revolution, is centrally about the critique of organized religion and the intrusion of dogmatic authority into what should really be terrestrial matters.[48]

After a closer look at Feuerbach's ideas on religion Marx concludes that Feuerbach's insights need to achieve a wider field of application to help understand how human energies, values and capacities come back to people in forms they fail to recognize as their own creations. In Marx's early writings, Feuerbach's critique of religion and the church hierarchy expands into a critique of democratic ideology and liberal-democratic mediating processes. This does not entail a rejection of democracy as much as it demands that the universal aspirations of liberal ideas be completed with institutions that would make genuine universality possible in relation to concepts like freedom, justice, humanism, etc., though not, it seems, as this relates to the liberal ideal of the separation of powers.[49] There is more to say about this below, since it relates to problems of emancipation conceived as re-appropriation. It is worth pausing to note that Marx regards Feuerbach's reflections on Hegel and religion as confirmation of the thesis that the objective bifurcation between questions concerning 'what is' and those concerning 'what ought to be', perpetuated in many guises throughout the ages by scarcity and

---

[48]Ludwig Feuerbach, *Das Wesen des Christentums* [*The Essence of Christianity*] (1841), Stuttgart, Reclam, 1969, chapters 4 and 20. The question as to the reasons why humanity projects its best qualities on alien entities, or why, for that matter, it will cease to do so, is not really answered by Feuerbach or Marx. This explanatory deficient may help explain why Marx sees emancipation as a question of re-appropriation.

[49]The implicit tendency to seek to re-unify alienated essences is explicitly stated in 'Der Bürgerkrieg in Frankreich' ['The Civil War in France'] (1871), where Marx praises the Paris Commune for being executive and legislative at the same time. See Karl Marx und Friedrich Engels, *Studienausgabe (IV): Geschichte und Politik 2*, Iring Fetscher (ed.), Frankfurt, Fischer, 1990, pp. 209–10.

poverty, loses the bases of its real objectivity under conditions of steadily increasing industrial productivity. In other words, although Feuerbach is an original thinker, his chief significance resides in drawing attention to the mounting evidence that industrialization and the foreseeable end of scarcity indicate that the repression needed to conquer scarcity becomes superfluous in a situation evolving towards post-scarcity, and that this assessment is sociologically grounded and not based on wishful thinking. The likely advent of another structural transformation of social reality and individual experience is therefore a result of increasing complexity and contingency, and is not, in the first instance, a possibility that exists despite complexity. The corollary is that the systematic extraction of surplus value at the point of production also ceases to have a natural raison d'etre. From there it is a short step to seeing that it is possible to distinguish between potential autonomy from unnecessary ignorance and dependence, on the one hand, and more or less successful modes of passive adaptation to unnecessarily rigid norms, on the other: surplus repression is no more accidental than the extraction of surplus value is casual. This dimension of Marx's political economy has undoubted contemporary relevance. The same cannot be said of his notion of praxis as the effort of a collective subject to re-unify itself with its alienated powers. It is at this point that critical theory emerges and engages with Marx without becoming embroiled in questions about reform/revolution, revisionism, the dictatorship of the proletariat, etc. If the first generation could not afford to indulge in such futile debates, it is even truer of critical theory today.[50]

The first practical consequence of the widespread acceptance of the state in the Hegelian sense is a split between the individual as a private, labouring *self*, and the organs of estranged *government*. Marx thinks that this kind of alienation is no less paralysing for praxis than the suppression of human potential by obscurantist religious authority. He reckons that the transition from representative government (political emancipation) to self-government (human emancipation) will be accomplished by finding an expansively democratic form that reunites the private self of civil society with the abstract citizen effectively debarred from meaningful political participation in the state. As in the case of religious alienation, exclusion from active engagement in the workings of government results in widespread de-politicization and passivity. Looking beyond Marx's day to a period more familiar to theorists of the Frankfurt School attempting to synthesize Marx and Nietzsche, passivity means exploited workers consuming increasingly uniform products under

---

[50]This is not to deny that the young Max Horkheimer had a Leninist phase or to say that Marcuse gave up on revolutionary politics. See Wiggershaus, *Die Franfurter Schule*, chapter 1.

conditions of effective exclusion from more than largely symbolic legitimation of authority. The intensification of the processes of extracting value from the producers results in their progressive interchangeability as well as in a homogenization of culture. This logic culminates with the widespread expectation that only 'experts' removed from the pressures of accountability are fit to make important policy decisions for the masses of people with no effective overview of what is going on. As effective subordination becomes an internalized reality principle for most people, they come to scale back or even renounce their demands of what is possible despite the realities of a potentially post-scarcity and post-surplus repression social order. The limits of what is considered possible are in turn reinforced by the maintenance of relatively arbitrary boundaries between expert and non-expert knowledge and the enforcement of unnecessary sanctions against sensual knowledge and experience detached from narrowly defined criteria of competence.[51]

Marx attempts to apply to politics Feuerbach's thoughts on the anthropological origins of religion. He remarks that to the extent that adjectives such as rationally deliberative, universal, impartial, democratic, etc., are widely accepted as attributes of the state, civil society becomes the site of contractually mediated exploitation, unfair competition, fraud and the arbitrary exercise of power, that is, the civil sphere perpetuates collective human dependence on external nature while suppressing the unique, historically evolving nature of individual humans. In the course of the development of his thought after 1843–4, Marx shifts attention from the state to the labour process. He observes that production and consumption are regulated by exchanges through which humanity's inability to recognize its own religious and political creations finds its counterpart in its frustrated attempts to recognize its artistic capacities in wage labour, commodity production and the consumption of commodities. In comparison with the relation between the serf and lord, the relation between capitalist and worker appears to be free from direct, naturalized domination. Marx welcomes the transition from feudal-agrarian to modern-industrial society as preparation for a subsequent transition from the division of humanity into capitalists and workers, to a global community of truly autonomous individuals. Although he does not mention Nietzsche, he hopes that the reunification of intellectual planning and sensuous materialism will engender a new individual and collective subject that has much more in common with Nietzschean notions of self-overcoming and the revaluation of all existing values than it does with the traditional relations between lords and serfs or the competence-based instrumental reason guiding the highly

---

[51]Karl Marx, *Das Kapital*, Vol. I [Volume I of *Capital*] (1867), Berlin, Dietz, 1998a, chapter 23, section 3.

predictable behaviour of capitalists, workers, technocrats and managers. But the point that dependence is now indirect might be more ambiguous than Marx supposes. As a result of the modernizing processes through which dependence becomes indirect and mediated, form takes on a much greater significance than it had at the time when domination was more personal and social structure was relatively undifferentiated. Marx acknowledges this to the extent that he suggests that power and oppression are exercised through the instances of law, politics, culture and ideology, and that these enable a class of appropriators to buy the labour power of a directly opposing class through contracts and labour markets. The labour-power-buying class appropriates surplus value and at the same time relies on governments to pass laws which enact compromises between the buyers and sellers of labour power which privilege the former, lest the permanent threat of capital flight be carried out. Hence Marx is alive not only to the fact that socially created wealth is privately appropriated; he also notes that capital must reduce the role of labour to that of a passive executor and at the same time expand the forces of production. But it cannot do this with the help of merely passive executors, which is why he thinks that capital and labour will have to enter into a partnership of genuinely autonomous individuals in what would amount to a decisive step towards human emancipation.[52]

It is in large measure correct to argue that within a legal framework that permits labour power to be bought and sold like any other commodity, workers are forced into the roles of subservient executors at work and passive consumers when satisfying their household and leisure needs. While the mode of production transforms labour into commodities which are bought and sold on the market, the mode of consumption, which Marx for the most part neglects or reduces to the sphere of circulation, transforms individual and collective needs into commodities that must be bought and sold in order to guarantee the smooth functioning of the mode of production. This suggests although there is much scope for a sustained critique of what capitalism does to labour power and creativity more generally, it is futile to try to identify a collective-subjective version of the dialectic of humanity and nature, that is, a subject–object of history or some such model that identifies a collective actor external to the mode of production and disruptive of its operations. The problem is not so much with individual thinkers like Marx and Lukács as it is

---

[52]Karl Marx, *Lohnarbeit und Kapital* [*Wage-Labour and Capital*] (1847), Berlin, Dietz, 1998b, pp. 18–21, and *Das Kapital*, Vol. I [Volume I of *Capital*], pp. 85–108. There are problems raised by the analysis that oppression is exercised through the *mediating* instances of law, politics, culture and ideology, and the notion that social classes exist in a relation of *direct* opposition. That is to say that Marx at times neglects his own insights about the reality of form and the third instance inherent in the dialectical structure of an antagonistic social reality.

with the paradigm of alienated essence/re-appropriated essence, which is a tautological paradigm of re-naturalization, where the return to nature in this case implies relations of re-feudalized political obligation. Moreover, from the moment that one attributes a wide range of predicates to the people in an attempt to distil its essence in a secular idiom, one can speak in terms of the national people, the socialist people, the national socialist people, the most popular class of the people, etc. Marx believes that the separation of civil society and the state secures the emancipation of the state from religious demands without emancipating humanity from religion or the state in more general terms (leading Arendt and others to argue that Marx wants to emancipate humanity from politics altogether).[53] But emancipating humanity from the state would in important respects be an emancipation from mediations which, from Adorno's modified Hegelian perspective sketched above, would be tantamount to emancipation from reality. It is likely to be a reactionary or ideological emancipation from the dialectics of mimetic form to oppressive proximity with nature, either in terms of a community of fate or as (a)historical inevitability. In these debates Adorno is correct to signal that the project to eschew oppressive proximity and obscurantist distance in epistemology and politics depends in part on an aesthetic theory that re-articulates the relations between social criticism, mode of production, mode of reception, negative dialectics, social differentiation and de-traditionalization.[54]

Perhaps Marx thinks that once humanity has re-appropriated all of its alienated essences it becomes truly human. But this says little more than that humanity is alienated from what it alienates from itself. If there is a politics of self-overcoming, it surely embraces the idea of a healthy estrangement from the 'human, all too human' as this manifests itself in fatuous celebrations of already existing ways of being a 'normal' or 'successful' person. There are striking parallels between becoming normal and successful as modes of passive adaptation, on the one hand, and 'graduating' from worker without money and education to bourgeois with money and education, on the other; conventional notions of macro-economic growth go very well with accepted ideas about individual 'upward' mobility. The critique of political economy stipulating what is objectively possible in a given epoch must be re-articulated in relation to the critique of identity thinking and not, as so often in the past, tagged on to highly problematic accounts of collectivist re-appropriation of static, supposedly alienated anthropological properties.

---

[53]See section 3 on 'Action' in Arendt, *The Human Condition*, Chicago, University of Chicago Press, 1958.

[54]Christoph Görg, *Gesellschaftliche Naturverhältnisse*, Münster, Westfälisches Dampfboot, 1999, chapter 5.

The latter have usually been authoritarian and populist, as can be expected from institutionalized false proximity, or simply vague, as in the case of 'the multitude'.[55] Despite the problems with Marx's approach, he helps illuminate a number of important methodological issues that arise from different possible ways of trying to read Hegel in a materialist vein without abandoning dialectics. Hegel helps show why some of the conditions of understanding and autonomy are external to the subject. He may have been wrong to see this condition in the state as the mediating instance between private and public, when in fact the conditions (a constellation of plural social processes) as well as the subject, however conceived, are far more decentred than the terms 'state' and 'individual' generally imply. But in making contact with the real, mediated objectivity of this externality, he offers a reminder, albeit in an idealist idiom, that whether one is referring to individual or collective subjects, one cannot assume autonomy to be part of the definition of the subject without becoming caught up in tautologies.[56] If it is true that this problem is very apparent in the young Marx, this does not change the fact that it is nonetheless problematic to argue that the conditions of autonomy are external to the subject but can never be known, as is sometimes claimed in regard to Being. According to this view autonomy is a chimera because of humanity's condition of being thrown into the world. *To know* that the conditions are external means that the event and processes of mediation are real and happening: the subject cannot be categorically and irredeemably cut off from knowledge of the conditions of autonomy even if, at the same time, the latter cannot be re-appropriated as alienated essence. Yet it is also problematic to invoke a notion of essence and then backtrack from it. Whereas essence might normally be contrasted with form as the content contained or framed by form, Kant's version of negative liberty, for example, offers a good example of the somewhat misleading technique in much liberal thought to sketch a formal theory of essence. By refusing to countenance a positive definition of freedom, and simultaneously insisting on the primacy of liberal legal form over democratic legitimate essence, Kant and other liberals defend a formal conception of human essence that never discloses

---

[55]For a characteristically un-critical celebration of this amorphous and sociologically chimerical figure, see Michael Hardt and Antonio Negri, *Empire: The New Order of Globalization*, Cambridge, Harvard University Press, 2000.

[56]This confirms the point that if Hegel's methodological promise can be redeemed in non-idealist terms without resorting to one-sided materialism, humanity will receive renewed impetus to recommence the Enlightenment project of emancipation from all instances of unnecessary dependence. Critical philosophy and modernist aesthetics offer sociologically relevant ways of ascertaining how these instances arise, and the different ways in which they might be addressed. It is in this sense that the approach adopted here shares marked affinities with Robert B. Pippin's *Idealism as Modernism*.

what that essence might be. The challenge is to bear in mind the different problems relating to every notion of essence without renouncing knowledge with normative implications. Hence the politico-epistemological project implied by the affirmation that the critique of knowledge is also social critique is still actual and rational. It is related to the attempt to draw on aesthetics emancipated from religion and tradition in order to situate the subject of the study of reality and reality as the object of that study within a framework insulated from both oppressive proximity to nature and obscurantist distance from mediation processes.[57] This leads the discussion back to the possibility of aesthetic theory capable of illuminating the structures constitutive of socio-historical reality, not by glorifying the subject's essences or hiding them, but by outlining the contours of a method that strengthens the objective, socio-historical dimension of the dialectic of mediations while also tempering the individual, subjective dimension. The brief discussion of the modernist component of this endeavour outlined in the preceding pages can now be developed in Chapter Two with a more comprehensive discussion of montage dialectics, reciprocal interactive exchange, and constellational thought.

[57]For an example of this line of thinking see Maurice Merleau-Ponty, 'Cézanne's Doubt', in Michael B. Smith (ed.), *The Merleau-Ponty Aesthetics Reader: Philosophy and Painting*, Chicago, Northwestern, 1994, pp. 59–75; Diana Coole, *Merleau-Ponty and Modern Politics after Anti-Humanism*, Plymouth, Rowman & Littlefield, 2007, chapter 8; and Deborah Cook, *Adorno on Nature*, Durham, Acumen, 2011.

2

Dialectics, de-naturalization and social differentiation (II): From the cognitive content of aesthetics to critical theory

Towards the end of the previous chapter it is suggested that social theory with an aesthetic dimension offers an example of how *Erkenntniskritik* is social critique and conversely, bearing in mind that theory and society have evolved since Adorno defended this claim at the end of the 1960s. In the discussion of Hegel and Adorno it is suggested further that the aesthetic aspect includes dialectical and historical moments, such that it is not a question of stabilizing the integrity of social theory against encroachments by aesthetic theory and vice versa, nor a question of supplementing the analytical rigour of one with the suggestive power of the other. This chapter attempts to clarify in more detail the specific ways in which *Erkenntniskritik* is social critique by analysing the mediations between epistemology, sociology and aesthetic modes of cognition in late modern society. By way of introduction it can be said that from its inception up to its most recent examples, critical theory reflects on the cognitive content of aesthetics and the qualitative dynamics of inequality, in order to generate testable theses concerning the political possibilities available in each historical epoch.[1] It would be inaccurate and methodologically

[1]This way of approaching aesthetic cognition and sociological method is evident in the recent work of Fabio Vighi and Heiko Feldner. See their essays in Fabio Vighi and Heiko Feldner (eds), *Did Someone Say Ideology? On Slavoj Zizek and Consequences*, Newcastle, Cambridge Scholars Publishing, 2007, as well as the contributions in that volume by Ceren Ozselcuk and Yahya M. Madra. Another original contribution to the renewal of critical theory in the twenty-first century is made by Sarah Reichardt in *Composing the Modern Subject: Four String Quartets by Dmitri Shostakovich*, Aldershot, Ashgate, 2008. These authors indicate in different ways how

imprecise to say that there is an a priori analogy between social structure and aesthetic reason simply because the reality of form is common to both. Form achieves an enhanced epistemological valence in an historical period such as modernity and our current late modernity, in which form in epistemological, sociological and aesthetic enquiry is no longer centrally concerned with framing the timeless essence of natural harmony or organic order. In a number of important instances, form problematizes its relation with ostensibly form-giving subjects. Form begins to resist instrumental manipulation, and strives towards an investigation of objectivity and the impossibility of restoring the lost harmony that had previously been the condition of valid knowledge and the guarantor of aesthetic tradition.[2] Key works of modern art question the presumed symmetry between individual experience, 'the people', and the ethnicity and culture of the nation. Instead, aesthetic reflexivity leads to the development of a technical and conceptual vocabulary capable of critically analysing experience, political authority and social relations. In a series of observable processes that need to be examined together, the similarities as well as the differences mediating 'high', classical art, on the one hand, with 'low', folk, or popular art, on the other, become increasingly difficult to discern. With the demise of tradition as the foundation of quality and originality, the art critic assumes a new role in matters of aesthetic judgement. Changes in the mode of artistic reception and the social composition of the art public make aesthetically rational and politically democratic distinctions possible between art, kitsch and ideology. It will be seen in what follows that Baudelaire, Simmel and Benjamin are key figures in this regard.[3]

---

political economy, cinema, psychoanalysis and music theory can be articulated in a plurality of combinations in order to re-pose the fundamental questions of critical theory. Although the patterns of historical development alluded to in the text may change direction at some point in the future, the argument in this book stresses the continuing relevance of aesthetics for a social theory that aspires to help bring about political change. The aspiration to change is nurtured by the possibilities offered by the recognition that epistemological critique and social critique are closely linked in complex, functionally differentiated societies. Those possibilities are forfeited if it is assumed that this is an unchanging state of affairs or a natural right.

[2]While Adorno, Heidegger, Foucault and Derrida provide four of the most notable philosophical explanations of lost harmony in this regard, critical theory from the Frankfurt School to the present seeks to draw out the juridical and sociological implications. On the path-breaking role of these three thinkers, see the essays in Iain Macdonald and Krzyztof Ziarek (eds), *Adorno and Heidegger: Philosophical Questions*, Stanford, Stanford University Press, 2008; and Robert Hullot-Kentor, *Things Beyond Resemblance: Collected Essays on Theodor W. Adorno*, New York, Columbia University Press, 2006, as well as Christoph Menke, *Die Souveranität der Kunst; Ästhetische Erfahrung nach Adorno und Derrida*, Frankfurt, Suhrkamp, 1991.

[3]Robert Nisbet, *Sociology as an Art Form*, Oxford, Oxford University Press, 1976, pp. 61–7; Marshall Berman, *All that is Solid Melts into Air: The Experience of Modernity*, London, Penguin, 1988, chapter 3, and Peter Nicholls, *Modernisms: A Literary Guide*, Berkeley, University of California Press, 1995, chapter 1. There will inevitably be disagreement about which works of

Philosophy, aesthetics and cognition – Possible paths towards a rational society

In accordance with discernible patterns of historical development, especially the de-naturalization of hierarchy and the differentiation of function beyond the rudimentary levels of complexity denoted by the terms private, public and public sphere, the aestheticization of consciousness becomes increasingly observable in various models of explanation. This aesthetic tendency in consciousness and explanation can be seen at work in the novel, film, advanced mathematical models and in social theory as well.[4] But it can also be seen in society proper, with the appearance of a stratum of artists and writers whose methodological sophistication is symptomatic of a rupture in the traditional ties between classical art and folk art. It is possible to regard the emergence of the public sphere as a premonitory sign of this break: the intrusion of rational principles into the construction of legal norms in a period of rapidly changing social structure corresponds to a parallel, if somewhat later movement, towards constructivist art and urban planning in line with the demographical changes accompanying industrialization. Although works of high art were once widely regarded as more or less systematic and codified articulations of folk or popular art, virtually all artistic manifestations could be seen as diverse articulations of the creative spirit of different members of the same nation.[5] Within an ethnic community these instances of elite–popular

---

modern art demand new political and aesthetic forms in order rigorously to record changes in the truth content of art and the autonomy-enhancing potential of politics. Baudelaire, Simmel and Benjamin are instructive in that they approach these questions from a plurality of methodological standpoints.

[4]For an interesting account of these developments, see George Spencer-Brown, *The Laws of Form*, London, George Allen and Unwin, 1969. Brown's book is often cited by Luhmann as a decisive influence in the latter's original interpretation and further development of systems theory. While Lukács' notion of the proletariat as subject–object of history and embodiment of the unity of theory and praxis is criticized in this book, his *Theory of the Novel* (written in 1914–15, published in 1920) stands the test of time much better. See György Lukács, *Die Theorie des Romans*, Hamburg, Luchterhand, 1963, especially chapters 2 and 5, which discuss the relations between changes in aesthetic form and changes in consciousness and social structure from ancient Greece to nineteenth-century realism and romanticism. Whether or not the current period is best characterized as modern, late modern or postmodern is a matter of some debate. For some elucidatory remarks see Anthony Giddens, *Modernity and Self-Identity: Self and Society in the Late Modern Age*, Cambridge, Polity, 1991.

[5]If one takes music as the primary example, one sees striking parallels between classical music and codified law, on the one hand, and some of the more informal registers of legitimacy and folk music, on the other (though it may be the case that sport now rivals music in importance in some countries). The coherence of the parallels depends on the nation as a source of political and cultural unity. If in the first case classical music would not be able to flourish in isolation

unity were often regarded as typical expressions of emotional and physical character particular to the rigours of a specific climate, territory, and way of life. The interior beauty of the artist could be seen as a direct correlate to the natural beauty of the landscape of 'his' people. These tendencies reach a pinnacle in the build-up to and immediate aftermath of 1848–1918, when distinctly national traditions in art are harnessed to political aspirations to sovereign autonomy across Europe.[6]

But the gradual collapse of what remained of feudal hierarchy, as in the freeing of the serfs in Russia in 1861, as well as the ongoing differentiation of religious and political function according to markedly different tempos across European states, are indicative of the changed relationship between politics and knowledge wrought by breakneck industrialization and faltering democratization. These changes, in their turn, can be seen in the constantly evolving relationship between the people of a given country and the nation-state in post-feudal Europe. It is no accident that the nineteenth century was so fond of ideas of a national or ethnic genius in art and culture, at the very time when industrialization inexorably undermined national boundaries and simultaneously jeopardized the privileged epistemological status of the individual creator and the uniqueness of their (in almost all cases masculine) experience. The challenge this implies to ideas of ordained hierarchy, organic community, art as imitation of nature, and all rigidly conceived distinctions between fine art and popular art can be grasped as processes related to the

---

from ethnic folk traditions (at least up until World War I, as Bartók points out), legality would probably be unable to mediate between public and private interests without the supplementary cohesion furnished by instances of symbolic unity. In Chapter Four it will be seen that the logic of capitalist accumulation interrupts the continuities in these parallels. The ruptures involved are not simply synonymous with decline, however, since they offer the chance to think about different possible approaches to re-embedding art, reason and legitimacy in new regional and transnational institutions. That is, within the currently collapsing national constellation, reason is exercised primarily in the guise of instrumental reason and systemic communication, or, to a lesser extent, it is manifested as the sporadic expression of individual genius in an historical period where the latter has for the most part lost its objective raison d'être. New ways of thinking about re-embedding indicate that the waning of the organic paradigm of legitimacy is not synonymous with the end of individual creativity or collective learning and decisions. See Everett Helm, *Bartók*, Hamburg, Rowohlt, 1965, chapter 3, and Boaventura De Sousa Santos, *The Rise of the Global Left: The World Social Forum and Beyond*, London, Zed, 2006, chapters 3–4.

[6]Perhaps the most famous anecdote of more than anecdotal significance in this regard is the tale recounting the widespread practice of writing VERDI on the walls of Italian cities in post-Restoration, pre-Unification Italy, where Giuseppe Verdi's name stood for Vittorio Emanuelle II, Re d'Italia (Victor Emmanuel, King of Italy). See Mary Ann Smart, 'Liberty on and off the Barricades: Verdi's Risorgimento fantasies', in Albert Russell Ascoli and Krystyna von Henneberg (eds), *Making and Remaking Italy: The Cultivation of National Identity around the Risorgimento*, Oxford, Berg, 2001, pp. 103–18.

increasing implausibility of the premises of the territorial integrity of the nation-state, which, in turn, raise major questions about some of the foundational assumptions informing the liberal-democratic understanding of political representation. These developments also signal the equal implausibility of pristine notions of 'the political' articulated by observers who bemoan the supposedly nefarious influence of society, such as Carl Schmitt and Hannah Arendt. It is not so much that mass production and international markets destroy individuality and eliminate politics, as these two and many other thinkers at times suggest.[7] As a result of the specific developments through which art becomes less and less a matter of the imitation of nature or an expression of individual interiority, it becomes increasingly clear that the conditions of knowledge and autonomy are to be sought in spaces and on terrain not identical to supposedly unified individual juridical subjects or homogenous communities organized politically as nation-states. To the extent that aesthetic cognition de-constructs the ideological suppositions underpinning these supposedly self-sufficient individuals and imagined communities, it advances epistemological critique and sheds light on different aspects of this non-identity.[8] It will be suggested below that the capacity of aesthetic cognition to perform this task is enhanced in direct relation to what at first glance may look like a cultural loss, that is, it can do this better and more stringently to the extent that it is emancipated in two related senses already implied by the ongoing differentiation of religious faith, political authority, economic function and aesthetic reason. In order to fulfil its critical and normative potential, aesthetic cognition must be detached from the national-popular and ethnic premises underlying the framework making folk art and classical art mutually conditioning. Moreover, it must be re-conceptualized beyond the institutional parameters presuming the supposedly founding people of a state to be something approximating 'the natural majority' of democracy. This is an historical and sociological argument about processes which continue to unfold at an accelerated pace today – it is not an abstract normative argument

---

[7]See the conclusion to Schmitt, *Legalität und Legitimität* (*Legality and Legitimacy*, 1932), Berlin, Duncker & Humblot, 1993, and the section on 'Action' in Arendt, *The Human Condition*, chapter V, pp. 175–247.

[8]Without an illumination of these spaces and that terrain, mainstream theory tends towards essentialist and tautological accounts of alienation and emancipation. One sees this tendency in prevailing accounts of subjectivity, intersubjective communication, intersubjective recognition, and identity politics. Foucault suggests as much when invoking the need for a *pensée du dehors* (thought from the outside) as the preliminary step towards a viable politics of self-overcoming. See Foucault, 'L'expérience du dehors' ['The experience of exteriority'], (1966) in *La pensée du dehors*, Paris, Fata Morgana, 2003, pp. 15–21. The essay originally appeared in number 229 of *Critique* in 1966.

about what should be the case.[9] The aesthetic-cognitive capacity in question is an historically unique form of knowledge made possible by the abolition of the command to obey nature in art and national-popular politics. The 'alienation' or estrangement of aesthetic cognition from its popular base is one of a number of paradoxes relevant to an understanding of the origins and contemporary articulations of critical theory. The modernist avant-garde that emerges from the ruptures in question appears to be far more elitist and incomprehensible than the representatives of its classical/high art predecessor, but it is actually a libertarian and for the most part democratic-popular elite with concrete pedagogic principles in many cases. Hence this instance of alienation can be seen in a positive light as a sign of possible conceptual and institutional innovation. This point will be developed in more detail in relation to philosophical idealism towards the end of this section and in the next section of this chapter.[10]

Just as humanity has a better knowledge of causality and social process as a result of what film and photography reveal about the mechanics of simultaneity and sequence, so too do technological and social processes shape the conditions of aesthetic, scientific, and industrial production and research.[11] Hence from the standpoint of critical theory it is not sufficient to say that theorists must be reflexive and take into account that explanations of social reality are conditioned by the norms of the society that is being explained. Theory must be reflexive in a dialectical way that is conspicuously absent in traditional theory, in much dialectical materialism after Marx, and

[9]Just as there is some debate about whether the current period is best defined in terms of the modern, late modern or postmodern, there is comparable uncertainty as to whether post-Fordism or flexible specialization offers the most appropriate analytical tools for interpreting the current financial crisis, the Greek situation and the crisis of the Euro, etc. Mark Fisher offers a fruitful point of departure in *Capitalist Realism: Is there No Alternative?* London, Zero Books, 2009. Relevant in this context is Paul Claudel's comment that in Baudelaire one finds hints of Racine as well as the most current journalism of the period. Critical theory in this century is also likely to synthesize sophisticated theoretical analysis with contemporary cultural commentary. See Pierre Bertrand and Pascal Durrand, *Les poètes de la modernité de Baudelaire à Apollinaire*, Paris, Seuil, 2006, pp. 65–72.

[10]If one contrasts the innovations of the Bauhaus, Dada, surrealism and Situationism with the gesturing of Futurism in Italy (the Russian case is somewhat different) and English Vorticism, one notes that there is a clear correlation between aesthetic originality and libertarian politics among modernist art movements. On the case of Russian Futurism and its revolutionary politics, see Vladimir Markov, *Russian Futurism: A History*, Berkeley and Los Angeles, University of California Press, 1968. On Italian Futurism and Vorticism, see Peter Nicholls, *Modernisms: A Literary Guide*, chapters 5 and 8.

[11]In *La chambre claire: Note sur la photographie* (Paris, Gallimard, 1980), Roland Barthes offers a remarkably lucid account of these issues. Also see Herbert Read, *Art and Industry*, New York, Horizon, 1953, and László Moholy-Nagy, *Painting, Photography and Film* (1925), London, Thames and Hudson, 1991.

also in a number of other prominent approaches to empirical social research.[12] Stating the matter in these terms indicates that the initial impetus towards theoretical innovation taken forward by the Frankfurt School comes from some of the methodological inadequacies of Soviet Marxism as well as from earlier, unresolved issues in the nineteenth- and early twentieth-century debates about the specificities of historical explanation and the epistemological status of the human sciences. These debates are centrally concerned with the differences between natural scientific, historical and social scientific models of causality, and therefore involve an assessment of the role of aesthetic and textual interpretation in the formulation of hypotheses. For example, physics develops appropriately rigorous methodological criteria for the study of sequential succession as these criteria apply to the linear structure of events in nature. Critical theory by contrast is still evolving towards a stage of reflection in which it becomes feasible to define rigorous causal criteria as these apply to the multilayered and pluri-directional character of non-linear (and in some cases ongoing) events unfolding in history. It is perhaps somewhat curious that the concern to produce theoretical explanation commensurate with the heightened level of complexity of the socio-historical object of analysis vis-à-vis its natural counterpart can lead to what may appear to be anecdotal or whimsical arguments relying on intuition instead of rigorous documentation.[13]

This charge has been levelled at Walter Benjamin's monumental study of the rise and significance of the glass-covered indoor passages in nineteenth-century Paris. Despite the many ambiguities of his theoretical legacy, however, it is clear that Benjamin has a remarkable ability to shed light on the political implications of architectural changes. He asks if the most powerful political arguments are perhaps not directly political, and if, by extension, given a certain degree of functional differentiation, directly political arguments are in

---

[12]The most programmatic statement of this intention is offered by Max Horkheimer in his 1937 essay 'Traditionelle und kritische Theorie' ['Traditional and Critical Theory'], in Alfred Schmidt (ed.), *Traditionelle und kritische Theorie*, Frankfurt, Fischer, 1968, pp. 12–64. Although in many ways inadequate from a contemporary standpoint, Horkheimer's article helped initiate critical social theory with analytical method and normative content. The essay is reprinted in English in Andrew Arato and Eike Gebhardt (eds), *The Essential Frankfurt School Reader*, London and New York, Continuum, 1982.

[13]A prevalent and yet wholly inadequate alternative to a poetic response to complexity is to champion moral and normative arguments to the almost complete neglect of history and sociology, as is done in much of the analytical political theory to appear since Rawls' *A Theory of Justice*, Cambridge, Harvard University Press, 1973. For a review of several methodological approaches that strive to avoid the false choice between moral abstraction and empirical rigour, see Celine-Marie Pascal, *Cartographies of Knowledge: Exploring Qualitative Epistemologies*, London, Sage, 2011.

fact closer to propaganda and advertising than considered political reasoning. Hence rather than being anecdotal and eclectic in a pejorative sense, he indicates that there may be a way to assemble a montage of diverse and heterogeneous historical elements in order to meet the challenge of complexity rather than succumb to it with subjective impressionism. To the extent that montage and disruption are truer to late modern experience than linearity and continuity, his approach has relevance for the project of deconstructing economic and political justifications of austerity that are heavily reliant on notions of self-sufficient individuals and falsely imagined communities in need of steady growth and comprehensive protection from internal and external threats. The incorporation of a phenomenological moment into socio-historical explanation enables Benjamin to analyse a socio-historical object or event from a plurality of standpoints, though without this elastic pluralism breaking down into relativism or a banal exercise in human interest. His reflections set a standard of methodological stringency that is as fundamental to critical theory as Adorno's statement about epistemological critique and social critique.[14] While physics and other natural sciences had to be emancipated from religious tutelage in order to reach mathematical precision, critical theory continues to seek to transcend the confines of the academic humanities and of naively empirical social enquiry, in order to attain the greatest possible interpretative precision. This is an ongoing struggle for complex clarity, carried on by investigating a series of historical, political, social and aesthetic processes of de-coupling and re-coupling that are discussed in Chapter One in terms of the dialectics of differentiation. That struggle has its own history which can be briefly summarized here in order to introduce some of the themes dealt with in this chapter. The project introduced in this book builds on the work of Benjamin and Adorno by re-articulating the relation between critical hermeneutics, montage methodology and dialectical mediation in ways that are relevant to twenty-first-century realities and readers. Although there would seem to be little that is less reconcilable than the fleetingness of montage and the larger claims of dialectics, it will be seen in the second part of this chapter and then in Chapters Four and Five that Baudelaire, Simmel

[14]This interpretation of Benjamin's methodology is ably defended by Joseph Fürnkäs in *Surrealismus als Erkenntnis: Walter Benjamin – Weimarer Einbahnstraße und Pariser Passagen* [*Surrealism as Knowledge: Weimar One-way Streets and Paris Passages*], Stuttgart, J. B. Metzler, 1988, and more recently by Samuel Weber in *Benjamin's Abilities*, (see in particular chapter 15). Susan Buck-Morss provides a brilliant analysis of Benjamin's study of Paris in *The Dialectics of Seeing*, Cambridge, MIT Press, 1989. David Frisby notes that Benjamin's originality and sensitivity to sociological detail are largely attributable to his particular way of reading Simmel, whose work will also be discussed in this chapter. See David Frisby, *Fragments of Modernity: Theories of Modernity in the Work of Simmel, Kracauer and Benjamin*, Cambridge, MIT Press, 1986, pp. 3 and 93.

and certain aspects of systems theory offer ways of reconsidering this issue. While Benjamin's concept of *Rettung* (rescue or recovery) is adjusted in order to rethink missed transitions as political possibilities that may have been obscured, but are not irredeemably lost, Adorno's negative dialectics inform the attempt to rescue the concept of non-identity from political obscurity.[15]

In order to propel epistemology beyond the impasses reached by the empiricists and rationalists, Kant inquires into the conditions of possible knowledge. Rather than seeking absolute knowledge in the mind and the functions of consciousness, or in nature and the world external to consciousness, he maintains that the fundamental condition is a subject that can reflexively unify itself with reason and have objective knowledge of the phenomena that appear to the subject in time and space, by way of the mediating instance provided by the 12 categories of the understanding. Another way of saying this is that absolute, essential knowledge is impossible in Kant's view, because all objectivity is mediated by subjectivity and the forms in and through which knowledge is transmitted. Hegel counters by asking under what conditions subjectivity is possible, and concludes that all subjectivity is mediated by historical and social objectivity as it assumes tangible form in constantly changing institutions such as the family, civil society and the state. He prepares the ground for critical theory by implying that if an appropriate set of mediations can be discovered, the dialectic of individual subjectivity and institutional objectivity could become genuinely revolutionary. Marx intuits this, and looks into the conditions under which industrial production and aesthetic production might mutually enforce one another in such a way that work no longer issues from the necessity to overcome scarcity confronting humanity in the domain of external nature, and, in a parallel development, art becomes a reliable expression of the mediated unity of humanity and individual, internal nature. Following Hegel, Marx thinks that all of reality is constituted by the mediated unity of humanity and nature in both senses, but also, famously, Marx demands that reality change. Reading Marx as a critical theorist *avant la lettre*, one could say that changing reality in this context is not synonymous with seizing power by any available means that will produce a new set of leaders or an arbitrary alteration of property relations. It means adjusting the structure of mediations so that institutions no longer perpetuate a predominantly antagonistic unity of humanity and nature born of scarcity and the suppression of sensual, historically evolving nature in humanity. But the fact that the unity is predominantly antagonistic rather than

---

[15]Readers are asked to excuse the repeated emphasis on epistemology. This is enlisted to show that almost all practices of freedom and autonomy are shaped by a conception of knowledge rather than, in the first instance, by a conception of authority or equality, as is often affirmed.

wholly instrumental or completely misconceived is important. It suggests that at a certain stage in the evolution of collective humanity's relations with external nature, as well as in that of each member of the species' relations with individual, internal nature, normative questions about autonomy can no longer be dissociated from social and juridical questions concerning rights, different possible modes of production, varieties of property, etc., without becoming ideology: 'ought' questions no longer need to be approached from a hypothetical state of nature or from behind a veil of ignorance. What 'is', in the sense of actually existing institutions, and what is politically possible, are thenceforth impossible to separate categorically. This marks a moment in which it becomes possible to entertain non-speculative ideas about missed and possibly recoverable transitions to new political forms.[16]

Marx anticipates Adorno by intuiting that if all societies have been oppressive to greater and lesser extents, this fact is not best explained in terms of the ontological status of fear, or a supposed innate tendency towards aggression, or any other ahistorical invariant that leaves out of consideration *how* each particular society is oppressive in which *different* ways. Generalizations of this kind fail to explain the likely consequences of specific policies on human and non-human life: without this degree of nuance in method there can be no adequate discussion of the choices involved in assessing different possible political alternatives. Adorno observes that if society and reality are constituted in and through the synthetic unity of humanity and nature, Enlightenment depends on the institutionalization of a non-antagonistic synthesis rather than a romantic fusion or a retreat to rationalist separation. In his work the interplay of the collective human, extra-human natural and individual natural-human provides the framework for communication, society and knowledge in the broadest sense. As will be seen in Chapter Three, Adorno's methodology incorporates a plurality of elements that do not admit of any easy reconciliation or even of mediated unity in Hegelian terms. In Adorno's estimation such unity depends on an untenable presupposition of an originary, underived wholeness, the existence of which does not stand the test of analytical scrutiny or empirical verification. The most rigorous instances of critical theory from Adorno to the present attempt to discover an epistemology capable of subverting antagonistic, untruthful totalities and the ways in which they are represented, while at the same time finding plausible ways of reintroducing fragmentary evidence of struggle and knowledge – usually incompatible

---

[16]Alfred Schmidt, *Der Begriff der Natur in der Lehre von Marx* [*Marx's Concept of Nature*], Frankfurt, Europäische Verlagsanstalt, 1962, and Jörg Stadlinger and Dieter Sauer, 'Marx und die Moderne: Dialektik der Befreiung oder Paradoxien der Individualisierung?', *Prokla*, 159 (2010), pp. 195–215.

with most conceptions of mediated unity – into a broadly dialectical model of socio-historical explanation. In a number of important cases this entails supplementing certain features of Marx's analysis of capitalism with insights from modernist experiments in aesthetic cognition. One could say that while aesthetics obliges dialectics to move towards montage without becoming relativist and arbitrarily eclectic, dialectics obliges aesthetics to acknowledge the effects of social conflict on prevailing models of knowledge, political legitimacy and artistic innovation. If montage materialism effectively challenges existing practices of representation and presumed unity in a variety of fields, critical political economy monitors the tendency of the logic underlying one particular form of exchange to colonize extra-economic dimensions of social existence. The aspiration of this particular form to become synonymous with the only feasible form can thus be challenged in ways that are analytical and stringent instead of simply plaintive and shrill.[17]

Marx proceeds along the path laid bare by Hegel concerning the dialectical unity of 'is' and 'ought' research questions. He is guided by the demonstrable fact that the objective possibility of post-scarcity, and therewith of non-antagonistic individual and collective autonomy, is a realizable chance opened up as part of the same set of processes that demand a differentiated analysis of family, civil society and state. This is not to say that the opportunity in question is redeemed with a politics of dedifferentiation and the re-composition of a fragmented totality that was supposedly once whole, for this would amount to authoritarian re-feudalization of the kind practised in the former USSR, with which Marx would have had little sympathy. The point is to change the structure of mediations rather than to close them down and thereby forfeit the libertarian potential of increased self-organization offered by complex de-naturalization. There is undoubtedly a certain degree of contingency implied by the difficulties of agreeing on the best way to approach this change in the structure of mediations. But contingency does not mean chance, destiny, accident or the infallibility of supposedly self-regulating markets. The qualified autonomy of the modern economy unleashes unprecedented productive capacity, but it does so according to a very specific systemic logic, as the young Marx notes, and it does so by abolishing what had been the political character of production when it was presided over by guilds and other corporate bodies in late feudalism.[18] Hence the argument sketched in the

---

[17]Adorno, *Ästhetische Theorie* [*Aesthetic Theory*], pp. 244–74 and pp. 487–90, and Bertolt Brecht, *Brecht on Theatre*, ed. and transl. by John Willett, London, Methuen, 1978, chapters 11–13.

[18]Marx, 'Zur Judenfrage' ['On the Jewish Question'] (1843), in Marx und Engels, *Studienausgabe Vol. I. Philosophie*, ed. by Iring Fetscher, Frankfurt, Fischer, 1990a, pp. 43–7 and 53–5. Needless to say the systemic logic in question proceeds from highly antagonistic premises in societies

Dialectic of Enlightenment is to some extent implicit in Marx's ambivalence about economic expansion. Industrial economic growth certainly offers qualified potential for emancipation from dependence on external nature, and prospective release from coerced integration into disciplined socio-political units capable of combating scarcity. Adorno or Benjamin might add that failure to realize this potential is likely to intensify this dependence, and therewith the mythical content of mainstream art and politics. In other words, with this qualified potential comes the risk of a missed transition, if, that is, the project to overcome scarcity is detached from the project of a timely dismantling of unnecessary industrial discipline. Without such a dismantling, discipline of this kind is likely to become widely and deeply internalized despite being demonstrably superfluous at a specific historical juncture, and passive adaptation may gradually become synonymous with reason. Interpretative precision and complex clarity are needed in order to see that a transition has been missed without, however, being completely lost and gone. Hence the fact that the social bond at a particular time and place is predominantly antagonistic rather than wholly instrumental or completely misconceived is related to the fact that missed transitions are not lost transitions in all respects. In both cases the distinction between what is and what could still possibly be is preserved in fragmentary form as historical evidence and an injunction against forgetting and simply 'getting on with things'. The dictum that distortion of the past is tantamount to distortion of the present and vice versa thus attains greater clarity.

In this regard it is clearly important to distinguish between the real contingencies and unknowns inherent in assessing political alternatives, on the one hand, and myth and fatalism, on the other: if growth becomes the main prerequisite for marginalizing scarcity, and the presupposition of the particular kind of growth required to do this becomes political non-interference in the form of economy that made the initial steps forward towards potential post-scarcity, there are few legal obstacles to the evolution of economic growth in the direction of an end in itself, and its supra-political justification

marked by deeply entrenched stratification. Although codified in ostensibly neutral, factual terms such as profit, loss, property, interest, credit, rent, breach of contract, etc., the categories of capitalist exchange are underwritten by inequality and latent conflict. More theoretical research is needed in order to determine the extent to which profit and loss would shed their adversarial character in a post-commodity economy in which consumer interests and needs become important productive criteria before investment is made, that is, in de-centralized planning bodies. Whereas most current instances of 'market research' factor in the consumer in speculative terms as a potential source of profit, consumer interests could be aggregated in democratically elected consumer councils of the kind broadly envisaged by G. D. H. Cole. See Chris Wyatt, *The Defetishized Society: New Economic Democracy as a Libertarian Alternative to Capitalism*, London, Continuum, 2011, pp. 20–4, 83–7 and 214–18.

as a new form of necessity. At that moment one form of economy raises its 'scientific' status to *the* economy and the only feasible and rational way to organize the relations between humanity and external nature. The initial steps are then allowed to mark out the path of the entire journey, and the entire range of possible experience and knowledge is considerably narrowed. As a consequence, individual and collective learning is reduced to a technical adjustment to a trajectory that has been mapped out to a significant extent before the youngest travellers even set out. These macroeconomic tendencies are reinforced by the contradictions inherent in a conception of individual autonomy predicated on *enforced* political *non-interference* in people's daily lives. Taking into account the improbability of the invisible hand of the market and the implausibility of enlightened self-interest as a guide to rational action (if the guide is itself extra-rational, how can the outcome be rational, except in the drastically pared-down sense of a utilitarian aggregation of fairly random preferences?), Adorno builds on Marx and Hegel by developing a form of theory that is aesthetic in the double sense explained in the previous chapter. Such theory strives towards explanation capable of illuminating the structure of objectivity in Hegel's sense, which means revealing something defining about the character and quality of socio-historical objectivity at a particular juncture in the history of collective learning processes. For Adorno these include developing the capacity to investigate non-rational phenomena systematically with an eye towards addressing rationality deficits. Examples include Protestantism in Weber's account of the rise of capitalism and dreams in Freud's understanding of the unnecessary repression of individual internal nature. These analyses can serve to formulate guidelines for the project of increasing the degree of rationality shaping imperfectly rational institutions, such as universities, health systems and economies. If rationality deficits can be approached in this way, one may realistically begin to envisage the gradual devolution of knowledge-transmission processes from the state to an autonomous society in Castoriadis' sense of self-institution and generalized *auto-gestion*.[19]

Learning in this context also means designing collective living spaces which do not oppress individuals, and understanding complex and in some cases atonal music. Hence Adorno advances the project of strengthening the objective, socio-historical dimension of Hegel's dialectic while tempering the individual, subjective dimension subsequently collectivized by Marx and

---

[19]While Jeff Klooger interprets Castoriadis' sociological thinking in this vein in *Castoriadis: Psyche, Society, Autonomy*, Leiden/Boston, Brill, 2009, Dirk Braunstein interprets Adorno's economic thinking in these terms in *Adornos Kritik der politischen Ökonomie* [*Adorno's Critique of Political Economy*], Bielefeld, Transcript, 2011.

Lukács, and more recently given a social psychological, intersubjective twist by theorists of communicative action, recognition and performance. This is worth stressing, since if it is true that the best political arguments are not necessarily directly political in an obvious way, it may also be true that the most promising path towards non-antagonistic subjectivity does not necessarily pass in the first instance by way of direct empowerment of the subject or the uncritical celebration of intersubjectivity or intersubjective communication. This point is illustrated by specific features of Bauhaus pedagogy. These suggest that at a determinate moment in the production of modern industry and democratic consciousness, organized cooperation in production and art becomes the basis of real individuality, and not, as is often supposed, the other way round. Championing the communicative and agonistic potential of individuals bereft of the larger network of cooperative production and consumption distracts attention from the real possibility that without these coordinating ties, communication and agonism in most cases amount to little more than futile exercises of self-affirmation.[20] Stated in these terms, it is not difficult to imagine that the argument for dismantling superfluous industrial discipline on the basis of objective post-scarcity is not primarily about nationally calculated rates of growth or an enhanced autonomy that turns out to be passive adaptation and commodity fetishism. In Chapters Four and Five it will be suggested that it is more centrally concerned with initiating better communication between different social systems, where the optimal functioning of an individual system (in this case the economy) is predicated on its relations with other systems (educational, health, environmental, etc.), rather than isolation from them. Reform in this direction would offer a practical example of changing the structure of mediations in accordance with the de-centred and plural logic of differentiation, rather than trying to do it on the basis of an assumed mediated unity between citizens, law and the state. As societies learn they can take on such tasks without recourse to an organizing centre with the steering capacities of the kind that the post-1789 state may have always aspired to, but only fleetingly, if ever, possessed.[21] All evidence suggests that within existing institutional arrangements, nationally defined

---

[20]See Walter Gropius, 'Programme of the Staatliches Bauhaus in Weimar' (April 1919), reprinted in Anton Kaes, Martin Jay and Edward Dimendberg (eds), *The Weimar Republic Sourcebook*, Berkeley, University of California Press, 1994, p. 435; and Eric D. Weitz, *Weimar Germany*, Princeton, Princeton University Press, 2007, chapter 5.

[21]Peter Fuchs, *Die Erreichbarkeit der Gesellschaft: Zur Konstruktion und Imagination gesellschaftlicher Einheit* [*The Attainability of Society*], Frankfurt, Suhrkamp, 1992, chapters 4–8. The crisis of contemporary social democracy is better explained as one consequence of these decreased steering capacities rather than in terms of political apathy, supposedly post-ideological worldviews, creeping conservatism, etc. This phenomenon is analysed in Chapter Four of the present book.

states are now irreparably overburdened, thus making a qualitative shift to decentred and non-identity thinking possible and urgent. One can see the contours of this evolution at the theoretical level in the movement from the public sphere and civil society to notions of reciprocal interactive exchange and constellations. As the discussion in this and the previous chapter on the public sphere and epistemology indicates, Kant offers a very relevant account of the public sphere in this respect.

Kant posits that humanity is neither identical with nature nor separate from it. He breaks with the pragmatic sensuality of the empiricists and the intellectual humanism of the rationalists in order to develop an approach which is synthetic in several senses. Kant constructs knowledge out of heterogeneous elements by building a conceptual space in which a priori and experiential moments coexist. Despite his methodological rigour, however, not all readers are entirely convinced of the solidity or beauty of the resulting geometry of the space in question. A number of critics have been keen to point out that there is something somewhat mechanical and ahistorical about his account of the encounter between human consciousness and external nature, so that at times it looks like an awkward attempt to make Newton serviceable for philosophy. Hence the attempt to demarcate a field of inquiry which adopts the stringency of the natural sciences while acknowledging that philosophy and history are concerned with respectively different sets of questions often takes shape as a response to what are thought to be Kant's inadequacies in this regard.[22] But his *Aufhebung* of empiricist and rationalist approaches is not a simple case of pick, mix and hope for the best. The fact that for Kant humanity does not have *direct* knowledge of nature or objects is a large part of the reason why humanity can have *real* knowledge of them through experience. This is related to the political point about arguments being more real when they are not directly political, and also related to the unorthodox mimetic principle that landscape paintings and poems are more

[22]Walter Benjamin, 'Über das Programm der kommenden Philosophie' ['On the Tasks of the Coming Philosophy'] (1918), in *Angelus Novus* (contained in English in the volume *Reflections*, New York, Schocken, 1976b), Frankfurt, Suhrkamp, pp. 27–41. Part of the difficulty involved in coming up with a comprehensive and accurate analysis of Benjamin and his continued relevance for critical theory is that he builds on hermeneutical traditions going back to Schleiermacher, as well as Kantian idealist, theological and Marxist traditions. There is little doubt that the epistemological status of Kantian philosophy played a major role in the debates about the specificities of the *Geisteswissenschaften* (usually translated as the human sciences). The neo-Kantians, as well as Dilthey, Weber and Simmel are either positively or negatively influenced by Kant's critical philosophy and its impact on Hegel, Marx, Nietzsche and beyond to twentieth-century hermeneutics and phenomenology. See Herbert Schnädelbach, *Philosophie in Deutschland, 1831–1933* [*Philosophy in Germany, 1831–1933*] (published in English by Cambridge University Press, 1984), Frankfurt, Suhrkamp, 1983.

real, and in some sense more true, than landscapes. This reality should not be mistaken for a traditional humanist view of art or knowledge, as will be seen in the discussion of Baudelaire in the next section. It is not through direct imitation or unmediated unity with nature that humans have experience, and by extension, knowledge. It is through the reality of third instances that the conditions of objective knowledge – and autonomy – become ascertainable. References to such instances indicate that reality includes but is not reducible to the mediated unity of humanity and nature; this is an idealist discovery that is never really fully explored by idealist philosophers. Within the idealist tradition the third instance is at times thought of as an unknowable limit, as in the Kantian problem of the thing in itself. At other times, as in Hegel's case, it is intrinsic to the process mediating between the other two terms, and is constantly transformed and re-articulated, and then alienated and re-appropriated by mind on its journey towards self (re-)discovery. One can interpret this movement as a part of an attempt to grasp three realities simultaneously: those of form, mediation and dialectics. The enduring legacy of idealism is its acute sensitivity to the movement of thought as it relates to the dynamism of historical socio-economic processes. This is evident especially when theorists propose their thinking as post-idealist, as in the sociology of Marx and the phenomenology of Husserl and Heidegger. It will be seen in the next section of this chapter that Baudelaire and Benjamin add something distinctive to the theory of three realities, to wit, a theory of form as a hermeneutic of non-forgetting relevant to the project of making missed transitions palpably visible, and thereby, potentially recoverable.[23]

In closing this section, the question arises of how one ought to assess the residual relevance of idealism for critical theory in the twenty-first century. If the relation between humanity, nature, and their conceptual and practical mediation is one of non-identity, then contingency and fragmentary forms of experience cannot be eliminated from epistemology or politics. But this does not mean that knowledge starts where contingency and indeterminacy stop, but rather, that a certain degree of contingency is required for there to be something approximating post-dogmatic knowledge in science, politics, law and aesthetics. If this is the case, it becomes increasingly implausible to claim that politics starts where law and philosophy stop, or that aesthetics

---

[23]On the idealist legacy in social and political thought see Robert Pippin, *Kant's Theory of Form: An Essay on the Critique of Pure Reason*, New Haven, Yale University Press, 1982, chapters 7–8; and Henry E. Allison, *Kant's Transcendental Idealism: An Interpretation and Defence*, New Haven, Yale University Press, 1983, Part IV. Although Baudelaire and Benjamin are not really idealists as such, the dialectical dimension of their thinking resonates with idealist motifs. For an analysis of these issues see Rolf Tiedemann, *Dialektik im Stillstand: Versuche zum Spätwerk Walter Benjamins* [*Dialectics at a Standstill*] (available in English), Frankfurt, Suhrkamp, 1983, chapter 3.

begins where scientific rationality runs up against its outer theoretical limits. But this does not mean that things are an inextricable jumble of contrasting forces, interests and values. It is therefore imperative to develop a theory of society capable of articulating and re-articulating its composite elements in various combinations. In this way it may be possible to generate hypotheses, remain open to new evidence, and to produce and evaluate rival hypotheses about autonomy, legitimacy, conflict, reason, power, the causes of public financial deficits, etc.[24] The enduring link between a qualified form of idealism and critical theory today can be forged by marshalling historical evidence in support of the following claim: the experience of autonomy is very different if the degree of contingency in question is allowed to assume institutional form as the resurrection of fate and destiny (i.e. left to the haphazard decisions rendered by the play of market forces in the provision of goods and services and the allocation of labour power), than if, by contrast, it can be framed so as to establish a plurality of open-ended approaches to collective growth and individual development.

Kant suggests that experience synthesizes consciousness and nature, and, at the same time, that experience is a synthesis of consciousness and nature. This movement or play of consciousness, experience and nature is captured in the Kantian concept of subjectivity.[25] In the previous chapter it is observed that Kantian subjectivity is to a significant extent liberal juridical subjectivity, and that within this framework private property is a primary condition for reflexive, autonomous thought and communicative rationality. For Kant the conditions of knowledge and subjectivity inhere in the subject, so that it is unproblematic for him to ground autonomy in the defensive functions of private, if not necessarily isolated individuals. Yet his ideas on the reality

[24]Howard Caygill, *A Kant Dictionary*, Oxford, Blackwell, 1995, pp. 382–5. A number of post-Kantian idealist socialists have plausibly suggested that the self-organizational capacities of society are actually enhanced rather than undermined by the fact that individual subjects do not have direct access to knowledge or, for that matter, 'their own' experience. Hegel makes a similar point when observing that citizens do not have land, houses, etc., but instead have rights to those things. If as a consequence it can be shown that experience is demonstrably social, it can be argued further that this should be reflected in organizations and institutions. See the articles on Paul Natorp, Hermann Cohen, Friedrich Albert Lange and Karl Vorländer in Helmut Holzhey (ed.), *Ethischer Sozialismus: Zur politischen Philosophie des Neukantianismus* [*Ethical Socialism*], Frankfurt, Suhrkamp, 1994.

[25]Kant, *Die Kritik der reinen Vernunft* [*Critique of Pure Reason*] (1781, 1787), Frankfurt, Suhrkamp, 1990, pp. 267–85; and Hermann Cohen, *Kants Theorie der Erfahrung* [*Kant's Theory of Experience*] (1871), Berlin, Bruno Cassirer, 1918, pp. 123–5. The term 'play' is deliberately repeated in order to underscore the affinities between Kant's epistemological and liberal political positions. To do so is not to attribute sinister or conspiratorial intentions to the philosopher. What is noted is a rationality deficit that can be addressed with the argument that too much of what is often described as contingent is actually the indirect consequence of insufficiently historical and sociological theorizing.

of third instances and his views on the mediating capacities of the public sphere mark a qualified departure from some of his own presuppositions in this regard.[26] This turns out to be a fecund contradiction, however, because the origins of critical theory can be found in Hegel's critique of Kant and the Hegelian notion that all subjectivity is grounded in socio-historical objectivity. The contradictions in Kant are indicative of latent socio-historical conflicts and institutional disequilibria, and are not merely controversial episodes in intellectual history. A more recognizably sociological approach to theorizing conflict is found in Marx and Lukács. Their hypotheses point towards the subsequent founding of the Institute for Social Research in 1924 and the rise of Western Marxism, though as will be seen below, there is some doubt about the extent to which Marx and Lukács offer properly sociological accounts of conflict, communication, exchange and of society more generally.[27]

From 'correspondences' to *Wechselwirkungen* and constellations

Hence some of the initial impetus towards the development of a critical theory of society can be found in Kant, Hegel, Marx and Lukács. But it can also be traced to Benjamin's reading of Baudelaire on modern art and his analyses of the mode of artistic reception particular to post-feudal societies. Benjamin's ideas on these topics are closely related to his interpretation of the significance of the Paris arcades and his reflections on the changing boundaries between the interior and exterior manifestations of consciousness in poetry, as well as the evolving architectural and spatial organization of industrial cities. In Benjamin's estimation Baudelaire is a landmark figure in the rupture between low art and classical art which, if only indirectly,

---

[26]These ambiguities are skillfully highlighted by Wilhelm Teichner in *Kants Transzendental philosophie: Ein Grundriss*, Munich, Karl Alber, 1978, chapter 7–8, and by Simon Jarvis in *Adorno: A Critical Introduction*, Cambridge, Polity, 1998, chapter 7. Adorno provides a lengthy exposition of the problems involved in his 1959 lectures on Kant at the University of Frankfurt. See his *Kants Kritik der reinen Vernunft* [*Kant's Critique of Pure Reason*] (available in English by Stanford University Press), Frankfurt, Suhrkamp, 1995, especially lecture 19.

[27]For an analysis of the relations between critical theory and Western Marxism see Schecter, *The History of the Left from Marx to the Present: Theoretical Perspectives*, chapters 2–3; and Martin Jay, *Marxism and Totality: The Adventures of a Concept from Lukács to Habermas*, Berkeley, University of California Press, 1984. These accounts indicate that while Lukács' theory of reification had a major impact on the subsequent development of critical theory, his defence of aesthetic realism against modernism left him somewhat isolated from the Frankfurt School and thinkers like Brecht.

anticipates a more general rupture between citizens, law and the state. He also offers keys for interpreting the related rise of an avant-garde of aesthetic and political experience aware of the unfolding crisis of previously operative unities, including the precarious juridical-political bond between citizens and the post-1789 territorial nation-state. If Baudelaire is an urban thinker who reckons that the rhythms of industrial manufacture make for readers with short attention spans, to Benjamin his poetry also symbolizes the irrevocable end of the symmetry between private property, individual autonomy and reflexive rationality that may have fleetingly characterized the Kantian period of public sphere rationality. Benjamin suggests that it is not advisable to deduce natural rights or sociological constants from realities that may have been operative at one particular moment in history: that instant needs to be captured, in the manner of a photograph, and then compared with similarly captured instants before and after the specific moment in question. Moreover, Baudelaire's verse resonates with the unfulfilled expectations raised by the revolts of 1848 as well as the spectre haunting Europe evoked by Marx and Engels in that same year. Benjamin notes that to this extent Baudelaire clearly anticipates Rimbaud's notion that although in many ways a failure, 1848 would by no means be the final attempt to see the ideals of 1789 through to their logical, radically republican and libertarian socialist conclusions.[28]

One might ask what the relation is between the phenomenon of shortened attention spans, increasing impatience with poetry, the demise of the bourgeois public sphere, and the rise, in its stead, of professional political parties and mass electorates. Benjamin intuits that it is unlikely to be merely coincidental in ways corresponding to explanatory relativism. Nor is it likely to be foreordained in ways broadly corresponding to the imposition of authoritarian dogma, the plotting of conspiracies, or historical determinism. He attempts to develop a methodology that is elastic enough to relate micro phenomena concerning art and the structure of experience to macro phenomena like economic downturns and changes in the structures of political compromise

[28]Walter Benjamin, *Das Passagen-Werk*, Vol. I [*The Paris Arcades Project*] (written 1927–40), Frankfurt, Suhrkamp, 1982, pp. 311–16, and 'Über einige Motive bei Baudelaire' ['On a Number of Motifs in Baudelaire'] (1939), in *Charles Baudelaire: Ein Lyriker im Zeitalter des Hochkapitalismus* [*Charles Baudelaire*], ed. by Rolf Tiedemann, Frankfurt, Suhrkamp, 1974a, pp. 103–9. A comparison between Benjamin's analysis of Baudelaire with Sartre's is revealing of the different approaches to literature taken by critical theory and Western Marxism, and is indicative of the theoretical sophistication of the former. See Sartre, *Baudelaire*, Paris, Gallimard, 1947, pp. 40–1 and 100–1, where he squeezes Baudelaire into some very narrow and conventional Marxist categories. For a look at the role of 1848 in the poetry of Baudelaire and the literary oeuvre of other writers, see Dolf Oehler, *Ein Höllensturz der alten Welt: Baudelaire, Flaubert, Heine, Herzen*, Frankfurt, Suhrkamp, 1988. For an analysis of Rimbaud's poetry and radical republican politics, see Kristin Ross, *The Emergence of Social Space: Rimbaud and the Paris Commune*, Minneapolis, University of Minnesota Press, 1988.

and interest aggregation. In so doing Benjamin intimates that it is possible to retain Marx's emphasis on political economy, without which sociological analysis is likely to have a significant critical deficit, though without, however, converting this emphasis into economic reductionism or class fetishism, as Marx and his followers sometimes do. He perceives that a crisis of symbolic and political representation is at work. This is exemplified on a grand scale by stock market uncertainty and looming trade wars, but it is also manifested in less spectacular ways in the poetry and person of people like Baudelaire, who are caught between the cultural aspirations of the gradually declining haute bourgeoisie, and the daily realities of mundane money worries and the possibility of general downward mobility for the members of intermediate social strata. The task for Benjamin in the 1920s and 1930s, as well as for contemporary critical theory, is to explain the causes and institutional logic of these crises in macro-sociological and micro-aesthetic terms, bearing in mind too that the macro may at times manifest itself at the micro level and the other way round.[29] Benjamin's context is defined among other things by the Wall Street crash of 1929 and the collapse of parliamentary democracy in Germany. He sees that culture, economy, politics and consumption patterns are all related, but not in the manner suggested by the base and superstructure model or any related notion positing a causal centre and an epiphenomenal periphery. Benjamin believes that some kind of unusually configured totality is at work, but the one he has in mind is decentred and plural, that is, it is a constellation rather than a primary object or essence reproduced in manifold secondary reflections or shadows that owe their existence to a single causal factor or the interests of one social class. His research into the inner workings of nineteenth-century Paris is guided by the hypothesis that Baudelaire's poetry reveals something important about the structure of this constellation. His verse and essays in aesthetic criticism illuminate some of the reasons for the permanent instability of liberal forms of democracy that attempt to coexist with capitalism, just as, in a related context some years later, Alfred Döblin's *Berlin Alexanderplatz* (1929) confirms that suspicion of political volatility in relation to the crisis of the twentieth-century novel.[30]

---

[29]Siegfried Kracauer's study of German films in the Weimar period provides an outstanding example of this kind of methodology. See his *From Caligari to Hitler*, New Haven, Yale University Press, 1947. What Benjamin manages to discern in architectural trends, Kracauer detects in the political implications of permutations in cinematographic form. Though both authors enjoy continued relevance for critical theory, there has been little in the way of comparative research on them, with the notable exception of Frisby's *Fragments of Modernity*.

[30]Benjamin, *Das Passagen-Werk*, Vol. I [*The Paris Arcades Project*], pp. 316–18, 'Das Paris des Second Empire bei Baudelaire' ['Second Empire Paris in Baudelaire'] (1938), in *Charles Baudelaire*, pp. 108–9, 'Paris, die Hauptstadt des neunzehnten Jahrhunderts' ['Paris, Capital of the Nineteenth Century'] (1938), in *Illuminationen* (available in English as *Illuminations*), Frankfurt,

Yet Benjamin's analysis of the momentary congruity between private property, individual autonomy and reflexive rationality – and its definitive demise – is no more Hegelian–Marxist or straightforwardly dialectical than Baudelaire's work. The poet gives expression to what at this specific historical moment becomes a discontinuous and disharmonious trajectory from subject, experience, thought, concept and object to institution. This raises doubts about the plausibility of a credible re-unification of thinking and historical being of the kind envisaged by Hegel, Marx, and many of Hegel's ostensibly materialist critics after Marx, while also raising the possibility of a method nuanced enough to theorize discontinuity in thinking as well as discrepancies between thinking and institutions.[31] With few exceptions, from Kant to Lenin, Lukács and beyond, the reunification of thought and being, like the reunification of experience and memory or theory and praxis, is proposed as the work of an exceptional individual genius in art, or on the basis of the self-affirmation of a collective subject in society. In both cases, the subject restores the wholeness of an imputed original unity or teleological tendency towards unity through *Geist*, labour freed from the wage system, the party, revolution, etc. While the issues touched on by Baudelaire might be considered troubling for Marxists, he raises more general questions about aesthetic and political representation that have implications for the relations between language and truth, and between visibility and explanatory validity. There certainly are a number of unresolved issues between Marxism and critical theory. But dialectics, especially in Adorno, has far from exhausted its socio-political explanatory power. Benjamin has reasons for thinking that

---

Suhrkamp, 1976a, pp. 179–81, and 'Krisis des Romans: Zu Döblins Berlin Alexanderplatz' ['Crisis of the Novel: On Döblin's Berlin Alexanderplatz'] (1930), in *Angelus Novus* (available in English as *Reflections*), Frankfurt, Suhrkamp, 1988, pp. 437–43. In the 'Theses on the Philosophy of History' (also in *Illuminations*), Benjamin describes this permanent instability in juridical terms as a permanent state of exception. This idea has been taken up by a number of contemporary theorists, including Judith Butler and Giorgio Agamben.

[31]It might be objected that in positing an unknowable 'thing in itself', Kant concedes that there is no uncontested post-metaphysical symmetry of thought, concept and being, that is, that post-metaphysical objectivity is subject to external limits just as, by political analogy, theory and praxis are not easily mediated without law. This has prompted some thinkers to counter that objectivity is not genuinely post-metaphysical if the unity in question is reproduced, albeit with the acknowledged limits implied by the thing in itself, in the definition of subjectivity. In his work up until 1932 Heidegger proposes abandoning subjectivity for *Dasein* and jettisoning objectivity for ready-to-hand-ness and present-to-hand-ness, so that the difference between thought and being can be ontologically understood instead of anthropomorphized. See Heidegger, *Sein und Zeit* [*Being and Time*] (1927), Tübingen, Max Niemeyer, 1993, paragraph 4, as well as Heidegger, *Kant und das Problem der Metaphysik* [*Kant and the Problem of Metaphysics*] (1929), Frankfurt, Vittorio Klostermann, 1998, paragraphs 36–8. For a very thorough elucidation of these issues see Theodore Kisiel, *The Genesis of Heidegger's Being and Time*, Berkeley, University of California Press, 1993.

Baudelaire's uniquely allegorical dialectics is of vital importance for the project of reformulating historical materialism beyond the constraining parameters of reformism, voluntarism and determinism, and he also believes that Baudelaire's poetry points beyond the dubious juxtaposition of the individual/aesthetic with the collective/social. Central to the argument developed in this chapter and the next is that the renewal of critical theory today depends at least in part on re-articulating the relation between non-identity thinking and modernist aesthetic and political practice. The challenge is somehow to retain a central epistemological role for various instances of mediation, though without recourse to notions of alienated essences that can be re-appropriated by a monolithic subject, or unifying foundations that can be re-established by a liberal-democratic, republican, fascist, authoritarian, communist or any other type of General Will. The Marxist critiques of political economy and commodity fetishism remain relevant. But the project cannot dispense with a critique of organic unity or a broadly conceived account of social communication which insists on the non-reducibility of individual internal nature to private, liberal-democratic autonomy.[32] The more general point is that from the moment philosophical investigation credibly establishes the reality of third instances, the Hegelian–Marxist dialectic of alienation and re-appropriation becomes problematic in the sense that it depends on the highly improbable ability of a subject to reclaim the externalizations of its conscious sensual and intellectual activity. Since the facticity of non-identity makes this approach to overcoming alienation unrealistic, critical theory must now try to shift the focus of theory and practice from musings about revolutionary subjectivity – whether as universal class, multitude, vanguard party or any other honorary group – to an understanding of the qualitative and sociological distances between subject and institution, as well as the intermediary instances structuring the multiple flows of that trajectory (experience, thought, concept, object). If it fails in this endeavour, there will not be a great deal of difference between critical theory, fundamental ontology and deconstruction.[33]

---

[32]For the continuing relevance of the Marxist critique of commodity fetishism, see Chris Wyatt, *The De-Fetishised Society*, London, Continuum, 2012. Pioneering work in this field has been done by Wolfgang Fritz Haug. See his *Kritik der Warenästhetik* [*Critique of Commodity Aesthetics*], Frankfurt, Suhrkamp, 1971. On the dialectical quality of Baudelaire, see Bertrand and Durrand, *Les poètes de la modernité de Baudelaire à Apollinaire*, pp. 64–5. Considerations of space preclude a textual analysis of the poems, but interested readers should read 'Correspondences' and 'The Swan' from *The Flowers of Evil*, and consult Nicholls, *Modernisms*, chapters 1–2 and F. W. Leakey, *Baudelaire and Nature*, Manchester, Manchester University Press, 1969, chapter 6.

[33]This is the corollary of investigating the poetic quality of the spaces between words and the political dimension of the spaces between buildings. Benjamin, following Freud's attempt to make dreams readable, describes his own project as making readable what has never been written, much in the way that Baudelaire might claim to be imitating something that has no

Though Baudelaire does not refer directly to Kant, he retains Kant's notion that humanity is neither identical to nature nor separate from it. But he carries out a minor revolution in poetic form by hinting at a mode of mediation – and a correspondingly open dialectic – that neither depends on a fixed centre, nor seeks grounding in a stable synthesis. This constitutes a formidable, if subtle challenge to mainstream notions of juridical and political mediation between private and public spheres, that is, it presents a challenge to the theoretical bases of the liberal-democratic *Rechtsstaat* that does not despair of the possibility of an altogether different set of mediations. Hence it is in no way a retreat to anodyne notions of communicative competence or art for art's sake. At first glance Kant seems to do something similar with respect to rationalist and empiricist epistemology by depicting subjectivity as the free interplay of consciousness, experience and nature. But in answer to the question how knowledge is possible, he concludes that the condition is a subject that orders their experience of objects in time and space by way of the 12 categories of the understanding. Somewhat uncharitably, perhaps, but incisively, Nietzsche remarks that for all the originality of his 'Copernican revolution', Kant ultimately proposes that knowledge derives from a subjective faculty. Hence the condition of objective knowledge is an object-knowing subject (a tautology). From Nietzsche's perspective, this is typical of a particular kind of liberal-democratic egalitarian pathos determined to see the same mental processes at work in all people, as if there was something like a flawed but dignified universal human nature. This avowed identity of mental process vouches for the validity of the general laws of experience as well as for the rational legislative foundations most in keeping with bourgeois universality (a contradiction in terms).[34]

In Baudelaire, by contrast, Benjamin glimpses a re-articulation of Hegel's project of arriving at a method of analysing reality that is inherent in the structure of the real, though with the important caveat that reality reveals the logic of its unfolding evolution in a series of movements informed by the mimetic principle mentioned at the outset of this section and its corollary, which is that nature alone, whether in humanity or in the natural world, does

original. See Leena Petersen, *Poetik des Zwischenraumes* [*Poetics of the Space in Between*], Heidelberg, Winter, 2010, chapter 5. In the *Passagen-Werk* (Vol. I, pp. 592–5), Benjamin declares his hope to make this methodology fruitful for the project of seeing the ruins of things and regimes before they become ruins.

[34]Baudelaire, 'Le cygne' ['The Swan'], in 'Tableaux parisiens' ['Parisian portraits'], reprinted in Charles Baudelaire, *Œuvres complètes*, Vol. I, Paris, Gallimard, 1975, pp. 85–7; Friedrich Nietzsche, *Die fröhliche Wissenschaft* [*The Gay Science*] (1882), Stuttgart, Reclam, 2000, p. 258, and *Der Wille zur Macht* [*The Will to Power*] (posthumously published in 1906), Stuttgart, Alfred Kröner, 1964, pp. 334–6; Benjamin, *Das Passagen-Werk*, Vol. I [*The Paris Arcades Project*], p. 321.

not suffice to know nature. Benjamin reckons that Baudelaire discovers a de-naturalizing corrective to all suppositions of original organic unity which, while complex and at times allegorical, is never obscurantist or mythological. These movements, or *correspondances* as Baudelaire calls them, are not comparable to the Hegelian stages in the journey from consciousness to self-consciousness, in which *Geist* discards its own successively obsolete forms on the way to a mediated unity of humanity and nature in philosophy, and the mutual recognition of citizens in politics. In Baudelaire's work the discovery of third instances is respected and directed towards an investigation of unsuspected mediations, rather than repudiated in favour of an exaltation of the subject's capacity for conceptual thought and masterful re-appropriation. From Benjamin's perspective this confirms the point that the contradictions in Kant and the problems in Hegel are indicative of latent socio-historical conflicts and the impending crisis of the liberal-democratic state form. It is not merely the case that the Kantian period of public sphere rationality has passed: even Hegel's historical finesse starts to look a bit like grasping at theoretical straws, as the young Marx shows in relation to the problems with the model of state/civil society relations outlined in the *Philosophy of Right*. But the crises of reason and legitimacy registered in idealism are not adequately addressed without integrating a number of conceptual insights from aesthetics. Even the most sophisticated innovations in political economy will not suffice, which is why Baudelaire attains political as well as literary importance.[35]

But how is knowledge possible for Baudelaire if nature cannot know nature, and the objective knowledge accessible to an object-knowing human subject is for the most part illusory? Baudelaire does not direct the mediation processes back to Kant's anthropological subject, Hegel's spirit, or Lukács' historicized collective subject. He suggests that mediated unity might be a

---

[35]Baudelaire, 'Correspondances', in *Les fleurs du mal* [*The Flowers of Evil*] (1857), reprinted in *Œuvres complètes*, Vol. I, Paris, Gallimard, 1975, pp. 11–12; F. W. Leakey, *Baudelaire and Nature*, pp. 195–217; Benjamin, 'Über einige Motive bei Baudelaire' ['On a Number of Motifs in Baudelaire'] (1939), in *Charles Baudelaire*, pp. 114–19 and 'Über das Programm der kommenden Philosophie' ['On the Tasks of the Coming Philosophy'] (1918), pp. 29–30. It may seem contradictory to stress the political possibilities opened up by social differentiation, which would seem to demand academic specialization, and simultaneously to emphasize the need for interdisciplinary research integrating historical, sociological, aesthetic and juridical methodologies. The argument about what remains actual in Hegel's thinking is that the possibilities in question are unlikely to materialize unless method can keep pace with complexity. While specialization that is not tempered and enriched with heterogeneous elements tends to retrench in hermetic closure, and thereby become meaninglessly complex, critical theory strives to think the reality of form in conjunction with the reality of mediation. Thus at times it seems ungainly and disjointed. In its best instances, however, it demonstrates the reality of what it is powerless to prove in full at a precise historical moment. This will become clearer when the discussion shifts to non-identity in the next chapter.

reliable epistemological and poetic principle when, as in the classical world, there may have been an intrinsically poetic relation between linguistic signs, the objects they represent, and the forms in which the objects appear. Representation as direct imitation and reiteration is reliable in poetic and political terms as long as an underlying unity can be supposed to obtain in the network binding together words, things and images, and there exists a subject that can comprehend that unity in ways that yield sense or meaning. As long as these conditions hold, it is plausible to believe that literary beauty has its laws, and that the poet orders words accordingly to let that beauty shine forth just as, in the polis, the good life has its own laws, which the philosopher can deduce from the ontological order of things.[36] The socio-economic realities of modern urban life undermine the symmetrical network that once facilitated un-coerced syntheses, thus making a new approach to poetic and political mediation necessary. Discovering correspondences can be likened to sounding out extra-sensual affinities between entities that are normally perceived or experienced as being physically similar, when in fact the similarity between them is neither physical in the sense of crude materialism, nor metaphysical in the sense of consistent idealism. Baudelaire, Benjamin and Adorno indicate distinct ways of investigating the relations between conceptual and non-conceptual knowledge in terms of mimetic similarity and hermeneutical dialectics, without subsuming these discrete instances of knowledge under an overarching concept, or separating them according to arbitrary and ultimately instrumental categories. For Benjamin this has important implications for developing different possible ways of researching the interconnectedness of macro and micro sociological change without subsuming both into a meta-cause or single origin that distorts explanation, and therewith, critical evaluation of possible alternatives to existing institutional configurations. Baudelaire thus anticipates and contributes to the development of Benjamin and Adorno's reflections on constellational thinking, about which more will be said presently.[37]

While Lukács and other Marxists acknowledge that the industrial era marks a rupture in epistemological, literary and political tradition, they generally tend

[36]Baudelaire, 'De l'idéal et du modèle' ['On the Ideal and the Model'] in 'Salon de 1846', reprinted in *Œuvres complètes*, pp. 454–6, Aristotle, *The Politics* (335–322 BC), Books VII–VIII, ed. and trans. by John Warrington, London, Dent, 1959, and Aristotle, *Nicomachean Ethics*, in Reginald E. Allen (ed.), *Greek Philosophy: From Thales to Aristotle*, New York, Macmillan, 1966, pp. 362–74.
[37]Baudelaire, draft introduction to *Les fleurs du mal* [*The Flowers of Evil*], reprinted in *Œuvres complètes*, 1975, pp. 181–6. The theoretical production of non-arbitrary similarities offers new ways of conceptualizing the relations between modern legality, which holds out the promise of a rational alternative to traditional command, on the one hand, and legitimacy, which is usually associated with collective socio-economic, welfare, and security needs, on the other.

to ascribe the break to private property, commodity fetishism, reification and other consequences of an entrenched division between mental and manual labour that is made more entrenched still by industrial capitalism.[38] Benjamin is inclined to accept these accounts of the causes of de-traditionalization and the fragmentation of experience to some extent. But he is markedly less sanguine than Lukács about the possibility of re-constituting a linguistic harmony between things, images and meaning through a change in property relations or the ascension to power of a political party. He is also adamant that vague notions of historical progress, social reform, etc., encourage wishful thinking about the likelihood of this re-reconciling revolution.[39] Reading Baudelaire from a perspective informed by Simmel as much as by Marx, Benjamin concludes that the poet is obliged to re-arrange and unscramble the relations between language, humanity and nature. One can compare this to a kind of micro re-embedding operation that preserves the moment of truth in contingency without embracing agnosticism or passivity. Whereas sense and communication in Western Europe have been dependent on tradition since the time of Homer, Baudelaire writes at a time when tradition is being undermined by commodity production and the ascension of the commercial fashion industry. Under the then newly emerging conditions, communication can no longer proceed on the basis of a reliable set of fixed points within a stable representational order of meaning. In anticipation of montage methodology, Baudelaire hints that communication is constructed from analogies and affinities between the sensual, intellectual, objective, subjective, individual, collective, written, acoustic, natural, social, contemporary and past dimensions of reality.[40]

Benjamin advises that the best approach to Baudelaire is to think about what may seem obscure in *The Flowers of Evil* and other writings, that is, mediation without an identifiable central mediator, as an attempt to articulate an enriched form of post-anthropological materialism, and to attain a higher degree of interpretative clarity than was previously reached by progressive humanist philosophers such as Feuerbach. Where imitation of nature as the

---

[38]György Lukács, 'Die Verdinglichung und das Bewusstsein des Proletariats' ['Reification and Proletarian Consciousness'], in *Geschichte und Klassenbewusstsein* [*History and Class Consciousness*] (1923), Amsterdam, De Munter, 1967, pp. 193–5.

[39]As the term re-reconciling suggests, there is a markedly conservative dimension to some of Lukács' ideas. This can be seen in his refusal to engage with modernism, and his dismissal of a number of important thinkers, including Nietzsche and Simmel, as irrational harbingers of fascism. See György Lukács, *Die Zerstörung der Vernunft* [*The Destruction of Reason*] (1954), Berlin, Aufbau, 1954, pp. 254–8.

[40]Baudelaire, 'Reflexions sur quelques-uns de mes contemporains: Victor Hugo', reprinted in *Œuvres complètes*, Vol. II, Paris, Gallimard, 1975, pp. 129–40, and 'Salon de 1859', p. 665, as well as 'Le peintre de la vie moderne', pp. 694–5 in the same volume; Benjamin, *Charles Baudelaire*, pp. 113–14.

basis of art breaks down, and presupposed unity as the basis of linguistic and political representation collapses, the possibility of knowledge depends on the construction of a non-verbal language out of actual and metaphorical ruins, dreams, memory, and other fragments of experience that defy linear interpretation and hierarchical ordering in terms of importance. It is in the poetic method of research suggested by Baudelaire's *correspondances* that Benjamin glimpses the possibility of a sociological approach to understanding the reciprocal interaction between micro-aesthetic phenomena concerning the structure of experience and knowledge, on the one hand, and macro-political phenomena relating to economic, architectural, juridical and political changes, on the other. Benjamin regards Baudelaire's poetics of the city to be particularly innovative, in that the poet indicates paths of research pointing beyond distinctions like private/public and base/superstructure.[41] While it might sound esoteric to try to construct a visual language out of fragments and different kinds of ruins, Benjamin follows Freud's fairly stringent method of making dreams and other products of the unconscious readable. Hence there is nothing esoteric about tracing the correspondences between sensual and conceptual knowledge, or making legible phenomena that have never been written. The parallel project pursued by Benjamin is to make missed transitions as well as unsuspected political possibilities visible, even if they are not objects of perception in the usual sense. Hence for Benjamin, Baudelaire's correspondences have to be alloyed with Marx's historical materialism in order to enable people to read and interpret extralinguistic historical phenomena.[42]

In the opening lines of the first chapter of Volume I of *Capital*, Marx notes that in a capitalist society, although wealth appears as piles of commodities, value is derived from labour power. He adds that plausible explanations for this state of appearances must take into account the particularities involved in capitalist forms of exchange.[43] To say that the commodities *are* labour power is to argue that one can figuratively *see* the processes through which labour power is transformed into commodities, and to see too, that these processes can be modified. This presents considerable methodological difficulties, because it entails seeing many snapshots at once, and to doubt, if need

---

[41]Benjamin, *Charles Baudelaire*, p. 114.

[42]It is more than a casual detail that Baudelaire (1821–67) and Marx (1818–83), like Kant (1720–1804) and Hegel (1770–1831) before them are more or less contemporaries, and that *The Flowers of Evil* and the *Grundrisse* both appear in print in 1857. The issues raised by idealism are taken up first by poets and philosophers, and then by sociologists (Simmel) and the critical theorists of the Frankfurt School. Building on this history of critical interpretation, contemporary critical theory articulates a vision in which philosophical, historical, sociological and aesthetic moments are all interrelated.

[43]Marx, *Das Kapital* [*Capital*] (1867), Vol. I, Berlin, Dietz, 1947, p. 49.

be, what they seem to say when arranged in chronological order. Stated in these terms, one can perceive how the aspiration to see surplus value is related to the project of remembering an event that has not yet happened. To experience the world in this way is to understand that the structure of mediations can be altered in both subtle and large-scale ways. The project thus implies more than simply 'overcoming' reification with correct party doctrine and strategy, or waiting for 'the contradictions of capitalism' to impose crises on internal and external nature. To make a modest start it can be noted that if it was not possible to see in this theoretical-historically informed way against the overwhelming weight of the 'natural facts', one would have to concede that the only real difference between one commodity and the next, like the only difference between the labour of one person compared to that of any other person, is its size and the price it fetches, that is, money in the form of wages (in accordance with a traditional theoretical account that dovetails with the 'common sense' notion that only the market can make this decision in a non-authoritarian way). Similarly, if one city consists of nothing than the same streets, buildings, underground systems, etc., found in any other city, the only meaningful difference between cities is their respective number of inhabitants. In this case one has the objectivity of sheer number at the macro level, which *corresponds*, in a provisionally negative sense, to individual whim at the micro level: everybody has their own opinions about the differences between cities. Benjamin concludes that what is common to these two examples is the tendency to obscure the specific histories relating to the way things are made and what makes each place unique. To counter these depoliticizing and history-effacing tendencies, one needs to develop a form of memory that does not simply remember in terms of linear sequence, as such, but actually creates a real image of what has not yet happened and could still happen. Hence in the aftermath of 1848 it is no longer simply the case that the real/actual is rational and vice versa: the rationality of the real is no longer synonymous with the actuality of the real. There is a kind of hermeneutical remainder of non-actualized reason that is excluded from the institutionalization of objective spirit. This shift in emphasis becomes necessary because the visible appearance of the excluded, yet-to-happen, has been blocked – but not destroyed – in the sense that Marx means in relation to the appearance of wealth in one particular, now increasingly international kind of society. What has happened is that diverse instances of labour power have been homogenized by a system of exchange as part of the same ensemble of processes that render the differences between places increasingly meaningless, that is, by the technological and monetary modification of distance and the way it is experienced. If, on the one hand, late capitalist technological and monetary approaches to the alteration of space do not exhaust the possibilities of changing spatio-temporal relations, what has not yet happened is not a matter of fantasy, on the other. It is directly related to what has happened, just as, after Hegel, normative questions are framed by actual events and institutions, and, after Freud, dreams cannot be dismissed as irrelevant mental detritus. So the task is somehow to see (an empirical, sensual process) in extra-empirical, conceptual terms. Certain strands of modernist thinking grasp this possibility while also bearing in mind that its practical realization depends on correcting the division of labour between mental, conceptual thought, on the one hand, and manual, sensual labour, on the other. To the extent that individual examples of intuitive genius achieve this non-coerced synthesis in works of art and philosophy under conditions of anticipated post-scarcity, the works in question implicitly demand realized post-scarcity as a constitutional condition of generalized, as opposed to merely sporadic epistemological and political validity. In this regard the critique of institutionalized instrumental reason is as politically relevant as pragmatic struggles about the distribution of money and property. This means that the poetics of correspondences must be rendered sociological at the same time that the historical dimension of mediation is rendered hermeneutic. In contrast to those who insist on regarding him as a mystic, Benjamin wants to develop a hyper-materialistic approach to the history of what has not yet happened. Although this sounds like contradictory nonsense, he invokes the dialectical argument that there is no history of the 'already has been' without a history of the 'not yet': if the past has simply occurred and is irredeemably gone, then so too must the future be already written, and this linear determinism, he insists, is falsified by experience.[44]

The implication is that practical-conceptual sight may evolve to the point where one can see labour power and the extraction of surplus value at the same time that heaps of goods come into the focus of what is gradually becoming the cinematographic eye of individuals in much wider circles than the avant-garde initially typified by figures such as Vertov and Eisenstein. This is a way of perceiving that connects the immediately visible with what is mediated by the documentation of historical experience. For example, the fall of the Berlin Wall does not actually happen until the Wall is smashed by

---

[44]Benjamin, 'Über den Begriff der Geschichte' [usually translated as 'Theses on the Philosophy of History'] (1940), in *Illuminationen* [*Illuminations*], pp. 251–3 (Theses 1–6), and 'Über einige Motive bei Baudelaire' ['On a Number of Motifs in Baudelaire'] (1939), in *Charles Baudelaire*, pp. 133–40. In making this argument Benjamin relies on Baudelaire, Bergson, Proust, Marx, surrealism, the history of nineteenth-century Paris, and a number of other sources. For a concise exegetical overview, see Howard Caygill, *Walter Benjamin: The Colour of Experience*, London, Routledge, 1998. The reality of the 'not yet' is a central feature in the work of Ernst Bloch, author of *Das Prinzip Hoffnung* [*The Principle of Hope*, 3 vols, 1954–9], 5th edn, Frankfurt, Suhrkamp, 1998.

hammers and bulldozers, but it is patently misleading to say that hammers and bulldozers brought down the Wall, even if this is as true as the fact that London has more inhabitants than Berlin at the moment. Historical reconstruction of actual events and still possible events is required. But the question is, with what kind of evidence, and with what kind of language? If one is going to get beyond approaches stuck between factual numbers of inhabitants and whimsical matters of individual taste, one needs a method that explains the real in terms of movement and process rather than as incarnations of a supposedly timeless human nature (fear, greed) or as mythologies of progress, legal impartiality, technological neutrality, decline, salvation, inevitability, etc. Hence rather than speculating about the possible differences between 'false' consciousness and 'true' consciousness, or between 'reactionary' or 'reformist' social action versus 'revolutionary' social action, critical theory, drawing on idealism, Baudelaire, Marx, Nietzsche, Freud, Benjamin and Adorno, attempts to develop criteria for assessing what is arbitrary and modifiable in relation to what presents itself as socio-historical objectivity and fact.[45] In order to do this adequately, the theory of correspondences needs to evolve towards a more systematic theory of constellations. Simmel's ideas on mutual interactive exchange and the drifting apart of subjective and objective culture provide a good starting point. The path from the cognitive content of aesthetics to critical theory passes by way of sociological theory and not, as is sometimes argued, by way of the detours of Western Marxism or postmodernism. The theory that there can be an ensemble of mediations without a central or foundational mediating subject finds its counterpart in Simmel's thesis that in modern societies there is objective social form, but no discernible collective form-giving source or legislative centre that generates forms and laws. Building on Baudelaire and anticipating systems theory, one could say that for Simmel, forms have their own extra-natural and extra-human life force or streams of life. The analogies with Hegel on objective spirit and with Marx on alienation stop at the point where Simmel retains an extra-subjective dimension to society, but dispenses with all recourse to discourses of re-appropriation. The originality of this approach becomes clearer if one bears in mind that in the formulation of epistemological arguments, Kant relies on a transcendental subject that is

---

[45]Though not all critical theories make explicit reference to this specific set of thinkers, their ideas nonetheless help form the broad matrix out of which critical theory continues to develop. Weber, Lukács and Freud are of course also key figures. For the Weberian legacy, see the articles contained in Asher Horowitz and Terry Maley (eds), *The Barbarism of Reason: Max Weber and the Twilight of Enlightenment*, Toronto, University of Toronto Press, 1994. On the impact of Freud and later Freudians such as Lacan, see Joel Whitebook, *Perversion and Utopia: A Study in Psychoanalysis and Critical Theory*, Cambridge, MIT Press, 1995.

subsequently humanized by Feuerbach, historicized by Dilthey, and grounded in labour by thinkers in the Marxist tradition. In Simmel's work, social form persists independently of human essence conceived in transcendental, humanist, class, or, to update the analysis, communicative terms. He does not pronounce judgements on possibly 'false' consciousness, 'reformist' practice, or the plausibility of arguments based on structure versus those based on agency. He aims instead to re-cast the relations between philosophy and sociology in an attempt to sketch the conditions of existence of a non-positivist objectivity that is neither idealist nor one-sidedly materialist.[46]

In the *Philosophy of Money* (1900) Simmel analyses the processes through which money, which initially functions as a means of exchange, takes on additional functions due to the various reciprocal interactive exchanges (*Wechselwirkungen*) that money sets in motion. In ideal-typical terms, the feudal system is legitimized by laws and traditions thought to have a divine origin above and a natural order on earth. Simmel submits that money facilitates a spatio-temporal separation between the feudal unity of individuals, the status they acquire at birth, and the particular plot of land where they are identified as lord, serf, or some intermediate figure in the fixed hierarchy of ranked positions. He then reminds readers that this *separation* has more to do with differentiation and de-naturalization than it does with *alienation* or even exploitation.[47] An economy based on the exchange of money and the

---

[46]Simmel's originality highlights the ambiguity of Marx's legacy as well as the sociological deficit in Adorno and the first generation of critical theory. Marx's theory of alienation can be regarded as a radicalized version of the natural right to property in a period where property has to a significant extent been converted into capital. According to this view, labouring humanity has collective rights to the alienated labour power it has sold to heteronomous class forces. Later Marx embraces the opposed view that people simply are bearers of economic relations. Whether or not one designates this volte-face as an epistemological shift is unimportant. What is clear, however, is that a class with nothing to lose but its chains is as problematic as faceless bearers of economic relations. Simmel is not at all hostile to historical materialism as an approach to explaining socio-historical change, but also sees that it cannot be made to answer normative and political demands for revolution. See Georg Simmel, *Die Philosophie des Geldes* [*The Philosophy of Money*] (1900), Frankfurt, Suhrkamp, 1989, chapter 1. Adorno badly underestimates Simmel's relevance for critical theory. One glaring example is provided by the disparaging comments he makes about Simmel in 'Henkel, Krug und frühe Erfahrung' ['Handle, Jug and early Experience'], in Theodor W. Adorno, *Noten zur Literatur* [*Notes on Literature*] (posthumously edited by Rolf Tiedemann), Frankfurt, Suhrkamp, 1974, pp. 556–66. Benjamin's reflections on the ways in which the differences between places become increasingly meaningless due to the socially mediated modification of distance is indirectly derived from Simmel's sociology of money and his ideas on the drifting apart of objective and subjective culture. Simmel offers a sociological alternative to alienation which stresses that inherent in the processes that alienate are differentiation processes that de-centralize. Given the appropriate juridical framework, the latter could actually enhance autonomy while streamlining bureaucracy.

[47]To say these elements are separated but not alienated is somewhat akin to saying that they are related but not identical, hence the task of the sociological theorist is to clarify the quality of

circulation of capital, labour power and commodities introduces a dynamic element that is not simply imposed by an emerging class of entrepreneurs or popularized by theological-philosophical notions about the natural rights of man and citizen. Just as dynamism and instability are not simple by-products of economic changes, economic changes are not reducible to increased social and geographical mobility. Simmel's attempt to enrich historical materialism focuses on the processes and institutions regulating acts of trade as specific instances of the exchange of values. This sets him apart from Nietzsche, Dilthey and, to a certain extent, Marx. He maintains that the result of trade is not merely a use value or exchange value in Marxist terms. Whereas Nietzsche employs the term value in psychological-aesthetic terms, and Dilthey uses it to try to explain cultural specificities, Simmel explains that a careful approach to exchange indicates that it creates a social value, that is, a third element brought into existence by the trading partners that neither could foresee. However, in contrast with Hegel, it is not this third instance which confers normative and juridical validity on the contract established between buyers and sellers. Without referring to Baudelaire, Simmel tries to provide what could be described as a consistently sociological account of the correspondences theory found in the *The Flowers of Evil.* He does this by tracing the movement of money and other phenomena that resist exact determination within a subject–object or humanity–nature framework, but are nonetheless palpably at work in shaping the micro and macro conditions that structure the way individuals think about autonomy and reason. While money has certainly played a major role in structuring the conditions of reason and autonomy in modern societies from the industrial revolution to the present, Simmel's thought raises questions about the alternatives to money in this regard.

One might say that if a reciprocal interactive exchange is dialectical to the extent that it mediates between trading partners, it is not a closed dialectic that is already certain about what mediates, and with what effect (and from a number of vantage points it can be argued that money and capital guarantee one specifically possible kind of flexibility within existing institutional arrangements). Hegel, for example, is confident that history mediates between subject and object; by extension, the modern state is that historically engendered political form that mediates between private and public spheres in ways that reconcile autonomy and community. Marx

---

the relation, while bearing in mind that a relation holds several terms without conflating them. Arguments about alienation tend to drift towards tautology as a result of the fact that alienation almost invariably denotes something that is alienated or estranged from itself. See Simmel, *Die Philosophie des Geldes* [*The Philosophy of Money*], pp. 55–8.

is similarly confident that labour power mediates between humanity and nature in accordance with historical stages of economic development, and believes too that a stateless society of spontaneous mediation is the likely result of the historical process once, that is, labour power can freely unfold and transform nature according to post-scarcity human design. Hegel thinks that he has refuted the social contract theorists by demonstrating that a valid contract between two trading partners presupposes a valid state. Thus while he defends the reality of third instances, it is a somewhat static and all-encompassing reality that constantly returns to its form-giving origins. This is evident in Hegelian–Marxist notions of the proletariat as subject–object of history and the fetishized agent of historical change. However historicized, idealism tends to make some kind of subject the measure of objective reality. In consequence, idealists tend to think of separation as a loss in need of repair, and the chance of thoroughly immanent thinking and theory is displaced by resurrected figures of transcendence (the state, the proletariat, the nation, etc., in much thinking that styles itself as post-idealist). If Hegel's thought seems to be suppler than empiricist, rationalist, and even Kantian philosophy, Simmel follows the decentring rhythms of de-naturalized social form considerably further than Hegel or Marx. This leads him to develop a model of exchange that points beyond tautological accounts of action based on self-interest. He thus develops ideas that can be elaborated into an outline of new mediations. It is in this regard that Simmel illuminates the movement of modernist aesthetic theory towards sociological critical theory in two ways. First, he points out that form exists as value objectified in market exchanges, but, he also explains that these exchanges are more than simply economic. This is exemplified by the development and changes in the structure of manners, gambling, fashion, competition, and the structure of aspirations in the broadest terms. These phenomena are in turn affected by the metamorphoses money undergoes (cash, capital, rent, credit, stocks, etc.). Secondly, he indicates that modernity is best interpreted as a polycentric overlapping and intersection of values and institutional forms, that is, of constellations, and that these configurations are not concentrated in foundations like the subject, state, history, proletariat, etc. Reality is dispersed in historically changing imbrications of subject, object, humanity, nature, reason, instinct and a variety of other protean factors. The state cannot mediate these constellations any more than a single social class (or its party-political representatives) can preside over and direct them. By 1989 this was painfully evident with regard to state socialism. There are indications to suggest that as the logic of systemic differentiation continues to unfold, however, parliamentary systems will soon be regarded as similarly unwieldy and ill-adapted to increased levels of complexity and contingency.[48]

Simmel agrees with Marx that capitalism is characterized by the existence of distinct social classes, each with its respective milieu or *habitus*. But he rejects the notion that one class can directly oppress another in any intelligible way. The problem with the base–superstructure model, like the reduction of history to class struggle, is that both visions imagine that a small number of people confront a large number of people in an arena of struggle over the same thing. In reductionist versions of Marxist–Leninist historical materialism, the struggle is mediated by a state that adjudicates in favour of the minority in at times open (fascist) and at times concealed (parliamentary-democratic) ways. While this tendency is most clear in the *Communist Manifesto*, where the state is pilloried as an executive committee for managing the affairs of the entire bourgeoisie, it is also discernible in the more nuanced historical pieces, such as the *Eighteenth Brumaire of Louis Bonaparte* and *The Civil War in France*. Marx introduces a sociological element to dialectical thinking that remains insufficiently theorized. He materializes the Hegelian concept of mediation, when in fact it is necessary to develop a pluralist theory of mediations, without which dialectical thinking remains residually idealist. Idealism in this context interprets the de-naturalization of feudal society as a process of simple humanization, as if there was a sliding scale between the purely natural and the perfectly human. Simmel anticipates later developments in critical theory and phenomenological ontology by analysing the idealist claim that humanity is part of nature but not reducible to it, and that there is more at work in the world and social relations than the natural or the human. He notes that this qualitative difference or surplus is not derived from a composite balance of their relative proportions, as if one could say, for example, that humans are 60 per cent natural, 20 per cent historical and 20 per cent social. A political leader like Lenin thinks in terms roughly analogous to such percentages when affirming that communism and the smashing of the state are twin projects because the state is a distributor of homogenous power units that distributes them unequally, or, as he also at times suggests, the state appears as the armed force three quarters of the way to the top of a power pyramid, where it protects the small number of people 'above' from the very much larger group of people 'below'. Here the demos is interpreted in class terms, with the proletariat tautologically identified as the most popular class of the people.[49]

---

[48]Simmel, *Die Philosophie des Geldes* [*The Philosophy of Money*], pp. 209–10; and *Soziologie* [*Sociology*] (1908), Frankfurt, 1992, pp. 723, 765–6.

[49]Lenin, 'The State and Revolution' (1917), in *Collected Works*, Moscow, Progress Publishers, 1975, chapter 3.

Employing the pyramid as a model of stratification is somewhat like interpreting class struggle as tug of war engaged on a vertical axis, with the 'higher' classes enjoying the backing of the state to pull the rope downhill, against the more numerous side of the 'lower' classes, waging an uphill battle against the privileged minority. If this were so, as Second and Third International rhetoric at times appears to suggest, workers could perhaps seize the state, occupy language and use it for their own purposes, and smash money. Whether conceived as pyramidal struggle or tug of war conflict over the same thing, naturalist metaphors tend to creep into dogmatically materialist explanatory models of the causes of conflict: power is often understood in physical terms as the equivalent of gravity, leverage and weight, while resistance is thought of in terms of friction, overturning, seizing, etc. It is suggested in this chapter that although such models aspire to be post-idealist, in important respects they are not idealist enough, and misconstrue political possibilities as a result. Simmel does not caricature social relations in terms of alienated, exploited, democratic majorities (whose natural interests drive them to socialism, but whose pragmatic necessities force them to settle for democracy until the party clarifies things) versus underhand, exploiting, anti-democratic minorities (whose natural interests drive them towards fascism, but whose pragmatic interests in stability compel them, albeit provisionally, to accept democracy). Since such schemata offer merely pyrrhic victories over Kant and Hegel, Simmel intimates that a modified form of idealism, articulated in conjunction with the asymmetrical dialectics of reciprocal interactive exchanges, is likely to provide a better methodology for social enquiry.[50]

On this reading one might be tempted to think that although Simmel raises important questions about philosophy and Marxism, his sociology lacks contemporary resonance. But in addition to posing the question about possible alternatives to money as a medium of communication, his ideas on the drifting apart of subjective and objective culture anticipate and in some ways point beyond the argument developed in the *Dialectic of Enlightenment*. For Simmel one of the most salient aspects of money is not so much that some people have more than others. Money disseminates unwritten lies about the way things are made and how they are made, and it is silent about the social relations money-based economies presuppose and reinforce. While Benjamin takes up the challenge of trying to make these untruths and ideologies readable, Simmel concentrates on the specific ways in which money initiates and perpetuates a separation of production from exchange and consumption in modern cities, thus attesting to a qualitative transformation in the texture

[50] Simmel, *Die Philosophie des Geldes* [*The Philosophy of Money*], pp. 209–10, 428, 449–51; and *Soziologie* [*Sociology*], pp. 665, 831–2.

of the social fabric in comparison with previous ways of living together and making collectively binding decisions. In commodity production objects lose their particularity, and, in a parallel development, places lose their specificity. This is clear in more recent sociology of everyday life focusing on phenomena that appear well after Simmel's period, such as shopping malls, supermarkets and other spatio-temporal locations that could almost literally be anywhere. Another way of saying this is that commodified objects and interchangeable places lose their objectivity and distinctiveness, thus effectuating a kind of Hegelian inversion from quality back to quantity that is indicative of a missed or only partially realized transition to new institutions. In the face of verifiable post-scarcity one can designate this development as regressive without engaging in the rhetoric of decay that one sometimes finds in the Frankfurt School.[51]

Within this matrix of ideas, values and institutions, money functions like an elastic form rendering possible the investment of an object or relation with an almost infinite range of subjective meanings and values. This neatly encapsulates Horkheimer and Adorno's argument, though without, however, the pathos of decline that characterizes their work at times. Simmel shows that money disperses the feudal unity of individual destiny, position at birth, and obligatory belonging to a caste-like stratum within a territorially circumscribed unit of space. Money breaks down the personal, naturalized forms of hierarchy and obedience that prevail under these conditions, and can thus be seen as autonomy-enhancing. Yet the subjectivization of value goes together with the privatization of experience, so that personal satisfaction, caught in a potentially limitless cycle of consummation–renewal–consummation, becomes the ultimate standard of quality. The criteria for a meaningful appreciation of quality become increasingly difficult to discern due to this privatization and the corresponding metamorphosis of the social bond. The pervasiveness of money-based instrumental relations decreases the capacity of isolated individuals to make reliable judgements about the unique qualities of objects, other people, or the distinguishing characteristics of particular places, and so can be seen as autonomy-negating. In anticipation of Benjamin's argument in the *Work of Art in the Age of Mechanical Reproduction* (1935), one could say that the phenomena in question lose their aura. But instead of acting on the decline of aura in order to launch a comprehensive critique of institutions still guided by auratic principles of

[51]On this and related issues see Edward W. Soja, *Postmodern Geographies: The Reassertion of Space in Critical Social Theory*, London, Verso, 1989; Edward S. Casey, *The Fate of Place: A Philosophical History*, Berkeley, University of California Press, 1997; and Henri Lefebvre, *La production de l'espace* [*The Production of Space*], Paris, Anthropos, 1974.

tradition and obedience, the objectively discernible capacity for enhanced autonomy remains for the most part frustrated by the absolute relativization of value, which, as this term suggests, ushers in an historically new kind of market-enforced dogmatism. The continuing relevance of this approach is clear: instead of simply re-articulating the *Dialectic of Enlightenment* and the theses of total administration and one-dimensionality, innovative critique needs to develop a sociology of privatization that avoids the dead-ends of outdated 'debates' about privatization versus nationalization. These remain locked within a framework assuming the validity of state sovereignty and the necessity of party-political management of authoritative decisions. Marx's argument that socially created wealth is privately appropriated remains relevant but not sufficient. The recent financial crises indicate that more work has to be done on the mechanisms through which privately created debts are falsely socialized in ways that amount to a privatization of the distribution of individual and collective responsibility. Although the ways these measures affect individual households are very different to the ways they affect private banks, government-backed banks, and corporations, international financial institutions continue to regard the debt phenomenon as a national problem that cuts across all distinctions related to the distribution of capital and access to participation in investment decisions.[52]

Simmel does not try to deduce changes in fashion, the succession of one art movement by another, or the professionalization of sport, etc., from changes in the economy or objective spirit, nor does he regard these changes as being unrelated. Benjamin and Lukács thus follow him in attempting to analyse cultural innovations as phenomena embedded in the economy, rather than trying to insist on the economy as the cause of diverse cultural, legal and political orientations. It has been seen that Simmel's interest for contemporary critical theory lies in his ability to combine montage and dialectical elements in constellations, and that the guiding principle of constellational thinking and research is that the mediations between micro and macro phenomena should be re-articulated in ways that redeem the importance of the micro moment without isolating it and distorting its relation with macro-level developments. Future theoretical endeavour cannot get stuck in attempts to draw attention to the dignity of de-objectified objects or restore the originality of a particular

---

[52]Simmel, *Die Philosophie des Geldes* [*The Philosophy of Money*], pp. 177–81; and 'Die Arbeitsteilung als Ursache für das Auseinandertreten der subjektiven und der objektiven Kultur' ['The Division of Labour as Cause of the Drifting Apart of Objective and Subjective Culture'] (1900), in *Schriften zur Soziologie*, ed. Heinz-Jürgen Dahme and Otthein Rammstedt, Frankfurt, Suhrkamp, 1983, pp. 95–128; Benjamin, 'Das Kunstwerk im Zeitalter der mechanischen Reproduzierbarkeit' ['The Work of Art in the Age of Mechanical Reproduction'], pp. 136–69.

city, as Benjamin sometimes seems to suggest is possible with his somewhat obscure ideas on language and naming.[53] If one considers this obscurity in conjunction with some of the more culturally pessimistic pronouncements of the *Dialectic of Enlightenment*, *Minima Moralia*, and other writings, it might seem justified to argue that there is an irreparable sociological deficit in critical theory that demands rectification with theories of communicative action, recognition, performance, care of the self, etc. But the validity of this charge is far from self-evidently valid. One might counter by observing that to the extent that these more recent theories neglect political economy, they suffer from a glaring critical deficit which is as unsatisfactory as the sociological deficit of the early Frankfurt School. It is no coincidence that the newer ideas are relatively anodyne and mainly appreciated in restricted academic circles.

The alternative between melancholic theory and mainstream academic theory is inadequate. Instead of opting for one of these, it is time to work on bridging the theoretical gap dividing critical evaluations of autonomy-negating and autonomy-enhancing processes, so that research on recoverable transitions ceases to seem forlorn or speculative. To begin this rapprochement, it will be helpful to examine a potentially fruitful contradiction between two verified tendencies discussed in this chapter. On the one hand, the subjectivization of value goes together with the privatization of experience and the relativization of quality. Within a contemporary context this means that previously endured natural scarcity is reintroduced in the guise of capitalist market forces and other measures deemed to offer individuals the only acceptable criteria of quality and choice. Individual freedom and choice thus appear to be the bedrock of legitimate law. Yet within a constellation largely defined by the private appropriation of publicly created wealth and the socialization of privately incurred debt, individual choice is patently ideological: since political control of such an economy supposedly is inevitably bureaucratic and authoritarian, 'we' simply have to dig in and eliminate the debt, which in the end is all of 'our' problem. In an imaginary dialogue on this point, the first generation of critical theorists and contemporary critics of the specifically neo-liberal instantiation of globalization may well have agreed: neo-liberal globalization proceeds on the basis of decisions taken in cumbersome, partially de-centred (private) and partially centralized authoritative (public) bodies such as the IMF, World Bank, EU Parliament, the White House and the Central Committee of the Chinese Communist Party. On the other hand, it has been seen that in modernity

[53]Benjamin, 'Über die Sprache überhaupt und über die Sprache des Menschen' [On Language in General and on the Language of Humans'], in *Angelus Novus* (now contained in the English volume of Benjamin's works entitled *Reflections*), pp. 9–26. For an in-depth study of Benjamin's ideas on language, see Winfried Menninghaus, *Walter Benjamins Theorie der Sprachmagie*, Frankfurt, Suhrkamp, 1980.

and late modernity it is possible to make aesthetically rational and politically democratic distinctions between art and kitsch, as well as between ideology and reason. This second tendency confronts market-dogma relativism with forms of non-instrumental reason that are part of the same differentiation processes that have detached the economy from unwieldy political control. The bank bail-outs and threats to Greece and other countries indicate that this detachment is far from complete, and far from anything remotely democratic. One of the challenges facing critical theory in the twenty-first century is to take up key questions of political economy, while also engaging with the findings of cultural criticism and cultural studies. Critical theory can begin to do this by developing socio-historical criteria relating to de-naturalization, differentiation, mediation, dialectics and form. In this way it can analyse processes and institutions that are demonstrably too formal or not formal enough, differentiated or not differentiated enough, etc., and to do so in a way that is neither plaintively normative nor speciously objective. Money continues to function as a de-centred, elastic social form guaranteeing rapid decision-making and deployment of resources and investment. But money cannot guarantee that the decision-making processes fulfil even minimum democratic standards of consultation, or that resources are not monopolized, or that investment is efficient according to analogously elastic criteria of necessity, possibility and creativity. The re-articulation of the theory of non-identity in the next chapter attempts to outline what such criteria might be in ways that are relevant for an analysis of political economy and an evaluation of different conceptions and practices of legitimacy.

3

Critical theory and mediated non-identity

In Chapter One it is observed that much mainstream political theory from the Reformation to the present is informed by the premise that if there was no unity at all between citizens and the state, political representation would be impossible, and, by extension, if there was identity between citizens and the state, representation would be superfluous. The recurrent argument across a broad spectrum of thinkers is that just as in subject–object relations, where absolute separation is as untenable as complete fusion, mediated unity accurately describes the relationship between citizens and the institutions of political authority aspiring to be post-feudal, secular and juridical: it is the condition and outcome of the processes that balance freedom and authority in a post-traditional world in a manner that is rational, predictable and transparent.[1] Among many liberal-democratic thinkers one encounters

[1]One should remember that there is still much theoretical and historical debate about what constitutes a state, as opposed to a loose conglomeration of corporate bodies, each with their own semi-private, semi-public legal status (church, nobility, courts, finance/taxation, military, bureaucracy, guild, university, etc.), and there is also continuing disagreement about when, exactly, states arise out of empires, manorial kingdoms and absolute monarchies. It could be argued, for example, that despite the epochal significance of the French Revolution, the events of 1848–51 mark a return to authoritarian executive power and the temporary interruption of state-building processes in modern France. It is relatively uncontroversial to maintain that this process only comes to a definitive close in the aftermath of the Franco-Prussian War and the consolidation of the Third Republic (still the longest lasting of the five, at the time of this writing). See Robert Gildea, *The Third Republic from 1870 to 1914*, London, Longman, 1988, chapter 1. It may seem to many observers that the price to pay for the early modern wave of political centralization required to enact the positivization of law and the erosion of differential status is extremely high; it can be summed up in Weber's assertion that the modern state is a monopoly on the legitimate use of force within a given territory, and certainly nothing remotely approximating a rational ideal made real in historically generated institutions. Chapters Four and Five of the present book investigate whether or not relaunching the project of Enlightenment might best be approached by initiating a second wave of egalitarian legal positivism, though

the argument that the inequalities that remain should be a reflection of differences in individual talent rather than arbitrary assignment to a fixed status in an ordered hierarchy. Bearing in mind the divergences stemming from distinct national legal traditions and territorial history, liberal democrats defend the view that inhabitants of modern societies should be free to live in accordance with laws and institutions that facilitate the meritocratic empowerment of what are assumed to be inherently autonomous individuals, and, by extension, empowerment should be enacted under conditions of maximum respect for and recognition of the greatest possible diversity of life projects. Attempts to palliate inequalities stemming from merit should stop well short of 'correcting' them, lest merit itself fall victim to illegitimate interference in citizens' lives, and in any case, such attempts should be kept to the bare necessary minimum required to maintain order.[2]

---

with the important caveat that egalitarianism will be more bureaucratic and instrumental the second time round unless it is enacted in decentralized and *social* constitutional forms (see Sciulli, *Theory of Societal Constitutionalism*, chapter 6). It will be suggested that making good on the emancipatory potential of differentiated social ensembles is not so much a question of pragmatically balancing meritocratic considerations of individual liberty with the need for egalitarian redistribution (the assumption is that social cleavages need to be 'healed' to preserve the stability of national communities, which inevitably result in appeals to 'buy French' or whatever the national 'community' in question may happen to be). The more pertinent issue, given the contemporary crisis of the welfare state and social democracy, is finding ways to promote feasible modes of individual autonomy that are no longer tied to stipulations of value for money based on considerations of 'what can be afforded'. Modern societies are evidently in need of more flexible and multi-entrance-point modes of integration than those suggested on the basis of payment in kind and generic representation presupposing mediated unity. In formal-political terms, representation is certainly about power sharing to some extent. But from a more sociological standpoint, it is also about less and more functional modes of adaptation to particular instances of contingency at specific historical junctions, and it concerns ways of integrating people without consigning them to fixed places or marginal roles. This is precisely the point where contingency and complexity may be able to foster non-oppressive modes of social integration, if, that is, contingency and complexity are not instrumentalized to generate precarious and inexpensive forms of employment. In this context it can be argued that the dialectic of Enlightenment thesis should cede to a series of investigations into what might be called the ambiguities of flexibility.

[2]In very broad terms, therefore, one can say that liberal-democratic Enlightenment requires that reason indicate the boundaries of legitimate state intervention and also that the claims of reason and legitimacy stop with the delineation of those coordinates. These points demarcate the epistemological and political limits beyond which reason becomes irrational and states become illegitimate. Legislation must acknowledge the limits of reason and restrict itself to legitimate intervention and enforcement of a form of law that is a neutral, purely formal means of adjudicating between competing conceptions of legitimacy. Such auto-limitation is the indispensable precondition for the establishment of the same freedom of all, and a fundamental precondition of the specifically juridical universality without which liberal democracy would lapse into pre- and post-liberal dogma. Liberals therefore claim to *know* the conditions of liberty for all, and to know this from a perspective that is *already* emancipated from illegitimate political intrusion. The only way to make this claim, however, is to separate knowledge from experience, since in reality it is

In anticipation of the critical theoretical perspective on these issues offered here, one might add that difference that translates directly into inequality rather than pluralist diversity must be considered evidence of insufficient differentiation and, therefore, an inability to translate liberal norms into institutional reality. There is some debate as to whether the dynamics of differentiation, inequality and political rights are to be explained in terms of structural limitations on democratic inclusion, incompetent decision-making by the governing coalition in question, or contingency. In any case, liberal-democratic governments must make sure that rationally mediated unity does not regress towards oppressive, that is, badly mediated unity of the kind that arises in authoritarian and antagonistic corporatist guises. In the authoritarian case, mediation deficits can result in a movement towards citizen–state fusion. This happens when the individual rights needed to realize personal conceptions of freedom are usurped by governments compelled to generate some sort of cohesion out of manifest inequality and other forms of conflict which, broadly following Hegel, one might designate as the mediated disunity between citizens and the institutions of government. If governments arrogate to themselves the privilege to decide what freedom is, they artificially engineer a return to unwieldy forms of quasi-feudal stability, realized through the vertically ordered hierarchies of the kind prevalent in the twentieth century under fascism and state socialism. This is harmful and unnecessary due to the fact that in liberal-democratic society, at least in principle, political stability and economic growth are achieved horizontally through the buying and selling of capital, property, labour power, ideas, information and many other instances of exchange. Since talents are distributed unequally according to innate differences, these attempts are akin to bureaucratic plans to meddle in the random distribution of intelligence and the spontaneous coordination of exchange through money and markets. In the anarchic corporatist case, mediation cedes to antagonistic negotiations between the different branches of government, between government, industry and other lobbies, between industry and education, etc., so that instead of becoming too strong and centripetal, as in the case of what one might call the creeping identity of individual and state, the bases of the state are undermined by centrifugal forces

---

not possible to determine what is knowable without already knowing what knowledge is, and that is inseparable from lived history, that is, experience. It is not uncommon for early modern liberal theorists to maintain that reason mediates between the a priori dimensions of knowledge and what is taken to be the *naturally legitimate* private sphere of marriage, property and exchange. In this case reason does not so much mediate as it conflates, that is, identifies, just as, by extension, appeals to the immediacy of experience against the abstraction of knowledge run the risk of uncritically conflating alternative subjectivities with whatever seems to run counter to liberal-democratic norms.

creeping towards ungovernability.[3] In order for modern liberal-democratic government to achieve the full potential of individual liberty in practice, in sum, a continuous battle has to be carried out on two fronts. It must be waged against government intervention in spheres and sub-systems that in theory can be self-governing according to the horizontal model of continuous exchange (against neo-feudal paternalism). But it must also safeguard against concessions to special privileges, idiosyncratic demands for independence of all kinds (local, regional, personal, etc.), and differential status (against neo-feudal particularism). Both paternalism and particularism predate the consistent positivization of law initiated across Western Europe with the imposition of the Napoleonic Code, and thus should no longer be necessary tools for the manufacture of order and consent. Liberal-democratic doctrine from its earliest articulations to the present is not always explicit about these suppositions, and the emphasis is of course different from thinker to thinker. In addition, Anglo-Scottish liberalism is informed by different theories of political economy and commercial society, French and North American liberalism are buttressed by an emphasis on republicanism, Central European liberalism has a marked philosophical orientation, etc. Despite these differences, however, one can discern a core of epistemological arguments relating to the limits of reason as these relate to the boundaries of legitimate state intervention in the economy and other areas of society and politics.[4]

There will be more to say below about the ambiguities inherent in a mode of mediation enacted on the basis of a condition that is then ostensibly reproduced as an outcome. There will also be more to say about the compositional arrangement of the elements forming a constellation of mediations that is meant to produce simultaneous unity and non-interference, and there will be observations to make about the quality of the unity in question. Although this dialectical characterization of post-Reformation political theory is particularly relevant to the idealism of Kant and Hegel that is subsequently developed by Marx and later thinkers in the Marxist tradition, it is also articulated in the social contract theorists' reflections on the fictitiously unanimous agreement

[3]The techniques involved in managing the unstable dynamics of *dirigisme* and un-governability are now often analysed by invoking the notion of governance and drawing on the work of Foucault. See Alan Hunt and Gary Wickham, *Foucault and Law: Towards a Sociology of Law as Governance*, London, Pluto, 1994. The idea that this relation can be 'managed' with the appropriate 'techniques' may be indicative of a tendency in this type of literature to overstate the centricity of power and the steering resources of governments (or, more anonymously, of discourses).

[4]For a more detailed discussion focusing on Kant, Simmel and Freud, see Darrow Schecter, 'Liberalism and the Limits of Knowledge and Freedom: On the Epistemological and Social Bases of Negative Liberty', *History of European Ideas*, 33 (2007), pp. 195–211.

guiding humanity's exit from the state of nature. With the notable exception of Rousseau, one finds recurring hypothetical consensus about the need to limit the scope of agreement, such that whatever consequences may affect individuals in practice as a result of compulsory non-interference, citizens have in principle agreed that the risks involved are part of the price of freedom: this is quite simply the price to pay for transforming licence in the state of nature into juridical freedom. That is, one has consented to and is responsible for one's own problems and misfortunes, because one has agreed to the terms stipulating what living together according to just principles entails; natural inequality of talent is preserved and given a solid framework through politically equal rights. These are formal rights, however, the bounds of which must be respected, lest a violation of formalism be allowed to stifle independent initiative, and thereby compromise juridical neutrality. It is worth recalling that for most of the social contract theorists, the legitimacy of post-feudal government is not directly founded on a calculation of interest. It is founded instead on the supposedly spontaneous and collective decision made by people with uncertain powers in the state of nature to become citizens with secure rights in civil society. The key texts of Hobbes, Locke, Rousseau, Kant and Rawls indicate that arguments about political authority presuming mediated unity as a universally valid starting point as well as a legitimate outcome can be made in terms of the notion of a social contract, and that the social contract, in turn, can be articulated in authoritarian-conservative, liberal constitutional, authoritarian republican, liberal-democratic and welfare democratic frameworks. Despite the somewhat discrepant views of the thinkers in question as regards the conditions under which civil disobedience might be justified, they all posit a moment of supra-contractual agreement that makes the contractual moment of understanding possible, or, to put it slightly differently, they rely on a supra-contractual moment of agreement to guide the exit from a pre-contractual, pre-social condition.[5]

Civil society and the state are synonymous until Hegel and Marx abandon the state of nature construct in favour of their respective theories of history as a series of simultaneously diachronic and synchronic processes. In their writings, the politics of mediated unity is articulated in more straightforwardly dialectical terms than is the case with the social contract theorists. Albeit for

---

[5]Dante Germino, *Machiavelli to Marx: Western Political Thought*, Chicago, University of Chicago Press, 1972, chapters 4–7. Epistemological critique which is also social critique is obliged to deconstruct the anthropological and naturalist assumptions in social contract thinking from its earliest articulations to the present. One of several reasons why Hegel remains relevant to critical theory in the twenty-first century is that he has an acute ability to deconstruct supposedly supra-contractual moments of agreement and other fictions enlisted to give political obligation atomist foundations.

different reasons, Hegel and Marx think that history can be understood as the movement from unmediated unity (the undifferentiated unity of the family in the *Philosophy of Right*, corresponding to rudimentary classlessness in Marx's account of early human society), to mediated disunity (civil society in Hegel's text of 1821, corresponding to caste and subsequently more complex class-based stratification), and from there to mediated unity between humanity and nature in the Hegelian state and the arrival of social relations one can designate as complex classlessness in Marx. While the Hegelian state is mind objectified, complex classlessness characterizes a society in which the transformation of nature through labour ceases to be a barometer of natural scarcity and the rigid hierarchies required to turn scarcity into the basis of subsistence. Labour power released from the strictures of wage labour becomes the basis of un-coerced agreement, whereby agreement does not mean romantic fusion in which mediation gives way to traditional organic unity. Marx intimates that once the trajectory from scarcity to subsistence is carried through to abundance, there will no longer be any objective reason why a rigid division of labour must be maintained, and no objective reason why executive and administrative personnel cannot be subjected to citizen recall on demand. At this point in human history it is reasonable to expect that production becomes spontaneous, sensual and creative, and that politics can be integrated into daily life to such an extent that its formerly repressive and military dimensions gradually wither away. Consensual is to be understood in this context in the pluralist sense of qualitatively increased transparency as regards the grounds of disagreement, and does not mean that disagreement disappears in favour of unanimity or passive withdrawal from public affairs.[6]

One may thus question Arendt's thesis that traditional political theory begins with Plato and Aristotle, and ends with Marx. It can be argued that Marx criticizes political theory with objections that do not break radically with its traditional assumptions. Marx's relation with the history of political thought is in any case more complex than Arendt suggests.[7] These issues will be

---

[6]Marx, *The German Ideology*, pp. 196–7, the *Manifesto of the Communist Party* (with Friedrich Engels), p. 491, the *Critique of the Gotha Programme*, pp. 537–8, and *The Civil War in France*, pp. 632–4, in *The Marx-Engels Reader*, ed. by Robert Tucker, New York, Norton, 1972. There is a tendency to exaggerate the potentially apolitical implications of Marx's notion in the *German Ideology* that in communist society people will hunt in the morning, fish in the afternoons, and exercise their critical faculties in the evenings. A cursory look at *The Civil War in France* and other writings offers a more republican vision.

[7]Arendt, 'Tradition and the Modern Age', in *Between Past and Future: Eight Exercises in Political Thought*, London, Penguin, 1954, p. 17. Rather than constituting a flaw in his theorizing, one might explain Marx's position within the tradition as the logical consequence of his analytical commitment to immanent critique. Immanent critique is epistemologically preferable to ahistorical, abstract speculation about human nature and forms of government appropriate for it.

discussed in more detail in what follows. The first part of this chapter poses a series of questions about the ways in which the concept of mediated unity functions in much liberal-democratic, Hegelian–Marxist, and some recent and contemporary social theorizing about politics and legitimacy.[8] The second part goes on to explain how and why, carrying on from the discussion of the epistemological modernism of Baudelaire, Benjamin and Simmel in the previous chapter, contemporary critical theory defends the explanatory power of the concept of mediated non-identity against the explanatory deficits inherent in the concepts of mediated unity and unmediated non-identity.[9] It will be seen that there are very good reasons to retain a sociological methodology grounded in dialectics and mediation, and indeed, the dialectical concept of mediated unity is central, if not always explicit, in much liberal-democratic, Hegelian–Marxist, and contemporary thought, that is, in almost all political thinking in general. It will be seen further that a consistently critical approach to normative questions must dissociate every analysis of the reality of mediation in philosophy, art, politics, aesthetics, law, etc., from the presumption of unified essences.

Mediated unity between liberal abstraction and populist mobilization

The liberal-democratic version of mediated unity alluded to above is usually articulated in conjunction with a defence of negative liberty and of

---

But immanent critique runs the risk of becoming historicist and conformist if it is not tempered by a hermeneutic of the 'not yet' or the 'not fully actualized'. See the 'Introduction' to Theodor W. Adorno, *Zur Metakritik der Erkenntnistheorie* (strangely translated into English as *Against Epistemology*, written in exile in Oxford during 1934–7), Frankfurt, Suhrkamp, 1990, and pp. 106–7 below.

[8]Reasons of space will limit the length of the discussion on contemporary thought. But it is clear that much of this theorizing is indebted to Hegelian notions of recognition and/or Marxist or post-Marxist accounts of collective agency presupposing a mediated unity between 'the people', laws, governments and states or, as it sometimes turns out, as indicative of an emerging unity between the alienated people of international, stateless communities in search of radically cosmopolitan political form. Negri and Hardt's *Multitude* offers a convincing case in point.

[9]For two of many examples see Hauke Brunkhorst, *Critical Theory of Legal Revolutions: Evolutionary Perspectives*, New York, Continuum, forthcoming in 2013, in the same series as the present book, and Andreas Fischer-Lescano and Gunther Teubner, *Regime-Kollisionen: Zur Fragmentierung des globalen Rechts*, Frankfurt, Suhrkamp, 2006. See also Andreas Fischer-Lescano, 'La théorie des systèmes comme théorie critique', *Droit et Société*, 76 (2010), pp. 645–65. A similar caveat to the one invoked in the previous footnote is relevant here as well: reasons of space will limit the discussion of instances of non-mediated non-identity. In the conclusion to this chapter Heidegger will be briefly looked at as an emblematic advocate of this current of thought, which is often associated with notions of radical alterity.

representative as opposed to direct government. The advocacy of negative liberty and representative government is reinforced by the conviction that in modern industrial societies, commercial republics tend to be more peaceful than the political republics of antiquity, such as Athens, and also tend to be more viable than Renaissance political republics, such as Machiavelli's Florence. This belief is evident in the writings of Benjamin Constant and in a number of the Scottish Enlightenment thinkers, whose works had a notable influence on Hegel's conception of civil society. In other words, these thinkers advocate trade as a response to the problem of post-metaphysical order and of horizontally structured authority, and not, in the first instance, as a natural right to acquisition.[10] Hegel neither celebrates the supposed virtues of exchange, nor does he endorse a contractual vision of liberty. But he does share a number of the preoccupations of some British and French liberals regarding the feasibility of republican government under conditions of incipient industrialization. Hegel suspects that if stability and rational authority will not be generated spontaneously by commerce, they are equally unlikely to result from an artificially resurrected version of Athenian democracy that has been foisted upon the vast majority of citizens residing in large modern states, whose primary concern is realizing their personal vision of autonomy rather than achieving intensive political community with others. This is why he thinks that the post-feudal aspiration to participation is best addressed by the associations of civil society, whereas government, for the most part, should be left to the universal class of civil servants cooperating with representatives of the agricultural and business classes.[11] In 'On the Liberty of the Ancients Compared to that of the Moderns' (1819), Constant evokes Montesquieu and anticipates the mature Hegel by affirming that the direct government of the ancient states and some of the Renaissance Republics praised by Machiavelli is no longer possible, and not even desirable in a number of significant ways.

---

[10]In his well-known essay, 'The two Concepts of Liberty', Isaiah Berlin distinguishes between negative liberty (individual liberty as non-infringement, or freedom from impediment), and positive liberty (communal freedom or freedom to realize specific instantiations of the good life). While negative liberty is closely associated with liberalism and liberal democracy, positive liberty is linked with republicanism and different varieties of communitarianism. See Isaiah Berlin, 'Two Concepts of Liberty', in Henry Hardy and Roger Hausheer (eds), *Isaiah Berlin: The Proper Study of Mankind*, London, Pimlico, 1998, pp. 191–242. The essay is Berlin's inaugural address as Chichele Professor of Social and Political Theory at Oxford University, delivered on 31 October 1958, and originally published by the Clarendon Press in Oxford in the same year.

[11]Hegel, *Grundlinien der Philosophie des Rechts* [*The Philosophy of Right*] (1821), paragraphs 295–7. Hence it is mistaken to label Hegel a liberal, conservative, elitist or theorist of organic political community. He is really an early thinker of differentiation who has too much confidence in the ability of the state to mediate dysfunctional conflict between social systems. See Darrow Schecter, 'Unity, Identity and Difference: Reflections on Hegel's Dialectics and Negative Dialectics', *History of Political Thought*, 33 (2012), pp. 258–79.

It is no longer possible due to the implausibility of Rousseau's insistence that a people is not democratically sovereign unless its legislature is in constant session, and unless the people enjoy conditions of general socio-economic equality and interpersonal familiarity. Constant remarks that modern societies are too complex to admit of any such degree of cultural homogeneity or political unity. However different their respective political orientations and views of the state may be, Hegel and Constant implicitly agree that Rousseau is probably the last person seriously to consider the identity of citizen and state to be a precondition of genuine democratic legitimacy. Against Rousseau's republican vision of unmediated unity between citizen and state they propose their more attenuated versions of mediated unity.[12]

Like Hegel, Constant was forced to reflect on the long-term implications of the Terror during the French Revolution.[13] For both thinkers the theoretical excesses of Rousseau are reproduced in the real atrocities committed by the Committee of Public Safety. The violence of the French case raises a number of questions about the prospects for the general application of the principles of the Glorious Revolution to wider contexts. The difficulties involved in assessing these prospects stem in part from the evident reality that the Glorious Revolution itself was not without ambiguity. While Locke is happy to declare that sovereignty resides with the people, Milton is wary of the possibility of populist and demagogic distortions of popular sovereignty by Presbyterians, Catholics, dogmatic republicans and others he considers to be intriguers. These more cautious thinkers of early liberalism are more likely to temper their support for popular sovereignty with a defence of inheritance, freedom of conscience, and civil rights calling for absolutely minimal interference in the life of each adult citizen. It is possible that a fairly robust culture of post-feudal toleration and dissent is somewhat peculiar to states like Holland and Britain, where the transition from absolute monarchy to constitutional monarchy is achieved without major upheavals.[14] Whether in revolutionary France or later, in Germany immediately following World War I and during the Weimar Republic, the transition from traditional authoritarian monarchy (*Obrigkeitsstaat*) to republican democracy elsewhere

[12]Constant, 'De la liberté des anciens comparée a celle des modernes' ['On the Liberty of the Ancients compared to that of the Moderns'] (1819), reprinted in *Benjamin Constant: Ecrits politiques*, ed. by Marcel Gauchet, Paris, Gallimard, 1997, pp. 591–619.

[13]See in particular paragraphs 590–2 of Hegel's *Phenomenology of Spirit* (chapter 6, part B, section III).

[14]Richard Ashcroft, 'Locke's Political Philosophy', in Vere Chappell (ed.), *The Cambridge Companion to Locke*, Cambridge, Cambridge University Press, 1994, pp. 226–51. One would not want to overstate the point, however, given the fate of Charles I in Britain. See J. P. Kenyon, *Stuart England*, London, Penguin, 1978, chapters 1–5.

was considerably more abrupt and dramatic. In these cases, the principle of popular sovereignty is no longer the negative articulation of the aspiration to non-conformist freedom from Absolutism and becomes, instead, a positive affirmation of the will of the mobilized people, incarnated in the state. From the French events onwards, liberalism in Britain and well beyond divides along lines defined by conservative defenders of cultural particularity, traditional rights and inheritance, such as Burke, and the ostensibly more democratic proponents of abstract, universal rights of citizenship, such as Paine. In the aftermath of the Terror, Constant and Tocqueville come to accept the broad lines of the argument outlined in Burke's *Reflections on the Revolution in France* (1790). But the French thinkers are compelled to develop ideas appropriate for a situation in which neither the monarchy, nor the House of Lords, nor the church could be called upon to restrain the people's supposed appetite for redistribution and revenge, or what one might call the vindictive will of the people. This probably appeared all the more urgent in view of the fact that the events of 1792–4 seemed to suggest that Burke's sobriety was more accurate than Paine's optimism.[15]

Somehow the modern revolutions championing individual rights and popular or parliamentary sovereignty needed an ongoing series of consolidating sequels. Otherwise, the states that were brought about to create a stable set of individual and collective rights might re-appropriate what they had been called on to enact against the vagaries of vertically structured feudal authority.[16] Here one notes a remarkable prescience in early liberal thought that is subsequently echoed in Marx's *Eighteenth Brumaire*, and then verified as historical reality in the 1920s and 1930s: the post-feudal state necessary to establish (falteringly) generalized rights of franchise and freedom of expression is unstable, for the most part, and beset with latent authoritarian tendencies. These become manifest in periods of economic and political crisis, though the particular state form eventually assumed in each crisis differs, depending on a broad range of institutional dynamics, including the cycles of the world economy at each juncture in question. There are a number of distinctions to be made between state-socialist and fascist practice in these areas, and there are also differences between state-socialist and fascist regimes in different countries at distinct historical moments. The general point is that state-socialist and fascist governments attempt to compensate for the limited

---

[15]For a dissenting and staunchly republican interpretation of the events of 1789–93, see Jules Michelet, *Histoire de la révolution française* [*History of the French Revolution*] (1847), Vol. I, Paris, Gallimard, 1952, chapter 3.

[16]Edmund Burke, *Reflections on the Revolution in France* (1790), Oxford, Oxford University Press, 1993, pp. 158–63; Raymond Aron, *Les étapes de la pensée sociologique* [*Main Currents in Sociological Thought*], Paris, Gallimard, 1967, pp. 240–51.

steering possibilities offered by the legal form of legitimacy institutionalized in most liberal democracies, which tends uneasily to vacillate between normative allegiance to natural law and general enforcement of positive law. While one might associate the idea of permanent revolution with thinkers in the Marxist tradition such as Trotsky, it is nonetheless clear that liberal-democratic governments are obliged to organize a constant watch against what is referred to above as the creeping identity of individual and state, while also guarding against creeping ungovernability.[17] State socialism and fascism tend quickly to gravitate towards extra-legal forms of legitimacy that opt to steer the economy and polity with more transparently authoritarian means than those permitted by liberal-democratic constitutions. Steering of this kind provides concrete examples of highly flawed instances of mediation, and undoubtedly discredits state socialism and fascism as viable alternative state forms to legal forms of legitimacy. Nevertheless, a careful look at the causes for the need to steer in the first place yields insights into the discrete dialectical tensions simultaneously binding and separating the specifically liberal and the specifically democratic dimensions of liberal democracies. An analysis of these tensions can contribute to outlining the objective, socio-historical dialectics of institutional transformation discussed in Chapter One, and in the process, help redefine the relations between the analytical and normative components of critical theory.[18]

It would be naïve to imagine that state violence is not bound up with the different forms of conflict particular to industrial societies, such as those related to capital and class, which affect state-socialist, fascist and liberal-democratic legal systems in distinct ways. But many of the nuances involved are overlooked if one assumes mediated unity between citizens, laws and governments, and asks if capitalism is unstable because the state is in debt, or if the state is unstable because capitalism incurs debts. Simmel's sociology indicates why it would be equally naïve to think that the distribution of property and income is the unique source of social conflict in modern industrial societies, or that there could even be such a thing as 'a unique source' in

[17]Benjamin's analysis of these unstable dynamics is summarized in his essay, *Zur Kritik der Gewalt* [*On the Critique of Violence*] (1921), now in *Reflections*. The critique of everyday life associated with surrealism, Lefebvre, de Certeau and Situationism can be seen as a response to this constant watch. See Michael Sheringham, *Everyday Life: Theories and Practices from Surrealism to the Present*, Oxford, Oxford University Press, 2006.

[18]Marx, *The Eighteenth Brumaire of Louis Bonaparte*, in Robert Tucker (ed.), *The Marx-Engels Reader*, p. 607. The works of Otto Kirchheimer, Franz Neumann and Ingeborg Maus are very adept in this regard. See the essays by Kirchheimer and Neumann collected in William Scheuerman (ed.), *The Rule of Law under Siege: Selected Essays of Franz L. Neumann and Otto Kirchheimer*, Berkeley, University of California Press, 1996; and Maus, *Rechtstheorie und politische Theorie im Industriekapitalismus*, Munich, William Fink, 1986.

this regard: unique sources of conflict would only be plausible if there was such a thing as a unified foundation of authority that had somehow been split apart, or alienated from a social subject–object.[19] Political representation and the separation of powers should have been able, in theory, to operate on two fronts simultaneously, providing a break on executive power while also stipulating limits to the exercise of unmediated popular sovereignty at the point(s) of its post-feudal origins and fictional founding agreements. All of this had to be constitutionally organized at a symbolically prioritized political level ('the state'), highlighting the differences between liberal democracy and other modes of representation and mediation, while at the same time creating the bases for the adjudication of social conflict along multiple axes. It is becoming increasingly clear that multiplicity in this sense is incompatible with the juridical foundation ascribed to the supposedly self-governing demos. This is one good reason why the pluralist premises of systems theory must be taken seriously by critical theorists (see Chapter Five). The more immediate point is that the conflicts and forces in play rarely lend themselves to adjudication by way of traditional parliaments and parties. Recent events in Greece and the 'occupy' movements all over the world confirm the thesis that key liberal-democratic institutions are not particularly well suited to translating difference into pluralist diversity, that is, that under current arrangements, difference almost invariably means inequality. There can be little doubt that effective political representation is dismantled through coerced integration in state-socialist and fascist state forms, which leads to the centralization of power and correspondingly high levels of volatility. But generic political representation now seems an unlikely candidate to perform the task of non-instrumental, egalitarian mediation in liberal democracies. The situation has evolved to the extent that it currently seems moderate rather than radical to claim that only substantially reformed modes of production and mediation will have a good chance of stabilizing industrial and post-industrial societies in the twenty-first century. There are good theoretical and empirical grounds to suggest that this is the case.[20] These will now be looked at in turn.

At the theoretical level, the point about the relation between *fair mediation* of conflict and presupposed *mediated unity* is analogous to the one concerning unified foundations and fixation on ostensibly unique sources of

---

[19]Simmel, 'Soziologische Apriori' ['Sociological a priori'], in Otthein Rammstedt (ed.), *Georg Simmel: Individualismus der modernen Zeit*, Frankfurt, Suhrkamp, 2008a, pp. 290–302; 'Die ästhetische Quantität' ['Aesthetic Quantity'], in Ingo Meyer (ed.), *Georg Simmel: Jenseits der Schönheit*, Frankfurt, Suhrkamp, 2008b, pp. 248–57.

[20]For two cases in point, see Nick Dyer-Witherford, 'Net, Square, Everywhere', and Howard Caygill, 'Also Sprach Zapata: Philosophy and Resistance', *Radical Philosophy*, 171 (2012), pp. 2–6 and 19–26.

social conflict. Western Marxism would appear to be discredited for relying on a central axis of conflict in order to conjure up a monolithic, class-populist account of collective agency in response to the fundamental conflict between capital and labour. If the manifest absence of that fundamental axis seems to raise insoluble questions for Western Marxists and Marxist–Leninists, it also raises major questions for liberal democrats about the possibility of justice and legitimacy beyond punishment and minimal levels of redistribution. The fact that there is no unique source of conflict and no unified foundation of legitimate authority would seem to make liberalism preferable to all other forms of governance. In principle liberalism responds to these realities with the separation of powers and a consistent refusal to champion any particular conception of human flourishing. But it remains a form of governance all the same, indeed, what some might say is a more efficient and stable one than other known political forms of governance.[21] It offers palliative consolation for injustice in the guise of modest redistribution and the vigilant punishment of offenders, but it cannot legislate reconciliation or justice because of its own inconsistently respected injunction to refrain from a positively defined conception of liberty. In the manner of the Kantian thing-in-itself, substantive justice is there, but not for us. This is a telling point with regard to the dynamics of inclusion and exclusion particular to liberal democracies, especially at a time when palliative consolations are increasingly regarded as expensive luxuries from the perspective of overburdened states.[22] Liberal democracies rely, depending on national traditions and historical period, on variously formulated conceptions of mediated unity for the purposes of limited inclusion (without which legitimacy deficits become glaring); but they must simultaneously distance themselves from real political commitment to more than tenuous mediation because of their avowed aversion to determinate political commitments. This vaguely defined reliance is necessary in order to enforce one of the central juridical conditions of liberal-democratic stability, to wit, a

[21]In Weberian terms taken up by first-generation critical theory, one could say that legal–rational legitimation comes closer to establishing the conditions of truthful autonomy, in that it breaks with the personal forms of dependence associated with charismatic and traditional legitimation. But the legal–rational mode of mediation, of which liberal democracy is a key example, is also more anonymous and therefore more difficult to oppose than the other two modes. Here one sees parallels between the Frankfurt School and Foucault. See Thomas Lemke, *Foucault, Governmentality and Critique*, London, Paradigm, 2011, chapter 4.

[22]Hence it is sometimes affirmed that one should really talk about the political system as one of many systems, rather than in terms of the state, mediating between public and private. See Luhmann, *Die Politik der Gesellschaft* [*The Politics of Society*], Frankfurt, Suhrkamp, 2002, especially pp. 423–4 and 433–4. Luhmann was working on this (and many other manuscripts) at the time of his death in 1997. The 2002 version is edited by André Kieserling on the basis of an unfinished manuscript dating back to October 1996.

legal form of legitimacy protecting individual autonomy against all instances of what is deemed to be arbitrary state power. In other words, the possibility of more than formal inclusion is discarded as inherently authoritarian.[23]

In terms of ideal types, pure legality without regard to the legitimacy of the socio-economic content of the law is as politically risky as pure legitimacy unmediated by legal form. The former might be able to provide a detached, abstract framework for the production of a disciplined workforce and steady economic growth, but it cannot generate a legitimate democratic consensus, or secure the conditions required for rational political will formation. If the latter would be able by definition to secure very high levels of citizen support, it would be unsuited to the task of creating a docile workforce out of the same highly motivated and involved citizens, and as such, it is highly unlikely that it could sustain continuous growth or conditions propitious to what is likely to be regarded as opportunistically private or hostile foreign investment. Command, in various guises seen throughout the twentieth century and into our own, offers the undoubtedly wrong answer to what are important questions, such as: what principles should govern job sharing and income sharing? Liberal-democratic commercial republics and constitutional monarchies may have survived the dilemmas bound up with these questions through a combination of colonialism and periodic warfare followed by economic growth, Keynesian macro-economic management, and welfare provision. Yet few if any commercial republics can confidently rely on being able to secure any of these factors today. Moreover, the nation-state framework in which they initially appeared is not likely to play a stabilizing role in the world society that is now taking shape.

The point concerning the continuing relevance of the *Eighteenth Brumaire* is that liberal democracies claim to renounce explicitly normative political visions because these allegedly tend to force states to gravitate towards extra-legal neo-feudalism of the right, left or corporatist centre. Many of these states have nonetheless needed periodic recourse to crisis management techniques ranging from Louis Bonaparte's militarist demagoguery to the bank bail-outs of today. Bearing in mind that recourse to such negotiable means

[23]So while there was unanimity of political purpose in the state of nature or when temporarily donning a 'veil of ignorance', all subsequent unity of political purpose is regarded as incompatible with individual freedom. Although the concept of unity rightly alarms many people, it may be time to reconsider the Bauhaus notion that cooperation is the basis of genuine autonomy and independent thinking, rather than the other way round. If individualist autonomy is allowed to become the basis of cooperation, and votes are allocated according to the principle of political rewards for services rendered, then thoroughly instrumental socio-economic relations and commercialized art forms tend to prevail. See Victor Margolin, *The Struggle for Utopia: Rodchenko, Lissitsky, Moholy-Nagy*, Chicago, University of Chicago Press, 1997, chapters 2 and 4.

undermines the neutral status of the non-negotiable end of impartiality, liberal democracies have periodically had to embrace mediated unity in the form of varying degrees of populism, in desperate attempts to shore up legitimacy. Simultaneously, they have rejected mediated unity as too costly, thus paring down unity to a level approaching organized indifference. This dynamic unfolds according to the principle that more than minimal levels of inclusion/unity create educational, housing, health, energy, labour-market, etc., commitments and therefore costs that are comparable to the security risks created by less than minimum levels of inclusion. Managing such a dynamic can be likened to dealing with a permanent state of emergency. In theory, the mediated unity of citizens and the state is the condition for rational practices of representation, fair norms regulating conflict adjudication, and discursive political will formation beyond mere voting for candidates from different parties. Yet mediated unity also implies a metaphorical juridical proximity between citizens and their state that casts serious doubt on the feasibility of government and state-level indifference to the life plans of its citizens. One of the central problems is the discrepancy between hypothetical mediated unity, and the diverse legal and extra-legal means required to make legal systems mediate in the palpable absence of socio-economic and political unity, that is, without widespread equality, solidarity and other indicators of non-coerced integration that are incompatible with merely minimum levels of inclusion.

In other words, mediation processes cannot possibly mediate rationally if they are little more than an instrumental means for securing the legitimacy of imposed austerity and other ostensibly necessary sacrifices that quite obviously affect different individuals, age groups, social classes, geographical regions, genders, races, etc., differently: analysing this discrepancy is revealing as regards the difference between the actual practice of legal forms of legitimacy, and the possibility of legitimate forms of law. The contradictory and incoherent rules balancing the ideology of comprehensive inclusion in the demos with the reality of socially differentiated, multi-entrance point inclusion, often leave individuals without clear explanations for the precariousness of their lives. They might compensate for this uncertainty with confident affirmations about their free (even if poorly informed) choices, and deliberate (even if precipitate) decisions, in the belief that they are autonomous and not largely responding to external commands. Put too simply, for the moment, they may have internalized and individualized a range of issues that are not straightforwardly individual-subjective or internal-subjective, though the questions may appear in that light if the only alternatives seem to be collectivist, bureaucratic and foreign. This is not a matter of false consciousness: there is admittedly a fine line between the politics of collective learning from the *objective*, socio-historical dialectics of systemic differentiation and normative integration, that is, mediation which must possess some measure of non-ideological authority, on the one hand, and widespread submission to what are perceived or simply accepted as *external* commands, on the other.

Few, if any political parties are likely to draw attention to the choices and consequences implied by these markedly different approaches to understanding the mediated non-identity of individual consciousness and society. That is because the parties mediating between governments and citizens are, with few exceptions, trapped within a logic that is instrumental and centrist in two related senses that raise major questions about the fate of reason in any liberal democracy. First, each party is likely to assume that the state is a centre from which the fundamental conflict between individual freedom and social equality can be managed, and second, parties are obliged to follow the principle that centrist electoral strategies accommodate this apparently self-evident reality. Before returning to this point below, it might be observed that liberal-democratic rules are contradictory in a complex manner that make individuals seem incoherent, incompetent or simply at fault, while also equipping this particular form of governance with an economically liberal bail-out clause that says, 'we cannot afford this', and/or a democratically populist one that warns that 'you are threatened by internal enemies and external foreign elements'.[24] Liberal democracy may be the most elastic and supple of the heretofore known ostensibly democratic state forms, that is, it may be demonstrably more plural than Soviet socialist democracy or left- and right-wing authoritarian democracies, all of which, from a liberal vantage point, offer examples of extra-legal legitimacy committed to a determinate conception of the good in political terms. There is nonetheless an evident clash between the solidaristic cooperation required in advance to make fair mediation possible as an outcome, and insistence on the neutrality of juridical procedure and impartiality in the face of divergent conceptions of the good life. Hence to focus on the supposed clash between liberalism, which respects individual rights but is also complicit in the perpetuation of entrenched inequality, and democracy, which safeguards the sovereignty of the demos at the potential expense of the individual, is tantamount to resurrecting a chimerical central axis of conflict. But it is not altogether chimerical to the

---

[24]'We cannot afford this' and 'you are threatened by internal enemies and foreign elements' is well complemented by the retort on the part of big commercial firms offering products of dubious originality and quality that they are simply 'giving the people what they want'. Here one sees the affinities between critical social theory and Gramsci's ideas on the contradictions of common sense. For a detailed discussion, see Peter Ives, *Gramsci's Politics of Language: Engaging the Bakhtin Circle and the Frankfurt School*, Toronto, University of Toronto Press, 2004b; and Michel Foucault, *Sécurité, Territoire, Population: Cours au Collège de France*, 1977–8, Paris, Gallimard, 2004, pp. 31–56.

extent that conflict appears to arise as a technical-administrative matter of welfare and redistribution. Within this framework equality and justice are for the most part reduced to a question of 'sharing' the spoils of the national effort geared towards international competitiveness. An impasse often ensues at this juncture: the distinction between the naturally national and the legitimately democratic becomes blurred, thereby producing various instances of barely mediated identity, that is, populism, rather than mediated unity. Alternatively, the demand for social control is hijacked for the purposes of constructing a new political centre dominated by a state-socialist bureaucratic elite.[25]

The theoretical evidence just cited in support of the claim that only substantially reformed modes of production and mediation will be capable of stabilizing late industrial societies is complemented by empirical evidence, since it is clearly the case that fundamental changes in the social composition of the electorate have become manifest since representation was first introduced with considerable income and property qualifications.[26] Moreover, the constant recurrence of financial and budgetary crises in recent years raises doubts about the longer term viability of the liberal-democratic state form and about the future of the territorially defined nation-state in more general terms. These crises indicate that there are evident tensions within a juridical-political matrix shaped in part by the elective affinities between supply and demand models of interest aggregation, on the one hand, and models of legitimacy constructed according to contractual models, on the other. Demands for affordable housing and quality higher education, environmentally sound and efficient management of energy resources, etc., which are directed at the inadequacies inherent in the market provision of those 'goods', evidently exceed the supply of what can be provided by governments which, by liberal-democratic constitutional definition, are not meant to get too much in the way of 'letting markets work'. When markets do not work well enough, within the present institutional constellation, governments are required to make up the difference with the limited steering resources at their disposal. In the period following the 30 years of post-war growth and full employment, and especially after 1989–90, making up that difference seems an increasingly remote possibility for governments whose first political responsibility,

---

[25]A number of different possible ways beyond this impasse are outlined by Boaventura De Sousa Santos in *The Rise of the Global Left: The World Social Forum and Beyond*, 2006.

[26]Weber's analysis of the transformation of the social composition of the electorate and the corresponding evolution of the clubs of the early public sphere into mass political parties is one of the pioneering works of political sociology, and forms the background to the issues subsequently taken up by Benjamin, Schmitt, Neumann, Kirchheimer, Maus, Habermas and Luhmann. See Weber, *Politics as a Vocation* [*Politik als Beruf*] (1918), reprinted in H. H. Gerth and C. Wright Mills (eds), *From Max Weber*, New York, Scribner and Son, 1946.

regardless of their party political composition, is directed towards the banks and other financial institutions that have failed in recent times. Without the good functioning of these institutions and their investment, the centre referred to above threatens to collapse. One is nonetheless tempted to ask if it was ever there in real historical terms, as the first footnote to this chapter cautions.

But what alternative institutional constellations are currently available? Might there be one in which citizens' rights are not, figuratively speaking, returned to them with the label of private needs that must respect the ostensibly pre-political boundary that separates individual, private existence from public, juridical inclusion? That figurative threshold is currently designated as pre-political in liberal democracies; defenders of this arrangement can claim that it was the abolition of the threshold that set the state-socialist societies on the road to ruin. So should one redefine 'the political' to include 'welfare', or should the threshold be relocated, or is the very invocation of the normative concept of 'should be' simply irrelevant in view of the 'fact' that governments cannot indefinitely spend more than they have? Part of the problem is that recourse to the necessity of steering is bound up with supply and demand models of interest aggregation and contractual models of legitimacy. Political difficulties arise because what is aggregated is not undifferentiated interest, as such. It is an unstable montage of individual and group interest, a variety of instances of aspiration, inter-group solidarity and many-sided communication that is not commensurable with the technocratic rationality of government ministries and related bureaucratic chains of command. Much theoretical and empirical work still needs to be done in order to clarify these complex dynamics, but there are nonetheless good reasons for thinking that change is necessary and possible.

For a start, the apparent trade-off between affordability and inclusion is less straightforward than it may seem. A very different set of questions is raised as soon as it has been demonstrated that currently, the pursuit of different life-plans involving housing, transport, health, education, use of energy, etc. alternatives translates directly into inequality rather than pluralist diversity. Where empirical evidence in support of this theoretical claim can be supplied, it can be shown that mediated unity in practice tends to be rather less mediated, and rather more ideologically unified, than is generally suggested by most social scientific accounts of legitimacy and those ministerial documents pertaining to accountability that are accessible to the public. One is clearly confronted with insufficiently differentiated mediation processes that have destabilized the separation of powers and continue to do so, thus re-creating the need for authoritarian steering in conjunction with a range of constantly evolving bio-political modes of governance. This is a telling point, for while economic steering is rejected with the warning that this would stifle individual liberty, executive prerogative amounting to steering in matters of policing and public order is allegedly responsible political foresight. The *calculated risk* of ensuing instability and potential crisis is an integral part of an intricate system of governance in which elected politicians owe their political responsibility to failing financial institutions rather than to the project of facilitating the empowerment of autonomous individuals, and cannot be confused with *contingency* as such. Given substantially reformed socio-economic and political priorities and social rights, synchronized with the reality of unfolding differentiation, however, terms like efficiency, merit, etc., could be redefined beyond decisionist crisis management, early retirement plans and budgetary cuts. The historical and sociological availability of the enabling conditions for this transition to a redefinition of the key concepts of political economy is discussed in Chapter One in terms of the emergence of the public sphere and civil society, and considered in Chapter Two in terms of the qualified autonomy of aesthetic cognition vis-à-vis religious tradition and naturalized forms of hierarchy. This chapter indicates that efficiency and other concepts can now be revised to include, for example, the institutional facilitation of innovation with respect to reconciling environmental resource management with feasible economies of scale. The implication is that the potential normative gains of differentiation can only be redeemed with a corresponding move towards *qualitative* decentralized political decision-making, not, that is, towards privatization and/or de-regulation, which one can liken to quantitative decentralization. Addressing the choices involved requires an assessment of alternative constellations and new mediations. It is certainly not addressed by complacently writing off mediation as a barrier to the unity of theory and practice that is overcome by universal social classes or vanguard parties. Nor is it addressed by insisting that decentralized mediation in theory is paternalist intervention in practice that deprives individuals of the autonomy to make the relevant decisions for themselves. With few exceptions, liberal democracies do not adjudicate between various conceptions of a good life without prejudice, nor do they enforce respect of the (universal) right before the (personal, arbitrary) good. But it is wholly inadequate to respond by challenging liberal prejudice with non-liberal prejudice, or by exalting more or less arbitrary conceptions of the good life because of the inconsistencies of what is currently presented as consistently legal form and equal consideration of all conceptions of the good. Critical theory remains committed to immanent critique and non-dogmatic objectivity. It therefore does not abandon the Enlightenment ideal of a rational society free of prejudice, obscurantism, and the arbitrary exercise of power. It seeks to analyse how reason, obscurantism and the arbitrary exercise of power actually function in liberal-democratic and post-liberal-democratic societies, and it seeks to investigate the ways in which populism and hegemony tend to undermine democracy.[27]

The examples of housing, education, health, transport and energy could easily be extended to include many other fields in which it is patently ideological to construe the citizen as a private consumer of personal goods. Given the socio-economic potential made possible by advanced industrial economies, it is evidently the case that a formally consistent practice of inclusion of the entire demos – without which a glaring democratic deficit emerges on juridical rather than on welfare grounds – would also have to be a differentiated one which recognizes demographic differences in respect of population density, average age of citizens, and regional history with regard to climate, energy and other natural and synthetic resources, migration patterns, etc. One fruitful avenue of research may be opened up by examining the increasing incommensurability of social conflict and communication, on the one hand, and the long-standing institutions of political representation, interest aggregation, and political will formation emerging from the Glorious and French Revolutions, on the other. To anticipate what follows in the second part of this chapter, it can be noted here that incommensurable does not mean unrelated or altogether separate, but conveys instead part of what is meant by the term mediated non-identity. The discrepancy between social reality and political representation becomes acutely problematic when there is no longer enough overlap between them to characterize that relation plausibly as one of mediated unity. There are three related observations to make in this regard. For a start, it is questionable if this metaphorical overlap really existed for substantial periods in the life of any modern state, and it is highly doubtful that it ever existed at all under conditions of mass democracy. This means that the central premise underlying prevalent notions of democratic representation has rarely been operative in real historical terms.[28] Second, the metaphor itself relies on the notion of an organizational force capable of channelling social values and conflicts towards a political centre which is empowered to mediate, adjudicate, redistribute, etc. Third, and crucially, it is this imaginary centre that is still being called

[27]Brunkhorst's *Critical Theory of Legal Revolutions: Evolutionary Perspectives*, 2013, makes this argument in convincing terms, as does Werner Bonefeld in *Critical Theory and the Critique of Political Economy: On the Subversion and Negative Reason*, also forthcoming in the series.

[28]See Chris Thornhill, *A Sociology of Constitutions: Constitutions and State Legitimacy in Historical-Sociological Perspective*, chapters 3–5; and Chris Thornhill, 'Sociological Enlightenments and the Sociology of Political Philosophy', *Revue Internationale de Philosophie*, 1 (2012), pp. 55–83. Also see Jean Clam, *Was heißt, sich an Differenz statt an Identität orientieren: Zur De-ontologisierung in Philosophie and Sozialwissenschaft*, Constance, UVK, 2002, pp. 32–4; and Jean Clam, *Aperceptions du présent: Théorie d'un aujourd'hui par-delà la détresse*, Paris, Ganse Arts et Lettres, 2010.

upon to re-present and re-unify what is assumed to have been an originally unified presence, that is, the sovereign people as the foundation of the state. The beginnings of a realistically alternative, de-centred perspective on legality and legitimacy that are tentatively sketched here can yield a far more incisive analysis of the apparent trade-off between affordability and inclusion than the usual focus on the 'contradictions' between capitalism and democracy. The fact that power and authority are much more protean and discontinuous than foundational accounts maintain helps explain why social democracy is facing such a profound period of crisis and transformation. But it also indicates why some of the potential solutions to the problems of overburdened states and apathetic electorates are likely to be decentred and post-foundational, though not relativist and postmodern. As a consequence, the solutions envisaged will have to break decisively with the political anthropology of left, right and centrist democratic essentialism. Humanist essentialism and socio-historical complexity have for the most part coexisted to the detriment of the latter in terms of standard practices of political representation. By the time of this writing, complexity has seemingly developed to such an extent that it is demanding political change, but it is unclear, as yet, what form change will assume, that is, whether authority will be devolved to an increasingly politically mature and self-managing citizenry, with all that this entails in terms of policy innovation at a number of levels, or whether there will be a re-centralizing, folkloristic reaction. This raises the question concerning the likely alternatives and their respective consequences for the project of post-scarcity autonomy.[29]

To regard relations between polity and economy as somehow contradictory is to posit the existence of a fictitious centre – either in the existing state or in the one that is meant to be coming after the revolution – and endowing it with the obligation and capacity to resolve the imbalance between socio-economic inequality and political equality, as if there was some kind of continuum between inequalities in some spheres and the more fundamental, overarching equality of citizenship. These observations are not put forward as part of an argument in favour of 'free' markets instead of command planning. Nor do they constitute an argument in favour of the commune as 'the political form at last discovered to work out the economic emancipation of labour', as Marx put it in relation to the Paris Commune. The real argument is not so much about generic juxtapositions like capitalism, which is 'run' by a minority,

[29]See, for example, the different scenarios envisaged by *The Invisible Committee* in *The Coming Insurrection*, Los Angeles, Semiotext(e), 2009, and by the different contributors to Alessio Lunghi and Seth Wheeler (eds), *Occupy Everything! Reflections on why it's kicking off everywhere*, New York, Minor Compositions, 2012.

versus democracy, which is 'run' by the majority, nor is it about related arguments about the extent to which expertly trained minorities are needed to run things. It has more to do with notions of undifferentiated inclusion reliant on a chimerical central axis which presupposes and produces mediated unity, and which can be imagined in liberal-democratic, social-democratic and communist terms (and the different versions of natural rights implied by each), versus a transition to more sociologically sophisticated practices of inclusion with qualitatively enhanced legitimacy. If such a transition can be initiated, one can anticipate forms of integration that are sensitive to the non-identity of identity and difference; without this sensitivity, autonomy is likely to be more about damage limitation and self-preservation than about affirmation. Instead of presupposing a central foundation or human nature, the juridical principle of differentiated inclusion, like the social philosophical stimulus to think mediated non-identity, retains the dialectics of mediation. But it does this without forcing the discrete, mediated elements of the dialectic into the identity (coerced, oppressive unity) towards which mediated unity tends in practice. This kind of dialectic implies, among other things, diverse kinds of communication with uncertain outcomes, about which more will be said in due course. In conclusion of this section of the chapter it can be added that steady growth, full employment and steadily rising wages did much to forestall systemic crises until the early 1970s.[30] During this period, consistent trade union involvement in policy decisions as well as Cold War politics provided further stabilizing influences into the early 1990s. But we are now clearly in a period requiring new thinking about constellations and the possibilities for re-structuring interactive reciprocal exchange that can reach beyond the simplified rubrics implied by political republics, commercial republics, welfare states, the withering away of the state, the multitude or 'the event'.

Towards a sociological dialectics of non-identity

Liberal-democratic thinkers across national boundaries and historical epochs tend to proceed on the hypothetical basis that all human beings are born

---

[30]Habermas initially diagnoses these dynamics in the early 1970s as part of a process of simultaneous depoliticization and re-politicization. His argument at that juncture is that the corporatist welfare state depoliticizes to the extent that Keynesian redistributive measures 'buy' political legitimacy by blunting social conflict. But this only serves to politicize the situation by creating demands for more government intervention and planning in socio-economic spheres that have been differentiated from the polity with the rise of the modern state. See his *Legitimationsprobleme im Spätkapitalismus* [*Legitimation Crisis*], Frankfurt, Suhrkamp, 1973, and available in English by the Beacon Press, Boston, 1975.

free and equal, and that they have a right to retain their innate freedom and equality. Hence one may ask: what principal institution or set of institutions do inherently free people have an obligation to obey, if any? The standard liberal response is that they owe a qualified allegiance to those institutions that guarantee their freedom and security, that is, to those that protect their most basic natural rights. To return to the reflections at the start of this chapter, the question of rights is often thought of in conjunction with a number of suppositions about the kind of unity needed to make the re-presentation of unity possible. It has been seen that traditionally conceived representation offers a form of mediation that does not so much mediate as search for means tautologically to reiterate, integrate and command, especially if mediation and representation are conceived in terms of monolithic foundations such as 'the individual', 'the people' or 'the nation'. A critical theory of mediated non-identity can begin by pointing out the anthropological assumptions underlying liberal and democratic conceptions of mediated unity. Within the terms of such discourses it is often posited that humanity is part of nature and subject to natural forces due to mortality and a variety of other factors that for the most part have to do with need and mechanical/biological causality beyond human control. Gravity, environmental realities and sheer chance therefore place limits on human autonomy. But humanity is not identical to nature or completely subordinate to natural forces. To varying extents, reason embedded in law and other institutions can be enlisted in order to enable citizens to transcend need in the guise of poverty and resist arbitrariness in the guise of authoritarian government. As the examples mortality and reason indicate, and as the word 'extents' suggests, there is a great deal at epistemological and political stake depending on what kind of dialectic one invokes to explain how humanity might rise above the necessities of the life cycle without becoming completely detached from nature. The account of qualified transcendence of necessity one defends decisively shapes the theory and practice of freedom and politics that one is likely to endorse. Needless to say, individuals and classes pitted against each other in a bitter struggle for survival are likely to reproduce the highly limited forms of transcendence particular to archaic, relatively simple social ensembles, in which the struggle for survival demands a clear chain of command, and conflict with other communities may well seem inevitable.[31]

[31]Stated in these terms, there seem to be good reasons for critical theorists to continue to articulate the concerns of sociology, legal theory, political theory and political economy in conjunction with philosophy, much in the manner that this was undertaken by the first generation. But philosophy can only survive if it is more, so to speak, than merely an academic exercise or analytical dissection of purely epistemological questions, for these, in their turn, are likely to turn on un-decidable debates about the psychology of cognition, and indeed, some of the

Within liberal-democratic states it is an instance of transcendence rooted in what one might call a weak or formal dialectic in humanity–nature relations. Whether explicit reference is made to Kant or not, liberalism elaborates a theory of freedom broadly in accordance with the Kantian idea that humanity has access to formal, objective knowledge rather than access to absolute, metaphysical knowledge. The more directly political point is that the formal limits to cognition find their institutional counterpart in formal limits to freedom and a correspondingly limited transcendence of necessity. In order to prevent the critique of the metaphysical unity of subject and object from turning into a critique of the possibility of knowledge of any kind, subject and object had to be separated, in a first step, and then conditionally re-united by way of mediation, in a second. Much rides on the terms under which the conditions governing this separation and re-unification are set out. Adorno, for example, is highly ambivalent, in that while he would like to imagine the political possibilities opened up by post-metaphysical thinking and post-national community, he regards the idealist solution – which may well be the best on offer until further notice – to be fraught with difficulties. It may be that some kind of subject–object separation is a necessary condition of post-metaphysics, and for thinking the priority of the object as well as the socio-historical conditions of objectivity. It may also be the case that the idealist tradition approaches the issue with analytical stringency and dialectical flair. Unfortunately, however, subject–object dichotomy in Kant and many other philosophers prior to Hegel is achieved on the basis of a defensive, antagonistic subjectivity whose implicit resentment towards the schism predisposes subjectivity either towards instrumental manipulation of the surrounding world, or towards resigned passivity, or a volatile alternation between these two false positions. Adorno intimates that this defensive reaction orients thinking towards the identification of ostensible similarities for the purpose of ordered classification, thus neglecting parallels and non-sensual similarities that could be conducive to a mimetic approach to the ongoing constitution of objectivity. The possibility of rational reciprocity and other instances of open-ended communication in subject–object relations and beyond recedes before the reality of a rationalized drive towards self-preservation. As the term suggests, a rationalized drive can be understood as a thoroughly contrived synthesis of nature and reason that flourishes to the detriment of knowledge of objects and other people, and which is institutionalized as a series of threats,

---

debates within twentieth-century phenomenology would seem to bear this out. For an overview see Michael Lewis and Tanja Staehler, *Phenomenology: An Introduction*, New York, Continuum, 2010.

rewards and compensations.[32] This is not the singular cause of capitalist or state-socialist exploitation, as such, given the intricate web of mediations between consciousness and what Hegel refers to as objective spirit. But in a manner analogous to Weber's understanding of the relationship between Protestantism and capitalism, it helps create a matrix in which thinking and impulse can be colonized by a non-natural reflex to perform according to certain rules and standards, and to obey. The corollary, in Kant and other thinkers, is an abstract and formal normative orientation which retreats to vague invocations never to treat people as means, and passive contemplation of the sublime.[33] Hegel's historically destined reunification of subject and object fares little better in Adorno's view, in that it collapses the distinction between the rational and actual, thus paving the way for a theoretical pseudo-overcoming of metaphysics that becomes an acute practical problem in Hegelian–Marxist accounts of revolutionary class consciousness and the unity of theory and practice. If humans are not separated from the objective world, they are also not alienated from it or from one another according to the model suggested by a series of estranged forms that are gradually overcome in mediated unity, that is, in perfected form.[34] Therefore one could say that

---

[32]See Adorno, *Kant's Kritik der reinen Vernunft* [*Lectures on Kant's Critique of Pure Reason*] (given at the Johann Wolfgang Goethe University of Frankfurt in 1959), Frankfurt, Suhrkamp, 1995, especially chapter 19. The previous chapter attempts to show why a change in the relations of production, as a key component of the external conditions of autonomy, could help mediate between the cognitive content of modernist aesthetics and the normative dimension of critical theory. This endeavour can be considered part of the project to think beyond the liberal-democratic separation of system and life-world, and the equally problematic notion of their re-unification in state socialism. Preliminary theoretical steps in this direction are taken by Fredric Jameson in *Late Marxism: Adorno, Or, The Persistence of the Dialectic*, London, Verso, 1990.

[33]Whereas liberal post-metaphysics of Kantian inspiration tends to be articulated as a series of dichotomies (subject–object, theory–practice, legality–legitimacy, etc.), post-liberal post-metaphysics (Lukács, Heidegger, etc.) attempts to overcome these dichotomies without resurrecting metaphysics. Adorno regards these as instances of reconciliation under duress that inevitably lapse into informal idealism that cannot even boast of Kantian rigour. Transcending idealism in the name of materialism or ontology may seem like a positive step. But one needs an idea of truth, justice, etc., in order to think about and eventually dismantle falsity and injustice. Hence the problem is not so much that concepts are an impediment to thought and action – there is an inherently conceptual dimension to thinking. Epistemological and political problems begin when, as Horkheimer and Adorno somewhat crudely put it, the imaginative processes involved in the conceptual syntheses of the intellect and senses are taken away from potentially autonomous individuals, and are entrusted, in a manner of speaking, to commercial corporations who do the synthesis on their behalf by pre-forming experience, choice and communication. See 'The Culture Industry', in *The Dialectic of Enlightenment* (1944), New York, Continuum, 1978, pp. 123–5.

[34]It can be argued that Adorno should be more careful in distinguishing claims made in the *Phenomenology* from those made in the *Logic* and the *Realphilosophie* (of nature and spirit). See Angelica Nuzzo, 'Dialectic as Logic of Transformative Processes', in Katerina Deligiorgi (ed.), *Hegel: New Directions*, Chesham, Acumen, 2006, pp. 85–103.

if separation of subject and object fosters reified thought and oppressive formalism in law and the state more generally, premature or coerced unity foments oppressively informal, that is, extra-legal unity tending towards falsely imagined, mobilized community, or state fetishism.[35]

The formal limits to cognition find their institutional counterpart in formal limits to freedom, such that when hegemonic in consciousness and institutions, the weak dialectic of humanity and nature compels liberal-democratic law to regulate and then respect the boundaries framing citizen–government–state relations – at least until the boundaries are shifted anew as the structure of political compromise is modified over time. It has been seen so far in this chapter that in practice, 'respect' translates into a precarious balancing act between liberal formalism (forced separation of citizens as a condition of their fungibility on labour markets and misleadingly termed autonomy, analogous to the figurative prying apart of subject and object deemed necessary for post-metaphysical epistemology), and 'democratic' integration (coerced unity of citizens needed to produce post-traditional, enforceable obligation, analogous to the makeshift reconciliation of subject and object required in order for there to be knowledge of some sort, however instrumental, following the demise of metaphysical unity).[36] Despite its inherent problems, however, this particular mode of thinking and governance has been considerably more effective in shoring up legitimacy deficits than the strong dialectical approach associated with state socialism and a number of other movements, which reject the cognitive and political limits of formalism in favour of a series of more organic links structuring citizen–government–state relations. Historical evidence suggests that though this

---

[35]In the essay 'Subject and Object', Adorno explains why what he refers to as the 'priority of the object' can in part be characterized as an attempt to retain dialectics without having to embrace a Hegelian position on the rationality of the actual. Since thought is an object of a kind, and objects partake in thought, subject and object must be thought together as a non-hierarchical series of objective, subjective, natural, socio-historical and aesthetic moments. His hope is that the individual elements are not simply indistinguishable bricks in an edifice built according to a plan derived from instrumental reason, that is, where concepts rule over their non-conceptual elements. If the non-conceptual elements and singular moments can be rearranged, it may be possible to dismantle hierarchical thinking and institutional leveling of individual difference, without this leading to chaos. See Adorno, 'Subject-Object' in Arato and Gebhardt (eds), *The Frankfurt School Reader*, pp. 497–511 (originally published in *Stichworte*).

[36]This formulation sketches the broad contours of a tentative sociology of negative idealism of the kind that is hinted at in Adorno's writings. It is an experimental sociology that awaits further elaboration beyond his somewhat fragmentary endeavors in this field. Two notable attempts to do so can be seen in Gillian Rose, *Dialectic of Nihilism: Post-Structuralism and Law*, Oxford, Blackwell, 1984, and in Beatrice Hanssen, *Critique of Violence: Between Poststructuralism and Critical Theory*, London and New York, Routledge, 2000.

organicism may appear to be a leap beyond the reified boundaries of lifeless liberal form, it proves to be a retreat to naturalist accounts of spontaneous action, that is, voluntarism.[37] While one needs to be aware that there are important nuances that distinguish their writings from each other, Western Marxists such as Lukács and Korsch can be said to abandon the ahistorical state of nature argument in favour of what they take to be the materialist ground of history. This means that for them, it is class struggle that defines the terms of possible agreement between citizens with markedly different starting points and not, emphatically, a model of negotiation based on a fictitious assembly of property holders seeking to make stable property out of their precarious possessions. According to the argument set out by proponents of the strong dialectical approach, it is the mission of the working class to abolish private property by collectivizing it. This kind of theory–praxis nexus supposes that private property is the fundamental obstacle impeding a transition from formal democracy and negative liberty, to properly communal democracy and positive liberty. Hence the revolution brings about the *Aufhebung* of commercial society. But instead of turning back the clock to reinstate the old political republics and their class antagonisms, revolution in advanced industrial society initiates a new kind of political republic with socialist content. If the *democratic* essence of the *people* is oppressed by the formal mechanisms consolidating liberal freedoms and parliamentary democracy, it is redeemed in the revolutionary breakthrough to the more consistent modalities of action and agreement that would constitute genuine legitimacy beyond a legal form of legitimacy. Hence as suggested on the preceding pages, the people–government–state totality can be conceived of in liberal (ostensibly 'more' liberal, less democratic) or socialist-communist (ostensibly more democratic, 'less' liberal) terms, as if there was a graduated scale linking liberal, democratic, socialist and communist positions along a political continuum that *unites* all the positions on the basis of a fundamental, underlying *unity*, where the concepts of totality and unity function as a mutually reinforcing conceptual system.[38]

The freedom to adopt any and by turns all positions on this 'demos-continuum' indicates that there is a markedly relativist dimension to the choices made. Arbitrariness of this kind is tempered but not fundamentally

---

[37]This argument is developed in Darrow Schecter, *Beyond Hegemony: Towards a New Philosophy of Political Legitimacy*, Manchester, Manchester University Press, 2005a, chapter 2.

[38]The tautologies in the text are deliberately underscored for emphasis, and to illustrate how, in relation to the observation about Arendt in the beginning of this chapter, Marx may actually be much closer to traditional political theory than Arendt and others suspect. See Schecter, *History of the Left*, chapter 2, for a detailed discussion of Western Marxism.

altered by outlawing some parties because of their potentially anti-constitutional views. All points on the continuum are identical to the extent that they derive from the same falsely imagined unitary source that permits a predictable degree of difference to be tolerated up to a certain point, beyond which, rather dogmatically, difference is either not recognized, or is punished. Through an original synthesis of sociological theory, negative idealism and dialectics, Adorno interprets the dynamics of relativism and dogmatism as part of a series of phenomena bound up with identity thinking, which, in its turn, is a consequence of assuming the existence of mediated unity in matters of epistemology, politics, representation, law and aesthetics. The argument developed in this chapter is that some of the problems inherent in presumed mediated unity can be addressed with the concept of mediated non-identity, and that future forays into critical theory would do well to explore the legal and political implications of the concept. It might be noted that there are less obvious yet related problems involved in attempting to defend the natural rights assumed to correlate to the most valuable of the marginalized values, however these might be measured in terms of lack of recognition, non-conformist performance, subaltern communicative action and disadvantaged habitus. In other words it is clearly a non-explanation to say that the dominators dominate the dominated, or that one is alienated from the essence one has alienated to another person, object, social class or institution, and there are obvious problems involved in attempting to distil the democratic essence of the most popular class of the people, where index of popularity, numerical superiority, and imputed interest are thought to coincide. There is nonetheless a comparable explanatory deficit in arguing that struggles for recognition can result in the recognition of non-recognized or under-recognized values or perspectives. One can attempt to challenge dominant identities and end up coming close to defending a modified form of identity thinking. If it is inadequate to defy liberal prejudice with non-liberal prejudice, it is doubtful that informal conceptions of essence adequately respond to the problems inhering in formal conceptions of essence. Hence the question is not resolved by contrasting formal essence versus informal essence. One must address the question of institutional form as an important external condition for practices of autonomy that do not tend to homogenize individuals or instrumentally integrate them for the sake of order. In terms of the actual functioning of institutions and possibilities for genuine autonomy, there are important differences between formal essence, the revealed essence of authoritarian regimes based on race, class, etc., and more contemporary practices of informal essence grounded in struggles for recognition and variously conceived notions of performance. These struggles are diverse, and should not be reduced to a single common denominator.[39] But even so it is not clear if they can project beyond identity in the double sense of relatively predictable group identities at the figurative margins of society, and identity thinking in more general terms.[40]

Before proceeding it is worth asking two questions. First, how and why does postulated mediated unity tend towards coerced, mediated identity in practice, and second, what role does the sociology of negative idealism have to play in illuminating the dialectics of non-identity? These are clearly interrelated questions, for if relativism and dogmatism can be seen as two sides of the same false coin, it is more than likely that the forced separation of citizens and their simultaneously enacted coerced integration is likely to produce a kind of unity which, in qualitative terms, is not conducive to the genuine autonomy of individuals or the rational legitimacy of states (leaving aside the question if mediated unity ever really existed for substantial periods in the history of any modern state, or if the notion of legitimacy is as fictional as the state of nature). At this juncture a number of strands in the argument developed in this book so far come together: one can see in concrete terms why epistemological critique is also social critique for reasons that have more to do with collective learning processes, possible alternative constellations, and potentially redeemable transitions, than it has to do with distinctions such as those guiding public/private and base/superstructure frameworks. One can also see why the valorization of subaltern groups and values is not necessarily a sufficiently reflexive political response to the hegemony of currently dominant elites. A rigorous critique of identity reveals that there is no natural majority of democracy. Nor is there a majority perspective from whose vantage point minorities are either simply resentful of their bad luck, and in denial about their own meritocratic deficits, or are systematically marginalized, and deserving of enhanced esteem from the majority. The valorization of subaltern groups is problematic if it assumes the persistence of archaic, zero-sum power struggles of the kind prevalent in relatively undifferentiated social formations,

[39]This remarkable diversity is evident in the theoretically fertile exchanges between Judith Butler, Ernesto Laclau and Slavoj Žižek in *Contingency, Hegemony, Universality: Contemporary Dialogues on the Left*, London, Verso, 2000. Also see the contributions contained in Seyla Benhabib (ed.), *Democracy and Difference: Contesting the Boundaries of the Political*, Princeton, Princeton University Press, 1996; and Oliver Marchart, *Die politische Differenz: Zum Denken des Politischen bei Nancy, Lefort, Badiou, Laclau und Agamben*, Berlin, Suhrkamp, 2010. Simon Thompson provides a very good overview of the main debates in *The Political Theory of Recognition: A Critical Introduction*, Cambridge, Polity, 2006.

[40]For a brilliant discussion of the problems involved see Judith Butler, *Gender Trouble: Feminism and the Subversion of Identity*, New York, Routledge, 1990; and *Excitable Speech: A Politics of the Performative*, New York, Routledge, 1997.

where it may have been plausible to suppose that the ascension of one group was somehow coterminous with the decline of another. The point can be illustrated by returning to the issue of merit and other concepts, and relating them to the sociological question of hierarchy: in a relatively undifferentiated social ensemble, one person or group's upward mobility will be virtually synonymous with another person or group's downward mobility. Under these conditions, subaltern groups are more or less compelled to aspire to take the place of the people 'above' them, so that challenges to existing hierarchies also affirm the necessity of hierarchy. The corollary, thinking forward to our period of objectively possible post-scarcity, is that demands for recognition may be utilized systematically to reproduce status hierarchies that are no longer objectively necessary. Much depends on whether the demands and impulses in question presuppose mediated unity.[41]

Earlier in this chapter it is remarked that in the twenty-first century, concepts like merit, efficiency and contribution to socially necessary labour can be redefined. That is, these ideas can now acquire a pluralist valence, while progressively shedding the ambiguously anti-hierarchical impetus they pretty much had to have under conditions of relative social homogeneity. Once the credibility of merit and other normative concepts has been detached from the compulsion to achieve ever increasing levels of statically measured growth – and these simplistic gradations were perhaps needed when the question of survival was more or less *the* question of human existence – it is reasonable to expect that the demand for reallocation of merit will begin to have consistently pluralist and anti-hierarchical institutional effects, if, that is, it does not become synonymous with inclusion under duress. This is a big if, of course, and one that is contingent on the institutional forms through which objective social process (juridical positivization, differentiation, etc.) and normative integration (individual rights) are negotiated. There is much at stake depending on whether these dynamics are negotiated on an exclusion-inclusion monetary model defined by zero sum trade-offs, where stability is precariously achieved through dubiously meritocratic hierarchies, or complexity can become the condition of decentred, elastic stability. In the second case Marx's claim that humanity only sets itself tasks for which the solutions are objectively attainable would be vindicated, though not in the sense in which his claim is usually understood. Instead of material abundance rendering the division of labour unnecessary, thereby enabling people to hunt, fish, criticize, etc., differentiation processes would educate humanity about the ecological limits on specific ways of creating abundance, and offer

[41]Thorsten Bonacker, *Die normative Kraft der Kontingenz: Nichtessentialistische Gesellschaftskritik nach Weber und Adorno*, Frankfurt, Campus, 2000, chapter 4.

instruction on more nuanced approaches to questions of growth, progress, interest aggregation, political will formation and other matters.[42]

It has been demonstrated that humanity and nature are neither identical nor separate, and that each individual human presents a unique instance of historicized human nature. Any attempt to harmonize humanity and nature according to a general juridical model will produce a reactionary, re-naturalized *romantic synthesis* stressing organic unity, or an instrumental, *rationalized synthesis* based on fictitious agreements on origins and procedures that simply have to be accepted as necessary fictions. More likely still, it will turn out to be a method of governance that draws on a combination of both techniques in ways that may seem to result from pure contingency, good or bad luck, destiny, justly rewarded individual desert, etc. But this does not negate the need for a new compositional arrangement of the human, natural, objective, sensual and conceptual, keeping in mind that these categories are never encountered as pure entities. It is therefore important to develop explanations for the discrepancy between social reality and political representation without recourse to fatalistic notions of inevitable incommensurability, or pragmatic interpretations of politics as 'the art of the possible', or cynical assessments of democracy as 'a terrible system, but the best one we've got'. Continuing along the paths opened up by Adorno, critical theory deploys the concept of mediated non-identity against the concept of mediated unity with conscious awareness of the reality that concepts are both insufficient and truly necessary in a way that is fundamentally different from the speciously necessary fictions referred to above. Thinking entails conceptual and synthesizing dimensions, even if thought is not reducible to its conceptual constituent, just as, by extension, under the conditions prevailing in political modernity, legitimacy assumes a legal form, even if legitimacy is not exhausted in legality. However flawed and problematic, arguments for mediated unity have the great merit of being articulated in a way that does not obliterate the space of possible mediation between what is currently reconciliation under duress (legitimation), and what might more closely approximate reconciliation (legitimacy). At the start of this chapter it is shown how arguments about political authority presuming mediated unity as a universally valid starting point as well as a legitimate outcome can be made in terms of the notion of a social contract relying on what has been referred to as a weak dialectic, and that a similar moment of supra-contractual agreement informs the strong dialectical approach to framing the relationship between

[42]Hansgeorg Conert, 'Umrisse der Ökonomie eines möglichen Sozialismus', in Iring Fetscher and Alfred Schmidt (eds), *Emanzipation als Versöhnung: Zu Adornos Kritik der Warentausch-Gesellschaft und Perspektiven der Transformation*, Frankfurt, Neue Kritik, 2002, pp. 251–67; and Dirk Braunstein, *Adornos Kritik der politischen Ökonomie*, chapter 13.

thinking and social being, that is, society. To abandon an analysis of thought, whether in the name of post-idealism, materialism, ontology, pragmatism, communicative action, etc., is to disrupt an historically informed and analytical discussion about the extent to which each individual human life need not be governed by heteronomous forces, without such autonomy translating into defensive self-preservation that ultimately undermines real autonomy. The immanent critique of weak and strong starting points is therefore not intended completely to undermine those positions, because each, in their own way, is asking the same question about heteronomy and autonomy, and each, in their own way, poses the question dialectically. Autonomy and heteronomy are concepts whose reality is not exhausted in their conceptuality. Instead of trying to deny the conceptual dimension of autonomy, or 'realize' the concept in practice, and thereby obviate the need for its theoretical articulation, negative dialectics seeks subtly but forcefully to direct cognitive and sensual attention towards the social processes that currently guide harmonization and synthesis in the senses used above, and asks if the processes in question can be consciously modified, rather than manipulated or naïvely accredited with spurious self-governing capacities that they patently do not possess.[43]

In *Negative Dialectics* Adorno remarks that utopia is best conceived of as a knowledge utopia in which it is paradoxically possible to make use of concepts in order to attain access to sensuous, mimetic non-conceptual knowledge.[44] The juridical-political corollary of this utopian epistemological paradox is access to extra-legal legitimacy by way of legal reform. In this regard it may be helpful to think of legality and legitimacy in the same vein as one might think about recognition and reconciliation, that is, in terms of quantity and quality, though without a demos-continuum or other comparable sliding scale that converts one into the other according to a unifying logic. It is this logic that uncritically assumes that a bourgeois is a worker with money, and that a worker is a bourgeois without money and, on an international scale, that someone in the under-developed world resembles and has similar aspirations as a more 'advanced' person in the developed world. Whether one is speaking about class, gender, race, region, (dis)ability or other categories, domination will prevail as long as concepts reign over the extra-conceptual, and difference is mediated through the technique of integration through conversion or forced assimilation. In each case, spurious universals – conceptual imperiousness, legal formalism, and money – colonize what they register as alien to them. But this is not to suggest that these systems can be re-appropriated in the manner of an alienated human essence, or that they are unnatural systems

---

[43]Theodor W. Adorno, 'Gesellschaft' ['Society'] (written in 1965), in Rolf Tiedemann (ed.), *Soziologische Schriften I* [*Sociological Writings I*], Frankfurt, Suhrkamp, 1972, pp. 9–19.
[44]Adorno, *Negative Dialektik* [*Negative Dialectics*], p. 21.

that must be held in check by some combination of life-world communication and natural rights. Discerning which conditions of knowledge are external to the subject, and fortifying the socio-historical dimensions of dialectical theory can thus be seen as complementary aspects of the project to emancipate humanity from dependence on external nature, without this backfiring in the twin guises of environmental ruin and domestication of historically evolving individual inner nature. It remains to be seen in Chapter Five why the injunction to respect increased complexity entails more effective communication between discrete systems of production, consumption, education, research, etc., and is not best accomplished by insisting on their hermetic separation: the modalities of collective learning and organizing shared resources are once again clearly a central concern.

Where does this leave critical theory in the twenty-first century, if there is no feasible or desirable return to pre-conceptual symbolism, extra-legal legitimacy or barter exchange instead of commodity production? All evidence suggests that the answer to the *mediated disunity* of polarized civil societies around the world first analysed in social philosophical terms by Hegel is not *mediated unity*, which tends towards *mediated identity* in practice. Surely, it could be objected on the basis of what is argued here, the idea of *mediated non-identity* is too ephemeral to be politically significant. But does this mean that the provisional answer to the problem of mediated unity is to be sought in some notion of *unmediated non-identity*? Might unmediated non-identity provide a coherent response to the problems of romantic and rationalized syntheses that does not fall back on anthropological essences and their conceptual counterpart in the guise of classificatory schemata? One of the main points in the preceding discussion is that mediation cannot be neutral, or, at least, that it can never really be a pristine means or empty form, whether conceived of as pure procedure or as obligatory non-interference. That is, of course, if knowledge is to be substantive rather than a relatively arbitrary demarcation of boundaries, and if legitimacy is to be focused on the reconciliation of internal and external nature, rather than a series of techniques for securing the ad hoc support of constantly mobilized electoral majorities. But it may also be objected that substantive knowledge and legitimate reconciliation must surely constitute lapses into dogma or utopian flight from reality. Leaving the matter at this impasse would not advance what has already been known for quite some time.

One possible way round this problem is to argue that *knowledge* is always, to varying degrees, instrumental knowledge, and instrumental knowledge, inevitably, comports varying degrees of manipulation. On this account knowledge is by definition the tautological, technical-pragmatic objective knowledge of an object-knowing subject in its search for reliable prediction and control of its surroundings. *Understanding*, by contrast, is made possible by something that is external to the subject, but which is not an object or an entity as such. It could be God and the Bible, as in the case of traditional hermeneutics, or it could be the face of the other, as in Levinas' formulation.[45] It might also be another transcendental subject, according to Husserl's theory of transcendental intersubjectivity, or a fellow communicative subject, as Habermas maintains at times. There are other possibilities, such as Luhmann's system, interacting with its environment, or Heidegger's concept of being. Heidegger is certain that any attempt to explain reality in terms of humanity–nature relations, however subtle and decentred the mediations may be, is metaphysics. His attempt to think being beyond identity and presence constitutes a non-Marxist response to the questions of instrumental reason, alienation, mass society and reification. A brief concluding word comparing the political projects implied by the epistemologies of mediated non-identity and unmediated non-identity indicates a number of the issues at stake when analysing possible alternatives to the politics of mediated unity.

At first glance Heidegger and Adorno seem to converge in their assessment of Hegel's attempts to break the limits of Kantianism. In keeping with the distinction between knowledge and understanding, Heidegger submits that metaphysical knowledge is founded on the assumption of a fundamental unity that is the condition for all subsequent examples of difference. Thinking, in contrast to knowing, thinks the ontological non-identity of identity and difference. Thinking is an event that happens or can happen as a result of a fundamental difference between being (*Sein*) and beings (*Seiende*) that makes understanding possible. If unity makes knowledge and objectivity possible, difference allows understanding to emerge in a moment of unconcealedness. According to Heidegger a subject can attain knowledge and objectivity without really thinking, but there is no understanding without the thought of a particular kind of being that is there, thrown into the world and aware of its mortality, that is, *Dasein*. The error typical of traditional knowing is to misconstrue each individual as an object-knowing subject within a subject–object universe, which leads to the parallel error of considering nothing to be non-existent precisely because it is a non-object, whereby the condition of non-existence is consequently satisfied as a result of it being no-thing. Adorno's and Heidegger's critiques of identity thinking once again seem to converge in Heidegger's lament that much of what is usually referred to as reason relates to the 'meta' of the physical rather than the 'extra' of the physical: the meta of the physical magnifies the presence of presence so that what is bigger (cathedrals, skyscrapers, etc.) seems more important, and closer to God than what is small and seemingly insignificant. Such pseudo-thinking fails to bear

[45]Emmanuel Levinas, *Totalité et infinité: Essai sur l'extériorité* [*Totality and Infinity*], Paris, Kluwer, 1971.

in mind Husserl's discovery that it is not as if there is a form behind which an essence is concealed, or an appearance behind which the thing in itself is hidden. Husserl's phenomenology explains that the forms and appearances of objects are the essential characteristics of those things. What really matters is the various ways in which they appear, and the plurality of meanings they have for us. Instead of asking whether a thing is there or is nothing, or if it is in consciousness as a thought or in nature as an object, Husserl examines how the thing is there in its immediate given-ness. Heidegger seizes upon Husserl's project to overcome the separation of the process of knowing from the things that are known, and concludes that pre-theoretical thinking is an event that refutes juridical anthropology's supposition of the primacy of theory over practice. He argues, in effect, against the reality of concepts by arguing that being – a concept – does not 'be', as it were.[46]

If we have pre-theoretical certainty, we do not have to ask if that of which we are certain represents a quantitative increment in knowledge and, by extension, we do not need theory or law to frame our understanding of community or of politics more generally. For Adorno, somewhat like Heidegger, the task of thinking after Hegel is not so much the materialist inversion of consummated idealism, since simply to invert what is flawed is an insufficiently dialectical response to the flaw in question. For Adorno the task consists in thinking without making foundational assumptions, or, to be more precise, to investigate the mediated quality and compositional characteristics of the unity of citizens and the state, and of humanity and nature, etc., as a specific moment in human history and in natural history, and not as an eternal truth, or an episode in the march of progress, or a stage on the way to the unification of form and essence. For Adorno non-identity thinking, somewhat like Benjamin's dialectics at a standstill, disrupts the continuity of the historical process at the same time that it questions the juxtaposition of rational history and irrational, ahistorical nature.[47]

Hegel's strong dialectical approach offers a robust juridical model of thinking in the *Philosophy of Right*. In his mature work, the mediated unity of subject and object is not possible without *Geist*, and the state is the condition of an individual rational will. One could interpret Adorno as a weak juridical thinker,

---

[46]Heidegger, *Sein und Zeit* [*Being and Time*] (1927), Tubingen, Max Niemeyer, 1993, section 2, chapter 2, paragraph 58.

[47]Husserl, *Die Phänomenologische Methode: Ausgewählte Texte I*, Stuttgart, Reclam, 1985, pp. 98–105, 131–48; Paul Ricoeur, 'Husserl', in Eduard Brehier (ed.), *Histoire de la philosophie allemande*, Paris, Vrin, 1967, pp. 183–96; Heidegger, 'Prolegomena zur Geschichte des Zeitbegriffs' ['Prologue to the History of Concepts of Time'] (1925), in Heidegger, *Gesamtausgabe*, Vol. 20, 1979, pp. 29–33; Adorno, *Ästhetische Theorie* [*Aesthetic Theory*], pp. 170–3, 1997a; and Theodor W. Adorno, *Drei Studien zu Hegel* [*Hegel: Three Studies*] (1963), Frankfurt, Suhrkamp, 1963, pp. 78–85.

though not in the formal sense of a weak dialectic discussed above in relation to liberal democracy. He maintains that tracing the mediated non-identity of subject and object is not possible without thinking the priority of the object against the background of anticipated reconciliation in epistemology and politics. By contrast, one might describe the Heidegger of *Being and Time* as an anti-juridical thinker of legitimacy who asserts that *Dasein,* as distinct from a traditional subject, understands events, where understanding and the event are not possible without the external condition of being. In other words Heidegger distinguishes between subjects knowing objects without bothering to think the being-ness of their being, and *Dasein*'s chance, if resolute enough, to think that difference in ontological terms. Adorno stresses that there is a marked difference between thinking and passive adaptation to reigning modes of recognition and integration, that is, what could be construed as social knowing; his continuing significance for critical theory can be seen in his insistence that thinking is not thinkable in abstraction from the repressive socio-economic, political and juridical institutions that illuminate the difference between thought and different strategies to fit in. Negative dialectics is weak juridical thinking of non-identity in that it shows why it is insufficiently dialectical to separate the political potential of the present, discussed in this book in terms of de-naturalization, de-traditionalization, differentiation, de-centred democratic constellations, etc., from their currently repressive character. To celebrate the former without a sustained critique of their present forms is to engage in a kind of superficial sociological cosmopolitanism. To bemoan these tendencies as the end of the nation, the rise of society, the inauthentic prattle of 'Das Man', that is, as a *Verfallsgeschichte* (a history of decline) and the forsaking of national-linguistic communities of fate, is to conjure up an unmediated and therefore inaccessible otherness in relation to what currently exists. The contrast between non-dialectical, anti-juridical thinking and negative dialectical, weak-juridical thinking illustrates how conformity and obscurantism mutually reinforce each other. Post-identity thinking only retains its critical incisiveness if it also retains its stress on dialectics and post-foundational mediation.[48]

---

[48]Some will want to question the criticism of non-dialectical, anti-juridical thinking put forward here, according to which the allegedly immediate, ready-to-hand, is actually the irredeemably inaccessible, and therefore largely chimerical. The notion that things disclose themselves in the plural event of *aletheia*, independently, that is, of the forms in which their essences are thought to appear, is to retreat to pre-Kantian epistemological positions. Knowledge does not 'begin' at a fixed point where uncertainty 'ends'. Similarly, norms are not pristine ethical postulates enforced by legitimate power that is free of normative content. To divorce concepts from the phenomena they conceptualize obscures the processes that the concepts imperfectly help to explain. Conceptual explanation has to be adjusted and refined to the point of redefining what concepts can do, not abandoned in the name of some kind of extra-conceptual purity.

4

Critical theory and political theory

The previous chapters indicate that a specific approach to critical theory emerges from the sustained engagement with idealism, Marxism, psychoanalysis, legal theory and modernist aesthetics undertaken by the various thinkers affiliated with the Institute for Social Research first established in Frankfurt in 1923–4. Other approaches are possible and do exist. Any analysis of knowledge and the corresponding study of the social and historical relations conditioning the production of knowledge that aspires to be critical and reflexive cannot simply re-phrase the ideas of the first generation of Frankfurt School thinkers, and this is not the aim of this study. Yet at the same time, the first-generation thinkers raise epistemological and political questions that are not easily dismissed as obsolete or overrun by events. It might be argued that they do not raise enough practical political questions. This would be somewhat inaccurate, in view of the fact that Neumann and Kirchheimer had practical experience as lawyers, Fromm and others practised psychoanalysis, Marcuse was directly involved in the upheavals of 1968, etc. Like Arendt and others who regularly published articles in *Die Zeitschrift für Sozialforschung* and *Die Gesellschaft*, but were not directly associated with the Institute for Social Research, many first-generation critical theorists experienced National Socialism and political exile in more than one host country.[1] There is a more important point, however, which is that some of the first-generation thinkers anticipate the need for a new kind of politics in the age of the definitive decline of commercial republics, that is, a political equivalent to philosophical solidarity

---

[1]See Martin Jay, *The Dialectical Imagination, A History of the Frankfurt School and the Institute of Social Research, 1923–1950*, Berkeley and Los Angeles, University of California Press, 1973; and Jean Michel Palmier, *Weimar en exil*, Paris, Payot, 1987 (available in English translation from Verso).

with metaphysics in the moment of its collapse.[2] This point is developed in greater detail in this chapter and the next. After examining the concept of mediated non-identity, one must ask what the politics of mediated non-identity could become. Although Adorno raises the question in critical hermeneutical terms, it is time to build on his theoretical legacy.

It could also be argued that critical theory needs to be more open, and able to assimilate other theoretical influences and methodological impulses. Many defenders of cosmopolitanism and advocates of the innovations implied by the 'linguistic turn', or, more recently, by the 'spatial turn', are likely to hold this view.[3] In what precise ways, in other words, is critical theory critical, and how does critical theory differ from other currents of thought that strive to integrate the analytical and normative aspects of rigorous social inquiry? Given the decidedly economic aspects of the Greek crisis, and the obvious ways that the Greek crisis could rapidly become a Spanish, Portuguese, Italian, etc., crisis, why should not proponents of critique opt for a return to some suitably modified version of Marxist analysis and socialist politics?[4] Given the academic popularity of recognition theory and invocations of the multitude, the event, 'the post-modern', etc., why not advocate an amalgam of these notions in some new theoretical synthesis? In terms of re-articulating the critique of instrumental reason and making the case for largely untested practices of reason and autonomy today, one must ask if the writings of the Frankfurt School continue to offer the most incisive analyses of social reality and political possibility available. Returning very briefly to some of the issues raised at the beginning of this book may help point towards a tentative answer, and provide an introduction to some of the questions to be taken up in this chapter.

---

[2]If the collapse of fascism marked the failure of state-centred and virulently nationalist approaches to shoring up legitimacy, it also signalled the end of a liberal-democratic way of doing so without extensive welfare provision of the kind that became the norm in Western Europe after World War II. The longer-term effects on political parties in liberal-democratic states are only now starting to become clear. See Marcuse, *Konterrevolution und Revolte*, Frankfurt, Suhrkamp, 1972, chapter 1.

[3]While the linguistic turn often associated with Habermas can be seen as an attempt to move beyond the crucial limitations attributed to the first generation due to their residual idealism and lack of sociological rigour, the spatial turn coined by Fredric Jameson can be regarded more as an attempt to give fresh impetus to Frankfurt School critical theory, and especially to dialectical theory. See Fredric Jameson, *Late Marxism: Adorno, Or, The Persistence of the Dialectic*, London, Verso, 1990, chapters 5–8, and his *Valences of the Dialectic*, London, Verso, 2009, Part I. On Jameson see Sean Homer, *Jameson: A Critical Introduction*, Cambridge, Polity, 1998.

[4]This perspective is ably defended by Alex Callinicos in *Imperialism and Global Political Economy*, Cambridge, Polity, 2009. Much of the international relations literature in recent years has distinct Gramscian overtones that point to a renewal of Marxist approaches to understanding conflict today.

If re-articulation means little more than re-stating the theses of the first generation on the totally administered society, the authoritarian personality, one-dimensional humanity, the culture industry, the possibility of profane illuminations, the potentially utopian dimension of 'the great refusal', etc., the answer must be negative.[5] The project, if one may call it that for the moment, is to understand contemporary society and assess the chances of transforming social processes in specific ways that reciprocally empower people, instead of pitting them against each other, and develop their capacities to transform themselves on their own terms, instead of demanding that they adapt to existing conditions if they want to survive. Such a project aspires to re-examine the prospects for Enlightenment without ignoring the *Dialectic of Enlightenment*, bearing in mind that credible answers to the questions raised by Horkheimer and Adorno cannot afford to skirt the issues of reason, communication, functional differentiation, legitimate legality, systems, modes of mediation, and, crucially, the relation between mediation processes and knowledge of society. This is not an arbitrary assortment of topics, but an attempted re-appraisal of a number of key philosophical, juridical and sociological concepts with contemporary relevance. In order to make a decisive contribution to this endeavour in the twenty-first century, critical theory must elaborate a number of theories that make brief appearances in the works of Adorno, Benjamin, Horkheimer, Neumann, Sohn-Rethel, Pollock, Kirchheimer, Marcuse, etc., but which must be refashioned. One promising approach to this reconstruction is indicated by the way the concept of mediated non-identity is discussed in the previous chapter and the rest of this book. The theories of the first generation must be re-interpreted not, however, to keep up with the pace of change, for this would amount to a major concession to a particular notion of *progress* that the founding members of the Institute rightly rejected. Their ideas need overhauling in the same way that these theorists were confronted with the task of re-reading Kant, Hegel and Marx while bearing in mind both the manifest

[5]This would be a bit like trying to defend the continuing relevance of Marxism by reiterating the timeless validity of the tendency for the rate of profit to fall, or maintaining that the state is still nothing other than an executive committee for managing the affairs of the entire bourgeoisie. Yet if it might be advisable to revise rather than reject Marx's thesis that humanity only sets itself tasks for which the solutions are objectively possible, one would not want necessarily to abandon the idea of a profane illumination. It could be argued that the idea of free-speech situations guided by a teleology of agreement is no less utopian than Benjamin's, and no more rooted in the real movement of history, which is towards objectively possible post-scarcity. Hence it becomes important to specify the conditions under which radically new thinking and uncoerced agreement might emerge, rather than to dismiss powerfully original thought as commercially untenable and politically unfeasible, that is, as a matter of merely private importance. For an analysis of how profane illuminations are linked with the capacity to recognize an imminent state of exception, see Thanos Zartaloudid, *Giorgio Agamben: Power, Law, and the Uses of Criticism*, Abingdon, Routledge, 2010, pp. 129–40.

inadequacies as well as the ongoing relevance of specific facets of idealist philosophy and Marxist political economy, and doing so in the light of ruptures and transitions in the course of *history*. Thus it is incorrect to say that progress is illusory, Enlightenment is myth, evolution leads from the slingshot to the atom bomb, or that democracy is a smokescreen for capitalism, and capitalism is pure domination. The idea that needs testing is that under conditions of objectively possible post-scarcity, each person can develop independent criteria for evaluating which innovations in art, science, technology, law, economy, etc., help them to distinguish between individual autonomy and 'successful' adaptation to social expectations, and to formulate judgements enabling them to assess if they are reacting to the dictates of various performance principles, or working out a suitably nuanced reality principle in line with the broad contours of their life experience. It is however mistaken to regard the matter as a question of working out private strategies that juxtapose individual choices with social facts, thereby transforming socio-economic and political questions into episodes of luck, fate, psychological disposition, and somewhat arbitrary cases of 'merit'. The entire network of interactive reciprocal exchanges must be carefully studied in order to show how, why and where individual aspirations acquire the appearance of subjective desires that inevitably clash with objective culture. There are certainly other plausible approaches to critical theory, some of which will be alluded to in this chapter and the next. But there are also a number of convincing grounds for modifying the guiding insights of the Frankfurt School, rather than abandoning their methodology in favour of ostensibly more radical or more 'up-to-date' versions of social theory. Elements of Gramscian and bio-political theory could certainly contribute to the reformulation of critical enquiry. But this book explains why it is important to retain, in suitably altered versions, several key aspects of the project as it was conceived from the Weimar period until *Legitimation Crisis* (and indeed, there may also be certain dimensions of the theory of communicative action that one would want to retain going forward).[6]

[6]The two volumes of *Theory of Communicative Action* first published by Suhrkamp in 1981 mark a decisive break from the Weberian Marxist themes of *Legitimation Crisis*. In the last chapter of volume 2 of *Theory of Communicative Action*, entitled 'The Tasks of a Critical Theory', Habermas explains why it is more accurate to speak of the colonization of the life-world by systemic imperatives than it is to discuss the preponderance of instrumental over other forms of reason. This introduces a salutary sociological dimension into critical theory. But it also raises many questions about the critique of systemic imperatives that will be taken up in Chapter Five. Within this framework, systemic demands seem to be insulated from critique for the same reasons that system and life-world have become differentiated, so that the price for a rational, post-traditional life-world is a qualified respect for and acceptance of the logic of money and power. See Jürgen Habermas, *The Theory of Communicative Action, Volume 2: The Critique of Functionalist Reason,* Cambridge, Polity, 1987, pp. 383–6.

The preceding chapters attempt to provide fresh impetus to the study of a number of glaring discrepancies between liberal-democratic theory and prevailing practice in most industrial democracies in the period roughly lasting from the French Revolution to the present, bearing in mind, of course, that a number of major structural transformations take place during those years. It is shown how presumed or *hypothetical pre-legal unity* among private individuals is credited with the spontaneous steering power needed to facilitate collective decisions between citizens and what they authorize to become universally agreed upon, binding norms, thus producing achieved, *legitimate unity* between citizens and governments in the legal state. Whether formulated as a unanimous exit from the state of nature, or fundamental agreement on the difference principle reached from behind a veil of ignorance, this line of argument can be analysed as a political tautology complementing the cognitive tautology according to which objective knowledge is attained by the innate faculties of an object-knowing, isolated subject. The analogy between belief in spontaneous steering and postulation of innate faculties captures something fundamental about a way of thinking by way of extrapolation from a central premise which is somehow insulated from critique. Interesting in this regard is that while the problem of object-knowing subjects is often casually dismissed as an idealist error that can be rectified with a bit of pragmatic common sense, the problem of spontaneous steering is rarely addressed as the serious politico-epistemological problem that it is, despite the crisis of 1929 and those of today. Both explanations, however, are centrally concerned with the relations between mediation, knowledge and unity; what is usually taken to derive from unity, that is, compromise and agreement, is of specifically political relevance. In the second case it is the mediated unity of subject and object, whereby the status of unity is qualified by the caveat that knowledge is limited and framed by the forms that knowledge takes, that is, that there are no direct subject–object relations that are not also metaphysical and therefore epistemologically unsound. In the first case it is the unity of the individual and state, whereby the status of unity is qualified by the caveat that each individual's freedom is mediated by law and government, so that one person's freedom is made compatible with the freedom of every other person. Both in theory and actual historical practice *the necessity* to 'make compatible' – to lawfully coerce, in other words – is explainable as a consequence of the likelihood that direct citizen–state relations are metaphysical and therefore as untenable as anarchic citizen–state relations without law, government, or collective consensus of any kind. But here again, the analogy holds: lawful coercion of citizens corresponds, roughly, to subjective manipulation of objective realities for fear of natural scarcity and unpredictability. A critical theory of politics and democracy cannot dispense with a theory of mediations. Accordingly, it will be argued in what follows that mediation, as opposed to populist-authoritarian immediacy and dichotomous polarity, demands continual negotiation between different social systems if, that is, the ongoing processes of mediation are to be translated into democratic, cross-systemic dialogue. It will be suggested that since systems exist and function without a unifying central system, and each individual system is by definition in a minority position in relation to the plurality of other systems that together constitute society, a critical democracy capable of replacing political republics and their successor commercial republics will be a non-foundational democracy organized by minorities in constant formation, dissolution and re-formation.[7]

There are evident links between individual epistemological irrationality, authoritarian collectivism and the search for unmediated knowledge and liberty. It has already been observed at various points in the preceding chapters that, whether unbeknown to the main protagonists in the decisive debates or not, the methodological discovery of the impossibility of essentialist immediacy, and the corresponding discovery of the mediating reality of institutional form, is a modern and a dialectical one that begins with Kant and Hegel. Despite frequent affirmations to the contrary conflating dialectics with either dogma or implicitly authoritarian speculative idealism, this theoretical advance is not peculiar to idealist, Marxist or critical theoretical approaches to knowledge and politics.[8] One of the tentative conclusions that follows is that (1) some kind of dialectic, to some substantial degree at least, accurately depicts the structure of the modern and late modern worlds, and the political possibilities they offer, and that (2) the structure of mediations (mediated unity, mediated disunity, non-mediated non-identity and mediated non-identity) appearing in response to dialectical realities can be analysed in terms of democratic potential and deficits. This provisional conclusion about dialectics, mediations and politics holds regardless of one's political orientations. Liberal democracy

---

[7]The history of modern states indicates that mediation can be arranged by government ministries in dialogue with various economic, political, military, religious, educational, etc., elites. There is therefore a necessary relation between mediation and politics, but there is no necessary relation between mediation and democracy.

[8]Although the most famous statement of this dogmatic repudiation of virtually all methodologies that do not conform to the postulates of analytical philosophy and logical positivism can be found in Karl Popper, *The Open Society and its Enemies* (1945), Bertrand Russell and a number of other thinkers tend to make similar disparaging generalizations about idealism, dialectics and dictatorship. Thomas Akehurst shows how many of these polemics assume a number of givens about analytical philosophy, democratic society, and political liberalism that really cannot be accepted as unproblematic. See his 'Britishness, Logic and Liberty: The Cultural Politics of Twentieth Century Analytical Philosophy', DPhil in History at the University of Sussex, 2007.

has been relatively successful in drawing attention to the affinities between dogma and dictatorship, depending on the country and period in question. But it has not always been consistent in doing so. Moreover, prominent liberal-democratic theorists and political leaders have not always been quick to acknowledge their own use of dialectical argument in their defence of a legal form of legitimacy. This problem is analysed at the end of Chapter One in terms of liberal reliance on a formal but undisclosed essence, and is taken up again at various points thereafter.

In its diverse guises, critical theory strives to show how this lack of clarity contributes to inconsistencies and compromises with dogma and dictatorship on the part of states that broadly define their institutions as liberal-democratic and juridical. In its more ambitious articulations critical theory strives to show why liberal-democratic institutions must decisively evolve if these periodic compromises are to be prevented from becoming recurring spells of organized oppression at home and abroad. Part of what that evolution entails is greater transparency (discussed in the next chapter as systemic re-coupling) about how agreement between citizens and governments is achieved and what counts as agreement, how and to what extent agreement is codified in law, how non-agreement and conflict are managed in legal and extra-legal ways, what counts as extra-legality, and why under certain conditions extra-legal measures are deemed to be necessary and therefore legitimate.[9] Some of these questions are as old as the history of political thought. Yet it would be wrong to suppose that tentative solutions would already have been proposed if there was anything approximating 'a solution'. Indeed, the term systemic re-coupling is preferred to the old-fashioned notion of people–government–state transparency because the unity required to make transparency a real option or critical criterion must now be re-considered, in the light of growing complexity and contingency. With this in mind, Chapter Four elaborates the discussion of mediated non-identity in the previous chapter. In opposition to the notion that the answers to these questions are as elusive as the questions are timeless, it is argued here that the cultural, socio-economic, technological and juridical resources developed in the late modern world

---

[9]It is fairly evident that oppression within liberal democracies is more likely to be bio-political rather than straightforwardly dictatorial or fascist. Theoretical and practical difficulties arise because even though liberal democracy often denotes a political party, the term can also refer to a state form, a body of ideas and values, or the dominant historical successor to feudalism. Hence even opposition parties are liberal-democratic to the extent that they operate within the legal parameters defined by liberal-democratic states, thus promoting the view that opposition that is not liberal-democratic is extreme, irrational and anti-democratic by definition.

offer unprecedented political possibilities that are somewhat obscured by the widespread assumption that a legal form of legitimacy defines the limit of political possibility, that is, that legitimate forms of law are impossible. Once it has been established that liberal democracy, as the hegemonic instantiation of a legal form of legitimacy, is structured according to dialectical premises about form, content, mediation and representation, the dialectical critique of a dialectically structured socio-political reality can proceed. Liberal democracy is not a pernicious doctrine that is hegemonic thanks to ideological deceit, the brutal imposition of norms, or its role in disseminating reified false consciousness. It is very much in touch with phenomena such as the dangers of dictatorship and the problem of contingency, and therefore truthful and objective up to a point, but only selectively so.[10] There will be more to say about selective processing of information, systems theory and critical theory in what follows.

Dysfunctional representation and instrumental legitimacy

Since Plato's *Republic*, the possibility of rational political authority grounded in knowledge of humanity, nature and society, as distinct from authority issuing from merely bargained compromises or the exercise of power, has engaged the imagination of philosophers, legal theorists and activists. If one accepts for the moment that rational law and lawful coercion are coterminous, lest one posit the existence of a divine source of purely normative juridical rationality, it becomes clear just how utopian the idea of rational political authority

---

[10]In principle liberalism defends each person's *chance* to develop independent criteria for discerning between individual autonomy and strategic adaptation to the rigours of different performance principles, and it is generally true that liberal democracy has been sensitive to the affinities between dogma and dictatorship. It seems however that the provisional victory over dogmatic essentialism has been won with the triumph of a rationalized formal essentialism that now represents a limit to what can be known and learned about the contemporary world. Although effective against dictatorship, the combination of rigorous scepticism and formal essentialism has been complicit in the transformation of a number of key socio-economic and political questions into myths of luck and just desert, so that real independence is undermined in many cases, that is, it becomes a matter of chance in a more recognizably pejorative sense. Some will say that this is the price to pay for living with the uncertainties of contingency, but a more serious approach will insist that rigorous scepticism must now be directed towards formalism without embracing new dogmas or postmodern relativism. The essays collected in Benjamin Noys (ed.), *Communization and its Discontents*, Wivenhoe, Minor Compositions, 2012, indicate a number of possible directions for research.

really is. But this utopianism is offset by the not so self-evident reality that power is juridically mediated and rarely directly exercised as pure violence. If reason and coercion are not antitheses, it would nonetheless be erroneous to suppose that their mutual dependence signifies the inherent violence or consistently extra-normative power of law. It is clear that at present, at least, power and knowledge are mediated by law and politics, and that there are no juridical norms free of power relations. This may be uncontroversial. But what is usually overlooked and potentially utopian in a concrete sense, is that in de-traditionalized societies, there are no power relations that are not susceptible to political discussion and juridical reform. The corollary of the postulate that there is no divine source of purely normative juridical rationality is not simply that coercion is required in order to make law binding. It can be argued that the more pertinent corollary is that there is no such thing as the exercise of pure power or coercion, and that given the right conditions, norms could become binding on the basis of their truthfulness and capacity to reconcile external nature and individual human natures. If one cannot assume the validity of norms without binding sanctions, it is equally implausible to assume the timelessness of the need for specific instances of coercive sanction. What has to be shown with greater clarity is that the need for coercive sanctions is closely bound up with historically antecedent, relatively undifferentiated forms of social organization, and that such repressive measures eventually outlive the historically discernible period of their necessity and efficient functioning. At that point the perpetuation of surplus repression can be analysed as ideology, myth, and archaic organization instead of being passively accepted as unfortunate but unavoidable human error. The use of terms such as norm, coercion and sanction will attain greater clarity and relevance for critical theory during this chapter and the next, when the discussion turns to the ostensible power of systems in relation to the implicit normativity of life-world communication. It will be seen that Habermas is certainly correct to emphasize that the historical evolution of Western societies is not fully explicable in terms of the transformation of traditional and charismatic power into legal-rational authority, as interpreters of Weber sometimes suggest, and that the division of labour is not synonymous with alienation, as many interpreters of Marx (who ignore Durkheim) assume. The de-coupling of law and religion, which plays a large part in the movement towards legal rationality, like the de-coupling of person and land-bound status, which plays an important role in the disarticulation of economy and polity, has been accompanied by a series of re-coupling movements. In many instances re-coupling has been badly organized in a manner more akin to attempted reunification. The politics of re-coupling, as opposed to those of inflexible reunification/re-nationalization, have only been discussed in as yet tentative terms.[11]

Although mediated unity is often posited as the presupposition as well as the outcome of rational law and functionally efficient secular political representation in much traditional political theory since the time of the first social contract theorists, in practice the real relations structuring unity of this kind resemble something much closer to badly mediated disunity. Within the context of democratic states in the industrial revolution and its long and ongoing aftermath, mediated disunity usually translates into race and other colonial and post-colonial antagonisms, as well as class and gender conflicts that consolidate the sway of instrumental over other forms of reason, entrench bureaucratic hierarchies, and perpetuate fairly arbitrary distinctions concerning what is meant to be good, efficient, objective, objectively necessary, etc., as well as what is 'normal'.[12] One would surely want to update these observations today with an analysis of the links between dysfunctional disunity and environmental crises.[13] The argument in Chapter Three is centrally concerned with explaining how instances of mediation affect forms of representation as well as reflexive knowledge of society: it is shown that where key mediating instances do not so much mediate as dictate, impose, marginalize and coercively integrate, as in the contemporary example of imposed austerity plans presented as necessary and therefore beyond negotiation, political representation tends to be institutionalized in unstable combinations marked by clientelism, populism and voter apathy. Empirical evidence related to

---

[11]Pat Devine and David Purdy remark that in contradistinction to corporatism, state-ownership, and private ownership, true social ownership, as they put it, has hardly been tried. See Pat Devine and David Purdy, 'Feelbad Britain', in Mark McNally and John Schwarzmantel (eds), *Gramsci and Global Politics: Hegemony and Resistance*, Abingdon, Routledge, 2009, pp. 182–4. Truly social ownership roughly corresponds to what is discussed in this chapter in terms of de-centralized, social re-coupling.

[12]As Nietzsche's work on good and evil shows, what is respectively valorized as good, efficient, objective, necessary and normal undergoes periodical change. Foucault adapts Nietzsche's method to the study of the evolution of techniques of normalization. His analysis provides ample evidence in support of the claim that if disunity, which alludes to fragmentation, and normalization, which evokes standardization, are contradictory in semantic terms, it is that contradiction which illuminates rather than obscures changes in the discursive dissemination of power. See Michel Foucault, *Les mot et les choses* [translated as *The Order of Things*], Paris, Gallimard, 1966; and Niels Akerstrom Andersen, *Discursive Analytical Strategies: Understanding Foucault, Koselleck, Laclau, Luhmann*, Bristol, Policy Press, 2003, chapter 1.

[13]For a general look at the issues involved, see Serge Latouche, *Pour sortir de la société de la consommation: Voix et voies de la décroissance* [*Beyond the Society of Consumption*], Paris, Gallimard, 2010, chapter 1. For a specific analysis of the case of water, a very incisive aggiornamento is provided by Yvan Renou in 'La rationalité dialectique à l'épreuve de la gouvernance de l'eau: une analyse des (en)jeux hydro-sociaux contemporains', *Droit et société*, 80 (2012), pp. 143–62.

this particular issue indicates that there is a profound credibility crisis for governments everywhere.[14] At any rate it is not a simple case of systemic steering needs accidentally straying into the domain of the life-world. To be more precise, and to explain in more detail what is meant by mediated identity, it is patently not the case of an agreed-upon norm being backed with the sanction of legitimate force: the norm is itself coercive because the mediation between citizens and governments committed to austerity is for the most part instrumental. Hence not only are there social philosophical explanations of phenomena as diverse as corruption and passivity; these phenomena are explainable in terms of dialectical movements that contain seemingly opposed terms, such as populist mobilization and citizen indifference. Badly mediated disunity, as the term suggests, denotes a qualitative assessment, but it is not an assessment formulated in normative abstraction from an analysis of how and why presumed mediated unity in practice really means imposed unity, or, in more contemporary terms, imposed austerity that is good, as is confidently claimed in some quarters, for all of the citizens in a crisis-afflicted or potentially crisis-afflicted nation-state, regardless of their individual capacities and needs. These capacities and needs can only be made visible and politically relevant as flexibly institutionalized relations characterized by non-identical political equality for all. Otherwise there is a marked tendency, under conditions of generalized mediated identity, for the ostensibly necessary to converge with the good, and for the in principle rational norm to converge with the exercise of power. It then seems that the real simply could not be more rational than it is when hardship is inflicted on those living today for the ostensible well being of future generations. This is not a language game, simulacrum, the multitude caught sleeping, or some kind of postmodern irony. It captures something real about contemporary politics, and attests to the urgent need for innovative social research with normative relevance and policy implications. On this point it can be said that the aims of the first generation of critical theorists address contemporary concerns. The fact that all states are potentially prone to crisis means that their budgets will each need to be scrutinized by the relevant international bodies set up for that purpose. The legitimacy deficits of these bodies have been debated in a wide variety of academic forums, and are the subject of controversy on a daily basis in newspapers, journals and books.[15]

---

[14]For the British case, see Seumas Milne, 'The Coalition's Phony War is an Exercise in Political Fraud', *The Guardian*, 26 September 2012, p. 30. On the Spanish case see Katharine Ainger, 'A Financial Coup d'Etat', on the same page of *The Guardian* of that day.

[15]The expression 'some quarters' is a slightly euphemistic way of referring to what has been called the troika formed by the IMF, the European Central Bank, and the EU Parliament. See Nikos Dimou, 'L'immobilisme dure depuis trop longtemps', *Le Monde*, 25 May 2012, p. 18, and Grit Beecken and Bernd Salzmann, 'Investoren legen Spanien trocken', *Frankfurter Rundschau,*

Although the empirical dimension of this analysis is key, there is not enough space in this volume to develop it. Other volumes in the *Critical Theory and Contemporary Society* series take up the task of integrating theoretical and empirical perspectives.[16]

The conclusion to Chapter Three analyses the different modalities of representation and legitimacy implied by the prevalence in any particular context of (largely absent) mediated unity (1), mediated disunity (2), mediated identity (3), non-mediated non-identity (4) and (perhaps faintly palpable at present, but potentially enhanced) mediated non-identity (5), all of which can be seen as theoretical attempts best to ascertain the relation between the conceptual analysis of political possibility and institutional realities at a determinate historical moment.[17] It is important to note the sociological transformation implied by the theoretical shift from the mediated disunity Hegel attributes to the civil society of his day, in which guilds and other corporations still play a significant role in socialization, education, occupational training and housing, to the more pervasive homogeneity of mass society signalled by the concept of mediated identity. Critical theory stakes its claim to continuing relevance by emphasizing that disunity and identity are not simply synonymous with inexplicable chaos, or something vaguely explainable in terms of 'the human condition'. The fact that the relations in question are mediated, and that the institutional logic of mediation undergoes historically verifiable structural transformations, indicates that conflict and cooperation are not simply inevitable, mysterious or inexplicable.[18] It consolidates that

6–7 June 2012, p. 12. For a detailed examination of the links between the politics of austerity, government bank bail-outs, the workings of international financial markets and staggering rates of unemployment in specific countries, see Sahra Wagenknecht, *Wahnsinn mit Methode: Finanzcrash und Weltwirtschaft*, Berlin, Das Neue Berlin, 2008.

[16]See Heiko Feldner's forthcoming volume on crisis theory in this series.

[17]Concepts are not really necessary to explain what is amiss in those rare cases where one is confronted with unmediated violence. Concepts become necessary when trying to disentangle and re-articulate the connections between the rational, sensual–corporeal, juridical and historical dimensions of events and phenomena such as injustice, inequality, solidarity, recognition and reconciliation. Adorno's remarks about the need for conceptual analysis of the extra-conceptual continue to stimulate reflection on these subjects.

[18]In this particular example it indicates that despite claims to the contrary made in the *Philosophy of Right*, mediated disunity in civil society is not unified in the political institutions of the state. This was certainly true in pre-unification Germany in 1821, and continues to be an accurate description in Germany and beyond. The young Marx clearly sees this, though it might be said that he comes up with the wrong solution to the right problem. The more pertinent point is perhaps that although one might normally distinguish between the first generation (Horkheimer, Benjamin, Adorno, Marcuse, etc.) and the second generation (Schmidt, Habermas, Wellmer, Honneth, Brunkhorst, Bonefeld, etc.), one should also bear in mind that within first-generation writers there are conflicting tendencies. There is the tendency towards trans-historical generalization and pessimism, which at times comes close to the speculations of Spengler and Heidegger about

claim to relevance by emphasizing the intricacy of social change, and by being cautious about assigning the task of 'putting things right' to any single social subject, category of communicative action, or to a performative or otherwise conceived identity. Another way of saying this is that post-feudal society is complex and constellational, despite what some of the Jacobins and their successors may seem to have thought and continue to think. It does not achieve unity by way of a supposedly democratic foundation such as the state, to which all political roads lead, nor is unity the spontaneous fruit of self-adjusting markets. Many may regret the passing of at least minimum standards of political control afforded by the nation-state in the period prior to globalization. From a contemporary vantage point it seems clear that for long periods, the political structure of the nation-state may have been partially suitable for limited degrees of social-democratic economic planning, welfare and redistribution, and that social-democratic governments directed these projects with moderate success. The state issuing from the French Revolution now appears to be incapable of performing these functions, thus casting doubt on the long-term future of that state-form and social-democratic politics within it. There will be more to say about the reasons why this might be the case in the second section of this chapter, but it could be noted here that the New Labour experiment in Great Britain provides solid evidence in support of this thesis.[19]

To many observers, liberals and Marxists alike, the French Revolution seemed to demonstrate that modernity, political emancipation, and democratic centralization were all interrelated and trans-national processes destined to restructure the relation between state and civil society everywhere in Europe and beyond. With this in mind one can see why Lenin and the Bolsheviks

---

decay and decline. But there is also the more historically sensitive work on the phenomenology of transitions, such as Benjamin's research on the appearance of the *Paris Passages*, and Neumann's and Kirchheimer's studies of the changes in the function of law in modern society. More historical work needs to be done on the shift from mediated disunity to mediated identity, in order to show why the prevalence of mediated identity in late modern societies is not simply synonymous with totalitarian identity but is, on the contrary, the condition of the possibility that mediated non-identity might become an operative principle of social organization. This possibility figures in consistently non-normative terms in some systems-theoretical writings, thereby conjuring up an apparently neat congruence between systems theory and neo-liberalism. There is a very different way of articulating the mutual concerns of critical theory, systems theory and post-foundational normative inquiry, however, as will be seen.

[19]See the articles by Pat Devine and David Purdy, Will Leggett and Jules Townsend in Mark McNally and John Schwarzmantel (eds), *Gramsci and Global Politics*, and Peter Kolarz, 'The Politics of Anthony Giddens' Social Theory: Utopian Realism and Late Modern Social Democracy beyond the Third Way', DPhil at the University of Sussex, 2011. Kolarz provides an adept analysis of the twists and turns of New Labour policy and the inconsistencies in Anthony Giddens' defence of what is sometimes referred to as the Third Way.

regarded their revolution as a consistent application of these ostensibly democratic principles against the Napoleonic turn of the first great break with the *ancien régime*, that is, the culmination of the Revolution in empire and political reaction. But events subsequently showed that post-feudal mediation cannot be achieved on the basis of a political party acting in the name of a social class that unifies theory and practice over and against functional differentiations. This is not to say that privatization and de-regulation solve the problems of cumbersome political control. On the contrary, it is improbable that the decline of apprenticeships or the commercialization of education and other aspects of socialization once performed by guilds can lead to the enhanced quality of those vital functions, which is why the study of the transition from mediated disunity to mediated identity should not be mistaken as an attack on mediation as such. It should be understood as a critique of dysfunctional, instrumental mediation. Critiques of mediated identity which are articulated as general critiques of the reality of institutional form usually amount to badly articulated demands for the privatization and commodification of public services, that is, demands for spurious immediacy that rarely come to grips with the fact that from the time of the *Critique of Pure Reason* onwards, and into our current late modernity, it is not immediacy or natural spontaneity that is at stake – and it has not been for some time now. The fact that some states, parties and professions have forfeited a number of their mediating functions means that mediation processes must be re-structured rather than neglected or usurped.

The celebration of immediacy can be seen as a retreat from the historical argument developed in the *Philosophy of Right*, and a reactionary return to the static dichotomy of state of nature vs. civil society. This dichotomy may have been linked to real events in the period starting with the writings of the first social contract theorists, subsequently leading up to the French Revolution, but really cannot be seriously invoked thereafter. Attempts to do so after the *Philosophy of Right* can be likened to calls for a return to the 'invisible hand' of the free market after 1929 and Keynes' *General Theory* (1936).[20] In any case it is not a coincidence that demands for privatization are often couched in terms of a return to natural spontaneity and non-interference in biological processes of self-regulation and auto-affirmation. The real issue is how to

[20]Contrary to what is often affirmed it is not idealism that seeks refuge from socio-historical developments. One is more likely to encounter this flight in empirical, pragmatic, and one-sidedly materialist attempts to establish some sort of immediate relation between an event and its sense, which often grasp at analogies between natural causality and notions of human essence. According to this logic capitalism 'works' because people are self-interested and competitive, just like the busy beavers. The problem with most varieties of idealism is not that they abscond from reality, but rather, they fail to ask under what conditions idealism could fully satisfy its own epistemological claims. For a defence of idealism along these lines, see R. G. Collingwood, *The Idea of History* (re-written in 1940 and published posthumously), Oxford, Clarendon, 1992.

develop historically sensitive criteria to analyse and evaluate qualitatively different possible modalities of differentiation and corresponding forms of political representation. Privatized, capital-driven markets do not provide immediacy so much as they mediate according to dictates that subordinate potential educational, housing and occupational diversity to a conceptual and institutional logic of accumulation and short-term profit, that is, they mediate instrumentally, and they therefore dictate and impose. Parties that follow this logic may think they are defending what they consider to be the best means to achieve efficiency and consumer choice. In most cases what becomes clear are the demonstrable links between conceptual tautologies, instrumental calculation and identity thinking: efficiency is invoked as an efficient way to be efficient. Although the 'how' of efficiency is discussed at length in all kinds of media, the 'why' of efficiency is skirted with appeals to various abstractions, such as growth, progress, the well-being of future generations, etc. The idea is championed with great conviction by governments who claim to have the best responses to international competition and 'changed circumstances' that apparently demand sacrifices and the renunciation of rights that are suddenly deemed to be luxuries.[21]

The critique of identity thinking and instrumental reason raises a number of practical and political questions, several of which issue from the Frankfurt School's various assessments of the problems and continuing relevance of a qualified form of idealism. It is clear that Adorno's dialectical critique of Hegelian dialectics is not an anti-Hegelian call for dogmatic materialism or a defence of unfettered, romantic expressivity. It is an attempt to salvage and re-articulate the realities of dialectics, form and mediation, emphasized by Hegel, against an equally Hegelian tendency to posit basic unity, allow for long periods of estrangement and conflict between humanity and nature in parallel with conflicts between a divided humanity in search of different kinds of recognition, and then see complex unity assert itself in epistemology and politics. Proponents of negative dialectics hold that as long as the empirical reality of mediated unity is contrived unity, that is, rather more like an unstable mix of mediated disunity and mediated identity in practice, one has to argue for the explanatory and normative superiority of mediated non-identity against both premature declarations of mediated unity, on the one hand, and against postures of unbridgeable disunity/difference, on the other.[22] It is

[21]See Pierre Dardot and Christian Laval, *La nouvelle raison du monde: Essai sur la société néolibérale*, Paris, La Découverte, 2009, and the brilliant essays collected in Susan Braedley and Meg Luxton (eds), *Neoliberalism and Everyday Life*, Montreal, McGill, 2010.

[22]The opening ceremony of the 2012 Olympic games in London offers a good empirical example of what one might understand as contrived unity. See the articles on the politics of the games in *Sociology*, Vol. 5 (2011).

noted at the end of Chapter Three that whereas a diagnosis of unity usually amounts to a defence of coerced reconciliation, invocations of non-mediated non-identity are likely to betray their lack of dialectical reflexivity with the pompous rhetoric of ontological difference, or somewhat pious appeals to the mystery and sanctity of the face or essence of 'the other'. It is more promising to develop a hermeneutical sociology of postponed transitions and as yet neglected forms of reason. However old-fashioned it may sound, it is argued here that post-idealism can contribute a dialectical dimension to this approach to understanding provisionally suspended historical possibility.[23]

Bearing in mind the considerable differences between them, Adorno and Hegel might well agree that the dynamics of subjective consciousness and socio-historical objectivity crystallize in institutional conflict and cooperation. To put the matter in more systems-theoretical terms, one could say that they examine various forms of communication, modes of information selection, and *Aufhebung* of information. Adorno is also very interested in analysing what kinds of communication are discarded as incidental, as well as investigating the mechanisms leading to the resulting homogenization of social interaction. The two thinkers might also agree that socio-economic, political and historical change develops in accordance with discernible patterns, and that the processes in question unfold according to logics that are neither one-sidedly subjective and random, nor predetermined in some crudely materialist way. Where Hegel and Adorno differ is on the questions of recognition and reconciliation. This discrepancy is centrally related to the discrete ways in which they assess the political and cultural repercussions of the socio-historical dialectics of identity, unity and difference, on the one hand, and those of centralization and dispersion, on the other. For Adorno the possibility of real freedom lies with the institutionalization of mediated non-identity and reconciliation between humanity and nature. Without reconciliation in this sense, freedom does not mean a great deal more than competitive success and consumerism – at least in the era of mediated identity. Real freedom does not depend on the consolidation of contrived unity between citizens and the state, or antagonistic recognition that ushers in an uneasy stalemate between mutually suspicious citizens. For Adorno this is as implausible as widespread citizen identification with the crown, army and civil servants who give substantial structure to

---

[23]For a discussion of this topic that avoids pathos and bombast, see Michael Theunissen, *Der Andere* [*The Other*], Berlin, de Gruyter, 1977. It would appear that rigorously theological approaches to the question of otherness fare better than most attempts to bring theology down to earth by converting it into social psychology. For a discussion of the work of Rudolf Bultmann and Karl Barth, see Leonard V. Kaplan and Rudy Koshar (eds), *The Weimar Moment: Liberalism, Political Theology and Law*, Lanham, Lexington Books, 2012, Part II. For a poetic if somewhat naïve portrayal of alterity and non-conformity, see Pier Paolo Pasolini's film *Theorema* (1968).

Hegel's version of ethical life. In his more optimistic pronouncements, Adorno intimates that the proliferation of instances of simultaneously mediated and non-identically structured communication could foster a process of reconciliation that is no longer achieved against the background of scarcity or forms of objectively obsolete command that have survived into post-scarcity because of missed/postponed transitions, and therefore attained under duress and compulsion.[24] It could be approached instead through de-centred mediating instances – and therefore juridically, to some extent – in nuanced terms which appreciate that each person is an instance of historicized nature rather than a typecast embodiment of a speciously universal human nature that is fundamentally interchangeable with others of the same type. The implication is that there are as many human natures and possible reconciliations as there are humans. But the chance to realize this diversity in practice no longer rests with the state – if it ever did – nor does it rest on an ahistorical natural right to non-interference or individual entitlement. As discussed in Chapter Two, the chance presents itself due to the historically unique political possibilities generated by the discovery of the dialectical dynamics of modern social forms, and the simultaneous persistence of non-identity within them. Whereas Hegel and Marx help illuminate the first dimension, Baudelaire and Nietzsche track the second. Simmel then paves the way for critical theory by studying the coexistence and reciprocal dependence of objective spirit and individual autonomy within a properly theoretical sociological framework. Since that time Frankfurt School critical theory has been constantly evaluating the status of the non-identical and measuring, in qualitative terms, the chances for persistence, in the sense just used, to become more than a fleeting avant-garde modernist aesthetic experience.[25]

But this raises a question that will be touched upon below: how can the project of disseminating non-identity avoid subsuming non-identical phenomena under a generic, somewhat banal concept that undermines the very notion of an extra-conceptual, extra-systemic, and nonetheless

---

[24]As far as potential transitions are concerned, the Greek crisis indicates that post-scarcity is certainly not synonymous with post-austerity, though it could well mean something like post-democracy. Focusing on the United States, Noam Chomsky explains this discrepancy in terms of a re-orientation of economic policy towards de-industrialization and de-development as a panicked reaction to the falling rate of profit in the West during the 1970s. For a very accessible analysis of how the decisions taken in these years relate to contemporary events, see his *Occupy*, London, Penguin, 2012.

[25]Some of these issues are explored in Walter Gropius, *The New Architecture and the Bauhaus* (1919), Cambridge, MIT Press, 1965; Victor Margolin, *The Struggle for Utopia*, and Gerald Raunig, *Art and Revolution: Transversal Activism in the Long Twentieth Century*, Los Angeles, Semiotext(e), 2007. It is important that theoretical work is substantiated by empirical and historical research.

epistemologically valid form of reason that may have important implications for new forms of political representation? This is a crucially important question for any social theory concerned with critique and change. However internally divided in terms of specifying the most fruitful paths of research for answering it, critical theory remains the most promising. This statement of the matter ties in with two of the main premises informing this study, as mentioned in the introduction. The critique of knowledge is social critique and vice versa, and, paraphrasing Marx without adopting an orthodox Marxist approach to praxis and revolution, humanity only sets itself tasks that it is capable of achieving: there are ways of reconciling law (strong dialectics) with non-identity (weak dialectics). If that reconciliation appears unlikely at the moment, the conditions of this unlikelihood can be examined and, eventually, deconstructed. This, in turn, will mean changes in the ways law is conceived of and practised.[26] Two points from the preceding pages will inform the discussion to follow: some kind of dialectic accurately depicts the structure of the late modern world and the political possibilities it offers; and the dialectical critique of a dialectically structured reality attains an enhanced socio-political density when directed towards the dynamics of legality, legitimacy, and the un-coupling and re-coupling of social systems.

Although Hegel's systematic dialectics had to be somewhat dismissive of non-identity in order to be coherent within an orthodox idealist framework, much opposition to Hegel, such as Stirner's for example, is not dialectical enough.[27] The history of social divisions recorded in the theoretical opposition between dialectical imperiousness and anecdotal critique takes a new turn by the time of Simmel's theorization of Marx, Nietzsche and reciprocal interactive exchange. In keeping with the critical theoretical approach to reading texts taken in previous chapters, however, the point is not to appreciate the *Philosophy of Money* as an original work in the history of ideas, but to see how it registers sociological changes as important as those implied by Kant's theory of the public sphere, or the movement from the reigning dichotomy between state of nature and civil society to the theory of ethical life in the *Philosophy of Right*. While Hegel's work is firmly rooted in the politics of post-revolutionary state building after 1789, Simmel sketches the contours of a more de-centred interplay of groups, values, interests, aspirations, allegiances, conflicts and agreements. The book explains why

---

[26]See Raymond Geuss, 'Dialectics and the Revolutionary Impulse' in Fred Rush (ed.), *The Cambridge Companion to Critical Theory*, Cambridge, Cambridge University Press, 2004, pp. 103–38.

[27]For an analysis of these issues see Karl Löwith, *Von Hegel zu Nietzsche* [*From Hegel to Nietzsche*], Zurich, Europa Verlag, 1941.

the individual is never fully included in society and never fully excluded from it either. Simmel helps clarify why, first, no person can be credibly represented in general political terms, and why, second, the modern individual is never reducible to any single caste, class, group or party. His sociology theorizes the significance of a situation in which the individual is emancipated from fixed status and organic community, though without being left to their fate. What is more, emancipation from assigned status comes at a time when the expansive development of the forces of production marks a point of no return to previously entrenched dependence on inflexible institutional responses to natural scarcity and contingency – except as reaction, myth, or both.[28] Hence at a broadly ascertainable moment in the development of the forces of production and a qualitative increase in socially accrued and transmitted knowledge, a possible symmetry arises between the complexity of individual capacities and needs, and elasticity of juridical response to the question of sharing responsibilities. One might regard job-sharing as just one of countless examples that reinforce the point. This is a political possibility that may be realized or may go begging, but it is also real because of its indeterminacy.[29] In other words it becomes realistic and feasible for each individual to develop an autonomous vision of life without thereby having to suffer socio-economic precariousness or isolation as the price for this independence, such that one can talk about individual and collective learning and growth in more complex ways than was previously possible. It is not a case of *Gemeinschaft* versus *Gesellschaft*, but rather the opportunity to reconfigure the social constitution of spatio-temporal relations such as distance, proximity, intimacy, rivalry and respect in a post-auratic way. Nietzsche's re-valuation of all values would thus be given sociological concreteness in ways that complement Marx's critique of political economy.[30]

---

[28]There is clearly a great deal at stake depending on whether myth and reaction prevail, or a politics of self-overcoming can be responsibly organized. Implementation of the latter will require an analysis of what would constitute reaction, and what educational and socio-economic changes are needed to promote flexible approaches to individual development. Major reforms of this kind are bound to meet with opposition from those who feel they are being left out, blamed for past injustices, etc., but will be necessary if large-scale change is going to take place.

[29]Previous discussions in this book intimate something analogous, where it is argued that knowledge does not 'stop' where contingency 'starts', and that the rationality of the consensual norm does not somehow subside where the extra-rationality of power is called upon to enforce. Non-identity is not the 'absent other' of reason and dialectics, but exists, however secluded for the moment, as a possibility within a constellation marked by mediated identity.

[30]The subtlety of his explanations in this regard place Simmel in another league compared to sociological theorists such as Sombart and Tönnies. See Siegfried Kracauer, *The Mass Ornament: Weimar Essays*, Cambridge, Harvard University Press, 1985, pp. 225–57.

However, there is a condition for the possibility of maintaining and enlarging this simultaneous distance from natural scarcity and social isolation, and it is difficult to know with precision to what extent the condition, operative at the time of the writing of the *Philosophy of Money*, remains operative today in new ways. This condition is the increasing importance acquired by money as a medium of communication, exchange and (generally poor) planning, which, in terms of the sociology of alienating distance/suffocating proximity, is of central importance in explaining the transition from mediated disunity to mediated identity. Exploring diverse modalities of communication and exchange is also important for assessing the prospects for the related possibility of non-identical equality, which one might liken to opening up times and spaces of non-discriminatory difference.[31] On this reading of Simmel, the possibility of mediated non-identity is closely connected with the same social fact that threatens to limit the scope of the non-identical to exceptional expressions of unorthodox creativity. Here one notes a number of striking parallels between the argument developed in the *Philosophy of Money* (1900) and the vision of history sketched in the *Dialectic of Enlightenment* (1944). Money de-naturalizes, de-traditionalizes, and creates forms of individual autonomy that have never existed prior to the full development of the money and commodity economy. But it also homogenizes and increases the social space between objective and subjective culture, thus preparing the transition from mediated disunity to mediated identity. Hence the flow of money, especially as capital, enjoys some of the self-steering capacities that a number of theorists attribute to advanced social systems. Although conducive to systemic autonomy, the latter are clearly not conducive to individual autonomy in any straightforward sense.[32]

What paths have been open to critical theory following the publication of the *Dialectic of Enlightenment*? Several distinct alternatives can be discerned. Some thinkers advocate a renewal of Benjamin's politics of revolutionary time and the juridical exception; this renovation has been attempted by Bloch, Agamben and others. A number of theorists have distanced themselves somewhat from the original aspirations of the first generation in favour of communicative action, recognition theory, notions of performance, the politics of friendship, etc. New forms of collective agency have been linked with social

---

[31]Some post-colonial and feminist theory has a great deal to say about this possibility. See in particular Judith Butler, *Bodies that Matter*, New York, Routledge, 1993.

[32]Simmel, *Die Philosophie des Geldes* [*The Philosophy of Money*] (1900), chapter 4. The parallel alluded to is implicit in Benjamin's analysis of the decline of aura in the 'Work of Art' essay, which can be analysed as a kind of farewell to the constellation comprised of mediated disunity within the nation-state, high modernism, Western Marxism and the radical political contestation of movements such as Dada, surrealism and left futurism.

movements, and, more recently, with 'the multitude'. Baudrillard and Rorty, among many others, have opted for post-modern irony against the supposedly grand narratives of History, emancipation, Enlightenment, modernity, reason and revolution. These examples clearly do not exhaust the entire range of options to explore today. In terms of assessing future directions, it might be promising to return to the questions posed in the preceding paragraphs, namely, what are the implications of the unprecedented capacity for people to be part of society without having to be one with it or directly subjected to society's material reproductive needs, and, what alternatives are there to money as the enabling condition of this flexibility? Might it be possible to restructure interactive reciprocal exchange so that communication is 'more' about individual and collective self-overcoming and learning, and 'less' about cash, property and financial markets? Whereas the bourgeois public sphere in the period examined by Kant and Habermas made financial independence and/or professional status the requirement for participation, political inclusion can now be guaranteed on the basis of non-identical equality. It is in fact plausible to go further and claim that late modern contingency and complexity require far more differentiated modalities of inclusion than the ones that facilitated the appearance of a relatively homogenous elite in the time from Kant to the first major crisis of democracy in the interwar period of the twentieth century. This perspective may enhance our understanding of the recent electoral decline of social-democratic parties in several countries, and cast some light on some of the dilemmas that most political parties are likely to face in coming years.

Blocked transitions from quantity to quality

Despite important differences between Scandinavian, German, Western European, British, South American and reformist traditions elsewhere, social-democratic politics across national boundaries for the most part remain committed to redistributive and other quantitative solutions to issues which, as is becoming increasingly clear, are matters demanding a qualitative approach. These include, for example, extra-university occupational training and assessment of the educational and technical qualifications of disabled people within a number of countries, as well as the design of aid programmes for developing countries at the international level. What is clear is that although there is no way back to mediated disunity and the role played by guilds and other semi-feudal corporations within it, political parties are gradually losing their capacity to mediate between individual, political and social concerns in mass society. But the causes of these changes are easy to misread. The electoral trends often explained in terms of the supposedly declining importance of social class as a mobilizing factor have far more to do with unnecessarily inflexible and unimaginative liberal-democratic and social-democratic responses to a changing political reality than they do with the late arrival of mediated unity to a post-Cold War world. Social class has not waned in importance because the vast majority of individuals are now successfully integrated consumer-citizens with good jobs and stable future prospects; the precariousness of many people's lives despite material abundance is impossible to ignore or euphemize, and, importantly, will eventually affect the parties of the centre and right the way it afflicts the centre-left at present. It is not difficult to see that for the same reasons that the Greek crisis could easily become an Italian, Spanish, Portuguese etc. crisis across states, the impasses and problems afflicting the parties of what used to be the far left and today's centre left will at some point embrace the gamut of official political representation within states.[33] The more that the issue is falsely diagnosed as a technical and administrative matter of balancing growth, austerity and tolerable levels of inequality, the more likely it is that instrumental, stop-gap solutions will be proposed by domestic political elites and their counterparts in international financial organizations. The usual litany of prominent voices will be raised to express concern that citizens feel cut off from these decisions and are becoming apathetic or embracing irrational protest parties. These lamentations are unlikely to shed much light on conflict in contemporary society, which is characterized neither by class equality nor citizen apathy. The emerging politics of mediated non-identity are and to an increasing extent will strive to become post-class politics because the de-naturalization processes which have guided the transition from caste to class have proceeded apace, just as, in a related vein, mediated disunity no longer accurately defines the specificities of socio-economic inequality today, to say nothing of the implausibility of mediated unity.[34]

---

[33]For a cogent analysis of the parallels between the crisis of the PASOK, Greek democracy and parliamentary democracy more generally, see Gerassimos Moschonas, 'Shooting Horses in Cold Blood', in *Policy Network Observatory*, 6 July 2012 (online article at www.policy-network.net/pno_detail.aspx?ID=4217&title=Shooting+horses+in+cold+blood), pp. 1–7.

[34]More than twenty years ago, in *La comunità che viene* [*The Coming Community*, Turin, Einaudi, 1990], Giorgio Agamben invokes the notion of a 'coming community' to describe a future politics of what he calls 'singularity'. Similar ideas can be found in a number of philosophical works in the years immediately following the end of the Cold War. See for example Jean-Luc Nancy, *La communauté désœuvrée* [*The Inoperative Community*], Paris, Christian Bourgeois, 1990; and Roberto Esposito, *Communitas*, Turin, Einaudi, 1998. Badiou and Rancière have elaborated on the ideas of Agamben, Esposito and their unorthodox way of thinking about non-instrumental politics. Agamben, Nancy, Rancière and Badiou touch on a number of questions raised by the critical theory of the Frankfurt School that are explored in this chapter. There are nonetheless important differences in

In the period of its ascendancy and stabilization, social democracy won major gains for its constituents within a framework in which conflict could be analysed in terms of a fragmented popular unity susceptible to legal adjudication and welfare reform within the borders of the nation-state. As one might expect, fairly predictable gender, ethnic, occupational, educational and income criteria defined who was entitled to redistributive justice, bearing in mind that such considerations of entitlement were usually preceded by strikes on the one side, redundancies on the other, and related shows of force. If normative consensus was largely absent from most contexts, the nation-state nonetheless provided an adequate framework for the mediation of conflict and the production of enough unity to at least achieve compromises between the diverse sectors of society. Following the breakdown of predictably ordered compromise in the interwar period of the twentieth century, social-democratic approaches to compromise and gradual change survived until the end of the 1970s, when one observes a second transformation – less visibly spectacular in comparison with those of the 1920s and 1930s – in the structure of political compromise and the function of law.[35] In the period leading up to the upheavals of 1968 and the subsequent neo-liberal assault on the principles of the welfare state symbolized by the electoral successes of Thatcher, Reagan and Kohl, the initially faint tremors of what was later to become the seismic shifts of globalization became visible. Despite the immense scope of change taking place in the years between the early 1960s and the mid-1980s, however, there is little solid evidence to suggest that people in Western Europe, North America and elsewhere suddenly became more conservative or hostile to experimentation, or that class-based forms of inequality and disunity were gradually disappearing.[36] If many social-democratic parties have been adept, depending on the party, country and years in question, at discerning recurring patterns in business cycles and the vagaries of boom and bust, their respective analyses of the relation between law and politics have been somewhat less robust. One notes a tendency on the part of social-democratic theorists and activists across states to liken the apparently natural cycles of boom and bust

their trajectories. Whereas critical theory moves from Marxism to sociology by way of a re-evaluation of idealism, the more recent theorists just mentioned move from Marxism to bio-politics and/or ontology. These distinct trajectories have a significant impact on the political implications of the theoretical conclusions reached in each camp. For very thorough overviews, see Keucheyan, *Hemisphère gauche*; Marchart, *Die politische Differenz*, and Nathan Widder, *Political Theory after Deleuze*, London, Continuum, 2012.

[35]See Schecter, *History of the Left from Marx to the Present*, chapter 3, for an exposition of the views of Kirchheimer and Neumann on the collapse of democracy in the interwar period.

[36]For an analysis see Saskia Sassen, *A Sociology of Globalization*, New York, Norton, 2007, chapter 6.

to analogous swings in human nature between conservatism and radicalism. According to this line of interpretation, it seemed reasonable to think that following the radical 1960s and the uncertain early 1970s, the conservatism of the late 1970s and early 1980s was likely to be followed by renewed receptivity to social-democratic ideals and policies. It was widely thought that the parties of the centre left simply needed to bide their time and wait for people to warm up and become less conservative again, which, like the changing seasons, would eventually happen despite unanticipated periods of prolonged political frost.[37]

What was happening and continues to happen, however, is the further unfolding of the processes differentiating social systems from one another that began quite some time ago with the separation of church and state. In the much more recent case at hand, what is particularly relevant is the partial de-coupling of politics and law. These dynamics have caught social-democratic parties by surprise and affected them more dramatically than other political parties. As stated, however, the longer-term consequences are likely to affect the party form as a political institution, and this, in turn, will raise many questions about the epistemological status of concepts like 'the people', 'the state' and democracy as the rule of the people incarnated in a state responsive to something as poorly articulated as the will of the majority. The structural differentiation of politics and law has been designated by some theorists as an apocalyptic sign of the coming post-democracy, and has been lamented by others as the twilight of democracy. It could be maintained that late modern societies are in some ways post-political if, that is, one understands politics in the way that Aristotle, Arendt and other republicans might, or construes it as a friend–enemy relation, as Schmitt and other decisionists do. In a related vein, some observers regard the fading capacity of political parties to manage conflict and compromise as synonymous with post-politics.[38] It can be countered that post-political need not necessarily mean post-democratic, and that in the near future the term democratic itself is unlikely to refer to vaguely articulated notions of popular sovereignty or the will of the majority. To speak with Durkheim and Deleuze, for the moment, the obsolescence of traditional theoretical conceptions of politics and democracy signals the demise of mechanical solidarity and the proliferation of new kinds of organic solidarity among heterogeneous minorities against the would-be natural majority of

[37]Maurice Agulhon, *Histoire et politique à gauche*, Paris, Perrin, 2005, Part II; and Donald Sassoon, *One Hundred Years of Socialism: The West European Left in the Twentieth Century*, New York, The New Press, 1996, Part III.

[38]See Colin Crouch, *Post-Democracy*, Cambridge, Polity, 2004; Emmanuel Todd, *Après la démocratie*, Paris, Gallimard, 2008, Mathieu Laine, *Post-politique*, Paris, JC Lattes, 2009; and Mario Tronti, *La politica al tramonto*, Turin, Einaudi, 1998.

populist democracy.[39] In this context organic denotes interpenetration and interrelation rather than ethnic homogeneity or closed community, such that new configurations of order as mutual dependence and cooperation will be able to challenge traditional notions of order based on the supposed stability-producing effects of hierarchy and respect for authority. As they become distinguished according to discrete developmental logics, politics, law, and other systems are separated in the basic sense that they are no longer unified or centralized. But this de-coupling is accompanied by re-coupling to the extent that there is constant communication, definition and re-definition of systemic boundaries. Centralization may have provided social-democratic and other parties with a conduit that appeared to unify state–party–people according to the party constituencies and *their* respective reliable electorates. Yet this kind of solidarity was often mechanically constructed according to the quasi-religious principle that whereas formal democracy incarnates, substantive democracy goes further by satisfying the corporeal needs of the incarnated. Historical evidence shows that such visions are not invulnerable to recurring organicist and racially intolerant interpretations and practices such as those that prevailed for a time in Italy, Germany, Spain and elsewhere in the last century. These practices have not disappeared in a number of parts of the globe. What may at first sight appear to be a post-political epoch is in fact highly politicized due to the apparent difficulties Western democracies seem to have with taking leave from the naturalist fallacy of the immediate corporeal legitimacy of '*our* people' at the expense of others. The reality of contemporary post-colonial world society convincingly refutes such ideology, and could be acted upon as the political corollary to the notion that (our) God is dead.[40]

A theoretical approach integrating specific aspects of systems theory and first-generation critical theory indicates that the clashing tendencies

---

[39]See Sassen, *A Sociology of Globalization*, pp. 183–9; and De Sousa Santos, *The Rise of the Global Left*, chapters 3–4, for just two of many studies providing empirical evidence in support of this line of theoretical interpretation.

[40]The point is that our people are dead in the political sense that like our God, they were never there as a unified presence in the first place. A synthesis of critical theory and post-colonial theory could effectively deconstruct what continue to be widespread exclusionist principles of belonging and hostility towards difference. Tentative steps in this direction are taken by Dipesh Chakrabarty in *Provincializing Europe: Postcolonial Thought and Historical Difference*, Princeton, Princeton University Press, 2000 and *Habitations of Modernity: Essays in the Wake of Subaltern Studies*, Chicago, University of Chicago Press, 2002. See also J. A. Mbembe, *On the Postcolony*, Berkeley, University of California Press, 2001; Gurminder K. Bhambra, *Rethinking Modernity: Postcolonialism and the Sociological Imagination*, London, Palgrave Macmillan, 2007; and Drucilla Cornell, *Moral Images of Freedom: A Future for Critical Theory*, Lanham, Rowman and Littlefield, 2008, chapter 4. As in the case of the brilliant work of Homi Bhabha, Gayatri Spivak, and Edward Said, the

towards de-naturalization and resurgent myths of natural belonging have been accompanied by the parallel and similarly contrasting movement of functional differentiation and renascent populist appeals to the unity of the people.[41] Hence far from being a post-political epoch, late modernity is highly politicized though not, however, in the increasingly outdated sense of presenting stark choices between different parties or between one clearly defined set of leaders and another. But it is not possible, for reasons sketched in the *Dialectic of Enlightenment* and other writings, to line up de-naturalization and differentiation against resurgent myth and populism, and simply opt for the former. The possibility of a politics of mediated non-identity arises for the first time in tandem with the continued unfolding of the processes that differentiate individual social systems and de-naturalize the conditions defining the terms of autonomy, community, majority and minority. Such politics have the potential to emancipate non-identity from coerced reconciliation through a series of constellational, de-centred mediating instances that could progressively detach material abundance from abstract growth imperatives and what one could designate as one-dimensional steering. To this extent it can be argued that there is evidence of a diffuse project to strengthen the objective, socio-historical dimension of dialectical enquiry in conjunction with the consolidation of materialist, non-identical equality.[42]

The potential for this kind of non-levelling solidarity increases as class is transformed into an increasingly elastic social relation, and the social bond becomes less mechanical in Durkheim's sense, so that egalitarianism is no longer necessarily tied to social-democratic political centralization or the far more cumbersome political centralization of state socialism in its various

---

aforementioned studies, with the exception of *Moral Images of Freedom*, tend to conflate critical theory with post-colonial theory or cultural theory, which is why they can be seen as somewhat tentative from the standpoint defended in *Critical Theory in the Twenty-First Century*. Sociological theory and political economy must play a more significant role in a critical theory of world society than they do in the aforementioned works.

[41]Nowhere is this more clearly the case than in Italy since 1994, where the political system has become increasingly insulated from other social systems. For years the Italian media have been focused on highly self-referential debates about the necessity of institutional reform that have excluded or taken little account of educational, economic, or legal systemic imperatives. Insulation has by no means produced systemic predictability or political stability, however. Berlusconi's nationalist rhetoric and his reliance on coalitions with the Northern League and the ex-fascist Alleanza Nazionale has resulted in an abundance of populist ideology and demagoguery. See Michael Huysseune, 'A Eurosceptic Vision in a Europhile Country: The Case of the Lega Nord', *Modern Italy* 15 (2010), pp. 63–75; and Anna Bull, Gian Luca Garbini et al., 'Italy: Reforms without Reformers', *Modern Italy*, 15 (2010), pp. 197–216.

[42]Latouche, *Pour sortir de la société de la consommation*, chapter 3; and Jean-Marc Durand-Gasselin, *L'école de Francfort*, Paris, Gallimard, 2012, pp. 436–51.

guises. Like the notion of democracy consisting in a free choice between parties with distinct programmes, social democracy and state socialism offer increasingly outdated ways of thinking about autonomy, justice and solidarity. This assessment is likely to seem counter-intuitive to those who regard social class as the primary locus of communal solidarity and collective action to emerge from the industrial revolution. To others it will appear to be a rapprochement with the New Labour approach to 'third way' politics. Spokespeople from both camps are likely to see the ostensible decline of class as tantamount to the end of any radical subjectivity and alternative to capitalism and liberal democracy. Yet these perspectives miss something fundamental about the sociological dynamics shaping historical change in the modern world. The imaginary sliding scale between non-egalitarian capitalism and egalitarian democracy that has informed much mainstream academic and party-political thinking on legality and legitimacy presumes an underlying unity of the people that is violated or infected by foreign bodies like capital and private property. The people, however, are divided on and across many lines (race, class, religion, gender, region, generation, etc.). It has become impossible to unite them and, crucially for the present crisis, impossible to represent them, except in fairly meaningless, or at most, symbolic ways. More importantly, however, is the theoretical and empirical evidence suggesting that underlying unity cannot be presupposed, in analytical terms, and that the passing of these foundational notions is not regrettable, in normative terms. At the end of Chapter Two it is shown how idealizations of foundational authority and undifferentiated conceptions of the people complement tug of war models of power, thus denying the reality of form and other mediating third instances. Due to its stress on mediation, idealism is not merely ideological. It tends towards ideology in certain idealist texts, when unity, reconciliation, objectivity or agreement are presupposed as premises and reproduced as outcomes (this tendency is not peculiar to idealism, but that is another matter). Throughout much of modernity, theoretical unity has really been about the history of stratified disunity, theorized in different ways by Marx and Weber, and about antagonistic identity between concepts and institutions, examined by Adorno. While the possibility of non-mediated non-identity is raised by theologians throughout the ages, and then again in the twentieth century by Heidegger, Levinas and Derrida, the concept of dialectical non-identity is not elaborated until the rise and development of critical theory. Hobbes famously declares that authority, not truth, makes the law, thus neatly expressing the idea that the central concern in the theory and practice of politics is guaranteeing the maintenance of legitimate order, rather than, say, institutionalizing freedom, reason, self-overcoming or justice. Yet there is no order without mediation, especially where more than minimum levels of complexity and contingency have been attained. The key point is that all modalities of order are not equally legitimate, and all modalities of mediation are not equally rational. Comparatively high degrees of complexity make these kinds of qualitative distinctions possible. They enable observers to distinguish, accordingly, between forms of *instrumental* legitimacy, relying on a calculation about the *means* most likely to establish a relatively stable order, and the possibility of legitimacy that is closer to truth in Hobbes' formulation. Can it thus be argued that with regard to more instrumental forms of legitimacy, characterized by varying degrees of disunity and identity, that law is mainly a formal means in the search for order? If this was unequivocally the case, it might help explain some of the resistance to the law from very heterogeneous social actors. But the matter is perhaps more complicated than it might seem.

It is too often supposed that whatever epistemological qualities one may ascribe to de-traditionalized legality, legitimacy is simply a functionalist concept devoid of rational content, and relevant only in terms of national unity. However, to separate legality and legitimacy into respectively normative-rational and non-normative, functionalist dimensions of order is to hold, in effect, that the individual citizen is a reflective juridical subject, whereas the nation is a potentially irrational, collective entity whose needs and appetites can be arbitrarily defined by perceived internal and external threats, that is, by the requirements demanded by constantly changing circumstances. Post-traditional law offers an example of a very particular kind of mediation, and exhibits an unusual formalism.[43] For example, in order to adjudicate distinct cases according to the same criteria, so that law is predictably applicable according to rules that distinguish law from custom, tradition and arbitrary command, legal formalism requires compliance with the distinction between legal and illegal. Ethical criteria (right/wrong) and epistemological criteria (true/false) are not centrally relevant within a legal form of legitimacy. Formalism refrains, almost consciously, one might say for the moment, from providing epistemological density – indicated by the term 'untrue' – to the category of 'illegal'. The converse would also seem absurd: otherwise one would have to say that legislation that conforms to juridical form is somehow just or true due to nothing more valid than its internal consistency. One of the provisional conclusions of this book that emerges

[43]Ernest J. Weinrib, 'Legal Formalism: On the Immanent Rationality of Law', *Yale Law Journal*, 97 (1988), pp. 949–1015. There is considerable textual evidence to suggest that much of what passed for formalism prior to systems theory was really more like an abstract anthropology of formal essence (see end of Chapter One) than a rigorous application of methodological formalism. My current formulation of these issues owes a great deal to my conversations with Ralph Kellas.

from the foregoing reflections is that critical theory can develop stringent criteria of non-hierarchical order and qualitative accounts of reason. These theoretical advances can in their turn provide fresh impetus to help reform existing mediation processes, so that formalism in law, economics, education, health, etc., will be modified in view of the fact that distinct cases are each unique. Hence demanding centralized political control of the economy may no longer be the best way to think about autonomy, solidarity and justice. It may now be more appropriate to demand constitutional guarantees that the economy, for example, operating in accordance with the formal distinction of wasteful/productive, is empowered to eliminate wasteful uses of human and natural resources, such as poverty, entrenched inequality and unnecessary pollution. In this context empowerment is closely bound up with the need for communication between the economy and other social systems.[44] Until relatively recently, instances of mediated non-identity (individual cases) could usually be dismissed, or they were forced to conform to the dictates of instrumental reason and reified objectivity. Given the right combination of theoretical innovation and corresponding adjustments in the functioning of exchange, legitimacy, and law, objectivity and reason will be compelled to orient their operations towards the singularity of non-identity in order to be formally stringent. At this juncture one can anticipate an at least partial symmetry between formal criteria of adjudication, individual rights, and collective needs at local, regional and eventually international levels. It is thus not wishful thinking to imagine that justice can evolve from a quantitative and largely self-defensive demand for punishment or redistribution, towards a qualitative epistemological affirmation of truthful objectivity.[45] This is undoubtedly an ambitious programme. But the suggestion that some combination of privatization, de-regulation, monetarism, Keynesianism, austerity and technocratic management can solve current crises is fantasy.

The project to strengthen the objective dimension of dialectical enquiry together with non-identical equality advances when it is demonstrated that the non-identical does not have anything to do with a supposed generic propensity for all things to swing in roundabouts, such that conservatism begets radicalism, which in its turn provokes a conservative backlash. Nor is it concerned with making good on the claim that the average worker is as intelligent and talented as the average bourgeois, and that this fundamental equality should be reflected in equal opportunities. This is sloppy psychological

---

[44]See the articles by Marcelo Neves, Hauke Brunkhorst, Christian Joerges, Andrew Arato and Philipp Dann in Hauke Brunkhorst (ed.), *Demokratie in der Weltgesellschaft, Soziale Welt*, Sonderband 18, 2009.

[45]Drucilla Cornell, *The Philosophy of the Limit*, New York, Routledge, 1992, chapter 6.

eclecticism that misses what is unique about each historical epoch in terms of its contradictions, potential and risks. The risk in the present context is the danger that abundance is re-coupled to undifferentiated, quantitative growth criteria, thus making the governments of the political system beholden to private banks and similarly functioning financial institutions that in the current economic system have little stake in addressing social and environmental problems. This kind of large-scale dysfunctionality curtails, and in some cases eliminates the scope for qualitative, extra-economic individual and collective growth and learning of the kind that is necessary to coordinate systems without amalgamating them. It arguably may also destroy the objective potential for post-scarcity by contributing to ecological degradation and resource depletion. The dialectics of differentiation, de-coupling and re-coupling can be seen at work in the institutional changes accompanying the transitions from the initial formation of the bourgeois public sphere, to the authoritarian re-coupling of the interwar period, and from there, following a war that can be interpreted as the second chapter of the same war, to the re-regulated de-coupling that followed the 'thirty glorious years' of post-war growth and social compromise, pursued under the broad rubric of neo-liberalism. De-centralized re-coupling will now be needed if the re-definition of systemic boundaries is not to be blocked in favour of a politics of re-amalgamation that ties political decision-making to economic criteria, that is, what amounts to a kind of neo-feudalism, though with the important difference that this time round economics dictates to politics instead of vice versa. To put the matter schematically for the moment, one can anticipate the contours of a constellation marked by the mutual dependence of mediated non-identity and de-centralized re-coupling. This may seem optimistic in some regards. It is contingent upon a number of factors that cannot be controlled or manipulated, but the preceding pages attempt to enlist analytical, historical and sociological argument in order to show that the possibility is not entirely speculative.

In short, de-centralized re-coupling (not fusion or separation) of law and politics holds one of the keys to redeeming the potential for new forms of autonomy implied by the unprecedented capacity for people to be part of society without having to be one with it or directly subjected to its material reproductive needs. The need to feed, clothe, house, etc., and beyond that, to educate, occupationally train, and prepare for autonomy, is a feasible task for any uncorrupted economic system operating under generalized conditions of late modern diversity and relative post-scarcity. The analytical steps leading up to this claim clarify what is meant by the extra-subjective conditions of knowledge and autonomy introduced at the start of the second section of Chapter One. A legitimate, non-hierarchical order will have somehow to preserve and enhance this slowly emerging pluralism without breaking down into chaos. But if allowed to flourish, it will be genuinely plural, and no longer based on a variety of more or less identical manufacturing brands, or on the electoral tactics of competing parties with little to distinguish them apart from their strategies for attaining control over officially recognized political power. These remarks should help elucidate further how mediated unity in theory tends in practice towards an historically specific form of mediated disunity in the transition from traditional feudal stratification to class stratification, registered in the writings of Kant, Hegel, Marx and Gramsci. More research needs to be done in order to show in some detail how this particular instantiation of mediated disunity evolves synchronically and diachronically towards mediated, antagonistic identity in the subsequent transition to mass society, theorized by Adorno, Kracauer, Foucault, Bourdieu and others. One can analyse Benjamin's 'Work of Art' essay as a pivotal moment linking the second and third transitions. In terms of collective learning processes and political possibilities, it is important to remember that the transition to chiefly class-based forms of stratification is marked by new forms of integration and inclusion. These include those initiated by the bourgeois public sphere. It is therefore erroneous to regard the demise of the guilds and the spread of class inequality as an all-encompassing process of exploitation, inexorable polarization and the eclipse of reason. As the allusion to movements across and through history suggests, elements of caste, class and mass continue to coexist, just as local, national and international realities do as well. At a certain point in the evolution of systemic differentiation, however, caste and class offer increasingly less cogent accounts of the modalities of the socially mediated difference between individuals. This is generally ignored by steadfast proponents of parties and states and by fetishists of meritocratic reward for successful conformism.

But there seems to be somewhat of a contradiction here. It is stated that there is a documented, unprecedented capacity for people to be part of society without having to be one with it or directly subjected to society's reproductive needs. So why and how is this capacity threatened by the same condition that creates it in the first place? If one can shed some light on this paradox, it will perhaps be easier to see how prevalent modes of mediation actually mediate to the detriment of non-identity, while others, perhaps more precarious and ephemeral in character at present, mediate with consciousness of their own mediacy and dependence on related mediating instances.[46] A central task of critical theory in the coming years is to show why, elaborating the insights

[46]In addition to the wealth of evidence provided by Occupy and similar movements in this regard, experience from border areas is extremely instructive. See Darij Zadnikar, 'Adorno and post-Vanguardism', in John Holloway, Fernando Matamoros and Sergio Tischler (eds), *Negativity and Revolution*, London, Pluto Press, pp. 79–94.

of Baudelaire and Benjamin, multivalent mediation may be inherent in the structure of socio-historical reality today in the way that Hegel and a great many others after him think that the structure of the real is best described as mediated unity or mediated disunity.[47] Although Hegel may have been partially correct in his assessment of the period 1807–21, Marx's insistence on the prevalence of mediated disunity is surely not illusory as regards the period directly thereafter. Where are we today? A sustained analysis of contemporary examples of multivalent mediation could serve as a starting point for convincing critiques of presumed mediated unity, real mediated disunity and mediated identity, and of largely imaginary non-mediated non-identity as well. Further, such analysis will certainly be able to contribute to an explanation of the current preponderance of money and instrumental reason in late modern societies. However flawed and homogenizing they may be in some respects, money and systems seem to operate in an uneasy, qualified symmetry with the principles of de-centred, multiple mediation and sensual-cognitive correspondences. But the way money and systems currently function also sheds some light on the enormous difficulties inherent in the impulse to intensify the valence of meditated non-identity without trying to channel and manage it. A second provisional conclusion is therefore that money and systems must be reformed in the sense above conveyed by the term re-coupling if, that is, mediated non-identity is to be more than a sporadic flash of truth that is dependent for its redemption on a collective profane illumination. One can also see why Habermas thinks that although sociologically grounded in the ongoing differentiation of systems and life-worlds, such finely tuned mediations between unique human natures can only flourish in limited life-world contexts. These are likely to be sustained because of the close relation between uniqueness and complexity, but never entrenched to the extent that they might challenge systemic logic on key matters of economic, security and administrative policy. Habermas' position in this regard is important, and merits sustained analysis. The discussion of Habermas and Luhmann that introduces Chapter Five offers a good way to explore a number of arguments pertaining to possible future directions in the ongoing re-elaboration of critical theory.

[47]More work needs to be done to explicate the relations between critical theory, reflexivity and all instances of stringent epistemological enquiry, including literary and poetic ones. For examples of the latter, see Fredric Jameson, *The Modernist Papers*, London, Verso, 2007b; and Luca Lavatori, *Dimmi che è stata una rana*, Milan, Codex, 2011.

5

New paths beyond the Marx–Freud synthesis

Habermas' work after *Legitimation Crisis* is guided by the conviction that the 'totally administered world' and 'one-dimensional man' approaches to history and social theory exaggerate the extent to which systemic power can marginalize differences and impose homogeneity upon individuals, objects, urban spaces, voting behaviour and consumption patterns amidst generalized late modern complexity and contingency. But he believes it would be equally imprudent to overestimate the potential political authority of non-identity by ignoring the systemic realities governing the distribution of money and power in an increasingly globalized world. This leaves him (and a great many others who are less coherent than he is) in a somewhat difficult position, since if in principle each instance of human nature is a non-identically equal citizen of the *Rechtsstaat*, non-identical equality should really be the source of all post-traditional political authority. This normative position is not easy to square with his more sociologically sensitive observation that the division of labour and other technical factors make representation indispensable in politics while also making iterative uniformity a condition of formal law. The latter should not be considered a break on democratic legitimacy, but rather, he thinks, as providing the juridical framework within which legitimacy can assume a rational form. In principle, formal consistency renders modern law resistant to *populist* excesses of nationalism, xenophobia, and other instances of contrived unity, and, at the same time, enables law to function as a reliable channel of informed *popular* opinion on important social and political matters. That is, rational law sorts, rejects and selects.[1]

---

[1]Habermas is in broad agreement with Arendt that the division of labour is economic and technical rather than political or simply coercive. Although his position in this regard does undergo changes, he remains committed to the view that one cannot simply politicize the economy or any other differentiated system without altering the meaning of politics and simultaneously blocking the

The implication is that a certain degree of identity must prevail if the exercise of legitimate power is to be regulated to an acceptably accountable extent, and if administration is to function in accordance with manageable criteria of predictability. But what happens if a certain degree of uniformity, deemed necessary for reasons of functional necessity and economic performance, is allowed to become a substantial degree of homogenization and conformity, as many of the first-generation critical theorists suspect is the case under conditions of advanced commodity production and mass culture? How do the quantitative and qualitative dynamics coordinating the aggregation of values and interests work towards widespread compliance with the demands of authority in industrial democracies, even when some of these demands are demonstrably not rational, coherent or legitimate? These become urgent questions if one bears in mind that the openly authoritarian fascism of the interwar period of the twentieth century is unlikely to resurface in the same way today, and if one considers too that a number of the imperatives are really commands that are not easy to square with the notion of popular sovereignty. They include collective submission to what is officially declared to be the necessity of economic growth, as well as individual adherence to various performance principles that reach well beyond a clearly delimited sphere of political accountability. What is at stake is nothing less than a sober assessment of the postulate that the people make the laws in democratic societies. It is widely believed and taught that to the extent that citizens elect representatives who make the laws, the citizens are indirectly involved in law-making processes, that is, they help make the laws that are then carried out by the elected representatives of the people, or those responsible to them, such as government ministries. However mediated their participation happens to be, they are the ultimate source of law and authority. But why would the people consciously subject itself to political and administrative tasks that leave it over-worked and under-represented? The theses of repressive tolerance,

---

flow of information required for the specific functions of the system in question. If his claim is correct, the open fields of communicative action and political equality coexist with the more closed workings of money, power and administration. In terms of the plausibility of this argument, much rides on the explanation of the exact nature of this coexistence. See Arendt, *The Human Condition*, Part III, and Habermas, 'Volkssouveränität als Verfahren' ['Popular Sovereignty as Process'] in Habermas, *Philosophische Texte, Band 4: Politische Theorie* [*Philosophical Texts*, Vol. 4: *Political Theory*], Frankfurt, Suhrkamp, 2009, pp. 35–69. The distinction between populist and popular is obviously a fine but important one which is invoked here in order to emphasize Habermas' belief that authoritarian political populism is a vestige of pre-rationalized life-worlds, that is, a phenomenon which he thinks democratic societies can marginalize if they manage to harmonize the communicative reason prevailing in the life-worlds of civil society with the instrumental imperatives governing social systems.

authoritarian personality, total administration, and one-dimensional order are perhaps somewhat overstated in their original formulation. A wide range of Marxist and non-Marxist thinkers have nonetheless drawn attention to the fact that economic crises do not often produce more profound crises of authority in complex social formations, thus producing the impression of passivity and manipulability on the part of the citizenry. In lieu of the openly authoritarian fascism of dictatorial tyranny, which might now seem to be inextricably bound up with an earlier historical period in which personalized rule was not exceptional, one observes a more subtle, if perhaps also more pervasive uniformity of political opinion and predictability of cultural expression.[2]

There are a number of competing explanations for these phenomena. These include the relative autonomy of the superstructure, imperfect communication between systems and their environments, systemic colonization of the life-world, the perennial domination of elites at the expense of the democratic aspirations of the people, the ostensible end of ideology and retreat to private life, further entrenchment of the tyranny of the majority, extension of the concentration camp to a model of peacetime social organization, the extension of government to governance and the bio-political control of individual human lives, etc. The evolution of Habermas' theoretical position on these

[2]Once again Italy provides an interesting case in point. Pasolini notes that while Mussolini's regime aspired to the total state theorized by Giovanni Gentile, postwar Italian consumer capitalism managed to impose a much more extensive model of social control than anything the Duce would have dreamed possible. In his *Pirate Writings* Pasolini offers the at first glance nonsensical hypothesis that if the fascist years were indeed authoritarian, the postwar period veered towards a level of control approaching totalitarian proportions. Despite the political aspirations of the corporate state to control all aspects of social life, fascist Italy was still a heterogeneous Italy in which regional dialectics flourished, the peasantry remained ungovernable in various parts of the country, and one could enter a piazza and distinguish a person's region of origin, social class and even their occupation by looking at their faces and bodies. By the early 1970s, however, the mechanisms coordinating modes of production and consumption had become inextricably enmeshed to the point where one could begin to detect the functioning of a potentially closed system hostile to cultural diversity, eccentric tastes and regional idiosyncrasies. In the process, the marked differences once visible on bodies and faces were gradually disappearing not, however, as a result of democratization, but rather as a consequence of the apparent reality that power could now integrate and homogenize at the same time it exploited and marginalized. There are clearly affinities between the approach to explaining the effects of creeping identity thought adopted in the *Pirate Writings* and *Lutheran Letters* (written in the early 1970s and first published in 1975–6), and the more sophisticated theories of bio-power subsequently developed by Foucault and Giorgio Agamben. See Pier Paolo Pasolini, *Scritti corsari* [*Pirate Writings*], Milan, Garzanti, 1990, and *Lettere luterane* [*Lutheran Letters*], Turin, Einaudi, 2003. The links with Foucault and Agamben are particularly evident when one compares Pasolini's essays and newspaper articles in the aforementioned collections with the main lines of argument in Foucault's lectures on bio-politics at the Collège de France in 1977–9 and Agamben's *Homo Sacer*. See Michel Foucault, *Sécurité, territoire et population: Cours au Collège de France 1977–1978*, Paris, Gallimard, 2004, and *Naissance de la biopolitique: Cours au Collège de France, 1978–1979*, Paris, Gallimard, 2004a; Giorgio Agamben, *Homo sacer: Il potere sovrano e la nuda vita*, Turin, Einaudi, 1995.

questions is of particular interest because of his links with the first generation of critical theorists and their diagnoses of economic problems, changes in the function of law, the ambiguities of mass culture, and the implications of various structural transformations affecting how people understand the demands of authority and how they imagine the possibilities for political change.[3] His work is also very important because of the potential practical conflicts implied by a normative commitment to non-identical equality, on the one hand, and simultaneous recognition of the coordinated uniformity of individual behaviour required for the regular operation of key social systems, on the other. Whereas the normative vision is implicitly pluralist, open and undetermined, the social scientific approach highlights causal factors that acknowledge limits to what can be changed through individual and group initiatives.[4] The potential conflicts are by no means limited to doubts about Habermas' theoretical framework, or to the explanatory efficacy of theory more generally. This is worth stressing, since of all mainstream and high profile attempts to arrive at a credible synthesis of normative and sociological perspectives, that is, a synthesis without which any social theory must be regarded as inadequate, Habermas' stands out for its theoretical, historical and

---

[3]Taking the arguments developed in Chapters Two and Five together, one can compare the contemporary constellation comprised of economic crisis, changes in the function of law, mass culture, and the implications of various structural transformations affecting how people understand the demands of authority and the possibilities for political change, on the one hand, with the nineteenth-century constellation defined by relations between shortened attention spans, increasing impatience with poetry, the demise of the bourgeois public sphere, and the rise, in its stead, of professional political parties and mass electorates, on the other. Just as society can be interpreted in diachronic terms as a series of mutual interactive exchanges, history can be interpreted as a succession of overlapping constellations in which the terms of the constellations shift, and are re-arranged and re-articulated. See Alfred Sohn-Rethel, *Geistige und körperliche Arbeit* [*Intellectual and Manual Labour*], Weinheim, VCH, 1989, Part I.

[4]In *Legitimation Crisis* (1973) Habermas notes that many political initiatives face the colonizing tendencies of systems. But in addition, it is enormously difficult for communicative action to resist the systemic steering of initiative, which tends to transform political projects seeking to change the architecture of the space between citizens into corporatist and welfare demands for more money. See in particular chapter 2 of that book. The enduring significance of Weimar debates on this issue is that there are few good grounds to retain democratic structures of collective rational will formation and accountability if, that is, legitimacy mainly becomes a question of rates of credit, capital gains tax, income tax and redistribution. In this case technical expertise will be more efficient than democratic debate and action. Political republicans are generally correct to observe that the line between the liberal-democratic notion of balancing equality of life-chances with equitable welfare, on the one hand, and the more frankly technocratic scenario just invoked, on the other, has become increasingly blurred. The problem intensifies to the extent that the state is called upon from various quarters to regulate the economy and also not interfere in it, that is, the state is assigned more tasks than it can possibly accomplish, thus leading to cries for more efficient, market-oriented policy (the problems with this view are well known). The far more pertinent project would consist in re-articulating the relation between life-chances and political will formation.

empirical breadth and vision. It is therefore a matter of some consequence that even a theorist with his sophistication is ready, as he seems to be at times, to come close to both Arendt and Luhmann on certain issues. From the time of the *Theory of Communicative Action* (1981) onwards, he accepts that it is not possible to politicize the economy (or any other differentiated sphere) without diluting the meaning of politics and simultaneously obstructing the flow of information required for the specific functions of the system in question.[5] In his defence it could be argued that by sounding out spaces between the facts and the norms, as he puts it, Habermas is less consistent but more ambitious than thinkers who rely on exclusively normative or primarily descriptive methodologies. On this reading coherence might actually be more akin to fetishism of conceptual purity than it is to actual methodological rigour. Whereas Arendt's celebration of republican virtues fails to engage with societal evolution, and insofar can be criticized as reactionary in some ways, Luhmann's account of systemic operations does not always stand up to close empirical scrutiny. For example, it would be absurd to imply that the ongoing economic crises of growth and unemployment can simply be solved with more resolute de-coupling of economic and political systems. Given currently prevailing institutional arrangements, property rights, growth imperatives and performance principles, this would mean little more than privatization and further economic de-regulation. These are the socio-economic and political measures that contributed to the latest round of problems in the first place.[6]

It is more convincing to construct a three-step argument explaining why, as is attempted in the previous chapter, (1) economic stability (not growth at all costs) can be coupled with non-identical political equality; (2) non-identical equality in practice will require a series of de-centred, cross-systemic operations, and therefore innovative and flexible approaches to ownership and planning; and (3) the educational, technical, cultural and political resources for this conceptual-practical synthesis may be available to many more citizens of world society at this current historical juncture than is generally acknowledged by governments beholden to the demands of the Central European Bank, IMF and European Parliament in Brussels.[7] The theoretical exploration of

[5]Habermas, *Nachmetaphysisches Denken* [*Post-Metaphysical Thought*], Frankfurt, Suhrkamp, 1988, pp. 234–41, and *Faktizität und Geltung* [*Between Facts and Norms*], chapters 5–6.

[6]Will Hutton, 'The Facts Are Clear: This Cruel Austerity Experiment Has failed', *The Observer*, 3 June 2012, p. 33. The aptly worded subtitle of the article adds: 'While the human cost of economic stupidity is all too visible, the world's leaders are paralysed by their dogma.' Hutton is far from offering an isolated assessment of this situation.

[7]Peter Kafka outlines the basic theoretical premises of this argument in *Das Grundgesetz vom Aufstieg: Vielfalt, Gemächlichkeit, Selbstorganisation: Wege zum wirklichen Fortschritt* [*The Constitution of Ascendancy*], Munich, Hanser, 1989. The claim that efficient investment decisions can be coordinated with differentiated rights of inclusion and democratic participation

this possibility is undertaken in the first two chapters of this book in terms of dialectics, social differentiation, de-naturalization and collective learning. That analysis needs to be supplemented with more historical, empirical and economic research that extends beyond the scope of this book. In anticipation of the discussion to follow in this chapter, however, it might be noted that towards the end of the 1970s and into the 1980s, with the accession to power of Thatcher, Reagan and Kohl, the institutional resources necessary to engineer a simultaneous retraction and extension of the role of the state in managing the economy and re-organizing policing were available and relied upon. Bearing in mind the different national contexts in play, the ground was prepared for the currently dominant neo-liberal version of globalization that was unleashed in the aftermath of 1989, that is, a model for the political organization of economic competition that is currently in complete disarray and in need of an alternative, to judge by events in Greece, Spain, Portugal and elsewhere. In a comparatively brief period, social-democratic welfare provision was curtailed, while the discretionary power of formal and informal law enforcement agencies was buttressed.[8]

This is a complex historical period that resists blanket political definition. The broader point holds, however. It was possible for certain governments in specific states to draw upon the knowledge and steering capacity required to pursue and accomplish determinate political aims. It may well be the case that governments are no longer equipped to do this – the issue must be analysed, researched and debated. But this incapacity does not obviate the need to question how, or according to which normative principles and sociological realities enhanced qualitative wealth and collective learning will be utilized in the coming years. Crucial questions arise concerning which projects will be chosen as worthy of investment in this extended sense of planning according to supple criteria of expansion, and which priorities will be invoked to decide how the information generated by wealth and resources

is confirmed by the Mondragon network of cooperatives in the Basque region of North-Eastern Spain. The confirmation indicates that cross-systemic operations are possible and can actually stabilize economic systems rather than consistently overloading them, as is often claimed. The Basque Country admittedly presents an unusual degree of effectively transmitted learning and collective appreciation of the qualitative dimension of social resources. But a number of studies show that Mondragon is by no means a one-off exception. See for example, Carmen Sirianni, *Workers' Control and Socialist Democracy*, London, Verso, 1982; Mark Holmstrom, *Industrial Democracy in Italy*, Aldershot, Averbury, 1989; Elaine Comisso, *Workers' Control under Plan and Market*, New Haven, Yale University Press, 1979; Robert Oakeshott, *The Case for Workers' Co-ops*, London, Macmillan, 1990; Alec Nove, *The Economics of Feasible Socialism*, London, Allen & Unwin, 1983, and especially Wyatt, *The De-fetishized Society*.

[8]See the articles contained in Mark McNally and John Schwarzmantel (eds), *Gramsci and Global Politics*, Part III.

will be selected.[9] Traditional theory and conformist common sense tend to deny the possibility of a rapprochement between steering of any kind with flexibility, just as mainstream voices appear to be unanimous when it comes to what they consider to be the objective limits to reconciling genuine political accountability and effective economic innovation. On this point conventional theory and common sense would seem to correspond to the timeless truths of reason and logic. Such lack of reflexivity, which quite conveniently accepts that 'the dull compulsion of economic forces' resists reform, underscores the continuing relevance of the attempt to break through to extra-conceptual knowledge by way of concepts, and to arrive at credible syntheses that do not suppress what is not easily assimilable to synthetic operations. Although the moment for the practical realization of idealist philosophy may have passed, a negative dialectical reading of idealism remains relevant to the study of democracy and to some of the assumptions and claims of mainstream theory.

In the previous chapter it is noted that despite their considerable differences, Adorno and Hegel might concur that the relations between subjective consciousness and socio-historical objectivity crystallize in the dynamics of institutionalized conflict and cooperation. That point is relevant to the discussion in this chapter: subjective consciousness and the production of synthetic concepts are not only closely related, they help constitute lived institutional reality. In other words common to both concepts and to institutions is the operation of mediating syntheses. The question is whether critical concepts can contribute to the deconstruction of prevailing common sense, in those instances when it is patently wrong, and contribute to the reform of institutional syntheses, where these are clearly wasting human potential and environmental resources. If so, conceptual work can participate in the construction of mediations that credibly envisage the future vitality of non-identity to be linked with the establishment of de-centred steering and new modes of cross-systemic coupling, re-coupling and de-coupling. It is implausible to argue that the conceptual unity of the cognitive and sensual dimensions of individual consciousness and nature is rational as long as it 'stops' before reaching the thing in itself, and refrains from questioning the sanctity of private property. Equally doubtful is the assumption that the

[9] Social differentiation undoubtedly constitutes a positive development in social evolution and an increment in learning and qualitative wealth. But just as there can be blocked and postponed transitions, there can also be periods of educational stagnation. These manifest themselves when fixations develop about what is necessary for a particular social system. See Pierre Guibentif, *Foucault, Luhmann, Habermas, Bourdieu: Une génération repense le droit,* Paris, Lextenso-Librairie générale de droit et de jurisprudence (Collection Droit et société [série sociologie] n° 53), 2010, pp. 369–70.

institutional synthesis of the individual and society is legitimate, even when it is an obvious case of mediated disunity that legislates and re-legislates an inviolable private right to exploit those categorized as foreign or less skilful/undeserving, and to damage the environment until evacuations and other inefficient post hoc measures are taken. It is instructive in this regard to return briefly to Hegel and Adorno on concepts and idealism, before moving on to Luhmann and Habermas on systems and communication.

On the possibility of cross-systemic operations and de-centred mediations

There is a lot at stake when assessing Adorno's reading of Hegel and Habermas' semi-Hegelian affirmation of the qualified convergence of facticity and norms in the modern legal state, which informs his critique of Adorno and first-generation Frankfurt School theory. These debates offer keys for interpreting and evaluating the actual extent to which proclaimed mediated unity and official democratic representation can, to differing degrees, tend in practice towards mediated disunity, mediated identity and dysfunctional, insufficiently democratic misrepresentation. They also offer valuable insights into the related reasons why expressions of mediated non-identity in aesthetic reason and political action are often obscured, or take on the semblance of eccentric irrelevance. It remains to be seen if the concept of mediated non-identity can offer diagnoses specifying how contrived unity and other implicitly populist syntheses can be analysed and, if possible, addressed, without resorting to the identity thinking that the non-identitarian impulse reflectively sets out to deconstruct. In general terms, consequently, one might say that just about every theory synthesizes and conceptualizes just as, by analogy, all democracies in principle integrate and constantly attempt to reconcile minority positions with what at any particular juncture is widely enough accepted to become prevailing common sense and legitimate authority. A critical theory, by contrast, strives to go beyond ethical abstraction and formalist description by analysing how the mediating dynamics at work in virtually all theorizing result in syntheses that exclude and silence dissident theoretical elements.[10]

---

[10]There are thus parallels between epistemological dissidence, musical dissonance, and the possibilities for democratic resistance. See Andrew Bowie, *Music, Philosophy and Modernity*, Cambridge, Cambridge University Press, 2007, especially chapter 9; and Stephen Toulmin, *Return to Reason*, Cambridge, Harvard University Press, 2003. It is particularly interesting that the analogies in question are not easily characterized as purely idealist, materialist, theoretical or practical. They are more akin to correspondences and reciprocal interactive exchanges.

Hence there is a fine line between critical theory that undermines itself by discrediting pretty much all of theory as inherently dogmatic, and critical theory that enlarges the domain of theoretical validity without becoming too eclectic and diffuse. Refractory theoretical impulses and practical movements arise whenever thought is rigorously suspicious of both overburdened concepts and quick or easy solutions to conflicting political proposals. Although these elements repeatedly leave traces that document their overlooked truthfulness, they are usually incompatible with conceptual systematicity and elegance. The parallel analogy, in very broad terms for the moment, is that many apparently democratic societies have a history of coercively integrating by excluding viable alternative courses of action, imposing certain solutions at the expense of others, silencing minorities and marginalizing dissident individuals and groups in the name of stability, security, tradition and the national interest. The link between oppressive theoretical syntheses and technocratic governance is therefore their common tendency to function on the basis of mediations that rely on unifying tendencies that gravitate towards, or in some cases actually culminate in levels of uniformity which can approach identity. This occurs when the rhetoric of freedom of democratic choice is belied by official policy announcements stating that there is only one feasible solution to a given issue, and politics effectively becomes fiat. In its best instantiations critical theory seeks to re-orient thinking in the belief, borne out by the experience of *diverse* human natures in the *common* medium of history, that conceptual imperiousness is no more the original sin of thinking, than oppression is the defining character of life in society. The qualified juxtaposition of theory in general and critical theory raises the possibility of a critical democracy in opposition to its generic and not particularly democratic manifestations.[11]

It is important not to reify this set of issues by positing a permanent contradiction between what is conceptual, abstract, systematic and legal versus what is extra-conceptual, concrete, experienced and legitimate. It is also likely to be wishful thinking, for the time being at least, to believe that

---

[11] Here one may hope (instead of wishfully thinking) that humanity sets itself tasks that only arise when the material conditions for their solution are already present or in the process of formation. See Karl Marx, *Preface and Introduction to a Contribution to the Critique of Political Economy* (1857–8), Beijing, Foreign Languages Press, 1976, p. 4. A critical democracy in this sense would have to function quite differently than a critical public sphere surrounded, as it were, by hostile economic and political systems. Castoriadis suggests that if the imaginary institution of society changes, a critical democracy could certainly be created. See Suzi Adams, *Castoriadis's Ontology: Being and Creation*, New York, Fordham University Press, 2011, and the special issue 3 (2012) of the *European Journal of Social Theory* on Castoriadis. Gramsci's ideas on what he refers to as a self-regulated society are also relevant in this context. See Gramsci, *Quaderni del carcere* [*Prison Notebooks*] (written in 1929–35, published in English by Columbia University Press), ed. Valentino Gerratana, Turin, Einaudi, 2007, pp. 693, 752–6, 882 and 937.

instances of non-conformist thought and art, or the politics of friendship, for example, might mediate between these two 'poles'.[12] What such instances can do is re-orient thinking and examine the ways in which prevalent syntheses and unities are constructed in epistemology and politics. Part of the task is to examine why these relationships take on the semblance of a dichotomy or a contradiction, or the appearance of an isolated pole. Habermas indicates that the problem of reconciling sociological facticity with normative validity is alleviated to a considerable extent because mediated unity and mediated non-identity co-exist in complex societies with solid constitutional foundations.[13] Although mediated unity and mediated non-identity are ideals, they also achieve a significant level of objectivity in the Hegelian sense of objective spirit. This is accomplished by enforcing the protection of abstract right, that is, individual autonomy, as the basis of mutual recognition and horizontal understanding, so that understanding can then be channelled vertically into democratic consensus, which, in turn, is made collective and representative in formal law. The formal component of positive law is complemented by various examples of post-traditional *Sittlichkeit* – most notably by communicative action. The danger of systemic colonization of non-instrumental reason in the life-worlds of civil society does exist, and does periodically threaten to interrupt finely tuned mediations between unique individuals. But civil society is partially insulated from systemic encroachment by the overlapping, imbricated interaction of different life-worlds and their diverse modes of communication, and protected too by the incommensurability of systemic rationality with life-world rationality. Habermas maintains that modern individuals are therefore self-legislating citizens and not isolated, sub-systemic consciousnesses. The real is still rational, but the rational is now sub-divided into its variegated instantiations, and therefore too polyvalent to be susceptible to absorption by any particular variant of reason, whether systemic, instrumental, communicative or mimetic.[14]

---

[12]The possibility of a 'politics of friendship' is explored by Derrida in his book with the same title (*Politiques de l'amitié*, Paris, Galilée, 1994, available in English). Some of the methodological and political affinities between critical theory and deconstruction are developed by Alex Thomson in *Democracy and Deconstruction*. Also see Peter V. Zima, *Deconstruction and Critical Theory*, London, Continuum, 2002, chapters 1–2.

[13]Nineteen years (1973–92) separate the critique of the late modern legal state in *Legitimation Crisis*, and Habermas' defence of constitutional law in *Between Facts and Norms*. One wonders about the extent to which his objections in the first book have been obviated by constitutional reform, and the extent to which he has chosen to try to re-route social theory in order to enter into a dialogue with a number of theoretical currents that were unknown to or largely ignored by Adorno, Benjamin, Marcuse, etc. See William Outhwaite, *Critical Theory and Contemporary Europe*, London, Continuum, 2012, chapters 6–7; and Jean-Marx Durand-Gasselin, *L'école de Francfort*, Part III.

[14]Habermas, *Faktizität und Geltung* [*Between Facts and Norms*], chapter 4.

In Habermas' estimation this high degree of complexity prevents modern social processes from succumbing to centripetal forces threatening to flatten reality into an imaginary, all-encompassing centre governed by a single principle such as one-dimensional existence or the unrelenting mastery of nature, and also stops them from unravelling into an equally improbable jumble of peripheries, disconnected private worlds, inconsequential language games, or colliding and scattering social systems. He thus distinguishes his position from what he takes to be the falsely imagined scenarios implied by the transformation of Enlightenment into total administration, which he associates with the first generation of critical theorists, and the theory of extra-normative, and therefore chronically illegitimate autonomous systems defended by Niklas Luhmann and other systems theorists. His point is that negative idealism, systems theory and many other approaches to understanding the contemporary world ignore the manifold learning processes through which modern societies have acquired the capacity to produce secular, post-metaphysical, binding norms. Habermas thus stresses the qualitative dimension of production at a given stage of social evolution and differentiation, and is right to point out that qualitative increases in knowledge and communication make humanity less dependent on or fearful of external nature. Hence a certain qualified continuity between early critical theory and critical theory in the twenty-first century can be discerned in his argument that the conditions have been established for a transition to rational life-worlds in which the cultural sources of meaning can eventually dispense with traditional norms, status hierarchies and pyramidal structures of authority.[15]

Habermas maintains that as this process unfolds, the respective claims of ethics and philosophy are progressively detached from institutionalized religion and theology. This path of development can be regarded in Weberian terms as rationalization, provided that one does not misconstrue rationalization as a completely instrumental phenomenon devoid of substantive meaning or content. The rationalization of religious beliefs produces a crisis in meaning while simultaneously generating democratically negotiable expectations about the right principles desired to guide the formulation of socio-economic criteria of productivity and non-discriminatory principles of political inclusion. This means that disenchantment has to be seen within a larger movement towards secularization and democratization, whereby disenchantment is not only a price worth paying for the prospect of genuine autonomy, it is the condition of

[15]The theses on differentiation, collectively transmitted learning and democratization link *Knowledge and Human Interests* [*Erkenntnis und Interesse,* Frankfurt, Suhrkamp, 1968], *Legitimation Crisis*, and *Between Facts and Norms* with Brunkhorst's *Critical Theory of Legal Revolutions: Evolutionary Perspectives*, forthcoming in this series, and some strands of the argument developed in *Critical Theory in the Twenty-First Century*.

norms free from the vestiges of metaphysical and religious justifications. If the demise of Western religions as overarching *Weltanschauungen* is indicative of cultural uncertainty, it is also evidence of the cognitive content (knowledge) of the political demand (human interests) that participation no longer rely on considerations of birth or hereditary rank. In the longer term, then, there are good grounds to believe in the prospects for bridging the claims of rational ethics with those of political order.[16] Habermas suggests that a democratic society with rational constitutional norms performs specific educational tasks that a formally democratic political system cannot do by virtue of formalism alone: it channels expectations into agreements, and eventually converts communication and agreements into rights. This is not a utopian scenario, but rather an at least partial convergence of facts and norms in keeping with the advanced conditions of material and cultural development of functionally differentiated modern societies. While the discrete dynamics of social evolution are ignored by idealists and most analytical philosophers, they are misconstrued as meta-biological cybernetic processes by many positivists and systems theorists. In sum, social theory in a democratic society requires methodological finesse. This subtlety is sorely lacking in complacent apologies for inequalities and other power asymmetries within the existing order, and is lacking too in much self-styled radical critique of that order. It is one thing to move beyond idealism and the philosophy of consciousness, but quite another thing, Habermas intimates, to abandon crucial anthropological categories such as language, communication, individual autonomy, etc., without which any victory over idealism surely must be pyrrhic. Hence Habermas appears to address the problem of moral abstraction he perceives in Kant and Rawls, while also redressing the critical deficit in Hegel's dialectics of mediated unity, which are too quick to conflate the actual with the rational. He believes that this enables him to salvage what is ephemeral but important in Adorno, while at the same time avoiding the normative deficits of Marxism, systems theory, post-structuralism and deconstruction.[17]

---

[16]Habermas, *Erkenntnis und Interesse* [*Knowledge and Human Interests*], chapter 3. There is a long-standing debate about the ways in which money, the division of labour, capital, advertising, etc. possibly neutralize or even undermine the collective 'cognitive gains' acquired through the demise of Western religion and hereditary status. The present book offers a perspective on this matter that differs from the culture industry and communicative action approaches.

[17]Habermas, 'Über den internen Zusammenhang von Rechtsstaat und Demokratie' ['On the Internal Connection between the Legal State and Democracy'], *Philosophische Texte, Band 4: Politische Theorie* [*Philosophical Texts*, Vol. 4: *Political Theory*], pp. 140–53. For a very good comparative analysis of Rawls and Habermas, see the essays collected in Gordon Finlayson and Fabian Freyenhagen (eds), *Habermas and Rawls: Disputing the Political*, London, Routledge, 2011, which includes texts by Rawls and Habermas, as well as critical essays on their work.

Luhmann looms as a key opponent. Like Habermas, and in contrast to many post-structuralists, bio-political theorists, and deconstructionists, Luhmann seeks to explain the dynamics structuring the relations between legality, legitimacy, reason, democracy and knowledge. Despite obvious differences in their respective manner of exposition, Luhmann is as stringent as Adorno in his refusal to prop up normative political ideas that have clearly parted way with institutional practice and historical reality. If dissident theoretical elements tend to be dissonant ones in Adorno's case, they tend to be consistently anti-foundational in Luhmann's. His approach is somewhat reminiscent of Simmel's critique of legal anthropology in this regard. Instead of denouncing legality as a smoke screen for the state of exception, or relativizing knowledge as a tool in the struggle for power, Luhmann carefully investigates the epistemological reliability of the essentialism underlying the dominant understandings of bedrock political concepts such as action, legitimacy, justice, the state and communication. Simmel performs a similar task in his analysis of money and the objectivity of social form. It is not necessary to condemn Kant or other liberals as cruel competition-driven individualists who fetishize formal concepts and lack any sense of solidarity. This kind of psychologizing critique is common, but ineffective. It is more analytically rigorous to explain how it is possible to discern objective social form without having recourse to subjective essence as the moral-epistemological foundation of objectivity. In this manner it is possible to avoid the pseudo-explanation according to which the discrepancy between social form and human nature represents a clear case of alienation, or an ontological difference about which nothing can be done. The discussion of Simmel, modernism and montage in Chapter Two confirms the point that dialectics are not exhausted in their subject–object form. By de-centring the subject–object totality into a polyvalent multiplicity of non-equivalent reciprocal exchanges, Simmel indirectly offers a plausible hypothesis of how knowledge of social form and process is compatible with a hermeneutic of non-equivalence and, by extension, with a hermeneutic of non-identity. This constitutes an important theoretical innovation if one considers that almost all preceding accounts of social and historical causality tend to be either non-dialectical or idealist, that is, incapable of thinking difference and differentiation as something other than a sub-category of unity, disunity, or estranged unity, as in the case of mediated unity and alienation.

Traditional theory generally ignores this innovation, with the consequence that it relies on normative concepts that are hostile to non-identity in a number of obvious and not so obvious ways. It re-sutures morality to knowledge with the implicit intent to anticipate and neutralize a set of potentially challenging questions about the relation between the order of things and the subject's acceptance of the validity of that order. Through supposed direct participation in the construction of an order of their own making, the subject knows and is morally beholden to what s/he has brought into existence. This is manifest in the case of a hypothetical civil society created in the unanimous exit from the state of nature and other similar theoretical constructions. Hence one should perhaps re-examine the widening gulf between citizens and authority before deploring it as a simple case of political alienation. Part of the problem is that depending on time and place, alienating disunity could be susceptible to overcoming by a unifying class, race, multitude, party or charismatic leader – in short, a vanguard subject representing a meta-subject – that manages to make it seem plausible that the alienated meta-subject can and should re-appropriate what was rightfully theirs or is somehow destined to be theirs. There are thus affinities between notions of originally unified presence, legitimacy through representation, protest against apparently dysfunctional representation which is typically diagnosed as alienation/disaffection, and attempts to re-appropriate and/or re-establish unified presence. The idealist fallacy of knowledge as re-presented presence complements the naturalist fallacy concerning the immediate corporeal legitimacy of *our* people, thus facilitating a transposition of subject–object unity into people–state unity based on an unstated, presumed continuum. Non-identity thinking resists these kinds of assumptions by signalling that in institutional practice, such transpositions often foment racism, resentment and ambiguous identification with contrived unities, such as the clichéd unions of Führer and Volk, vanguard and class, or of God, family, country and wage labour. Unity is thus constructed in ways that are not particularly unifying, that is, through mediations that are as likely to exclude or pathologize as they are likely to harmoniously integrate and synthesize. Critical theory investigates the mechanisms engineering largely symbolic syntheses, while simultaneously attempting to interrupt, wherever and whenever possible, the chain of associations that hold oppressively unifying identifications together. This approach links critical theory and deconstruction. Marxism and other critical disciplines sometimes revert to traditional theory when they locate the central, inherently exploitative mediator in capitalism, the state, or some other single sufficient cause that cannot explain the factors at work in specific cases and contexts.[18] Abstraction and

[18]For a Marxist approach that does not revert to traditional theory, see Moische Postone, *Time, Labour, and Social Domination: A Reinterpretation of Marx's Critical Theory*, Cambridge, Cambridge University Press, 1993. Despite the sub-title of the book and Postone's analytical rigour, Marx is a political economist, not a critical theorist. This becomes evident if one considers Postone's almost exclusive focus on questions of value, abstract time and abstract labour. Political economy has an important role to play in the reformulation of critical theory, but it cannot, by itself, satisfy the interdisciplinary claims of the latter. For a detailed analysis explaining why, see Werner Bonefeld's contribution to the *Critical Theory and Contemporary Society* series, forthcoming.

obscurantism offer equally inadequate responses to mediation processes that produce conflict, crisis and unnecessary mobilization. How does one best develop a methodology that is neither simplistic and conformist, or hopelessly abstract and of minor practical importance? This question is as relevant today as it was when the members and affiliates of the Institute for Social Research first attempted to re-think the relations between political economy, history, legal theory, philosophy, aesthetics and to a lesser extent, sociology. Going forward, critical theorists will have to redress the sociological deficit that deconstruction and recognition theory do not really address.[19]

Critical theory in the twenty-first century: Differentiation and difference in sociological perspective

There is an inevitable and potentially very salutary distance between citizens and political authority under conditions of systemic differentiation and comparative material abundance. These factors eliminate the need for a state-citizen symmetry envisaged as the most effective war machine available for conquering scarcity, poverty, and conducting other operations requiring militarized, un-reflective responses to uncertainty. It is ahistorical to equate the problems confronting societies adapting to natural scarcity with the problems of complex late modern societies, and therefore misleading to regard the current financial crisis as simply the latest episode in a long line of plagues binding archaic orders with advanced industrial ensembles, although problems in the Euro-zone are often portrayed in these terms in the mainstream media. Chapter Four indicates that once individuals can be part of society without being employed as full-time soldiers in what for centuries has been a war for survival, it will be feasible to regard wealth and productivity from more experimental perspectives. These resources can become measurable in terms of elastic responses to contingency, thereby obviating the need for imbalanced economies that are excessively geared towards standardized, wasteful accumulation. Waste of this kind can be regarded as an in-built overreaction to unpredictability that fails by rushing headlong, figuratively speaking, in the opposite direction. But it is definitely not best explainable as benign negligence or as a simple case of human, all too human

[19]The extent to which Habermas achieves this remains a matter of much contention. See Schecter, *The Critique of Instrumental Reason from Weber to Habermas*, chapter 6, for an assessment.

error that 'we', as democrats sharing responsibility in equal measure with all other citizens, have to 'learn to live with'.[20] The montage dialectic of concepts and institutions that oscillate between excessive formalism and insufficient formalism is relevant here. Instead of securing predictability, overreaction to unpredictability intensifies the problem the over-reactor sets out to solve. If societies set about problem solving with insufficient reflexivity regarding the mediated character of the phenomenon at hand, they are likely to ignore the reality that phenomena assuming an economic form are rarely purely economic. One cannot expect to produce the requisite reflexivity by calling in the right panel of experts, devising a magically efficient interest rate, or some similarly one-dimensional pseudo-solution. The 'right' panel of experts does not exist, as such, because no group of experts is capable of creating a theoretically credible and functionally efficient synthesis of facts and norms. The series of mediations needed to generate sufficient reflexivity and a workable synthesis depends on society-wide factors, that is, on a critical democracy coordinated by active minorities in the sense sketched at the beginning of the previous chapter. This qualitative intensification of democratization reaches well beyond the limited scope of reflexivity attributable to the early modern critical public sphere. At a given level of social complexity, increased production or more rapid production will not solve economic problems, any more than reductions in the cost of labour or outsourcing will. Hence austerity of the kind now being proposed from international financial experts will not work not because it is cruel, but because it is inappropriate at this historical juncture. In relation to blocked transitions, it is evident that quantity in production is impeded from evolving towards quality, that is, responsiveness to diversity of preference and individuality of need. Hence cross-systemic operations become necessary in order to adjust the economy to the requirements of other social systems, and for other social systems to adjust their functioning to the needs of the economic system. Otherwise systemic imbalances, wasted human potential and, eventually, environmental disaster, are likely to dictate the need for drastic political interventions that will almost certainly overburden the political system of the individual states of the emerging world society.[21] It is unclear

[20]While it is doubtful if any democratic characteristics can be attributed to this artificially constructed 'we', it is inimical to non-identical equality. There is a considerable difference between sharing responsibilities stemming from socially necessary labour time, and construing analysable dysfunctions to be the result of mysterious forces, such as what 'the financial markets' are said 'to want'. See Philippe Askénazy, André Orléan, Henri Sterdyniak and Thomas Coutrot, *Manifeste d'économistes atterrés* [*Manifesto of Dumbfounded Economists*], www.assoeconomiepolitique.org/spip.php?article140&lang=fr (accessed 12 November 2012)

[21]It is possible to regard the environment as a natural system with objective limits and boundaries with social systems. Although it is difficult to delineate these boundaries with precision, the point

how long these states will continue to exist in their present form. Traditional elites within their borders are likely to cite faltering growth, unemployment benefit, and other costs as causes for political overload, and argue further that these costs should be dealt with through de-regulation and massive cuts in public spending, so that the danger to democracy can be avoided in time. At present the political system may indeed be suffering from excessive inputs from other social systems. Apart from the fact that the economic system is just one of several of these, the economy continues to be overloaded with political expectations that it cannot fulfill. If one is going to argue in favour of relieving the polity of economic functions, one must surely also demand that the economy be exonerated from the huge task of acting as the primary source of political stability. Traditional cultural, political and economic elites may well resist, however, because the analysis points to the need to plan, distribute and coordinate in ways that will alter existing property rights in several areas, including intellectual property.[22]

Once the economic system is de-coupled from this kind of paradoxical blind steering posing as the free play of market forces, it can be flexibly re-coupled to political and legal sub-systemic participatory institutions through the exercise of differentiated rights. At this point autonomy can really mean something more than passive adaptation to external demands, and normative issues can be taken up outside of frameworks that cannot think the concept of difference, save as a function of underlying unity.[23] This should permit advanced societies to plan much more effectively in the light of increased complexity and other changes that have taken place in Europe and beyond since the end of feudalism. In this regard it might be more than merely remotely plausible to argue that the great modern revolutions are not necessarily the spectacularly visible ones proclaiming 'liberty, equality and fraternity', or 'all power to the Soviets'. It might really be the rather less visible and ongoing revolution in which pyramidal and personalized stratification is slowly being undermined by functional differentiation. This is not to say that liberty and equality have been achieved, or that the officially recognized

---

remains that in addition to political refugees and economic refugees suffering from systemic dysfunctions compounded by the arbitrariness of national boundaries, it is not fanciful to believe that there will be increasing cases of environmental refugees if the quality of cross-systemic mediation is not substantially enhanced. See Latouche, *Sortir de la société de consommation*, pp. 33–43.

[22]See David M. Berry, *Critical Theory and the Digital*, in the *Critical Theory and Contemporary Society* series, London, Continuum, 2013.

[23]Once again one thinks of Mondragon, but other examples exist. See Mary Mellor, Janet Hannah and John Stirling, *Worker Cooperatives in Theory and Practice*, Milton Keynes, Open University Press, 1988.

power invested in the person of a president or prime minister is illusory. It does however mean that there are post-foundational ways of approaching questions of rights, equality, merit, justice, autonomy and legitimacy.[24] These alternative conceptions will receive inadequate attention if austerity is imposed as the only possible solution to economic stability, or if some supposedly new social or political collective subject manages to resurrect pyramidal models of representation and authority. Such models may have been appropriate during some part of the historical period marked by the predominance of stratified social divisions, but they are increasingly unsuitable today. To ignore this is to respond to the current socio-economic, political and cultural malaise with populist stereotypes, such as those positing a French penchant for striking, or a Greek (and generally Mediterranean) tendency to shirk work. Mainstream media portrayals like to pit the austere Germans against the corrupt Greeks, thus perpetuating the impression that economic dysfunction is primarily a question of nations and national character rather than systemic.

Current attempts to impose economic austerity in the Euro-zone are being pursued as if the being of the whole of society, in terms of learning capacity, creative potential and future expectations, somehow culminates in a narrowly focused obsession with the question of economic performance. This instrumental strategy for consolidating hegemony overlooks the objective particularities of individual social systems, and is likely to induce further systemic dysfunctions as well as various forms of resistance. In the near future, and bearing in mind the differences in relevant criteria, doing justice to socio-historical objectivity, contingency and complexity will have to be considered as part of the same set of procedures implemented to do justice to individuals.[25] Generic slogans about how spending and saving are good for all of us and in any case the *only* option, will not offer any kind of viable substitute for re-thinking how these procedures operate at present. The only option is no option, but rather, the artificial cultivation of a culture of imposed scarcity. Apart from being a contradiction in terms, such simplifications disregard the fact that the ascetic 'solution' tends to result in contraction instead of growth, and is in any case of doubtful economic

---

[24]Richard Münch, *Die Struktur der Moderne: Grundmuster und differentielle Gestaltung des institutionellen Aufbaus der modernen Gesellschaften* [*The Structure of Modernity*] (1984) Frankfurt, Suhrkamp, 1992, pp. 11–71; and Niklas Luhmann, *Beobachtungen der Moderne* [*Observations of Modernity*], Wiesbaden VS Verlag, 1992, pp. 67–85.

[25]Adorno does not analyse these phenomena in explicitly sociological terms. But his notion of the priority of the object (Vorrang des Objektes) does offer a caution against subjective, instrumental manipulation of objects and their environments. See Adorno, 'Zu Subjekt und Objekt', *Stichworte: Kritische Modelle* 2 [available in English as 'Subject and Object', *The Essential Frankfurt School Reader*], and *Negative Dialektik*, p. 132; Helga Gripp, *Theodor W. Adorno*, Paderborn, Ferdinand Schöningh, 1986, pp. 101–6; and Jameson, *Late Marxism*, pp. 23–4.

quality. When foisted upon an extra-economic system it is almost certain to produce unpredictable effects in the latter that underline how poor this approach really is in terms of re-establishing a certain measure of material stability/predictability. The neo-liberal project to direct extra-economic systems through the use of international economic means such as the IMF–World Bank–Central European Bank troika therefore infringes upon systemic specificity. This may seem counter-intuitive to those accustomed to regard liberalism as boundary-setting rather than boundary-effacing. Although it undermines systemic autonomy in ways that are distinct from the old-fashioned socialist and social-democratic policies of exerting direct political control over the economy, the neo-liberal method is also at odds with evident developments shaping historical and sociological change. That is, the current instability of the neo-liberal model of global order provides good analytical and political grounds for cautious optimism: whereas stratification, by definition, necessarily entails hierarchy, differentiation does not. If differentiation processes can be de-coupled from the categorical growth imperative and instrumental reality principles based on narrowly quantitative notions of competitive advantage and efficiency, differentiation could help sustain what it implicitly promises, namely, difference in the extended sense of something sui generis and understood in its specificity. At the conceptual level there are certainly much greater affinities between differentiation, contingency, and non-identity than there are between stratification and non-identity. It can be argued that stratification metaphors have been closely linked with a number of fairly one-dimensional notions of justice/fairness and equality as upward mobility. This lack of finesse at the theoretical level tends to obscure non-identity in the practical monetarization of the types of equality normally prevalent where minimum standards of mobility are equated with or substituted for justice. Here one observes a clear example of how redistributive and other quantitative solutions are typically offered as solutions to problems that have become qualitative in significant ways. If the notion of restricted high status positions is retained along with that of limited upward mobility, one is back with the pyramid model and the related belief that the unequal distribution of identical units of power offers the best explanation of how stratified hierarchy is required to produce a stable foundation to accommodate the natural inequality reigning between inherently competitive individuals.

With the aforementioned in mind it is not difficult to explain why proposals to recover ancient and Renaissance republican political virtues are as likely to fail as any attempt to reinvent existing political parties as educational institutions with the cognitive and ethical charge of the political clubs operative in the early modern European public sphere. As seen in the previous chapter with regard to social democracy, this epistemological ballast has for the most part been displaced to individuals and social systems. Any critique of the defects of political republics and a correspondingly staunch defence of the virtues of commercial republics will offer very inadequate responses to what has been analysed in recent years in fairly sophisticated terms as the onslaught of risk society, *autopoiesis*, the colonization of the life-world and *Verrechtlichung*, bio-political medicalization of political difference, and most familiarly, as neo-liberal globalization.[26] At a far more modest level, it is even doubtful if commercial republics can be stabilized through the clumsy combination of economic austerity, de-regulation of public services, and the implementation of enhanced security measures that in some cases border on panicked miscalculation of risk. The discrepancy between the ideology of mediated unity and the realities of mediated disunity and identity is observable in the palpable attenuation of mediation instances and institutions such as guilds, political clubs, parties, public spheres, life-worlds and civil society more generally. Central to the argument developed here is that this thinning of Durkheim's notion of the social bond cannot be properly addressed with the pathos of decay or decline that characterizes some first-generation critical theory, because it has as much to do with functional differentiation as it does with the demise of integral experience or the commercial integration of once revolutionary avant-garde art movements. It has also been suggested in the preceding pages of this book that this thinning out is bound up with processes of de-naturalization and de-traditionalization that are not inherently inimical to individual freedom and which may, under certain conditions, actually help foster new forms of post-liberal autonomy.[27] If there has been a documented decline of expressly organic mediation and communal unity, the chances for asserting the linguistic and extra-linguistic claims of non-identity against coerced reconciliation have also been bolstered. The dynamics of these movements in flux are plural

---

[26]*Verrechtlichung* denotes an over-extension of (mainly executive) legal interventionism as a response to ruptures in what in principle should be the steady flow of juridical information between citizens, law makers and law enforcers. For an analysis of bio-political medicalization that draws heavily on the work of Foucault, see Nikolas Rose, *The Politics of Life Itself: Biomedicine, Power, and Subjectivity in the Twenty-First Century*, Princeton, Princeton University Press, 2007. For Foucauldian perspectives on bio-politics and law, see Thomas Lemke, *Foucault, Governmentality, and Critique*, London, Paradigm, 2011; and Ben Golder and Peter Fitzpatrick, *Foucault's Law*, London, Routledge, 2009.

[27]The figurative demotion of *the state* from foundational reconciler of private interests and public goods, to *the political system* as just one of several social systems, can be interpreted as part of the demise of over-arching discourses of legitimacy. But it also provides the chance to re-think legitimacy in far more plastic, nuanced terms than was possible during the hegemony of nation-state communities and their class and regional subcultures. In the short term this is likely to mean further difficulties for social-democratic parties. In the longer term it may signal the reconfiguration of individual and collective existence and of organic and non-organic life.

and constellational rather than vertical and hierarchical. That means that they are de-centred and dialectical, and as such, defy simple characterization in terms of steady democratic progress or inexorable cultural decline. The criteria societies use to assess the different possible ways of guiding the mediation between individual autonomy and systemic function, as well as the resulting consequences of those assessments and decisions, will be a key issue in the coming decades. If timely critical theoretical interventions in these debates are not made, there will be little to prevent autonomy from becoming little more than a matter of cash (pyramidal model of 'success'), on the one hand, and just as little to prevent systemic integrity from being raised to a fetishized principle of ahistorical fate and necessity ('reconciliation' under duress), on the other.[28]

This being the case, one can see why Habermas, Rawls and others are determined to jettison metaphysics while retaining select anthropological categories of action, and one can also see why they suspect that the legitimacy of any given nation-state will be chimerical without preserving the concepts informing the formulation of such categories. If that is generally correct, however, why not re-elaborate conceptual thinking in new ways that push traditional humanism beyond its religious, republican and nation-state political limits, as one can do with the concept of mediated non-identity? That path is surely more promising in epistemological and normative terms than settling for a very predictable set of incentives and rewards that might ideally obtain under conditions of mediating unity, such as those implied by the difference principle and other highly speculative scenarios.[29] Empirical

---

[28]Christoph Seils, *Parteidämmerung: Was kommt nach den Volksparteien?* Berlin, WJS, 2010. Interesting in this context is the likely future of the 'people's party', that is, of what in German is referred to as the *Volkspartei*, such as the Christian Democrats. The preceding discussion of mediated unity indicates that it is no longer possible to say, without sociological qualification, that individuals make the laws and the people are the democratic basis of the state, so that the people's parties, in conjunction with a free press and freedom of information, solidify the links between them. This does not mean that the state is nothing other than 'an executive committee for managing the affairs of the entire bourgeoisie', or that democracy is simply an illusion, etc. It does mean that collective learning and accrued resources will have to be re-organized and aggregated via new forms of representation as a matter of some urgency if, that is, these resources are not to be misused for the purpose of saving irresponsible banks and embarking upon similarly ill-advised projects that are officially declared to be necessary and without alternatives.

[29]Although the veil of ignorance and difference principle yield relatively predictable criteria of justice, more bold interpretations of Rawls' original position are possible. See Chris Wyatt, *The Difference Principle Beyond Rawls*, London, Continuum, 2008. For the broad outlines of an alternative economic system based on a dialogue between producers, consumers and citizens in the place of the current one and its dogmatic adherence to the principles of growth and austerity, see Wyatt, *The Defetishishized Society*. His New Economic Democracy offers an updated version of G. D. H. Cole's Guild Socialism, and a plausible account explaining how it is possible to move beyond generic conceptions of citizenship without entrusting management of the economy to the command of state planners.

and explanatory deficits suggest that it is by no means apparent that systems theory can explain, let alone help resolve the main problems and crisis tendencies characteristic of twenty-first century industrial and post-industrial democracies. The point for now is that if one is really serious about transcending positively formulated idealism in a way that is consistently pluralist and anti-foundational, one should be prepared to accept the probable demise of reigning notions of humanism and state-centred practices of democracy. Here as elsewhere theory outpaces practice: the critique of humanism initiated by Marx and Nietzsche, and subsequently taken up in diverse ways by Simmel, critical theory, Heidegger, Derrida, Foucault, Deleuze, Luhmann, Butler, post-colonialism, etc., has been more decisive than the evolution of nation-states towards a flexibly integrated world society. But globalization and economic crisis, changing migration patterns, shifts from stratification to differentiation, structural transformations in the mediations between individuals and social systems, etc., are slowly engendering high levels of individualization and systemic complexity that will at some point become incompatible with traditionally conceived unities, such as the organic bounds of nation and the legal legitimacy of states. Hence another provisional conclusion of this study emerges. To the extent that legal and political systems become increasingly differentiated, and the legal system takes its place among a number of other social systems, legality will no longer be able to provide the *overarching* form for the content of legitimacy. The consequences for prevailing ideas about people–government–state relations have still to be drawn out in all of their implications. Although it is as yet too early to ascertain with precision what new forms law, politics, economics, etc. will assume, one can safely say that the period of unifying, ready-made political forms and centralized, state-centred mediations is passing.[30]

Part of what this entails is being open to the possibility that rationality and autonomy might be properties of systems and are not the exclusive domain of individual, inherently autonomous citizens, and one must at least consider the possibility that communication may facilitate the operation of systems and is not, necessarily or primarily, about interpersonal communication or agreement between people. That is, if one wants to think beyond idealism without consistently de-anthropomorphizing one's thought, one has not

---

[30]Luhmann, *Ausdifferenzierung des Rechts: Beiträge zur Rechtssoziologie und Rechtstheorie* [*The Differentiation and Separation of Law*], Frankfurt, Suhrkamp, 1999, chapter 12, *Die Politik der Gesellschaft* [*The Politics of Society*], chapter 3; and Dirk Baecker, *Form und Formen der Kommunikation* [*Form and Forms of Communication*], Frankfurt, Suhrkamp, 2007, pp. 104–34. What will come in the place of general, ready-made forms may well be the proliferation of singular political forms whose instability is no longer perceived as a threat to the need for over-arching unity.

really risen to the challenges (or fully grasped the political potential) of post-traditionalism, de-naturalization and dialectical non-identity thinking. If one were to entertain the idea that communication takes place between social systems, that is, that communication does not yet really serve to realize communicative or creative human capacities beyond less and more sophisticated means of individual and collective self-preservation, then one might have to countenance the thesis that legitimacy has for quite some time been based on a precarious and ongoing series of adjustments between systems and their respective environments. With a few select exceptions, legitimacy has not been the result of a rational agreement between citizens and governments within the overarching symmetry between independent citizens, their legally empowered national governments, and state authority.[31] Just as the Hegel/Adorno comparison does much to clarify the issues at stake in any treatment of non-identity, the Luhmann/Habermas comparison helps illuminate the epistemological status of systems and evaluate the prospects for autonomy in the light of specific systemic realities. A close reading of these thinkers suggests that it is possible to reconfigure the metaphorical distance between citizens and political authority by re-coupling (not fusing) individuals with differentiated rights, and to do so while acknowledging (not absolutizing) the uncertainties arising from the indeterminacy of currently existing systemic boundaries.

Luhmann challenges the theory of overlapping life-worlds with his methodological observation of the diverse environments that form the outer boundaries of systems. This approach enables him to raise pertinent objections to the argument that rights discourses originate in speech-acts in the life-world, where they proliferate in communicative channels that establish and consolidate links between everyday life, scientific research, individual citizens, civil society and the state. The systems-theoretical account regards laws and rights as the results of a juridical social system operating as a series of closed, self-referential processes distinguishing between what is legal and what is not legal. Instead of acting as a conduit to the state via electors, parties and parliaments, law has detached itself from politics, depending on the national context, and is in the process of gradually becoming a social system co-existing with a range of related but distinct social systems, such as those producing and communicating value (economy), truth (science),

---

[31]However fleetingly, such agreement and symmetry have been achieved at the regional level in Spain during the Spanish Civil War. But even in that specific context, solidarity was communal and articulated as a unifying force against state power. See Schecter, *The History of the Left from Marx to the Present*, chapter 4. For an analysis of the affinities between the libertarian tradition of de-centralized self-government and Frankfurt School critical theory, see Charles Masquelier's forthcoming volume in this series (London, Continuum, 2014).

localizable government power (politics), intimacy (family), belief (churches and other religious organisations), etc. Instead of writing in terms of *Economy and Society*, Luhmann theorizes the *Economy of Society*, *The Law of Society*, *The Politics of Society*, etc., culminating with the publication of the two-volume *The Society of Society* in 1997. Within this theoretical framework, systems have the capacity to generate meaning in that they define their respective boundaries, reduce complexity, meet expectations to different degrees, and adapt to contingency. To the extent that this is true, it is more appropriate to speak of system rationality than value rationality or intersubjectivity.[32]

Luhmann describes the modalities of speechless communication between systems through which they successfully (or less successfully in some cases) reproduce the conditions necessary for their stable function and autonomy vis-à-vis other systems. From Habermas' perspective this approach to theorizing society amounts to a repudiation of the communicative action needed to sustain the non-instrumental reason of the life-world against systemic incursions of technical and administrative reason. But here again one notes that he is in something of a bind, since while his early work distinguishes between labour and interaction, his more mature formulations depend on the distinction between system and life-world. The distinction between system and environment is unacceptable in that it leaves no room for the compromises and agreements people make as individual actors in their everyday, extra-systemic lives. But Habermas needs some sort of similar distinction if he is somehow going to be able to theorize social complexity without abandoning republican notions of *phronesis*.[33] The life-world/system distinction attempts to do this while holding on to the primacy of law and politics in the constitution of legitimate order. But this marks a leap back to Hegel on the state and a step back to Kant on the public sphere. It is somewhat like arguing that despite the exploitation and alienation in civil society, and the prevalence of contractual rationality in the civil sphere, the state nonetheless transcends such conflicts and achieves mediated unity between family, civil society and state. Marx has already shown why this is unlikely to be the case. The argument that rights discourses originate as speech-acts that are then channelled towards the institutions of legislation, thus linking the life-world with the democratic organs of government, is very reminiscent of Kant's belief that although it is not possible to fuse ethics

---

[32]Luhmann, *Soziale Systeme* [*Social Systems*], chapters 11–12, and *Die Gesellschaft der Gesellschaft* [*The Society of Society*], Frankfurt, Suhrkamp, 1997, volume 1, chapter 2.

[33]For an elucidation of the differences between *techne* and *phronesis* in Arendt, Gadamer, Habermas and Rorty, see Richard J. Bernstein, *Beyond Objectivism and Relativism: Science, Hermeneutics and Praxis*, Philadelphia, University of Pennsylvania Press, 1983.

and politics, the public sphere transmits ethical inputs to lawmakers which they can only ignore at the risk of seeming incompetent and irresponsible. Habermas of course abandons the conservative conditions Kant attaches to entitlement to participate in public sphere discourse, and his account of the life-world is much more sociologically nuanced than anything one might find in Kant's or even in Hegel's writings. There is nonetheless a basic congruity in their respective approaches to reason, agreement and legality as the juridico-political form of legitimacy. Luhmann's account of speechless communication and his suspicion of political congruities and stable epistemological syntheses highlight a surprising affinity between some of his ideas on systems and their environments, and what is discussed in previous chapters in terms of the possibilities for post-foundational mediation. It has already been remarked that Luhmann and Adorno will not prop up ideas that have ceased accurately to describe how institutions work in practice. Hence despite the evident links between Adorno and Habermas as first- and second-generation critical theorists, there are several points of convergence between Adorno's critique of instrumental reason and Luhmann's more comprehensive doubts about the very possibility of rational as opposed to functional mediation. There are also notable divergences between negative dialectics and systemic autopoiesis on key issues. But both theories raise important questions about the feasibility of communicative action and reason in life-worlds that somehow manage to resist colonization by harmoniously co-existing with systemic realities. These questions add to what is probably a salutary confusion as regards what is left and right, politically, and what the categories conservative, liberal and democratic mean today. Which, if any of these terms, are still relevant to critical theory? How is the relationship between critical theory, legal theory and political theory going to evolve? The transformation of centralized, state-centred foundations and ready-made, natural political forms such as the nation, is set to carry on apace. What provisional conclusions can be drawn from these developments?

Conclusion: The mediations of society

Preceding chapters show that the critique of knowledge continues to have important implications for social criticism and political policy. More specifically, it is argued that epistemological questions attain particular resonance when focused on the assessment of different possible modes of mediation between humanity and nature. Because humanity is neither identical with nor separate from nature, the mediation between humanity and other humanity is both part of and different from that between humanity and nature. The parallel explored throughout this book between epistemological questions about the knowledge (and power) humans have in relation to the natural world, on the one hand, and political and sociological questions about the way humans relate to each other, on the other, is not of merely allegorical significance. While these questions each relate to distinct sets of mediations, they are strongly interconnected. Reflexivity is more obviously required whenever social research analyses and evaluates the diverse institutions mediating between humanity and other humanity. Hegel refers to such institutions as objective spirit, and indeed, it is difficult to overestimate the extent to which debate on these matters is marked by the various positions taken up in relation to Hegel. Whether one is examining the stipulations governing what can be known to be true and false, subject and object, possession and property, or public and private, one is often investigating the ways in which two terms are mediated by a third term. Depending on the phenomenon under consideration, the third term serves as the condition for the very possibility of the relevant difference. That is to say that it lays a foundation for that distinction, and lends conceptual form to the relation encompassing all three terms, thus conferring a provisional unity upon them. In what one may broadly characterize as traditional theory, then, underlying unity becomes the basis of difference and, in a related vein, notions of unity, foundations and origins are often loosely articulated together.[1] The point can be illustrated by recalling that if humanity and nature were completely cut off from one another without a mediating bridge between them, human knowledge of nature would be impossible. The converse is that if humanity and nature were fused and therefore interchangeable, knowledge would be superfluous. Moving from philosophy to political sociology, if there was no way to bridge the figurative distance between citizens and the state, politically democratic and rationally representative government would be impossible, and, as a corollary, if identity or fusion best described the relation between citizens and the state, government and representation would be unnecessary. A distinction between strong dialectical and weak dialectical approaches to the study of nature, history and society is made at the start of Chapter Three. This is done to show that although great emphasis on knowledge as mediation is often associated with Kant, Hegel and Marx, one finds a more attenuated or nuanced usage of dialectics in the writings of a wide range of other social and political theorists. In fact, it is plausible to argue that thinking generally concerns the relations between dialectics, the conditions of rational mediation, and the reliability of concepts in explaining mediations. Clearly, much depends on what is meant by rational, and how one understands the ways in which innovative thought and the historical evolution of institutional change condition one another. If these were not central methodological issues, theory would be largely irrelevant to understanding the dynamics of social process and phases of structural transformation. Where theory is relevant in this sense, method of study and object of study are rarely divorced. But if method and object are closely related, what becomes of the notion of neutral method as a condition of natural and social-scientific objectivity?

As far as the social sciences are concerned, methodological confusion and normative ambiguity often complement one another. The postulate that humanity and nature are neither fused nor separated is typically elaborated with a view to discerning what might be the optimal relations between citizens and governments. In the years broadly spanning post-feudalism to incipient globalization, the modern state is credited by mainstream theory with the capacity to provide the overarching unity of citizens and governments by reconciling legality and legitimacy. Reconciliation is accomplished through a legal form of legitimacy that can rationally mediate between individual aspirations to freedom and autonomy, on the one hand, and the necessity for order, binding decisions, and collective authority, on the other. Hence

[1]There is a marked tendency to conjecture in these terms about the state of nature and the imagined communities supposedly founding the nation-state. See Benedict Anderson, *Imagined Communities: Reflections on the Origins and Spread of Nationalism*, London, Verso, 1993.

rationality is synonymous with a neutral form of law that reconciles without coercing or imposing any determinate set of values or vision of the good life. The supposition of mediated unity in this historical period is not limited to humanity–nature or citizen–government relations; the presumption of an underlying congruity of epistemological form (concepts that become institutionalized in different ways) with what is held to be objectively known reality, can be seen at work in a wider range of phenomena in the arts, sciences and humanities. Chapter Two charts the crisis of the concept of political unity. It is seen that although seemingly impartial language may be used in the framing of methodological and substantive issues, as in the case of juridical procedure, one can nonetheless detect various instances of subjective manipulation of the mediating processes that separate and provisionally reunify citizens and states. The qualified convergence of analytical and normative perspectives is thus to some extent achieved when it can be convincingly shown that there is a close relation between subjectively manipulated mediation and political authoritarianism, and, conversely, that non-antagonistic mediation holds the key to the institutionalization of consistently non-discriminatory, emancipatory political form. Hence critical thought does not so much question science and objectivity in the name of relativism, as much as it seeks to point out where and how rigorous standards of verification are undermined by instrumental and strategic interventions, that is, by what can largely be seen as power struggles. Critical theory intervenes (1) by observing that thought becomes unwarranted extrapolation whenever it is asserted that mediation is inherently violent, or that power struggles are virtually the only constant throughout history, (2) by pointing out that thought becomes lazy apology whenever it is assumed that unity and neutrality can be taken as givens, and (3) by explaining why Marxism makes an important but ultimately limited contribution to the study of power struggles and how they could be re-organized in order to enhance our knowledge of the differences between natural necessity and socially embedded need that is reproduced as discrimination, hierarchy and command used to enforce spurious unity.[2]

[2]The emphasis on the parallels between presumed symmetry and subjective manipulation highlights the affinities between Adorno, Heidegger, Derrida and their respective critiques of metaphysics. All three indicate that secular humanist methodology is not necessarily post-metaphysical, and that metaphysics, in different ways, is complicit with violence and oppression by forging identity out of difference on the basis of an underlying unity that really cannot be accounted for. Adorno remains particularly relevant to the renewal of critical theory due to the analytical rigour of his analyses of the social ramifications of flawed epistemologies. This means that while he is willing to allow for contingency and complexity, he is also resolved to show that the affinities between what counts as valid knowledge and what is generally practised as autonomy, however mediated they may be by institutionalized notions of reason, merit, progress, efficiency and culture generally, are not accidental in late modern societies. There is a discernible,

Precise description of the logic and composition of the unity in question thus becomes a key concern that prompts a series of further interrogations. Can the unity most accurately be characterized as mediated unity, as Hegel maintains with regard to the institutions of ethical life in the *Philosophy of Right*, or does mediated disunity offer a better description of the relations between civil society and the state, in accordance with Marx's refutation of Hegel? Should *Dasein*'s relation with being be interpreted as non-mediated non-identity, as Heidegger seems to believe? Does the idea of mediated non-identity indicate new ways of thinking about un-coerced reconciliation, and therewith, the possibility of a legitimate form of law capable of synthesizing humanity and nature without damaging individuals? The matter becomes sociologically relevant once it is demonstrated that this particular synthesis affects socialization and the integration of individuals according to criteria that can range in quality from arbitrary to uniquely suited to individual ability and need. Most really important questions at the figurative points of contact between normative and empirical analysis will touch upon mediation and dialectics, as well as the conceptual and institutional reality of unifying form. This claim merits serious attention, especially if one considers that mediation is central to experimenters with such distinct preoccupations as Baudelaire, Hegel, Marx, Heidegger, Adorno, Foucault, Luhmann, Butler and Habermas. Baudelaire's methodological innovation, which is spotted by Benjamin and developed further by Adorno, is that in the wake of urbanization and functional differentiation, new modes of mediation arise, and along with them the possibility of correspondingly flexible dialectics that do not presuppose unifying foundations or rely on preformed syntheses. One implication is that in both conceptual and institutional terms, there are non-identical forms, as opposed to ready-made and dogmatic overarching ones. The former offer the chance to formulate individually suited criteria in the sense just used, and thereby address legitimacy deficits without resorting to populism and palliative ideologies. The latter are likely to integrate somewhat indiscriminately in accordance with the belief that things cannot be otherwise, given the 'necessities of order', and, within a contemporary context, the 'realities' of globalization. A further implication is that diverse practices of reconciliation are possible without recourse to a central mediating instance like the state, or

---

if tortuous and asymmetrical trajectory, from thinking to concepts, and from concepts to systems and back to thought. Thinking then comes up with conceptual innovations that influence the evolution of systems and institutions. Stringent critiques of presumed congruity and symmetry are always salutary safeguards against coerced reconciliation. But Adorno is generally correct to insist that such critiques tend to go astray and become obscurantist if they thereby conjure up images of immediate proximity and absolute otherness which demand authenticity in the face of uncertainty and reverence before the impersonal transcendence of being.

the presumption of foundational, natural unity, such as the nation. This book addresses an urgent problem: the potential for re-thinking a number of key sociological questions in light of these theoretical developments is far from exhausted in the existing literature on the subject.

It is therefore argued here that the reflexively idealist critique of idealism is still pertinent to the study of power, conflict and the prospects for a non-instrumentally rational society. Thinkers who broadly follow Kant and the main lines of modern philosophy accept that knowledge is mediated through the forms in which knowledge is framed. Consequently, human subjects can have knowledge of nature and objects, but they cannot have the objects 'in themselves', independently of the enabling frame. According to this approach, *mediating* form is provided, ready-made and ultimately *unmediated*, by a subject whose simultaneous proximity and distance from nature cuts it off from absolute, direct knowledge of nature, things and events, while giving it reliable access to the world of appearances. Although the subject is unable to penetrate the world of essences, the condition of being neither separated from nor fused with nature provides it with the possibility of real knowledge based on the interplay of universal synthetic a priori operations in consciousness, and the unique experience of each individual human life. What is real, therefore (not subjective nor absolute), is neither of the isolated individual terms in the polar juxtapositions of humanity or nature, subjects or objects, citizens or governments, etc., but rather their ever-changing relation and the third term that conditions the polarity at hand. One may regard this as the humanization of space and time. Rather than occupying a fixed place in a hierarchically structured order, the subject plays an active role in the ongoing creation of a stable, objective world that the subject can effectively manage up to that point where the enabling frame – the guarantee of neutrality and objectivity – prevents management from turning into irrational manipulation and subjective distortion of facts and other evidence. Humanity thereby transcends the epistemological limits of nature and delineates the contours of its own qualified autonomy from the mechanistic universe of cause and effect. By reconciling universal laws of cognition with individual freedom, one may also regard humanization in this context as juridical in an implicitly liberal-democratic way. Enlightenment reason mediates by reconciling; tradition, force, prejudice or command should in principle play no part. If the quality of the unity is a key concern when evaluating the elasticity of concepts and forms, the quality of reason becomes a key question when evaluating the extent to which prevailing mediations in any society are likely to be instrumental, functionally differentiated, communicative, mimetic, or, what is most likely to be the case in complex societies, an amalgam of all four forms of reason. But each unifying form of reason is articulated to the others, which means that some kind of dialectic is at work that provisionally reconciles and simultaneously distinguishes them. The same question pertaining to unity and reason thus arises: what kind of dialectic or plurality of dialectics mediates between instrumental, functionally differentiated, or other forms of reason? Adorno intuits that the implicit juridical humanization of time and space is likely to evolve towards overt politicization in times of socio-economic and constitutional crisis. His insight is inseparable from the Weimar period in which critical theory first developed. Yet previous chapters indicate that the issues he raises in relation to idealism, representation and legitimacy have much relevance for the contemporary world.[3]

An analysis of ostensibly direct, unmediated mediating form points to a number of different possible ways of deconstructing some of the dubiously universal anthropological assumptions informing what might be called traditional, as opposed to critical knowledge. It also offers ways of questioning a similar set of assumptions about traditional, as opposed to a critical democracy organized by many active and diverse minorities. Theory too often proceeds without really investigating the validity of ideas and intuitions that inadequately distinguish management from manipulation and similarly defensive reactions to the natural spontaneity and human vitality that are potentially destabilizing of hierarchy. These palpably biased and at times even traumatized reactions can then work their way into supposedly *neutral* concepts in disciplines like economics, law, population studies, psychiatry, criminology, paediatrics, and medicine, and are often effective in *neutralizing* different perspectives on what constitutes knowledge in these fields.[4] Foucault, Deleuze and Guattari, and a number of bio-political thinkers have developed this genealogical thesis in different directions by convincingly showing that power struggles are rarely frontal or direct clashes between easily distinguishable groups struggling over the same material and theoretical resources. Although a number of observers have already commented on the aesthetic implications of deconstructing the assumptions undergirding different notions of unmediated mediation, there is still much more to say about the questions that the bio-political thesis raises regarding the conditions for extra-conceptual knowledge, or, at least, for the elaboration of concepts that are less hostile to extra-conceptual realities than prevailing conceptual thought in the social and medical sciences cited above tends to be. In order to counter the identity thinking that disciplines individuals

---

[3]Adorno, *Vorlesung über Negative Dialektik* [*Lectures on Negative Dialectics*], delivered in 1965–6, and translated into English, chapter 3.

[4]The status of psychoanalysis is ambiguous in this regard. If it is not yet possible to have concepts free of the traces of trauma, it may well be possible to discern the traumatic moment in the origin and subsequent development of a given concept. See Joel Whitebook, *Perversion and Utopia: A Study in Psychoanalysis and Critical Theory*, chapter 3.

who live and think differently from established norms of thought and legal-scientific validity, critical theory can stimulate new ways of thinking about the regulatory role played by mediated unity in much mainstream political sociology and political theory. The crucial task, however, is to show how the institutional mediations between identity thinking and repressive integration function in practice. If unable to do so, critical theory will remain vulnerable to the charge of insufficient sociological grounding that recurs in the writings of the various proponents of the 'linguistic turn' in social and political thought.

The discussion of the parallels between unifying concepts and integrating institutions in Chapter Five makes a contribution to this endeavour. It is explained why it is more fruitful to provide idealism with a sociological framework than it is to pit idealism and philosophy against social science, and claim that the latter is superior on the grounds that it is somehow post-metaphysical and communicative. The aim is to clarify the continually changing mutual interactive exchanges between *extra-conceptual,* mimetic knowledge and communication, on the one hand, and the possibility of *cross-systemic* institutions that synthesize humanity and nature without harming individual, internal human nature through diverse instances of illegitimate integration, on the other. The pursuit of this line of inquiry offers the most promising path for critical theory in the twenty-first century, and an alternative to re-articulating the already well-known theses on the culture industry, the Marx–Freud synthesis, or the aging union of the critique of political economy and the critique of daily life. If it may sound somewhat fanciful to try to see ruins before they actually become ruins, it is perhaps not quite so romantic to observe how what passes for functional integration and efficient mediation can lead to war and wasted human potential in many cases. Common to most concepts and institutions is their reliance on form to manufacture synthetic unity out of disparate, and at times dissident theoretical and practical elements that can upset conceptual clarity and impede political governability. With these latent or overt conflicts in mind, one can qualitatively assess the extent to which synthetic unity is supple and adaptable, and the extent to which it may harden, so to speak, into contrived or authoritarian unity in the guise of different kinds of populism, nationalism, racism and gender oppression. The foregoing chapters indicate that where unity is organized in ways that are suspicious of difference, unusual reciprocal exchanges, and correspondences that resist the dominant modes of conceptualization, representation and institutionalization, it is more accurate to speak of mediated disunity and even mediated identity than of mediated unity in philosophy/epistemology or non-instrumental legitimacy in law/politics. Such ossification does occur and can result in blocked transitions and other regressively quantitative adaptations to the pressing need for change currently facing late modern societies in Greece, Spain, and many other parts of the world. Although the empirical research on these questions is limited in this book, a number of politically relevant hypotheses regarding sclerotic institutional form do emerge from the preceding pages. The main findings are that (1) there are potentially severe policy impasses stemming from the dogmatic defence of undifferentiated growth imperatives in an epoch demanding qualitative solutions; (2) the practical dilemmas facing social-democratic parties and political parties more generally are now impossible to ignore or ascribe to distinct national civic traditions or voter apathy; (3) cross-systemic operations and decentred mediations are needed to avert a looming environmental crisis that cannot be remedied with merely ad hoc measures and other inconclusive adjustments to prevalent ways of aggregating interests and values. Normative and analytical perspectives provisionally overlap where it becomes clear that mimetic knowledge and speechless communication are not simply lofty ideals: they are sociological realities as well as indispensable conditions for cross-systemic institutions that synthesize without damaging internal human nature. It is not easy to see how probing questions about human flourishing and problem-solving policy might otherwise be answered, if not through collective learning. The preliminary investigation of these phenomena offered here is intended to strengthen one of the main theoretical arguments of the book, that is, that law has detached itself from politics to an unprecedented extent. Two practical consequences are that legality can no longer be counted on to provide the overarching framework for legitimacy, and that real communication and mediation have, to a significant extent, been displaced from key institutions in civil society, such as parties, unions, universities, intellectuals, to individuals and social systems.

In order properly to address these issues, the structure of mediations between humanity and external nature will have to be re-organized in tandem with the re-organization of institutions structuring the collective life of humanity with other humanity. There is a pressing and to date unresolved political issue involved: how can one embark upon these processes of reform without embracing centralized planning that is likely to be bureaucratic, propagandistic, and therefore ineffective? Full-scale planning in this sense is roughly equivalent to conceptual imperiousness, the institutional corollary of which is coerced integration. Yet to oppose planning with an appeal to the natural adjustment of supply and demand or the spontaneous coordination of talent, merit and position, is to indulge in fairly obviously flawed deductions conflating the actual with the rational, and this, in turn, if widespread enough, is also likely to lead to coerced, illegitimate integration. If the outcomes are broadly similar, one may advance the tentative explanation that there is a parallel to strong and weak dialectics. That is the parallel between strong conceptual imperiousness and weak conceptual imperiousness. More importantly, however, in terms of the efficiency of governance, is that weak conceptual imperiousness, referred to at the end of Chapter One in terms of the paradoxes of formal essence, is more likely to be hegemonic in complex societies where strong conceptual arrogance and propaganda will be less effective. If one may suppose that humanity can know nature and achieve a degree of freedom not attainable in situations where natural need and necessity cannot be completely eliminated, one has to ask a further question: how does humanity know humanity? The ways in which one answers this question have important implications for any understanding one is likely to have of the relation between facts and norms, society and political legitimacy, and between ontology and anthropology. Humanization and juridification are marked by the appearance of new instances of conflict, cooperation and collective learning. As stated, most explanations of the relations between knowledge, freedom and necessity in society invoke a weak or a strong dialectic. The dialectic explains how constantly evolving normative standards of equality and justice coexist with causality and contingency. Where the latter broadly correspond to socio-historical facts and the changing limits to social knowledge, the former reflect humanity's capacity to transcend natural scarcity, and to learn to correct institutional responses to uncertainty and revise some of the inadequate solutions of the past. Inflexible and unimaginative thinking in these matters can retard possible transitions from quantitative (number of eligible voters) to qualitative (areas of social life affected by the vote as well as more nuanced criteria of accountability) freedom. On this issue the central concerns of critical theory complement practical attempts to marginalize scarcity and poverty without thereby reintroducing and even intensifying bureaucratic management and social control. Where it can be shown that such intensification has occurred, one can speak in fairly objective terms about normative deficits and integration problems that have at times led to revolutions.

Since the French Revolution, political constitutions in conjunction with the social sciences have been relied upon to answer the question concerning humanity's knowledge of humanity. The democratization of knowledge and the democratization of society can be seen to converge, at least partially, in the project to make power relations transparent to the greatest possible extent. Sieyès and the more moderate protagonists of change in eighteenth-century France had hoped that a constitutional monarchy would clarify the respective rights and obligations of the people, parliament and king. Clarification in this sense of maximum accountability was widely thought to be the key to combining the aspirations of the *demos* with the greatest possible neutrality and impartiality in all instances of adjudication. In much democratic theory, then, the *demos* provides the normative political foundation, which is then tempered by the objectivity of impartial mediation in the guise of law backed by popular sovereignty (the fact that the state can be characterized as democratic while society remains fundamentally undemocratic is not really a central problem until Marx). In this way the constituent power of the people equips itself with a self-regulating political brake on what could become the destabilizing exercise of legitimate essence, unfettered by legal form. The subsequent path of the 1789 Revolution and other upheavals in the course of modern state building, including the Paris Commune of 1871, confirm the thesis that the humanization of time and space also brings with it dramatic cases of politicization. By the time of the Russian Revolution, people begin to ask if rapid industrialization, world war and imperialism might make it possible to accelerate historical time and skip what had been taken as necessary historical stages. In accordance with the notion that the subject plays an active role in the creation of an objective, and nonetheless modifiable institutional world, the space between private and public is constantly redesigned in an effort to endow quantity–quality dynamics with signposts and guidelines. Catastrophic, in the Russian example, is the attempt to compress state and civil society into a 'higher synthesis' capable of absorbing the conflicts accompanying industrialization. The massive problems encountered by state-socialist societies in attempting to re-design and politicize existing temporal and spatial demarcations cannot be touched upon here. Regardless of the errors committed in specific contexts, it has become clear that it cannot be assumed that supposedly static, natural boundaries were simply manipulated by malevolent politicians like Stalin. Historical and sociological investigation indicates that what seems like the natural and eternal order of things can very quickly become obviously contingent, and further, that power relations constantly form and reform in new combinations and configurations. That history includes the separation of church and state, the ongoing and as yet incomplete differentiation of economic and political systems, and the relatively recently discovered boundary between system and life-world located by Habermas.

Yet as early as 1843, Marx begins to ask questions about the extent to which it is possible to defend the epistemological neutrality of boundaries, which is somewhat akin to investigating the political neutrality of mediating instances between spheres, systems, life-worlds and other regions of social life.[5] Critical theory attempts to build on Marx's early writings by carefully studying how mediation tends to become imposition in the name of some

---

[5]Previous chapters have analysed the view that it is perhaps more appropriate to speak in terms of differentiation and function than it is to do so in terms of spaces and regions. See Richard Münch, *Die Struktur der Moderne* [*The Structure of Modernity*], pp. 38–40.

combination of leadership, efficiency, necessity and contingency, so that various modalities of decree are reaffirmed to the detriment of epistemological and political democratization. Such democratization is not synonymous with cultural decline or 'dumbing down'. It is the very prerequisite of the de-centred pluralism required to respond flexibly to contingency and change without recourse to centralized steering or ostensibly more acceptable, 'democratic' versions of technocracy. Centralized steering will not work. Democratic technocracy, either as social-democratic Keynesianism or corporatism, has also shown itself to be ineffective. This book looks at the reasons why it is plausible to argue that both remedies rely on hierarchical command. It goes further by explaining why the propping up of hierarchical command is closely linked with the consolidation of different kinds of poorly constructed unity, and the concomitant marginalization of diverse articulations of mediated non-identity. Finally, it is shown that many of these instances of unity can be analysed and deconstructed, and that hierarchical command does not have good long-term prospects in the face of continuing de-naturalization and differentiation. Complex social formations offer the possibility for individual humans to exercise diverse forms of de-naturalized and post-traditional autonomy. Their success in doing so democratically, that is, without favouring particular individuals or groups, depends on the ability and desire of late modern societies to guide some of the advantages of complexity towards the effective renewal and redeployment of economic, political, pedagogical, scientific and cultural resources. The realization of this opportunity depends, in turn, on a transition from overarching forms of legitimacy to a densely articulated network of de-centred mediations that can coordinate needs, capacities and communication. The development of economic, political, legal and other systems is one particularly notable advantage of complexity that should not be lamented as unbridled rationalization. But it cannot be uncritically embraced as an automatically positive consequence of modernity. Systems are not endowed with self-steering properties in the manner or to the extent often attributed to them, which is why they must be guided. But they cannot be steered from a political foundation, or presided over by a small elite of systems experts, without forfeiting one of their chief virtues: they operate in a de-centred, pluralist way that could potentially foster civic responsibility and non-instrumental political action. A generic life-world cannot be relied on to do this spontaneously any more than Keynes offers a permanent stock of ready-made fixes. The task of cross-systemic coordination can best be performed by overlapping constellations of active citizens affected by the relevant systemic operations, so that people may fully develop the economic, political, legal and aesthetic capacities and knowledge required to become non-identical equals.

Bibliography

Adams, Suzi. *Castoriadis's Ontology: Being and Creation*, New York, Fordham University Press, 2011.

Adorno, Theodor W. *Drei Studien zu Hegel: Aspekte Erfahrungsgehalt Skoteinos, oder Wie zu lesen sei* [*Three Studies of Hegel*], Frankfurt, Suhrkamp, 1963.

—. *Negative Dialektik* [*Negative Dialectics*], Frankfurt, Suhrkamp, 1966.

—. *Stichworte: Kritische Modelle II* [*Key Terms II*], Frankfurt, Suhrkamp, 1969.

—. *Soziologische Schriften I* [*Sociological Writings I*], Frankfurt, Suhrkamp, 1972.

—. *Ästhetische Theorie* [*Aesthetic Theory*], Frankfurt, Suhrkamp, 1973.

—. *Philosophie der neuen Musik,* Frankfurt, Suhrkamp, 1976.

—. *Noten zur Literatur* [*Notes on Literature*], 6th edn, Frankfurt, Suhrkamp, 1981.

—. *Zur Metakritik der Erkenntnistheorie: Studien über Husserl und die phänomenologischen Antinomien* [*Against Epistemology*], Frankfurt, Suhrkamp, 1990.

—. *Kants Kritik der reinen Vernunft* [*Kant's Critique of Pure Reason*] (1959), ed. by Rolf Tiedeman, Frankfurt, Suhrkamp, 1995.

—. *Aesthetic Theory,* trans. and Introduction by Robert Hullot-Kentor, London, Continuum, 1997a.

—. *Minima Moralia: Reflexionen aus dem beschädigten Leben* [*Minima Moralia*] (1951) Frankfurt, Suhrkamp, 1997b.

Agamben, Giorgio. *La comunità che viene* [*The Coming Community*], Turin, Einaudi, 1990.

—. *Homo sacer: Il potere sovrano e la nuda vita*, Turin, Einaudi, 1995.

Agulhon, Maurice. *Histoire et politique à gauche*, Paris, Perrin, 2005.

Ainger, Katharine. 'A Financial Coup d'Etat', in *The Guardian*, 26 September 2012.

Akehurst, Thomas. 'Britishness, Logic and Liberty: The Cultural Politics of Twentieth Century Analytical Philosophy', DPhil in History at the University of Sussex, 2007.

Akerstrom Andersen, Niels. *Discursive Analytical Strategies: Understanding Foucault, Koselleck, Laclau, Luhmann,* Bristol, Policy Press, 2003.

Allison, Henry E. *Kant's Transcendental Idealism: An Interpretation and Defense,* New Haven, Yale University Press, 1983.

Antliff, Alan. *Anarchy and Art: From the Paris Commune to the Fall of the Berlin Wall,* Vancouver, Arsenal Pulp Press, 2007.

Antonioli, Manola. 'La machination politique de Deleuze et Guattari', in Alain Beaulieu (ed.), *Gilles Deleuze*, Paris, Presses Universitaires de France, 2005, pp. 73–95.

Arato, Andrew and Eike Gebhardt (eds). *The Essential Frankfurt School Reader,* London and New York, Continuum, 1982.

Arendt, Hannah. *Between Past and Future: Eight Exercises in Political Thought*, New York, Penguin, 1954.
—. *The Human Condition*, Chicago, University of Chicago Press, 1958.
Aristotle. *The Politics* (335–322 BC), Books VII–VIII, ed. and trans. John Warrington, London, Dent, 1959.
—. 'Nicomachean Ethics', in Reginald E. Allen (ed.), *Greek Philosophy: From Thales to Aristotle*, New York, Macmillan, 1966, pp. 362–74.
Aron, Raymond. *Les étapes de la pensée sociologique*, Paris, Gallimard, 1967.
Ashcroft, Richard. 'Locke's Political Philosophy', in Vere Chappell (ed.), *The Cambridge Companion to Locke*, Cambridge, Cambridge University Press, 1994, pp. 226–51.
Askénazy, Philippe, André Orléan, Henri Sterdyniak and Thomas Coutrot, *Manifeste d'économistes atterrés* [*Manifesto of Dumbfounded Economists*], www.assoeconomiepolitique.org/spip.php?article140&lang=fr (accessed 12 November 2012).
Baecker, Dirk. *Form und Formen der Kommunikation*, Frankfurt, Suhrkamp, 2007.
Barthes, Roland. *La chambre claire: Note sur la photographie*, Paris, Gallimard, 1980.
Baudelaire, Charles. *Œuvres complètes*, Vol. I, Paris, Gallimard, 1975.
Beecken, Grit and Bernd Salzmann. 'Investoren legen Spanien trocken', in *Frankfurter Rundschau*, 6–7 June 2012, p. 12.
Bello, Waldon. *Deglobalization: Ideas for a New World Economy*, London, Zed Books, 2004.
Benhabib, Seyla (ed.). *Democracy and Difference: Contesting the Boundaries of the Political*, Princeton, Princeton University Press, 1996.
Benhabib, Seyla and Maurizio Passerin d'Entrèves. *Habermas and the Unfinished Project of Modernity: Critical Essays on the Philosophical Discourse of Humanity*, Cambridge, MIT, 1997.
Benjamin, Walter. *Baudelaire: Ein Lyriker im Zeitalter des Hochkapitalismus* [*Baudelaire*], ed. by Rolf Tiedemann, Frankfurt, Suhrkamp, 1974a.
—. *Iluminationen*, Frankfurt, Suhrkamp, 1974b.
—. *Illuminations*, New York, Schocken, 1976a.
—. *Reflections*, New York, Schocken, 1976b.
—. *Das Passagen-Werk* [*The Paris Arcades Project*] (1927–40), 2 vols, Frankfurt, Suhrkamp, 1983.
—. *Angelus Novus*, Frankfurt, Suhrkamp, 1988.
Berlin, Sir Isaiah. 'Two Concepts of Liberty', in Henry Hardy and Roger Hausheer (eds), *Isaiah Berlin; The Proper Study of Mankind*, London, Pimlico, 1998, pp. 191–242.
Berman, Harold J. *Law and Revolution: The Formation of the Western Legal Tradition*, Cambridge, Harvard University Press, 1983.
Berman, Marshall. *All that is Solid Melts into Air: The Experience of Modernity*, London, Penguin, 1988.
Bernstein, Richard J. *Beyond Objectivism and Relativism: Science, Hermeneutics and Praxis*, Philadelphia, University of Pennsylvania Press, 1983.
Berry, David M. *Critical Theory and the Digital*, London, Continuum, 2013.

Bertrand, Pierre and Pascal Durrand. *Les poètes de la modernité de Baudelaire à Apollinaire*, Paris, Seuil, 2006.
Bhambra, Gurminder K. *Rethinking Modernity: Postcolonialism and the Sociological Imagination*, London, Palgrave Macmillan, 2007.
Bloch, Ernst. *Das Prinzip Hoffnung,* [*The Principle of Hope*], 3 vols (1954–9), 5th edn, Frankfurt, Suhrkamp, 1998.
Böckelmann, Frank. *Über Marx und Adorno: Schwierigkeiten der spätmarxistischen Theorie*, Freiburg, ça ira, 1998.
Boltanski, Luc. *De la critique. Précis de sociologie de l'émancipation*, Paris, Gallimard, 2009.
Boltanski, Luc and Eve Chiapello. *Le nouvel esprit du capitalisme* [*The New Spirit of Capitalism*], Paris, Gallimard, 1999.
Bonacker, Thorsten. *Die normative Kraft der Kontingenz: Nichtessentialistische Gesellschaftskritik nach Weber und Adorno*, Frankfurt, Campus, 2000.
Bowie, Andrew. *Music, Philosophy and Modernity,* Cambridge, Cambridge University Press, 2007.
Boyer, Robert and Jean-Pierre Durand. *L'après-fordisme*, Paris, Syros, 1993.
Boyer, Robert and Yves Saillard (eds). *Theorie de la régulation: L'état des savoirs*, Paris, La Découverte, 1995.
Braedly, Susan and Meg Luxton (eds). *Neo-liberalism and Everyday Life,* Montreal, McGill University Press, 2010.
Braunstein, Dirk. *Adornos Kritik der politischen Ökonomie* [*Adorno's Critique of Political Economy*], Bielefeld, Transcript, 2011.
Brecht, Bertolt. *Brecht on Theatre,* ed. and trans. John Willett, London, Methuen, 1978.
Breton, André. *Position politique du surréalisme*, Paris, Pauvert, 1971.
Bru, Sascha. *Democracy, Law and the Modernist Avant-Gardes: Writing in the State of Exception*, Edinburgh, Edinburgh University Press, 2009.
Brunkhorst, Hauke. *Theodor W. Adorno: Dialektik der Moderne* [*Theodor W. Adorno: The Dialectic of Modernity*], Munich, Piper, 1990.
— (ed.). *Demokratie in der Weltgesellschaft, Soziale Welt,* Sonderband 18, 2009.
Buck-Morss, Susan. *The Dialectics of Seeing: Walter Benjamin and the Arcades Project*, Cambridge, MIT Press, 1989.
Bull, Anna, Gian Luca Gardini et al. 'Italy: Reforms without Reformers', *Modern Italy,* 15 (2010), pp. 197–216.
Burckhardt, Wolfgang (ed.). *Luhmann Lektüren*, Berlin, Kulturverlag Kadmos, 2010.
Burke, Edmund. *Reflections on the Revolution in France* (1790), Oxford, Oxford University Press, 1993.
Butler, Judith. *Gender Trouble: Feminism and the Subversion of Identity,* New York, Routledge, 1990.
—. *Bodies that Matter,* New York, Routledge, 1993.
—. *Excitable Speech: A Politics of the Performative*, New York, Routledge, 1997.
Butler, Judith, Ernesto Laclau and Slavoj Žižek. *Contingency, Hegemony, Universality: Contemporary Dialogues on the Left*, London, Verso, 2000.
Callinicos, Alex. *Imperialism and Global Political Economy*, Cambridge, Polity, 2009.
Cambadélis, Jean-Christophe. 'Le moment social-démocrate' in *Le Monde*, 13 October 2006.

Casey, Edward S. *The Fate of Place: A Philosophical History*, California, University of Berkeley Press, 1998.
Castoriadis, Cornelius. *L'institution imaginaire de la société* [*The Institution of the Social Imaginary*], Paris, Seuil, 1975.
Caygill, Howard. *A Kant Dictionary*, Oxford, Blackwell, 1995.
—. *Walter Benjamin: The Colour of Experience*, London, Routledge, 1998.
—. 'Also Sprach Zapata: Philosophy and Resistance', *Radical Philosophy*, 171 (2012), pp. 19–26.
Celikates, Robin. *Kritik als soziale Praxis. Gesellschaftliche Selbstverständigung und kritische Theorie*, Frankfurt, Campus, 2009.
Chakrabarty, Dipesh. *Provincializing Europe: Postcolonial Thought and Historical Difference*, Princeton, Princeton University Press, 2000.
—. *Habitations of Modernity: Essays in the Wake of Subaltern Studies*, Chicago, University of Chicago Press, 2002.
Chomsky, Noam. *Occupy*, London, Penguin, 2012.
Clam, Jean. *Was heißt, sich an Differenz statt an Identität orientieren: Zur De-ontologisierung in Philosophie and Sozialwissenschaft*, Constance, UVK, 2002.
—. *Aperceptions du présent: Théorie d'un aujourd'hui par-delà la détresse*, Paris, Ganse Arts et Lettres, 2010.
Cohen, Hermann. *Kants Theorie der Erfahrung* [*Kant's Theory of Experience*], Berlin, Bruno Cassirer, 1918.
Collingwood, R. G. *The Idea of History*, Oxford, Clarendon, 1992.
Comisso, Elaine. *Workers' Control under Plan and Market*, New Haven, Yale University Press, 1979.
Conert, Hansgeorg. 'Umrisse der Ökonomie eines möglichen Sozialismus', in Iring Fetscher and Alfred Schmidt (eds), *Emanzipation als Versöhnung: Zu Adornos Kritik der Warentausch-Gesellschaft und Perspektiven der Transformation*, Frankfurt, Neue Kritik, 2002, pp. 251–67.
Constant, Benjamin. 'De la liberté des anciens comparée à celle des modernes' ['On the Liberty of the Ancients compared to that of the Moderns'] (1819), reprinted in *Benjamin Constant: Ecrits politiques*, ed. Marcel Gauchet, Paris, Gallimard, 1997, pp. 591–619.
Cook, Deborah. *Adorno on Nature*, Windsor, Arcoa, 2011.
Coole, Diana. *Merleau-Ponty and Modern Politics after Anti-Humanism*, Plymouth, Rowman & Littlefield, 2007.
Cornell, Drucilla. *The Philosophy of the Limit*, New York, Routledge, 1992.
—. *Moral Images of Freedom: A Future for Critical Theory*, Lanham, Rowman & Littlefield, 2008.
Crouch, Colin. *Post-Democracy*, Cambridge, Polity, 2004.
Dardot, Pierre and Christian Laval. *La nouvelle raison du monde: Essai sur la société néolibérale* [*The World's New Reason*], Paris, La Découverte, 2009.
Deleuze, Gilles. *Nietzsche et la Philosophie*, Paris, Presses Universitaires de France, 1962.
—. *Spinoza et le problème de l'expression* [*Spinoza and the Problem of Expression*], Paris, Minuit, 1968.
—. *Foucault*, Paris, Minuit, 1986.

Deleuze, Gilles and Félix Guattari. *Capitalisme et schizophrénie I: L'Anti-Œdipe* [*Capitalism and Schizophrenia I: Anti-Oedipus*], Paris, Minuit, 1973.
Demirovic, Alex (ed.). *Komplexität und Emanzipation: Kritische Gesellschaftstheorie und die Herausforderung der Systemtheorie Niklas Luhmanns* [*Complexity and Emancipation*], Münster, Westfälisches Dampfboot, 2001.
Derrida, Jacques. *Politiques de l'amitié*, Paris, Galilée, 1994.
De Sousa Santos, Boaventura. *The Rise of the Global Left: The World Social Forum and Beyond*, London, Zed, 2006.
Devine, Pat and David Purdy. 'Feelbad Britain', in Mark McNally and John Schwarzmantel (eds), *Gramsci and Global Politics: Hegemony and Resistance*, Abingdon, Routledge, 2009, pp. 182–4.
Dilthey, Wilhelm. *Der Aufbau der geschichtlichen Welt in den Geisteswissenschaften* [*The Construction of the Historical World in the Human Sciences*], Frankfurt, Suhrkamp, 1981.
Dimou, Nikos. 'L'immobilisme dure depuis trop longtemps', *Le Monde*, 25 May 2012, p. 18.
Dörre, Klaus (ed.). *Soziologie, Kapitalismus, Kritik: Eine Debatte*, Frankfurt, Suhrkamp, 2009.
Durand-Gasselin, Jean-Marc. *L'école de Francfort*, Paris, Gallimard, 2012.
Dyer-Witherford, Nick. 'Net, Square, Everywhere', *Radical Philosophy*, 171 (2012), pp. 2–6.
Eagleton, Terry and Drew Milne (eds). *Marxist Literary Theory*, Oxford, Blackwell, 1996.
Eder, Klaus. *Die Vergesellschaftung der Natur: Studien zur sozialen Evolution der praktischen Vernunft* [*The Socialisation of Nature*], Frankfurt, Suhrkamp, 1988.
Edwards, Claire. 'Foucault and Arendt: Beyond the Social/Political', DPhil at the University of Sussex, 2012.
Eickelpasch, Rolf. 'Bodenlose Vernunft: Zum utopischen Gehalt des Konzepts kommunikativer Rationalität bei Habermas', in Rolf Eickelpasch and Armin Nassehi (eds), *Utopie und Moderne* [*Utopia and Modernity*], Frankfurt, Suhrkamp, 1996, pp. 11–50.
Esposito, Roberto. *Communitas*, Turin, Einaudi, 1998.
Fetscher, Iring and Alfred Schmidt (eds). *Emanzipation als Versöhnung: Zu Adornos Kritik der Warentausch-Gesellschaft und Perspektiven der Transformation*, Liubljana, Neue Kritik, 2002.
Feuerbach, Ludwig. *Das Wesen des Christentums* [*The Essence of Christianity*], Stuttgart, Reclam, 1969.
Finlayson, Gordon and Fabian Freyenhagen (eds). *Habermas and Rawls: Disputing the Political*, London, Routledge, 2011.
Fischer-Lescano, Andreas and Gunther Teubner. *Regime-Kollisionen: Zur Fragmentierung des globalen Rechts* [*Regime Collisions*], Frankfurt, Suhrkamp, 2006.
Fisher, Mark. *Capitalist Realism: Is there No Alternative?* London, Zero Books, 2009.
Fohrmann, Jürgen and Arno Orzessek (eds). *Zerstreute Öffentlichkeiten: Zur Programmierung des Gemeinsinns*, Munich, Wilhelm Fink, 2002.

Foucault, Michel. *Les mot et les choses* (trans. as *The Order of Things*), Paris, Gallimard, 1966.

—. *La pensée du dehors* [*The Thought from Outside*], Paris, Fata Morgana, 1986.

—. *Naissance de la biopolitique* [*The Birth of Bio-politics*] (1978–9), Paris, Gallimard, 2004a.

—. *Sécurité, territoire et population* [*Security, Territory and Population*], Paris, Gallimard, 2004b.

Frisby, David. *Fragments of Modernity: Theories of Modernity in the Work of Simmel, Kracauer and Benjamin*, Cambridge, MIT Press, 1986.

Fuchs, Peter. *Die Erreichbarkeit der Gesellschaft: Zur Konstruktion und Imagination gesellschaftlicher Einheit* [*The Attainability of Society*], Frankfurt, Suhrkamp, 1992.

Fürnkäs, Josef. *Surrealismus als Erkenntnis: Walter Benjamin – Weimarer Einbahnstraße und Pariser Passagen,* Stuttgart, J.B. Metzler, 1988.

Germino, Dante. *Machiavelli to Marx: Western Political Thought*, Chicago, University of Chicago Press, 1972.

Gerth, Hans H. *Bürgerliche Intelligenz um 1800*, Göttingen, Vandenhoeck & Ruprecht, 1976.

Geuss, Raymond. 'Dialectics and the Revolutionary Impulse' in Fred Rush (ed.), *The Cambridge Companion to Critical Theory*, Cambridge, Cambridge University Press, 2004, pp. 103–38.

Giddens, Anthony. *Modernity and Self-Identity: Self and Society in the Late Modern Age*, Cambridge, Polity, 1991.

Gildea, Robert. *The Third Republic from 1870 to 1914*, London, Longman, 1988.

Golder, Ben and Peter Fitzpatrick. *Foucault's Law*, London, Routledge, 2009.

Görg, Christoph. *Gesellschaftliche Naturverhältnisse*, Münster, Westfälisches Dampfboot, 1999.

Gramsci, Antonio. *Quaderni del carcere* [*Prison Notebooks*], ed. Valentino Gerratana, Turin, Einaudi, 2007.

Gripp, Helga. *Theodor W. Adorno*, Paderborn, Ferdinand Schöningh, 1986.

Gropius, Walter. *The New Architecture and the Bauhaus* (1919), Cambridge, MIT Press, 1965.

—. 'Programme of the Staatliches Bauhaus in Weimar' (April 1919), reprinted in Anton Kaes, Martin Jay and Edward Dimendberg (eds), *The Weimar Republic Sourcebook*, Berkeley, University of California Press, 1994.

Guibentif, Pierre. *Foucault, Luhmann, Habermas, Bourdieu: Une génération repense le droit,* Paris, Lextenso-Librairie générale de droit et de jurisprudence (Collection Droit et société [série sociologie] n° 53), 2010.

Habermas, Jürgen. *Erkenntnis und Interesse* [*Knowledge and Human Interests*], Frankfurt, Suhrkamp, 1968.

—. *Legitimationsprobleme im Spätkapitalismus* [*Legitimation Crisis*], Frankfurt, Suhrkamp, 1973.

—. *Theorie des kommunikativen Handelns* [*The Theory of Communicative Action*], 2 vols, Frankfurt, Suhrkamp, 1981.

—. *Der philosophische Diskurs der Moderne: Zwölf Vorlesungen* [*The Philosophical Discourse of Modernity*], Frankfurt, Suhrkamp, 1985.

—. *Strukturwandel der Öffentlichkeit* [*The Structural Transformation of the Public Sphere*], Frankfurt, Suhrkamp, 1990.
—. *Faktizität und Geltung* [*Between Facts and Norms*], Frankfurt, Suhrkamp, 1992a.
—. *Nachmetaphysisches Denken: Philosophische Aufsätze* [*Post-Metaphysical Thought*], Frankfurt, Suhrkamp, 1992b.
—. *Philosophische Texte*, 5 vols, Frankfurt, Suhrkamp, 2009.
—. 'Reconciliation through the use of Public Reason: Remarks on John Rawls' Political Liberalism', in Gordon Finlayson and Fabian Freyenhagen (eds), *Habermas and Rawls: Disputing the Political*, London, Routledge, 2011, pp. 25–45.
Hanssen, Beatrice. *Critique of Violence: Between Poststructuralism and Critical Theory*, London and New York, Routledge, 2000.
Hardt, Michael and Antonio Negri. *Empire: The New Order of Globalization*, Cambridge, Harvard University Press, 2000.
Haug, Wolfgang Fritz. *Kritik der Warenästhetik* [*Critique of Commodity Aesthetics*], Frankfurt, Suhrkamp, 1971.
Hegel, Georg Wilhelm Friedrich. *The Philosophy of Right*, trans. T. M. Knox, Oxford, Oxford University Press, 1952.
—. *Grundlinien der Philosophie des Rechts* [*The Philosophy of Right*], Frankfurt, Suhrkamp, 1970a.
—. *Vorlesungen über die Philosophie der Geschichte* [*Lectures on the Philosophy of History*], Frankfurt, Suhrkamp, 1970b.
—. *Die Phänomenologie des Geistes* [*The Phenomenology of Spirit*] (1807), Stuttgart, Reclam, 1987.
Heidegger, Martin. 'Prolegomena zur Geschichte des Zeitbegriffs'['Prologue to the History of Concepts of Time'], *Gesamtausgabe*, Vol. 20, ed. Petra Jaeger, Frankfurt, Vittorio Klostermann, 1979.
—. *Kant und das Problem der Metaphysik* [*Kant and the Problem of Metaphysics*] (1929), Frankfurt, Vittorio Klostermann, 1998.
—. *Sein und Zeit* [*Being and Time*] (1927), Tübingen, Max Niemeyer, 1993.
Heine, Sophie. *Oser penser à gauche: pour un réformisme radical*, Brussels, Éditions Aden, 2010.
Heller, Agnes. *A Theory of Modernity*, Oxford, Blackwell, 1999.
Helm, Everett. *Bartók*, Hamburg, Rowohlt, 1965.
Hill, Christopher. *The Century of Revolution, 1603–1714*, New York, Columbia University Press, 1966.
Hoffmann, Hasso. *Legitimität gegen Legalität: Der Weg der politischen Philosophie Carl Schmitts* [*Legitimacy against Legality*] (1964), Berlin, Duncker & Humblot, 2002.
Holmstrom, Mark. *Industrial Democracy in Italy*, Aldershot, Averbury, 1989.
Holzhey, Helmut (ed.). *Ethischer Sozialismus: Zur politischen Philosophie des Neukantianismus* [*Ethical Socialism*], Frankfurt, Suhrkamp, 1994.
Homer, Sean. *Jameson: A Critical Introduction*, Cambridge, Polity, 1998.
Horkheimer, Max and Theodor W. Adorno. *Dialektik der Aufklärung: Philosophische Fragmente* [*The Dialectic of Enlightenment*] (1944), Frankfurt, Fischer, 1995.

Horkheimer, Max. *Traditionelle und kritische Theorie: Fünf Aufsätze*, ed. Alfred Schmidt and Gunzelin Schmid Noerr, Frankfurt, Fischer, 1995.
Horowitz, Asher and Terry Maley (eds). *The Barbarism of Reason: Max Weber and the Twilight of Enlightenment*, Toronto, University of Toronto Press, 1994.
Hui, Wang. *The End of the Revolution: China and the Limits of Modernity*, London, Verso, 2009.
Hullot-Kentor, Robert. *Things Beyond Resemblance: Collected Essays on Theodor W. Adorno*, New York, Columbia University Press, 2006.
Hunt, Alan and Gary Wickham. *Foucault and Law: Towards a Sociology of Law as Governance*, London, Pluto, 1994.
Husserl, Edmund. *Die Phänomenologische Methode: Ausgewählte Texte I*, Stuttgart, Reclam, 1985.
Hutton, Will. 'The Facts Are Clear: This Cruel Austerity Experiment Has Failed', *The Observer*, 3 June 2012.
Huysseune, Michael. 'A Eurosceptic Vision in a Europhile Country: The Case of the Lega Nord', *Modern Italy*, 15 (2010), 63–75.
Invisible Committee, The. *The Coming Insurrection*, Los Angeles, Semiotext(e), 2009.
Ives, Peter. *Gramsci's Politics of Language: Engaging the Bakhtin Circle and the Frankfurt School*, Toronto, University of Toronto Press, 2004.
Jameson, Fredric. *Marxism and Form: Twentieth Century Theories of Literature*, Princeton, Princeton University Press, 1971.
—. *Late Marxism: Adorno, or, The Persistence of the Dialectic*, Cambridge, Harvard University Press, 1982.
—. *Brecht and Method*, London, Verso, 1998.
— (ed.). *Aesthetics and Politics: Theodor Adorno, Walter Benjamin, Ernst Bloch, Bertolt Brecht and Georg Lukács*, London, Verso, 2007a.
—. *The Modernist Papers*, London, Verso, 2007b.
—. *Valences of the Dialectic*, London, Verso, 2009.
Jarvis, Simon. *Adorno: A Critical Introduction*, Cambridge, Polity, 1998.
Jay, Martin. *The Dialectical Imagination, A History of the Frankfurt School and the Institute of Social Research, 1923–1950*, Berkeley and Los Angeles, University of California Press, 1973.
—. *Marxism and Totality: The Adventures of a Concept from Lukács to Habermas*, Berkeley, University of California Press, 1984.
Jeanpierre, Laurent [Review of Keucheyan], *Le Monde des Livres*, 2 July 2010.
Kafka, Peter. *Das Grundgesetz vom Aufstieg: Vielfalt, Gemächlichkeit, Selbstorganisation: Wege zum wirklichen Fortschritt* [*The Constitution of Ascendancy*], Munich, Hanser, 1989.
Kant, Immanuel. *Kritik der reinen Vernunft* [*The Critique of Pure Reason*], 2 vols (1781, 1787), Frankfurt, Suhrkamp, 1968.
—. *Political Writings*, ed. Hans Reiss, Cambridge, Cambridge University Press, 1970.
—. *Schriften zur Anthropologie, Geschichtsphilosophie, Politik und Pädagogik I*, Frankfurt, Suhrkamp, 1977.
Kaplan, Leonard V. and Rudy Koshar (eds). *The Weimar Moment: Liberalism, Political Theology and Law*, Lanham, Lexington Books, 2012.

Kellner, Douglas. *Critical Theory, Marxism and Modernity*, Baltimore, Johns Hopkins University Press, 1989.

Kenyon, J. P. *Stuart England*, London, Penguin, 1978.

Keucheyan, Razmig. *Hémisphère gauche: une cartographie des nouvelles pensées critiques*, Paris, La Découverte, 2010.

King, Michael and Chris Thornhill. *Niklas Luhmann's Theory of Politics and Law*, London, Palgrave Macmillan, 2005.

Kisiel, Theodore. *The Genesis of Heidegger's Being and Time*, Berkeley, University of California Press, 1993.

Klooger, Jeff. *Castoriadis: Psyche, Society, Autonomy*, Leiden/Boston, Brill, 2009.

Kolarz, Peter. 'The Politics of Anthony Giddens' Social Theory: Utopian Realism and Late Modern Social Democracy beyond the Third Way', DPhil at the University of Sussex, 2011.

Kracauer, Siegfried. *From Caligari to Hitler*, New Haven, Yale University Press, 1947.

—. *The Mass Ornament: Weimar Essays*, Cambridge, Harvard University Press, 1985.

Laine, Mathieu. *Post-politique*, Paris, JC Lattes, 2009.

Latouche, Serge. *Pour sortir de la société de la consommation: Voix et voies de la décroissance* [*Beyond the Society of Consumption*], Paris, Gallimard, 2010.

Lavatori, Luca. *Dimmi che è stata una rana*, Milan, Codex, 2011.

Leakey, F. W. *Baudelaire and Nature*, Manchester, Manchester University Press, 1969.

Lefebvre, Henri. *La production de l'espace* [*The Production of Space*], Paris, Anthropos, 1974.

Lemke, Thomas. *Foucault, Governmentality and Critique*, London, Paradigm, 2011.

Lenin, V. I. 'The State and Revolution' (1917), in *Collected Works*, Moscow, Progress Publishers, 1975, chapter 3.

Lévinas, Emmanuel. *Totalité et infinité: Essai sur l'extériorité* [*Totality and Infinity*], Paris, Kluwer, 1971.

Lewis, Michael and Tanja Staehler. *Phenomenology: An Introduction*, New York, Continuum, 2010.

Löwith, Karl. *Von Hegel zu Nietzsche* [*From Hegel to Nietzsche*], Zurich, Europa Verlag, 1941.

Luhmann, Niklas. *Macht* [Power], Stuttgart, Enke, 1975.

—. *Soziale Systeme* [*Social Systems*] (1984), Frankfurt, Suhrkamp, 1987.

—. *Beobachtungen der Moderne* [*Observations of Modernity*], Wiesbaden VS Verlag, 1992.

—. *Die Gesellschaft der Gesellschaft* [*The Society of Society*], 2 vols, Frankfurt, Suhrkamp, 1997.

—. 'Globalization or World Society: How to Conceive of Modern Society', *International Review of Sociology*, 7 (1997), 67–80.

—. *Ausdifferenzierung des Rechts: Beiträge zur Rechtssoziologie und Rechtstheorie* [*The Differentiation and Separation of Law*], Frankfurt, Suhrkamp, 1999.

—. *Die Politik der Gesellschaft* [*The Politics of Society*], Frankfurt, Suhrkamp, 2002.

Lukács, György. *Die Zerstörung der Vernunft* [*The Destruction of Reason*], Berlin, Aufbau, 1954.
—. *Die Theorie des Romans* [*Theory of the Novel*] (1920), Munich, DTV, 1994.
—. *Geschichte und Klassenbewusstsein: Studien über marxistische Dialektik* [*History and Class Consciousness*] (1923), Amsterdam, Verlag De Munter, 1967.
Lunghi, Alessio and Seth Wheeler (eds). *Occupy Everything! Reflections on why it's kicking off everywhere*, New York, Minor Compositions, 2012.
Macdonald, Iain and Krzyztof Ziarek (eds). *Adorno and Heidegger: Philosophical Questions*, Stanford, SUP, 2008.
Marchart, Oliver. *Die politische Differenz: Zum Denken des Politischen bei Nancy, Lefort, Badiou, Laclau und Agamben*, Berlin, Suhrkamp, 2010.
Marcus, Greil. *Lipstick Traces: A Secret History of the Twentieth Century*, Cambridge, Harvard University Press, 1989.
Marcuse, Herbert. *Konterrevolution und Revolte*, Frankfurt, Suhrkamp 1972.
Margolin, Victor. *The Struggle for Utopia: Rodchenko, Lissitsky, Moholy-Nagy*, Chicago, University of Chicago Press, 1997.
Marinopoulou, Anastasia. *The Concept of the Political in Max Horkheimer and Jürgen Habermas*, Athens, Nissos, 2008.
Markov, Vladimir. *Russian Futurism: A History*, Berkeley and Los Angeles, University of California Press, 1968.
Marx, Karl und Friedrich Engels. *The Marx-Engels Reader*, ed. Robert Tucker, New York, Norton, 1972.
—. *Studienausgabe Vol. I. Philosophie*, ed. Iring Fetscher, Frankfurt, Fischer, 1990a.
—. *Studienausgabe Vol IV. Geschichte und Politik 2*, ed. Iring Fetscher, Frankfurt, Fischer, 1990b.
Marx, Karl. *Preface and Introduction to a Contribution to the Critique of Political Economy*, Beijing, Foreign Languages Press, 1976.
—. *Das Kapital* [*Capital*], Berlin, Dietz Verlag, 1998a.
—. *Lohnarbeit und Kapital* [*Wage-Labour and Capital*], Berlin, Dietz Verlag, 1998b.
Maus, Ingeborg. *Rechtstheorie und politische Theorie im Industriekapitalismus*, Munich, Wilhelm Fink Verlag, 1986.
—. *Zur Aufklärung der Demokratietheorie: Rechts- und demokratietheoretische Überlegungen im Anschluss an Kant*, Frankfurt, Suhrkamp, 1994.
Mbembe, J. A. *On the Postcolony*, Berkeley, University of California Press, 2001.
McNally, Mark and John Schwarzmantel (eds). *Gramsci and Global Politics: Hegemony and Resistance*, Abingdon, Routledge, 2009.
Mellor, Mary, Janet Hannah and John Stirling. *Worker Cooperatives in Theory and Practice*, Milton Keynes, Open University Press, 1988.
Menke, Christoph. *Die Souveränität der Kunst; Ästhetische Erfahrung nach Adorno und Derrida*, Frankfurt, Suhrkamp, 1991.
Menninghaus, Winfried. *Walter Benjamins Theorie der Sprachmagie*, Frankfurt, Suhrkamp, 1995.
Merleau-Ponty, Maurice. 'Cézanne's doubt', in Michael B. Smith (ed.), *The Merleau-Ponty Aesthetics Reader: Philosophy and Painting*, Chicago, Northwestern, 1994, pp. 59–75.

Michelet, Jules. *Histoire de la révolution française* [*History of the French Revolution*] (1847), Vol. I, Paris, Gallimard, 1952.
Mills, Jon. 'The I and the It', in Jon Mills (ed.), *Rereading Freud: Psychoanalysis through Philosophy*, Albany, State University of New York Press, 2004, pp. 127–63.
Milne, Seumas. 'The Coalition's Phony War is an Exercise in Political Fraud', *The Guardian*, 26 September 2012.
Moholy-Nagy, László. *Painting, Photography and Film*, London, Thames and Hudson, 1991.
Moschonas, Gerassimos. 'Shooting Horses in Cold Blood', *Policy Network Observatory*, 6 July 2012, www.policy-network.net/pno_detail.aspx?ID=4217&title=Shooting+horses+in+cold+blood (accessed 12 November 2012).
Münch, Richard. *Die Struktur der Moderne: Grundmuster und differentielle Gestaltung des institutionellen Aufbaus der modernen Gesellschaften* [*The Structure of Modernity*] (1984), Frankfurt, Suhrkamp, 1992.
Nancy, Jean-Luc. *La communauté désœuvrée* [*The Inoperative Community*], Paris, Christian Bourgeois, 1990.
Negt, Oskar and Alexander Kluge. *Öffentlichkeit und Erfahrung: Zur Organisationsanalyse von bürgerlicher und proletarischer Öffentlichkeit* [*The Public Sphere and Experience*], Frankfurt, Suhrkamp, 1973.
Nicholls, Peter. *Modernisms: A Literary Guide*, Berkeley, University of California Press, 1995.
Nietzsche, Friedrich. *Der Wille zur Macht* [*The Will to Power*], Stuttgart, Alfred Kröner, 1964.
—. *Die fröhliche Wissenschaft* [*The Gay Science*] (1882), Stuttgart, Reclam, 2000.
Nisbet, Robert. *Sociology as an Art Form*, Oxford, Oxford University Press, 1976.
Nove, Alec. *The Economics of Feasible Socialism*, London, Allen & Unwin, 1983.
Noys, Benjamin (ed.). *Communization and its Discontents*, Wivenhoe, Minor Compositions, 2012.
Nuzzo, Angelica. 'Dialectic as Logic of Transformative Processes', in Katerina Deligiorgi (ed.), *Hegel: New Directions*, Chesham, Acumen, 2006, pp. 85–103.
Oakeshott, Robert. *The Case for Workers' Co-ops*, London, Macmillan, 1990.
Oehler, Dolf. *Ein Höllensturz der alten Welt: Baudelaire, Flaubert, Heine, Herzen*, Frankfurt, Suhrkamp, 1988.
Outhwaite, William. *Critical Theory and Contemporary Europe*, London, Continuum, 2012.
Palmier, Jean Michel. *Weimar en exil* [*Weimar in Exile*], Paris, Payot, 1987.
Pascal, Celine-Marie. *Cartographies of Knowledge: Exploring Qualitative Epistemologies*, London, Sage, 2011.
Pasolini, Pier Paolo. *Scritti corsari* [*Pirate Writings*], Milan, Garzanti, 1990.
—. *Lettere luterane* [*Lutheran Letters*], Turin, Einaudi, 2003.
Petersen, Leena. *Poetik des Zwischenraumes* [*Poetics of the Space in Between*], Heidelberg, Winter, 2010.
Peukert, Detlev. *Die Weimarer Republik: Krisenjahre der klassischen Moderne* [*The Weimar Republic*], Frankfurt, 1987.

Pippin, Robert B. *Kant's Theory of Form: An Essay on the Critique of Pure Reason*, New Haven, Yale University Press, 1982.
—. *Idealism as Modernism: Hegelian Variations*, Cambridge, Cambridge University Press, 1997.
Poggi, Gianfranco. *The Development of the Modern State: A Sociological Introduction*, Stanford, Stanford University Press, 1978.
Postone, Moische. *Time, Labour, and Social Domination: A Reinterpretation of Marx's Critical Theory*, Cambridge, Cambridge University Press, 1993.
Raunig, Gerald. *Art and Revolution: Transversal Activism in the Long Twentieth Century*, Los Angeles, Semiotext(e), 2007.
Rawls, John. *A Theory of Justice*, Cambridge, Harvard University Press, 1973.
—. 'Justice as Fairness: Political not Metaphysical', *Philosophy and Public Affairs*, 14 (1985), 223–51.
Read, Herbert. *Art and Industry*, New York, Horizon, 1953.
Reichardt, Sarah. *Composing the Modern Subject: Four String Quartets by Dmitri Shostakovich*, Aldershot, Ashgate, 2008.
Reichman, Ravit. *The Affective Life of Law: Legal Modernism and the Literary Imagination*, Stanford, Stanford University Press, 2009.
Renou, Yvan. 'La rationalité dialectique à l'épreuve de la gouvernance de l'eau: une analyse des (en)jeux hydro-sociaux contemporains', *Droit et société*, 80 (2012), 143–62.
Ricoeur, Paul. 'Husserl', in Eduard Bréhier (ed.), *Histoire de la philosophie allemande*, Paris, Vrin, 1967, pp. 183–96.
Riedel, Manfred. *Theorie und Praxis im Denken Hegels: Interpretationen zu den Grundstellungen der neuzeitlichen Subjektivität*, Frankfurt, Ullstein, 1965.
Ringger, Beat (ed.). *Zukunft der Demokratie: Das postkapitalistische Projekt*, Basel, Rotpunkt, 2008.
Rose, Gillian. *Dialectic of Nihilism: Post-Structuralism and Law*, Oxford, Blackwell, 1984.
Rose, Nikolas. *The Politics of Life Itself: Biomedicine, Power, and Subjectivity in the Twenty-First Century*, Princeton, Princeton University Press, 2007.
Ross, Kristin. *The Emergence of Social Space: Rimbaud and the Commune*, Minneapolis, University of Minnesota Press, 1988.
Rousseau, Jacques. *Du contrat social* [*The Social Contract*] (1762), Paris, Éditions Garnier frères, 1960.
Rousselle, Duane and Süreyyya Evren (eds). *Post-Anarchy: A Reader*, London, Pluto, 2011.
Sartre, Jean-Paul. *Baudelaire*, Paris, Gallimard, 1947.
Sassen, Saskia. *A Sociology of Globalization*, New York, Norton, 2007.
Sassoon, Donald. *One Hundred Years of Socialism: The West European Left in the Twentieth Century*, New York, The New Press, 1996.
Schecter, Darrow. *Beyond Hegemony: Towards a New Philosophy of Political Legitimacy*, Manchester, Manchester University Press, 2005a.
—. 'Liberalism and the Limits of Legal Legitimacy: Kant and Habermas', *The King's College Law Journal*, 16 (2005b), 99–119.
—. *The History of the Left from Marx to the Present: Theoretical Perspectives*, New York and London, Continuum, 2007.

—. 'Liberalism and the Limits of Knowledge and Freedom: On the Epistemological and Social Bases of Negative Liberty', *History of European Ideas*, 33 (2007), 195–211.
—. *The Critique of Instrumental Reason from Weber to Habermas*, London, Continuum, 2010.
—. 'Unity, Identity and Difference: Reflections on Hegel's Dialectics and Negative Dialectics', *History of Political Thought*, 33 (2012), 258–79.
Scheuerman, William E. *Between the Norm and the Exception: The Frankfurt School and the Rule of Law*, Cambridge, MIT Press, 1994.
—(ed.). *The Rule of Law under Siege: Selected Essays by Franz Neumann and Otto Kirchheimer*, Berkeley, University of California Press, 1996.
Sciulli, David. *Theory of Societal Constitutionalism: Foundations of a Non-Marxist Critical Theory*, New York, Columbia University Press, 1992.
Schmidt, Alfred. *Der Begriff der Natur in der Lehre von Marx* [*Marx's Concept of Nature*], Frankfurt, Europäische Verlagsanstalt, 1962.
Schmitt, Carl. *Legalität und Legitimität* [*Legality and Legitimacy*], Berlin, Duncker & Humblot, 1993.
Schnädelbach, Herbert. *Philosophie in Deutschland, 1831–1933*, Frankfurt, Suhrkamp, 1983.
—. *Philosophy in Germany, 1831–1933*, Cambridge, Cambridge University Press, 1984.
Schuler, Philipp. *Rationalität und Organisation: Ein Vergleich zwischen Max Weber and Niklas Luhmann*, Norderstedt, Grin, 2007.
Schwartzberg, Melissa. *Democracy and Legal Change*, Cambridge, Cambridge University Press, 2007.
Seils, Christoph. *Parteidämmerung: Was kommt nach den Volksparteien?* Berlin, WJS, 2010.
Sheringham, Michael. *Everyday Life: Theories and Practices from Surrealism to the Present*, Oxford, Oxford University Press, 2009.
Simmel, Georg. 'Die Arbeitsteilung als Ursache für das Auseinandertreten der subjektiven and der objektiven Kultur' ['The Division of Labour as the Cause for the Drifting Apart of Objective and Subjective Culture'] (1900), in Heinz-Jürgen Dahme and Otthein Ramstedt (eds), *Schriften zur Soziologie*, Frankfurt, Suhrkamp, 1983, pp. 107–11.
—. *Die Philosophie des Geldes* [*The Philosophy of Money*] (1900), Frankfurt, Suhrkamp, 1989.
—. *Soziologie* [*Sociology*] (1908), Frankfurt, Suhrkamp, 1992.
—. 'Die ästhetische Quantität' ['Aesthetic Quantity'], in Ingo Meyer (ed.), *Georg Simmel: Jenseits der Schönheit*, Frankfurt, Suhrkamp, 2008a, pp. 248–57.
—. 'Soziologische Apriori' ['Sociological *a priori*'], in Otthein Rammstedt (ed.), *Georg Simmel: Individualismus der modernen Zeit*, Frankfurt, Suhrkamp, 2008b, pp. 290–302.
Sirianni, Carmen. *Workers' Control and Socialist Democracy*, London, Verso, 1982.
Smart, Mary Ann. 'Liberty on and off the Barricades: Verdi's Risorgimento Fantasies', in Albert Russell Ascoli and Krystyna von Henneberg (eds), *Making and Remaking Italy: The Cultivation of National Identity around the Risorgimento*, Oxford, Berg, 2001, pp. 103–18.

Smith, Adam and Howard Horne. *Art into Pop*, London, Methuen, 1987.
Sohn-Rethel, Alfred. *Geistige und körperliche Arbeit* [*Intellectual and Manual Labour*], Weinheim, VCH, 1989.
Soja, Edward W. *Postmodern Geographies: The Reassertion of Space in Critical Social Theory*, London, Verso, 1989.
Spencer-Brown, George. *The Laws of Form*, London, George Allen and Unwin, 1969.
Stadlinger, Jörg and Dieter Sauer. 'Marx und die Moderne: Dialektik der Befreiung oder Paradoxien der Individualisierung?', *Prokla*, 159 (2010), 195–215.
Stone, Lawrence. *The Crisis of the Aristocracy*, London, Penguin, 1968.
Surprenant, Céline. *Freud's Mass Psychology: Questions of Scale*, London, Palgrave, 2003.
Teichner, Wilhelm. *Kants Transzendentalphilosophie: Ein Grundriss*, Munich, Karl Alber, 1978.
Theunissen, Michael. *Der Andere: Studien zur Soziolontologie der Gegenwart* [*The Other*], Berlin, Walter de Gruyter, 1977.
Thompson, Simon. *The Political Theory of Recognition: A Critical Introduction*, Cambridge, Polity, 2006.
Thomson, Alex. *Deconstruction and Democracy: Derrida's Politics of Friendship*, London, Continuum, 2005.
Thornhill, Chris. 'Legality, Legitimacy and the Constitution: A Historical-Functionalist Approach', in Chris Thornhill and Samantha Ashenden (eds), *Legality and Legitimacy: Normative and Sociological Approaches*, Vol. 6, Baden-Baden, Nomos, 2010, pp. 29–56.
—. 'Re-conceiving Rights Revolutions: The Persistence of a Sociological Deficit in Theories of Rights', *Zeitschrift für Rechtssoziologie*, 2 (2010), 177–207.
—. *A Sociology of Constitutions: Constitutions and State Legitimacy in Historical-Sociological Perspective*, Cambridge, Cambridge University Press, 2011.
—. 'Sociological Enlightenments and the Sociology of Political Philosophy', *Revue Internationale de Philosophie*, 1 (2012), 55–83.
Tiedemann, Rolf. *Dialektik im Stillstand* [*Dialectics at a Standstill*], Frankfurt, Suhrkamp, 1983.
Todd, Emmanuel. *Après la démocratie*, Paris, Gallimard, 2008.
Toulmin, Stephen. *Return to Reason*, Cambridge, Harvard University Press, 2003.
Trevelyan, G. M. *English Social History*, London, Longmans, 1944.
Tronti, Mario. *La politica al tramonto*, Turin, Einaudi, 1998.
Vighi, Fabio and Heiko Feldner (eds). *Did Someone say Ideology? On Slavoj Žižek and Consequences*, Newcastle, Cambridge Scholars Publishing, 2007.
Wagenknecht, Sahra. *Wahnsinn mit Methode: Finanzcrash und Weltwirtschaft*, Berlin, Das Neue Berlin, 2008.
Weber, Max. *From Max Weber*, ed. H. H. Gerth and C. Wright Mills, New York, Scribner and Son, 1946.
—. 'Politik als Beruf' ['Politics as a Vocation'] (1919), in Johannes Winckelmann (ed.), *Gesammelte politische Schriften*, Tubingen, J.C.B. Mohr, 1988.
Weber, Samuel. *Benjamin's Abilities*, Cambridge, Harvard University Press, 2008.

Weinrib, Ernest J. 'Legal Formalism: On the Immanent Rationality of Law', *Yale Law Journal*, 97 (1988), 949–1015.

Weitz, Eric D. *Weimar Germany*, Princeton, Princeton University Press, 2007.

Werber, Niels. 'Kommunikation ohne Interaktion: Thesen zu einem zweiten Strukturwandel der Massenmedien', in Fohrmann, Jürgen and Arno Orzessek (eds), *Zerstreute Öffentlichkeiten: Zur Programmierung des Gemeinsinns*, Munich, Wilhelm Fink, 2002, pp. 43–51.

White, Stephen K. *The Recent Work of Jürgen Habermas: Reason, Justice and Modernity*, Cambridge, Cambridge University Press, 1988.

Whitebook, Joel. *Perversion and Utopia: A Study in Psychoanalysis and Critical Theory*, Cambridge, MIT Press, 1995.

Widder, Nathan. *Political Theory after Deleuze*, London, Continuum, 2012.

Wiggershaus, Rolf. *Die Frankfurter Schule: Geschichte, theoretische Entwicklung, politische Bedeutung* [*The Frankfurt School*], Munich, DTV, 1988.

—. *The Frankfurt School*, trans. by Michael Robertson, Cambridge, MIT Press, 1995.

—. *Wittgenstein und Adorno: Zwei Spielarten modernen Philosophierens*, Göttingen, Wallstein, 2001.

Williams, Raymond. *The Politics of Modernity: Against the New Conformists*, 2nd edn, London, Verso, 2007.

Wyatt, Chris. *The Difference Principle beyond Rawls*, London, Continuum, 2008.

—. *The Defetishized Society: New Economic Democracy as a Libertarian Alternative to Capitalism*, London, Continuum, 2011.

Zadnikar, Darij. 'Adorno and post-Vanguardism', in John Holloway, Fernando Matamoros and Sergio Tischler (eds), *Negativity and Revolution: Adorno and Political Activism*, London, Pluto Press, 2009, pp. 79–94.

Zartaloudid, Thanos. *Giorgio Agamben: Power, Law, and the Uses of Criticism*, Abingdon, Routledge, 2010.

Zima, Peter V. *Deconstruction and Critical Theory*, London, Continuum, 2002.

Index